Peers as Change Agents

Peers as Change Agents

A Guide to Implementing Peer-Mediated Interventions in Schools

EDITED BY TAI A. COLLINS

AND

RENEE O. HAWKINS

OXFORD
UNIVERSITY PRESS

OXFORD
UNIVERSITY PRESS

Oxford University Press is a department of the University of Oxford. It furthers
the University's objective of excellence in research, scholarship, and education
by publishing worldwide. Oxford is a registered trade mark of Oxford University
Press in the UK and certain other countries.

Published in the United States of America by Oxford University Press
198 Madison Avenue, New York, NY 10016, United States of America.

© Oxford University Press 2021

Library of Congress Cataloging-in-Publication Data
Names: Collins, Tai A., 1986– editor. | Hawkins, Renee O., editor.
Title: Peers as change agents : a guide to implementing peer-mediated
interventions in schools / Tai A. Collins & Renee O. Hawkins, (eds.).
Description: New York, NY : Oxford University Press, [2021] |
Includes bibliographical references and index.
Identifiers: LCCN 2020036528 (print) | LCCN 2020036529 (ebook) |
ISBN 9780190068714 (paperback) | ISBN 9780190068745 |
ISBN 9780190068738 (epub)
Subjects: LCSH: Behavior modification. | Peer mediation. | Peer counseling
of students. | School psychology.
Classification: LCC LB1060.2 .P44 2021 (print) | LCC LB1060.2 (ebook) |
DDC 370.15/28—dc23
LC record available at https://lccn.loc.gov/2020036528
LC ebook record available at https://lccn.loc.gov/2020036529

DOI: 10.1093/med/9780190068714.001.0001

9 8 7 6 5 4 3 2 1

Printed by Marquis, Canada

CONTENTS

CONTRIBUTORS

Victoria T. Babbs, MA, NCSP
Education Specialist, Special
    Education Solutions
Region 4 Education
    Service Center
Houston, TX, USA

Christerallyn A. J. Brown, PhD
Technical Assistance Consultant,
    Special Education
American Institutes for Research
Washington, DC, USA

Tom Cariveau, PhD, BCBA-D, LP
Assistant Professor, Department of
    Psychology
University of North Carolina
Wilmington, NC, USA

Erik W. Carter, PhD
Professor, Special Education
Vanderbilt University
Nashville, TN, USA

Tai A. Collins, PhD, BCBA-D
Associate Professor and Coordinator,
    School Psychology
University of Cincinnati
Cincinnati, OH, USA

Samantha Coyle, PhD
Assistant Professor, Psychology
Montclair State University
Montclair, NJ, USA

Evan H. Dart, PhD, BCBA-D
Associate Professor, Educational and
    Psychological Studies
University of South Florida
Tampa, FL, USA

Cara L. Dillon, MEd
Graduate Student, School Psychology
University of Cincinnati
Cincinnati, OH, USA

Lanae R. Drachslin, MS
Graduate Student, Educational
    Psychology
University of Texas
Austin, TX, USA

Bryn E. Endres, MEd
Graduate Student, School Psychology
University of Cincinnati
Cincinnati, OH, USA

Jessica F. Eshbaugh, MS
Graduate Student, Theory and Practice
    in Teacher Education
The University of Tennessee
Knoxville, TN, USA

Aaron J. Fischer, PhD, BCBA-D, LP
Dee Endowed Professor of School
    Psychology, Department of
    Educational Psychology
University of Utah
Salt Lake City, UT, USA

Douglas Fuchs, PhD
Professor and Nicholas Hobbs Chair
   of Special Education and Human
   Development, Department of
   Special Education
Vanderbilt University
Nashville, TN, USA

Lynn S. Fuchs, PhD
Professor and Dunn Family Chair in
   Psychoeducational Assessment,
   Department of Special Education
Vanderbilt University
Nashville, TN, USA

Mary Katherine Gerrard, MEd
Graduate Student, School Psychology
University of Cincinnati
Cincinnati, OH, USA

Erik J. Girvan, JD, PhD
Associate Professor, School of Law
University of Oregon
Eugene, OR, USA

Renee O. Hawkins, PhD
Professor and Director, School of
   Human Services
University of Cincinnati
Cincinnati, OH, USA

Todd F. Haydon, PhD
Professor, Special Education
University of Cincinnati
Cincinnati, OH, USA

Kate A. Helbig, PhD
Assistant Professor, Counseling and
   Psychology in Education
University of South Dakota
Vermillion, SD, USA

Stacy-Ann A. January, PhD
Assistant Professor, Department of
   Educational and Psychological
   Studies
University of South Florida
Tampa, FL, USA

Devin M. Kearns, PhD
Associate Professor, Department of
   Educational Psychology
University of Connecticut
Storrs, CT, USA

Alana M. Kennedy, EdS
Graduate Student, Special
   Education
University of Cincinnati
Cincinnati, OH, USA

Lori R. Kern, MEd
Graduate Student, Department
   of Educational Psychology and
   Learning Systems
Florida State University
Tallahassee, FL, USA

Hunter C. King, MA, MEd
Graduate Student, Educational
   Psychology
University of Utah
Salt Lake City, UT, USA

Angus Kittelman, PhD
Postdoctoral Scholar, College of
   Education
University of Oregon
Eugene, OR, USA

David A. Klingbeil, PhD
Assistant Professor, Educational
   Psychology
University of Wisconsin
Madison, WI, USA

Shelley Kathleen Krach, PhD, NCSP
Assistant Professor, Educational
   Psychology and Learning Systems
Florida State University
Tallahassee, FL, USA

Skip Kumm, PhD
Assistant Director of Special
   Education, Elmhurst Community
   Unit School District 205
Elmhurst, IL, USA

Heather L. J. Lewis, MEd
Graduate Student, Department of
    Educational Psychology
University of Utah
Salt Lake City, UT, USA

Timothy J. Lewis, PhD
Professor, Special Education
University of Missouri
Columbia, MO, USA

Daniel M. Maggin, PhD
Associate Professor, Special Education
University of Illinois at Chicago
Chicago, IL, USA

Christine K. Malecki, PhD
Professor, Psychology Department
Northern Illinois University
DeKalb, IL, USA

Elizabeth B. McCallum, PhD
Associate Professor, Department of
    Counseling, Psychology, and Special
    Education
Duquesne University
Pittsburgh, PA, USA

Dacia M. McCoy, PhD
Assistant Professor-Educator, Behavior
    Analysis
University of Cincinnati
Cincinnati, OH, USA

Sara C. McDaniel, PhD
Professor, Special Education and
    Multiple Abilities
University of Alabama
Tuscaloosa, AL, USA

Hannah McIntire, MEd
Graduate Student, School Psychology
University of Cincinnati
Cincinnati, OH, USA

Kent McIntosh, PhD
Knight Chair of Special Education,
    Special Education and Clinical
    Sciences
University of Oregon
Eugene, OR, USA

Paul Michael Meng, PhD
Assistant Professor of Early Literacy
    and Special Education, Special
    Education
University of Hawai'i at Mānoa
Honolulu, HI, USA

Tara Moore, PhD
Associate Professor,
    Special Education and Applied
    Behavior Analysis
University of Tennessee
Knoxville, TN, USA

J. Meredith Murphy, PhD, BCBA
Postdoctoral Fellow, Behaviroal
    Medicine and Clinical Psychology—
    Division of Developmental and
    Behavioral Pediatrics
Cincinnati Children's Hospital
    Medical Center
Cincinnati, OH, USA

Shobana Musti-Rao, PhD
Associate Professor, School of
    Education
Pace University
New York City, NY, USA

Laura A. Nabors, PhD
Professor, School of Human
    Services
University of Cincinnati
Cincinnati, OH, USA

Rhonda N. T. Nese, PhD
Assistant Professor, Special Education
    and Clinical Sciences
University of Oregon
Eugene, OR, USA

Christa L. Newman, MEd
Graduate Student, School Psychology
University of Cincinnati
Cincinnati, OH, USA

Michele M. Nobel, PhD
Assistant Professor, Education
Ohio Wesleyan University
Delaware, OH, USA

Julio Cesar Payan, MEd
Graduate Student, Educational
    Psychology
University of Utah
Salt Lake City, UT, USA

Sarah R. Powell, PhD
Associate Professor,
    Special Education
University of Texas
Austin, TX, USA

**Keith C. Radley, PhD,
BCBA-D, NCSP**
Associate Professor,
    Educational Psychology
University of Utah
Salt Lake City, UT, USA

Chelsea Ritter, PhD, BCBA
School Psychologist,
    Aurora Public Schools
Aurora, CO, USA

Ara J. Schmitt, PhD
Professor, Counseling,
    Psychology, and Special
    Education
Duquesne University
Pittsburgh, PA, USA

Meagan N. Scott, MEd
Graduate Student, School Psychology
University of Cincinnati
Cincinnati, OH, USA

Jessica N. Simpson, MEd
Postdoctoral Candidate, Special
    Education
University of Missouri
Columbia, MO, USA

Christopher H. Skinner, PhD
Professor, School Psychology and
    Applied Behavior Analysis
University of Tennessee
Knoxville, TN, USA

**Lisette Franklin Spraggins,
MA, MEd**
Education Specialist, Special
    Education Solutions
Region 4 Education Service Center
Houston, TX, USA

Julia N. Villarreal, MEd
Graduate Student, School Psychology
University of Cincinnati
Cincinnati, OH, USA

Jamie Leigh Yarbrough, PhD
Professor, Psychology
Appalachian State University
Boone, NC, USA

A New Conceptualization
of Peer-Mediated Interventions

TAI A. COLLINS AND RENEE O. HAWKINS ■

School teams are tasked with ensuring access to educational opportunities for all students, which often involves implementing evidence-based interventions intended to improve students' academic, social, emotional, and behavioral outcomes. The responsibility of implementing interventions in schools often falls on teachers and other school staff, stretching already limited resources (Collins, Hawkins, & Flowers, 2018). Decades of research has demonstrated that students can be mobilized to improve their peers' outcomes, whether as an implementation agent or as a vital component of interventions. As such, school-based peer-mediated interventions (PMIs) include a variety of strategies in which students serve as change agents in intervention delivery.

To date, no volume has included a comprehensive description of PMIs across academic, behavioral, and social-emotional interventions. As such, the purpose of this text is to consolidate our current knowledge of school-based PMIs into a collection of viable strategies that can be utilized in schools. First, we situate PMIs as a modern strategies with a variety of advantages, including increasing the developmental appropriateness, contextual fit, and cultural relevance of school-based interventions. Next, we update the conceptualization of PMIs since Kohler and Strain's (1990) seminal review. Finally, we present in-depth discussions of different PMIs, with a particular focus on implementation recommendations and the use of PMIs to promote equity in schools.

ADVANTAGES OF PMIS

Chapters 2 and 3 of this volume cover the various advantages of school-based PMIs. Chapter 2 discusses the critical role that children play in each other's lives with regard to social development and peer influence. Numerous advantages of PMIs are presented, including the efficient use of limited resources in schools. PMIs offer the opportunity for exponentially more opportunities to model appropriate behaviors and for students to practice and receive feedback on their performance than teacher-managed interventions. In this manner, teachers and other school staff can assume a supervisory role in a much more efficient, student-managed intervention rather than attempting to personally implement individualized interventions for target students. Another important advantage of PMIs discussed in Chapter 2 is programming for generalization, as the use of peers as change agents in schools allows access to naturally occurring reinforcement and increases the synergy between training and generalization settings.

Building off one of the advantages discussed in Chapter 2, Chapter 3 discusses the effectiveness of PMIs as culturally relevant school-based interventions. As school populations become increasingly more diverse with regard to language, acculturation, race/ethnicity, gender identity and expression, sexual orientation, religion, and a host of other factors, it has become more critical that school staff serve all students in a way that is consistent with students' and families' lived experiences. Chapter 3 presents an argument of PMIs as a critical component of culturally relevant service delivery, as they can promote to a positive, safe, and welcoming environment for all students, contributing to a community of learners whose success is interdependent (Ladson-Billings, 1994). As such, Chapters 2 and 3 identify the myriad advantages for utilizing students as change agents to improve their peers' outcomes.

A NEW CONCEPTUALIZATION OF PMIS

Kohler and Strain (1990) summarized the emerging research on PMIs (then referred to as peer-assisted interventions), indicating four types of PMIs in the educational and applied behavior analysis literature: (a) peer tutoring, (b) peer modeling, (c) peer management, and (d) group contingencies. In Kohler and Strain's conceptualization, peer tutoring interventions included all strategies in which students were tasked with improving their peers' academic outcomes. Peer modeling interventions involve students demonstrating appropriate behaviors for their peers to observe and repeat. Within peer management interventions, peers are trained to prompt and reinforce nonacademic behaviors in their peers, such as social engagement. Finally, group contingencies include a variety of strategies in which consequences (whether reinforcement or punishment) are based on the behavior of all or some members of a group, which incentivizes students to manage each other's behavior.

In the three decades since Kohler and Strain's (1990) seminal review, research has demonstrated new and innovative uses of peers as change agents within school-based interventions. These studies have also been produced within a changing landscape of education and school-based service delivery, particularly in the areas of multi-tiered systems of support and culturally relevant approaches to serving increasingly diverse student populations. This requires an updated, modern conceptualization of school-based PMIs given the current knowledge base. As such, we propose the following updated conceptualization of PMIs into three categories: (a) Peer-Mediated Academic Interventions (PMAIs); (b) Peer-Mediated Behavioral Interventions (PMBIs); and (c) Peer-Mediated Group Supports. Each of the sections of this book covers one of these categories, discussed in detail next.

THE LANDSCAPE OF PMIS

Peer-Mediated Academic Interventions

PMAIs include strategies in which students play a role as change agents in improving peers' academic outcomes. Chapter 4 reviews the research on PMAIs, including the strengths and challenges of implementing student-managed academic interventions. The following chapters in Section 2 detail four of the current types of PMAIs, including peer tutoring, peer-assisted learning strategies, game-based cooperative learning strategies, and peer-mediated writing interventions. Each of these chapters include practical recommendations for implementation of PMAIs, including selecting student interventionists and teams and managing tutor obsolescence in academic interventions.

Peer-Mediated Behavioral Interventions

PMBIs include strategies in which students are trained to implement behavioral interventions or otherwise serve as change agents within interventions intended to improve peers' nonacademic behaviors. Chapter 9 presents the research supporting each of the types of PMBIs covered in this text, including peer management and peer modeling interventions (both consistent with Kohler and Strain's [1990] conceptualization), as well as peer-mediated pivotal response training, restorative and conflict resolution interventions, peer support arrangements, peer-mediated social skills training, and peer-mediated play interventions. Each of the subsequent chapters covers implementation guidelines for school-based PMBIs.

Peer-Mediated Group Supports

The final section of this text covers Peer-Mediated Group Supports, which are a variety of class-wide and other system-wide supports involving peers as change agents. Chapter 17 introduces the use of peers within system-wide approaches such as multitiered systems of support. In addition to the group contingencies included in Kohler and Strain's (1990) conceptualization, chapters in this text also cover implementation and equity recommendations concerning the use of peers within School-Wide Positive Behavior Interventions and Supports, and classroom management strategies, both with and without incorporating technology.

THIS VOLUME

Students are an underutilized, but readily available resource in schools. This text is a comprehensive collection of the current knowledge base regarding the use of students as change agents within school-based PMIs. This volume includes both review chapters covering the research on PMIs toward a consolidation of the evidence base and practical chapters covering the implementation of PMIs within increasingly underresourced and diverse schools. As school staff continue to grapple with the real-world challenges of ensuring equitable opportunities for all students, we offer a variety of strategies utilizing students as change agents in their own learning communities.

REFERENCES

Collins, T. A., Hawkins, R. O., & Flowers, E. M. (2018). Peer-mediated interventions: A practical guide to utilizing students as change agents. *Contemporary School Psychology, 22*(3), 213–219.

Kohler, F. W., & Strain, P. S. (1990). Peer-assisted interventions: Early promises, notable achievements, and future aspirations. *Clinical Psychology Review, 10*, 441–452.

Ladson-Billings, G. (1994). *The dreamkeepers: Successful teachers of African American children*. San Francisco, CA: Jossey-Bass.

## 2

Peers as Change Agents

RENEE O. HAWKINS, MARY KATHERINE GERRARD,
CHRISTA L. NEWMAN, AND HANNAH MCINTIRE ■

Across theoretical perspectives, peers are recognized as having a significant role in child development (Gross-Manos, 2014). Peer interactions can support the development of a variety of cognitive skills, including language, problem-solving, and academic achievement (Parker, Rubin, Price, & DeRosier, 1995). Further, peers are critical for the social development of children, supporting the acquisition of social skills and facilitating overall socialization (Ladd, 2005). Research suggests that peer interaction can be important for learning and development at very young ages, as even infants can be influenced by peer models (Seehagen & Herbert, 2011). The imitation of peer models then continues throughout childhood and adulthood, with the influence of peers increasing with age (Gross-Manos, 2014). As children progress through adolescence, an increasing amount of time is spent with friends while less time is spent with family, providing more opportunity for peer influence (Brown, Bakken, Ameringer, & Mahon, 2008). There are strong correlations between a child's behavior and that of their peers and these associations are well documented in the literature (Gross-Manos, 2014).

Although much of the research on peer influence has focused on the negative effects of this influence in the context of problematic health and mental health behavior (e.g., smoking, violence, delinquency), research indicates that peer influence also can have positive effects on behavior (Brown et al., 2008). For example, research suggests that children are more likely to engage in prosocial behavior if their friends engage in similar behavior (Choukas-Bradley, Giletta, Cohen, & Prinstein, 2015) and children's views of their peers' academic performance are positively associated with their own performance (Lynch, Lerner, & Leventhal, 2013). Several theories have been proposed to explain the mechanisms behind peer influence, including behavioral theory focusing on reinforcement from peers and group socialization theory focusing on the process of assimilation wherein children become increasingly focused on fitting in the behavioral systems outside the home (Gross-Manos, 2014). Regardless of the specific mechanisms, it is clear that peers play a critical role in the developmental pathways of children. As such, when developing strategies to promote positive behavior and academic achievement in schools, the role of peers should not be overlooked. The research on the role of peer influence in child development provides another layer of support for the use of peer-mediated interventions (PMIs) for instruction and intervention across academic and social-emotional domains. The remainder of this chapter further highlights the many advantages of using peers as change agents, providing specific recommendations for implementation success.

ADVANTAGES OF USING PEERS AS CHANGE AGENTS

Readily Available and Free Resource

The limited number of qualified educators working in schools can serve as a potential barrier to successful intervention implementation across general and special education settings. Although hiring additional teachers and intervention specialists would be ideal, this is often not feasible. Factors such as a lack of additional funding for, and/or scarcity of, potential qualified hires create a barrier for many school districts (Black, 2017). Issues with teacher staffing, such as lower rates of qualified teachers and higher rates of turnover, are even more prevalent within urban and rural areas (Ingersoll, 2001; Mason-Williams, 2015); however, the use of peers as interventionists is virtually free. Resources needed for PMI implementation are limited to the time and personnel required to train students in procedures and possible tangible/edible rewards that may be used to reinforce students' behavior. Peers serve as an invaluable resource as they are readily available. With an estimated 16:1 pupil to teacher ratio (National Center for Education Statistics, 2019), there is an abundance of peers to choose from across classes and throughout the school day. By utilizing peers, teachers may maximize the number of students receiving an intervention and devote more time and resources to students who require additional, possibly more intense instructional and/or behavioral supports (Rohrbeck, Ginsburg-Block, Fantuzzo, & Miller, 2003). In addition, peers can be trained on a variety of academic or social skill interventions appropriate for small group or individualized implementation, depending on the needs of the teacher and classroom.

Increased Opportunities to Respond

Opportunities to respond (OTR) refer to the instructional technique in which an instructor enables the target student to actively participate by providing an instructional question, prompt, statement, etc. The target student emitting the correct response receives reinforcement whereas erroneous responses receive corrective feedback (Fitzgerald Leahy, Miller, & Schardt, 2019). OTRs are a critical component of effective instruction and intervention (Lentz, Allen, & Ehrhardt, 1996). OTRs provide the learning trials necessary for academic and behavioral skill development (Lentz et al., 1996). Increased OTRs are associated with higher levels of academic on-task behavior and lower levels of disruptive behavior (Simonsen, 2015). Increasing OTRs is exceptionally important to the academic and behavioral outcomes of students with disabilities. Students with emotional behavioral disorders (EBDs) often experience lower rates of OTRs to academic instruction (Sutherland, Wehby, & Yoder, 2002). When students with EBD have increased OTRs, they demonstrate higher rates of correct responses, increased task engagement, and decreases in disruptive behavior (Sutherland, Alder, & Gunter, 2003). Moreover, increased OTRs is associated with increases in positive academic outcomes for children with intellectual disabilities (IDs) in inclusive settings (Mortweet et al., 1999).

Through the use of PMIs, the instructor-to-student ratio essentially decreases. When this ratio decreases, target students may experience more OTRs to enhance learning. For example, in classwide peer tutoring (CWPT), the teacher–student ratio is reduced from 1:20 (or more) to 1:1. As a result of this reduced ratio, students can be afforded increased OTRs. Peer-mediated academic interventions (PMAIs), such as CWPT, enhance instruction for the target student and peer as both experience frequent OTRs; receive immediate, corrective feedback; and possibly benefit from increased time spent on the academic task (Bowman-Perrott et al., 2013). In addition to increasing academic OTRs, PMIs can increase OTRs for developing social skills through meaningful interaction during social skill intervention. PMIs can be socially significant for children who struggle with creating relationships with other peers by creating opportunities to engage and get feedback from their peers.

Promote Generalization

The goal of instruction is that a socially meaningful skill is acquired, generalized across settings and situations, and maintained over time; however, skill generalization cannot simply be assumed to occur.—It must be actively and extensively programmed. During the skill acquisition phase, generalization is programmed through the variation of stimulus and response targets, including instructors, materials, locations, times of the day, and stimulus cues (Smith & Gilles, 2003). Having peers serve as change agents allows for the target student to practice skills across settings, times, and people, especially in the context of meaningful social skill development (Watkins et al., 2015). Peers are typically present across instructional periods of the day and often are more available than teachers, who may be present for only certain times of the day and more limited in number.

When focusing on social skills, the use of peers is critical for the generalization of meaningful skills, such as initiation, turn-taking, or reciprocal conversation. Moreover, peers as change agents allow target students to practice skills with same-age peers. In a study conducted by Bambara and colleagues (2018), adolescents with Autism Spectrum Disorder (ASD) practiced conversational skills with typically developing peers during lunch using cue cards. The conversational skills then generalized to novel peers. Another appropriate context for teaching social skills includes the playground. Instead of solely practicing social skills during a pull-out instructional session with an adult interventionist, target students learn in vivo during peer-mediated play at recess (Mason et al., 2014). Furthermore, the use of peers as change agents enables the target student to access natural reinforcement contingencies through interactions with peers. In a recent meta-analysis of peer-mediated social skills, eight out of nine studies reported positive generalization and maintenance effects (Watkins et al., 2015). Interestingly, all studies that reported generalization reported similar peer interventionist selection criteria: typically developing peers with language and social skills, regular attendance, high rates of compliance, and an interest in working with target peers.

While a large breadth of research focuses on the generalization of social skills, PMI and instruction have been demonstrated to increase academic skill generalization. A study conducted by Campbell and colleagues (1991) targeted written language skills, including capitalization, using PMI within a special education classroom. The targeted students and peer instructors demonstrated increases in capitalization within their writing logs as well as response generalization after the intervention ended.

Socially Valid and Culturally Relevant

When choosing to implement an intervention, educators gauge the potential for positive outcomes and the extent to which adoption of a procedure is feasible and aligns with current professional practice (Carter & Kennedy, 2006). PMIs are viewed as practical and feasible by educators within alternative settings and general education settings (Carter & Kennedy, 2006). PMIs are considered socially valid for the peers implementing the intervention. According to a meta-analysis of PMIs for students with intellectual disabilities (IDs), peers across studies reported high levels of satisfaction with the intervention and interest in continuing the procedures. Additionally, peer implementers viewed individuals with ID positively at the end of the intervention, reporting that they perceived the individual with ID as a friend and that they had much in common (Schaefer, Cannella-Malone, & Carter, 2016). PMIs also yield social validity evidence for use with individuals with ASD, as teachers view procedures to be manageable, beneficial to the student, and appropriate for the peer (Chan et al., 2009).

PMIs hold potential to have cultural relevance as well. Peer interventionists can be matched based upon gender, racial/ethnic background, or ability status (see Chapter 3 of this volume for a more complete discussion). However, the majority of current research on PMI focuses on matching peers and target students with varying ability statuses, such as ASD, ID, and EBD. More research is needed to examine the effects of gender, race/ethnicity, or communication skills on academic outcomes for peer management interventions (Dart, Collins, Klingbeil, & McKinley, 2014).

Relying solely on a classroom teacher for instruction and intervention limits the demographic variables of the implementer (e.g., race/ethnicity, age, gender) to those of the teacher, whereas using peers as change agents expands these demographics to all represented by the pool of possible peer implementers, increasing the possibility that a student may work with an intervention agent more similar to themselves. This match may be particularly useful when supporting English Language Learner. Increasingly, teachers are providing instruction to students whose primary language is different than their own. Peers who speak the same language can help support instruction in the classroom throughout the day through PMI.

Increased Student Engagement with Intervention

At the core of all PMIs is that students are working together to promote positive academic and behavioral outcomes. Simply by the nature of the strategies relying on students working together, the procedures may be more engaging. As described earlier, peers play a critical role in child development and as children grow they generally show increased preference for peer interaction over adult interaction. By having students work with peers, instructional and intervention sessions may become more enjoyable than when they are led by an adult. Typically, peers have more shared interests and may feel more comfortable working with someone similar to themselves. As a result, students may be more engaged in sessions, increasing overall intervention effects. Greenwood and colleagues (1987) found higher rates of academic engagement and responding through PMI compared to teacher-mediated interventions. Similarly, Mortweet and colleagues (1999) found larger academic gains and higher rates of engagement during a CWPT program targeting spelling compared to teacher-led instruction.

Access Natural Reinforcement

Within PMIs, students can access several forms of natural reinforcement (Cooper, Heron, & Heward, 2020). First, students' behaviors are reinforced through the positive peer interactions that are core to PMI procedures. Peer interventionists not only provide praise for accurate responding but also provide supportive encouragement throughout implementation. Peers also encourage appropriate behavior from the target student and contribute to social reinforcement through positive interactions that occur during sessions. Second, generalization of the student's positive peer interactions during intervention sessions to other students within the classroom can aid in the formation of new friendships. Next, students may also access social reinforcement from teachers both within and outside intervention sessions. With improved academic performance or classroom behavior, students may experience more positive interactions with teachers as well. Finally, with improvements in academic skills and peer relations, students may find school to be a more positive and reinforcing experience overall.

Promote Social Skill Development

Regardless as to whether a PMI is designed to improve an academic skill or a specific social skill, PMIs have positive effects on students' social behavior (Dart et al., 2014). By their nature, PMIs set the stage for ongoing peer interactions, irrespective of the focus of the intervention. Through reciprocal interactions, peers shape each other's behavior by verbally or nonverbally reinforcing appropriate and acceptable social behavior and ignoring or punishing inappropriate behavior. For students who have social skills deficits, peer change agents can serve as models of appropriate behavior. In cases where students demonstrate appropriate social skills, PMIs provide continued opportunity to practice and further develop these skills through meaningful interactions with peers. Within the literature, Goldstein (1992) discusses the use of PMIs as one of the many strategies used to successfully increase appropriate social interactions between typically developing peers and peers with disabilities. Additionally, incorporating peers in the intervention has been shown to effectively increase social interactions (e.g., helping, sharing, cooperative play, empathy) with the target peers outside of the intervention setting (Goldstein et al., 1992). By using peers as change agents, there is an increase in social skills regardless of the targeted intervention because of the increased peer-to-peer interaction.

Support the Development of Peer Social Relationships

Beyond the targeted gains resulting from PMI implementation, an important secondary gain may be the development of friendships among students involved. PMIs involve ongoing interactions among peers that may evolve into positive social relationships outside the intervention sessions. This possibility may be especially important for students who do not have existing positive peer relationships, including students with disabilities. Fostering friendships that may not have naturally been formed can contribute to the target student making additional friends. Research suggests that school achievement and friendship quality affect each other (Zucchetti, Candela, Sacconi, & Rabaglietti, 2015). PMIs offer a method for potentially positively affecting both through one intervention plan.

RECOMMENDATIONS FOR IMPLEMENTATION

Selecting Appropriate Target Behaviors for PMI

Utilizing peers as interventionists can be an effective and efficient approach to addressing a variety of academic and behavioral concerns (Collins, Gresham, & Dart, 2016). Researchers have implemented PMIs to improve academic skills in reading, spelling, math, and social studies (Bowman-Perrott et al., 2013) as well as social skills including conversation skills, sharing, following directions, and engagement (Dart, McKinley, & Helbig, 2019). In theory, any behavior can be appropriate for PMI; however, it is critical that the behavior is clearly defined and the peer interventionist can accurately determine if the behavior has occurred or not. The target behavior should be defined in such a way that evaluation as to whether the response should be praised or corrected can easily be made by the peer interventionist. For example, if the peer is responsible for implementing a reading intervention, the peer needs to be able to accurately read the material themselves so they are able to provide accurate feedback to the target student. In another academic example, the peer may not have mastered the targeted math skills but could effectively provide feedback if they are provided a sheet with the solutions to the problems. Determinations of the appropriateness of PMIs for academic skills is arguably easier than determining the appropriateness of a PMI for social skills. Clearly defining social behavior while also including acceptable approximations may be challenging and, in turn, result in procedures that are difficult for peers to implement accurately. For PMIs targeting behavior, much attention must be given to creating clear, operational definitions so students inappropriate behaviors are not reinforced. Complex academic and behavioral skills should be broken down into steps to aid in teaching and evaluating a behavior, especially in the context of PMIs.

Training Students as Peer Interventionists

Training requirements vary across different PMIs. For example, peer-mediated group supports may require little to no peer training because they are often implemented by the classroom teacher (Dart et al., 2014). In contrast, peer tutoring, cooperative learning, and peer modeling interventions require that interventionists be formally trained to implement the intervention protocol (Dart et al., 2014). When crafting an intervention, much time and effort is focused on making sure there is a solid plan for the target student both in terms of introducing and implementing the intervention. When it comes to interventions where the peer has responsibility for implementation, significant time and effort should be dedicated to ensuring that the peer is appropriately trained. Intervention implementation can be complicated and involves many skills including giving prompts, providing positive reinforcement after desired target behaviors are demonstrated, and blocking specific target behaviors(Dart et al., 2014). One criticism of PMIs is the number of sessions and amount of time required to train and monitor the peers. Kohler and Strain (1990) advised researchers to include information about this in studies of PMIs so that feasibility could be weighed against intervention effectiveness. However, one could argue that PMI is efficient and will save time in the end. Once the peer is trained, teachers and staff will only be needed to monitor adherence and effects.

To ensure proper adherence to the intervention, one must thoroughly introduce expectations for the steps of the intervention using a detailed script and provide multiple practice opportunities. Examining several variables that may affect the outcomes of PMIs, Dart et al. (2014) found that the amount of time taken to train the peer was the only variable that meaningfully affected intervention effectiveness. Although it was unclear if intricate interventions that require more training are more effective than less intricate interventions or that simply more thoroughly trained interventionists are more effective, the results highlight the importance of preparing the peer interventionist in training (Dart et al., 2014). When creating a training plan, a good place to start is to use the gradual release of responsibility model, or "I do, you do, we do" approach, as it is straightforward and a highly effective plan for training (Pearson & Gallagher, 1983). This means first modeling the steps, then offering guided practice, and finally providing opportunities for independent practice (Kosanovich, 2012). Generous praise and corrective feedback should be utilized throughout this training model (Bear, 2010).

Careful Selection of Peers to Serve as Intervention Agents

There are many factors one must consider when selecting a peer to serve as an intervention agent; however, the most important is that the student is able to implement the plan as intended. The student must have the skills and motivation to follow the intervention script and accurately evaluate student performance. Previous research suggests that it is not critical that peers be matched by gender (Dart et al., 2014) or age (Wright & Cleary, 2006). However, based on social learning theory and the literature on children's social development, if all other factors are equal, it may be preferable to select a peer interventionist who is similar to the target student. The best models for learning are as similar as possible to the learner (Bandura, 2001). Further, students respond well to those who are their own age and are empowered by being able to solve problems without perceived adult assistance (Myrick, 2002). If a peer is similar to the target student and is modeling the desired behaviors, the target student may better relate to them. Thus, they will better envision themselves also engaging in similar, appropriate behaviors. In the next chapter, we will further explore this concept of crafting culturally responsive interventions by selecting similar peers for PMI.

Another important consideration is the value of the peer interactions. Ideally, the peer interventionist would be a preferred peer for the target student, increasing the chances that the target student is engaged in the intervention and experiences positive peer interactions. For example, if a student looks up to an older peer and finds their experience and opinions valuable, they may be the best choice for implementation. If a peer is similar to the target student, but the student does not get along with them, they may not be an effective interventionist. The target student must feel comfortable enough with the peer interventionist to follow instructions, accept feedback for errors, receive praise for accurate responding, and positively engage in the procedures.

Ongoing Monitoring of Adherence and Retraining

Peer adherence to the intervention steps should be monitored frequently to ensure the intervention is being implemented as intended. It is important to check in regularly and make sure the peer understands the different steps of the intervention. A major element to emphasize to the peer is providing ample opportunities for reinforcement to the target student. Monitoring adherence to this part of the intervention is key so that the student recognizes when they are accurately responding and to ensure that the intervention is a positive experience.

Developing a plan for collecting adherence data is vital. To aid in the evaluation of adherence, it is helpful to define each component of the intervention in observable and measurable terms so that the occurrence or nonoccurrence of each step can be readily recognized (Kazdin, 2001). When collecting adherence data, direct assessments of adherence are more reliable than indirect measures and should be utilized whenever possible (Mowbray, Holter, Teague, & Bybee, 2003). However, indirect measures like permanent product reviews or student self-ratings can provide valuable additional information about the intervention delivery. It may be useful to vary the days adherence data are collected so the peer is not always expecting to be observed during implementation. This will give a more accurate representation of how the intervention is truly being implemented. If it becomes clear that the peer has misunderstood or forgotten a step, retraining may need to take place. Having a refresher with the script and opportunities to practice can help resolve these issues. Going back to the aforementioned modeling, guided practice, and independent practice can make the retraining a simple and effective process. Adherence to the intervention steps and/or active participation in the training can be incentivized through a system of reinforcement.

System for Reinforcing the Peer Interventionist's Implementation

Although peers can serve as effective intervention agents, the real question is, will they? For PMIs to be effective, the peer must be motivated to participate. This means creating a system of reinforcement for the peer to make sure the role of interventionist is highly motivating. One should conduct a preference assessment with the peer and find what they are willing to work for to create an individualized plan for reinforcement. Praise and tangible rewards can be highly motivating, but there are other, more intrinsic motivators to consider as well. It is important to highlight the value and usefulness of the behaviors the intervention is targeting and then emphasize the importance of the peer's role, as this can be just as reinforcing (Bear, 2010).

CONCLUSION

School systems are under ever-increasing pressure to meet the academic, behavioral, and social-emotional needs of students with often limited and decreasing resources. Peers are a readily available resource who can be leveraged for the benefit of all students through the implementation of PMIs. Although time and careful planning are required to set the stage for success during PMI implementation, these efforts can be well worth it to improve significant outcomes for students.

REFERENCES

Bandura, A. (2001). Social cognitive theory: An agentic perspective. *Annual Review of Psychology, 52,* 1–26.

Bear, G. G. (2010). *School discipline and self-discipline: A practical guide to promoting prosocial student behavior.* New York, NY: Guilford Press.

Black, D. W. (2017). Averting educational crisis: Funding cuts, teacher shortages, and the dwindling commitment to public education. *Washington University Law Review, 94*(2), 423.

Bowman-Perrott, L., Davis, H., Vannest, K., Williams, L., Parker, R., & Greenwood, C. (2013). Academic benefits of peer tutoring: A meta-analytic review of single-case research. *School Psychology Review, 42*(1), 39–55.

Brown, B. B., Bakken, J. P., Ameringer, S. W., & Mahon, S. D. (2008). A comprehensive conceptualization of the peer influence process in adolescence. In M. J. Prinstein & K. A. Dodge (Eds.), *Understanding peer influence in children and adolescents* (pp. 17–44). New York, NY: Guilford.

Campbell, B. J., Brady, M. P., & Linehan, S. (1991). Effects of peer-mediated instruction on the acquisition and generalization of written capitalization skills. *Journal of Learning Disabilities, 24*(1), 6–14. https://doi.org/10.1177/002221949102400103

Carter, E. W., & Kennedy, C. H. (2006). Promoting access to the general curriculum using peer support strategies. *Research and Practice for Persons with Severe Disabilities, 31*(4), 284–292. https://doi.org/10.1177/154079690603100402

Chan, J. M., Lang, R., Rispoli, M., O'Reilly, M., Sigafoos, J., & Cole, H. (2009). Use of peer-mediated interventions in the treatment of autism spectrum disorders: A systematic review. *Research in Autism Spectrum Disorders, 3*(4), 876–889. https://doi.org/10.1016/j.rasd.2009.04.003

Choukas-Bradley, S., Giletta, M., Cohen, G. L., & Prinstein, M. J. (2015). Peer influence, peer status, and prosocial behavior: An experimental investigation of peer socialization of adolescents' intentions to volunteer. *Journal of Youth and Adolescence, 44,* 2197–2210. https://doi.org/10.1007/s10964-015-0373-2

Collins, T. A., Gresham, F. M., & Dart, E. H. (2016). The effects of peer-mediated Check-In/Check-Out on the social skills of socially neglected students. *Behavior Modification, 40*(4), 568–588. https://doi.org/10.1177/0145445516643066

Cooper, J. O., Heron, T. E., & Heward, W. L. (2020). *Applied behavior analysis* (3rd ed.). Hoboken, NJ: Pearson.

Dart, E. H., Collins, T. A., Klingbeil, D. A., & McKinley, L. E. (2014). Peer management interventions: A meta-analytic review of single-case research. *School Psychology Review, 43*(4), 367–384. https://doi.org/10.17105/SPR-14-0009.1

Dart, E. H., McKinley, L. E., & Helbig, K. A. (2019). Peer-mediated interventions. In K. C. Radley & E. H. Dart (Eds.), *Handbook of behavioral interventions in schools: Multi-tiered systems of support* (pp. 368–386). New York, NY: Oxford University Press. https://doi.org/10.1093/med-psych/9780190843229.003.0019

Fitzgerald Leahy, L. R., Miller, F. G., & Schardt, A. A. (2019). Effects of teacher-directed opportunities to respond on student behavioral outcomes: A quantitative synthesis of single-case design research. *Journal of Behavioral Education, 28*(1), 78–106. https://doi.org/10.1007/s10864-018-9307-x

Goldstein, H., Kaczmarek, L., Pennington, R., & Shafer, K. (1992). Peer-mediated intervention: Attending to, commenting on, and acknowledging the behavior of preschoolers with autism. *Journal of Applied Behavior Analysis, 25*, 289–305.

Greenwood, C. R., Dinwiddie, G., Bailey, V., Carta, J. J., Dorsey, D., Kohler, F. W., . . . Schulte, D. (1987). Field replication of classwide peer tutoring. *Journal of Applied Behavior Analysis, 20*(2), 151–160. https://doi.org/10.1901/jaba.1987.20-151

Gross-Manos D. (2014). The role of peers in children's lives and their contribution to child well-being: Theory and research. In A. Ben-Arieh, F. Casas, I. Frones, & J. E. Korbin (Eds.), *Handbook of child well-being* (pp. 1843–1863). Dordrecht, Netherlands: Springer.

Ingersoll, R. M. (2001). Teacher turnover and teacher shortages: An organizational analysis. *American Educational Research Journal, 38*(3), 499–534. https://doi.org/10.3102/00028312038003499

Kazdin, A. E., (2001). *Behavior modification in applied settings* (6th ed.). Belmont, CA: Wadsworth.

Kohler, F. W., & Strain, P. S. (1990). Peer-assisted interventions: Early promises, notable achievements, and future aspirations. *Clinical Psychology Review, 10*, 441–452. https://doi.org/10.1016/0272-7358(90)90047-E

Kosanovich, M. (2012). *Using instructional routines to differentiate instruction: A guide for teachers*. Portsmouth, NH: RMC Research Corporation, Center on Instruction.

Ladd, G. W. (2005). *Children's peer relations and social competence: A century of progress*. New Haven, CT: Yale University Press.

Lentz, F. E., Jr., Allen, S. J., & Ehrhardt, K. E. (1996). The conceptual elements of strong interventions in school settings. *School Psychology Quarterly, 11*, 118–136.

Lynch, A. D., Lerner, R. M., & Leventhal, T. (2013). Adolescent academic achievement and school engagement: An examination of the role of school-wide peer culture. *Journal of Youth and Adolescence, 42*(1), 6–19.

Mason, D. R., Kamps, A. Turcotte, S. Cox, S., Feldmiller, T. M., & Miller, T. (2014). Peer mediation to increase communication and interaction at recess for students with autism spectrum disorders. *Research in Autism Spectrum Disorders, 8*, 334–344. https://doi.org/10.1016/j.rasd.2013.12.014

Mason-Williams, L. (2015). Unequal opportunities: A profile of the distribution of special education teachers. *Exceptional Children, 81*(2), 247–262. https://doi.org/10.1177/0014402914551737

Mortweet, S. L., Utley, C. A., Walker, D., Dawson, H. L., Delquadri, J. C., Reddy, S., . . . Ledford, D. (1999). Classwide peer tutoring: Teaching students with mild mental retardation in inclusive classrooms. *Exceptional Children, 65*(4), 524–536.

Mowbray, C. T., Holter, M. C., Teague, G. B., & Bybee, D. (2003). Fidelity criteria: Development, measurement, and validation. *American Journal of Evaluation, 24,* 964–981.

Myrick, R. D. (2002). Peer mediation and conflict resolution. In S. E. Brock, P. J. Lazarus, & S. R. Jimerson (Eds.), *Best practices in crisis prevention and intervention in the schools* (pp. 181–211). Bethesda, MD: National Association of School Psychologists.

National Center for Education Statistics. (2019). *Digest of education statistics 2017* (53rd ed.). Washington, DC: U.S. Department of Education.

Parker, J. G., Rubin, K. H., Price, J. M., & DeRosier, M. E. (1995). Peer relationships, child development, and adjustment: A developmental psychopathology perspective. In D. Cicchetti & D. J. Cohen (Eds.), *Developmental psychopathology* (Vol. 2, pp. 96–161). New York, NY: Wiley.

Pearson, P. D., & Gallagher, M. C. (1983). The instruction of reading comprehension. *Contemporary Educational Psychology, 8*(3), 317–344.

Rohrbeck, C. A., Ginsburg-Block, M. D., Fantuzzo, J. W., & Miller, T. R. (2003). Peer-assisted learning interventions with elementary school studies: A meta-analytic review. *Journal of Educational Psychology, 95*(2), 240.

Schaefer, J. M., Cannella-Malone, H. I., & Carter, E. W. (2016). The place of peers in peer-mediated interventions for students with Intellectual Disability. *Remedial and Special Education, 37*(6), 345–356. https://doi.org/10.1177/0741932516629220

Seehagen, S., & Herbert, J. (2011). Infant imitation from televised peer and adult models. *Infancy, 16*(2), 113–136. https://doi.org/10.1111/j.1532-7078.2010.00045.x

Simonsen, B. (2015). Examining the effects of teacher-directed opportunities to respond on student outcomes: A systematic review of the literature. *Education and Treatment of Children, 38*(2), 211–239. https://doi.org/10.1353/etc.2015.0009

Smith, S. W., & Gilles, D. L. (2003). Using key instructional elements to systematically promote social skill generalization for students with challenging behavior. *Intervention in School and Clinic, 39*(1), 30–37. https://doi.org/10.1177/10534512030390010401

Sutherland, K. S., Alder, N., & Gunter, P. L. (2003). The effect of varying rates of opportunities to respond to academic requests on the classroom behavior of students with EBD. *Journal of Emotional and Behavioral Disorders, 11*(4), 239–248. https://doi.org/10.1177/10634266030110040501

Sutherland, K. S., Wehby, J. H., & Yoder, P. J. (2002). Examination of the relationship between teacher praise and opportunities for students with EBD to respond to academic requests. *Journal of Emotional and Behavioral Disorders, 10*(1), 5–13. https://doi.org/10.1177/106342660201000102

Watkins, L., O'Reilly, M., Kuhn, M., Gevarter, C., Lancioni, G. E., Sigafoos, J., & Lang, R. (2015). A review of peer-mediated social interaction interventions for students with autism in inclusive settings. *Journal of Autism and Developmental Disorders, 45*(4), 1070–1083.

Wright, J., & Cleary, K. S. (2006). Kids in the tutor seat: Building schools' capacity to help struggling readers though a cross-age peer-tutoring program. *Psychology in the Schools, 43*(1), 99–107.

Zucchetti, G., Candela, F., Sacconi, B., & Rabaglietti, E. (2015). Friendship quality and school achievement: A longitudinal analysis during primary school. *Journal of Applied School Psychology, 31*(4), 297–314. https://doi.org/10.1080/15377903.2015.1084963

## 3

Peers as Culturally Relevant Change Agents

TAI A. COLLINS, MEAGAN N. SCOTT,
JULIA N. VILLARREAL, AND BRYN E. ENDRES ■

The racial and ethnic makeup of U.S. schools continues to diversify, as students of color now make up over half the population of 63 out of 100 of the nation's largest school districts (Goldenberg, 2014). With projections indicating a continued increase in racially and ethnically minoritized students, it is concerning that the population of teachers in U.S. schools remains overwhelmingly White (Goldenberg, 2014; La Salle, Wang, Wu, & Neves, 2020). Also, given the number of opportunity gaps associated with minoritized students (e.g., achievement and discipline gaps; Goldenberg, 2014), it is now more important than ever that schools adopt a culturally competent approach to serving students of color. In particular, teachers must adapt their approach to serve increasingly culturally diverse classrooms and develop what Gay (2002) described as "critical cultural consciousness" (p. 619). School staff must be aware of their own culture, intersectional identities, and how their biases may affect their approach to serving minoritized students, especially in the realm of behaviors and social expectations (Cartledge & Kourea, 2008). This contributes to a social justice approach focused on advocacy, ensuring the rights of all students are protected and equitable opportunities for all students are available (Shriberg et al., 2008).

Culturally relevant service delivery in schools requires intentionality, as school teams must make deliberate efforts to become informed about the cultures, expected behaviors, motivations, and customs of the students and families they serve and incorporate this knowledge into their expectations and behaviors (Cartledge & Kourea, 2008). Cartledge and Korea (2008) identified critical elements of culturally responsive service delivery in schools, including intentionally reducing skill gaps, making data-based decisions with a particular focus on fairness and equitable access to resources, and utilizing direct instruction (i.e., prioritizing active responding, appropriate goals, and pacing, etc.). It is also important that schools attend to within-group heterogeneity, as individuals within groups are not monolithic and often differ widely in their ethnic identity and expression (Lopez, Edwards, Pedrotti, Ito, & Rasmussen, 2002). As such, schools must avoid "The New Prejudice," (Hayes & Taormino, 1995, p. 23) which is the assumption that all individuals within a group fit preconceived stereotypes. Rather, school staff should balance their knowledge of cultural norms for given groups with an analysis of individual students' lived experiences, expectations, contingencies, and skills.

CULTURALLY RELEVANT INTERVENTION ADAPTATIONS

Implementing culturally relevant interventions is a critical component of a social justice approach to serving minoritized students in schools. School staff often strive to implement evidence-based interventions; however, the criteria used to classify interventions as evidence-based do not require interventions to be implemented with minoritized students or demonstrated as generalizable to these populations (Ingraham & Oka, 2006). As such, interventions classified as evidence-based (i.e., without having been implemented with populations of color) can be adapted by infusing culturally relevant elements.

Brown, Maggin, and Buren (2018) identified three types of cultural adaptations to interventions: (a) procedural adaptations, including involving relevant stakeholders and reviewing intervention material for cultural fit; (b) content adaptations, such as the language, goals, representation, and metaphors utilized in the intervention; and (c) program delivery adaptations, including the intervention agent, method of delivery (e.g., online or face to face), and location of intervention delivery. These types of adaptations are grounded in the Ecological Validity Framework (Bernal, Bonilla, & Bellido, 1995), which includes dimensions of culturally responsive psychosocial interventions such as the goals, concepts, metaphors, content, language, context, and persons. The persons dimension focuses on the similarities and differences in ethnicity and culture of the intervention agent (e.g., therapist) and client, as therapists are encouraged to be intentional about improving their cultural competence, as well as facilitate an open dialogue with their clients about cultural similarities and differences (Bernal et al., 1995). Considering the demographic variables, cultural competence, and therapeutic relationship of the intervention agent is an often cited method of improving the cultural competence of interventions (Ingraham & Oka, 2006).

Researchers have identified factors that should be considered when adapting interventions to serve minoritized populations. Although Griner and Smith (2006) found that culturally adapted interventions were more effective than generic interventions (i.e., interventions that had not been intentionally adapted to fit the intended population), the reviews and meta-analyses on cultural adaptations are mixed, and more research needs to be conducted in this area. Researchers have indicated that simple translation of intervention and assessment content into different languages is not sufficient, as the translated language should then be adapted for appropriate use in the intended culture (Lopez et al., 2002). With regard to matching the intervention agent and client on demographic variables, Castro, Barrera, and Martinez (2004) cautioned that this use of surface structure should be accompanied by elements of deep structure, such as incorporating the cultural values, norms, and lived experiences of the client. In a review of school-based social-emotional intervention adaptations, Brown and colleagues (2018) found that matching the student and intervention agent on race or ethnicity was the most common type of program delivery adaptation; however, they also noted that matching on race/ethnicity may not be possible due to the lack of diversity in the teacher workforce. We posit that empowering similarly acculturated peers to implement interventions is a viable strategy to overcome this issue, as well as others.

PEERS AS CULTURALLY RELEVANT CHANGE AGENTS

Other chapters of this volume detail the utility of peers as interventionists in a variety of school-based academic, behavioral, and social-emotional interventions. Not only can students implement interventions, but research has also demonstrated that peers can be trained to reliably implement a variety of interventions with treatment integrity (e.g., Collins, Gresham, & Dart, 2016). As educators struggle to balance the issues of fidelity of evidence-based interventions and contextual fit of intervention adaptations (Castro et al., 2004), utilizing peers to implement interventions with both cultural relevance and fidelity is a promising option for serving minoritized students in schools. We posit that peers can be utilized as culturally responsive change agents in schools for four reasons: (a) communities of color often share a communal orientation emphasizing collaboration and mutual success; (b) studies in education and psychology have indicated that clients prefer to be matched with intervention agents on race and ethnicity; (c) peers can be used to overcome cultural mismatches in schools between students and staff; and (d) peers can be utilized as developmentally and culturally appropriate models.

Communal Orientation

Classrooms are not culturally neutral environments. They often reflect the mainstream, White American values consistent with the population of teachers rather than students (Boykin, Tyler, & Miller, 2005). Western White values typically emphasize independence, individualism, and competition, as success is often determined by surpassing others (Boykin et al., 2005; Coleman, Bruce, White, Boykin, & Tyler, 2017). In contrast, communities of color often adhere to a communal orientation emphasizing the "fundamental interdependence of people, where one places importance and priority on social bonds, mutuality, and proactive interconnectedness with others" (Boykin et al., 2005, p. 532). Issues of shared ownership, collaboration, and community are important characteristics of the communal orientation typically shared by minoritized groups such as Black Americans (Boykin et al., 2005) and Indigenous communities (McIntosh, Moniz, Craft, Golby, & Steinwand-Deschambeault, 2014). Clashes between individualistic and communal orientations may contribute to the tensions often seen between White teachers and students of color (discussed in the following text).

Ladson-Billings (1994) argued that culturally relevant service delivery for students of color should involve the establishment of *communities of learners* consistent with a communal orientation: "As members of an extended family, the students assist, support, and encourage one another. The entire group rises and falls together" (p. 76). In this manner, school cultures should become more consistent with the cultures of their students, as students should be encouraged to prioritize the learning and success of their peers rather than just their own (Boykin et al., 2005; Gay, 2002). A growing body of literature indicates that communal learning arrangements incorporating group seat layouts, and expectations and prompts pertaining to collaboration and shared accountability are more beneficial than individual learning contexts (i.e., involving individual seat layouts and not encouraging cooperation) for Black American students for academic skills in simulated classrooms (e.g., Coleman et al., 2017). In classrooms with a diversity of student ethnicities and races, it is critical that students learn from their peers who come from different backgrounds, and that a community of learners focused on collaboration be established (Gay, 2002). The utilization of peers in intervention implementation is consistent with a communal orientation, as peer-mediated interventions provide structured opportunities for students to support each other's development and success (Cartledge & Kourea, 2008).

Preference for Racial/Ethnic Match

Evidence in the educational literature suggests that racial/ethnic match between students and teachers is a protective factor. Greater academic gains have been demonstrated for both Black and White students when paired with a teacher of the same race/ethnicity rather than in mixed pairs (Egalite, Kisida, & Winters, 2015). Students and teachers have better perceptions of each other in same-race pairs, and lower absenteeism has been demonstrated (Rasheed, Brown, Doyle, & Jennings, 2020). Additionally, students indicate higher rates of college aspirations and more favorable perceptions of their teacher when matched on both race and gender (Egalite & Kisida, 2018). These studies indicate that race matters in the educational outcomes and perceptions of all students in terms of the match between teachers and students. Having similarly acculturated peers implement interventions may be a strong alternative, especially in situations in which a racial/ethnic match between teachers and students is unavailable.

Peer-mediated interventions may also be beneficial as culturally responsive interventions given the evidence from the psychotherapy literature about individuals' preference for interventionists of the same race/ethnicity. In a landmark meta-analysis of psychotherapy studies, Cabral and Smith (2011) found that racial/ethnic match of therapists and clients was not associated with significantly better treatment outcomes; however, studies demonstrated that participants indicated a preference for therapists of the same race/ethnicity. In Black American populations specifically, the study indicated a strong preference for Black therapists, as well as better therapeutic outcomes when paired with a Black therapist (Cabral & Smith, 2011). Cabral and Smith (2011) noted that similarity in race/ethnicity breeds credibility and trust, as clients assume that same-race therapists share their worldviews and lived experiences. Also, Griner and Smith (2006) found that mental health interventions adapted to specific populations and implemented with same-race participants were four times as effective as interventions implemented with mixed-race groups. As these studies indicate that client preference (and, to a lesser extent, client outcomes) is affected by the racial/ethnic match of clients and therapists, it is important to note that racial/ethnic matches are not always possible, especially when considering intersectionality (Ertl, Mann-Saumier, Martin, Graves, & Altarriba, 2019). Finding a peer who closely mirrors the intersectional identities of the target student is likely a more viable option than finding a teacher in schools given the racial/ethnic makeup of the teacher population.

Cultural Mismatches in Schools

The growing diversity of the school-aged population and the lack of diversity in the teacher population often leads to cultural mismatches that have negative implications for minoritized students. La Salle and colleagues (2020) found that fewer than 2% of schools in their sample had percentages of minoritized teachers matching or exceeding the population of minoritized students. Incongruence between the culture of students and teachers often leads to cultural clashes (Boykin et al., 2005; Goldenberg, 2014). In particular, teachers often misinterpret behaviors that are appropriate in students' cultures as inappropriate or disrespectful, resulting in the disproportionate use of punitive discipline such as suspension and expulsion with minoritized students (Blake et al., 2016; McIntosh et al., 2014). Blake and colleagues (2016) described the cultural synchrony hypothesis, which posits that the differences in culture between teachers and students, combined with stereotypes brought about by negative portrayals of Black Americans in the media, leads to teachers' misinterpretation of behaviors and overuse of punishment. No evidence suggests that students of color engage in higher rates of problem behavior than White students, yet disproportionality in discipline continues to persist (Losen & Skiba, 2010). In fact, minoritized students are at higher risk for being disproportionately punished when they are paired with teachers of a different race (Blake et al., 2016).

Culture clashes and punishment decisions are related to teachers' expectations of students, which are influenced by issues including race, socioeconomic status, and language, among others (Dee, 2005; McIntosh et al., 2014). Similarities and differences in race/ethnicity of teachers and students can have active effects, including both intentional and unintentional changes in teacher behavior, as well as passive effects, including positive effects of role modeling and negative effects of activating stereotype threat in minoritized students (Dee, 2005). Given the dearth of minoritized teachers, it is important that minoritized students who attended schools with higher percentages of other minoritized students reported higher perceptions of school climate (La Salle et al., 2020). This indicates the importance of cultural acceptance and connectedness among a community of peers, especially in cases in which teachers do not share students' race/ethnicity (La Salle et al., 2020). As minoritized students are much more likely than White students to go to schools with diverse populations of students (La Salle et al., 2020), having a similarly acculturated peer implement interventions may lead to more safe, positive, and equitable spaces for minoritized students. In situations where cultural clashes may be likely given the incongruence between students and teachers, peers provide a promising option to improve school climate and student outcomes in learning communities.

Peer Modeling

According to social learning theory (Bandura, 1997), individuals learn a variety of behaviors by observing others engage in behaviors. Evidence suggests that modeling is more effective when the model is similar to the observer in terms of race/ethnicity, gender, age, and ability (Bandura, 1997). Observers' self-efficacy in completing the modeled behavior is enhanced when a similar model achieves success, as their success is viewed as attainable (Bandura, 1997). As such, peers are often the next best option to the individual serving as their own model in school-based interventions (Richards, Heathfield, & Jenson, 2010). In the area of language development, Murphey (1998) described the use of near peer role models, who are similar in factors such as culture, ethnicity, language, gender, and age to the target student. Using near peer role models may limit stereotype threat and improve observers' self-efficacy as they learn from the successes and mistakes of similar peers (Bandura, 1997; Murphey, 1998). Compared to video self-modeling, peer modeling has the added benefit of being able to be used with multiple target students, as well as entire classrooms of students (Richards et al., 2010). Near peer role models can prompt, reinforce, and occasion appropriate behaviors in addition to both incidental and planned modeling in peer-mediated interventions, which makes them a viable alternative in intervention delivery.

CONCLUSION

As discussed throughout this volume, peers can be effectively utilized in a variety of school-based interventions. In this chapter, we posit four reasons why peers can be used as culturally relevant change agents within peer-mediated interventions. We argue that peers are a viable option in improving the cultural and developmental relevance of interventions, especially in situations in which there is a cultural mismatch between students and teachers. School staff often struggle to find appropriate adult mentors and models for minoritized students. We posit that similarly acculturated peers (e.g., near peer role models) are more often available and can be reliably trained to support the academic, social, emotional, and behavioral success of their fellow students.

REFERENCES

Bandura, A. (1997). *Self-efficacy: The exercise of control*. New York, NY: W. H. Freeman.

Bernal, G., Bonilla, J., & Bellido, C. (1995). Ecological validity and cultural sensitivity for outcome research: Issues for the cultural adaptation and development of psychosocial treatments with Hispanics. *Journal of Abnormal Child Psychology, 23*(1), 67–82. doi:10.1007/bf01447045

Blake, J. J., Smith, D. M., Marchbanks, M. P., Seibert, A. L., Wood, S. M., & Kim, E. S. (2016). Does student teacher racial/ethnic match impact Black students' discipline risk? A test of the cultural synchrony hypothesis. In R. J. Skiba, K. Mediratta, & M. K. Rausch (Eds.), *Inequality in school discipline: Research and practice to reduce disparities* (pp. 79–98). New York, NY: Palgrave MacMillan.

Boykin, A. W., Tyler, K. M., & Miller, O. (2005). In search of cultural themes and their expressions in the dynamics of classroom life. *Urban Education, 40*(5), 521–549. doi:10.1177/0042085905278179

Brown, C., Maggin, D. M., & Buren, M. (2018). Systematic review of cultural adaptations of school-based social, emotional, and behavioral interventions for students of color. *Education and Treatment of Children, 41*(4), 431–456. doi:10.1353/etc.2018.0024

Cabral, R. R., & Smith, T. B. (2011). Racial/ethnic matching of clients and therapists in mental health services: A meta-analytic review of preferences, perceptions, and outcomes. *Journal of Counseling Psychology, 58*(4), 537–554. doi:10.1037/a0025266

Cartledge, G., & Kourea, L. (2008). Culturally responsive classrooms for culturally diverse students with and at risk for disabilities. *Exceptional Children, 74*(3), 351–371.

Castro, F. G., Barrera, J. M., & Martinez, J. C. R. (2004). The cultural adaptation of prevention interventions: Resolving tensions between fidelity and fit. *Prevention Science, 5*(1), 41–45. doi:10.1023/b:prev.0000013980.12412.cd

Coleman, S. T., Bruce, A. W., White, L. J., Boykin, A. W., & Tyler, K. (2017). Communal and individual learning contexts as they relate to mathematics achievement under simulated classroom conditions. *Journal of Black Psychology, 43*(6), 543–564. doi:10.1177/0095798416665966

Collins, T. A., Gresham, F. M., & Dart, E. H. (2016). Peer-mediated check-in/check-out on the social skills of socially neglected students. *Behavior Modification, 40*(4), 568–588. doi:10.1177/0145445516643066

Dee, T. S. (2005). A teacher like me: Does race, ethnicity, or gender matter? *American Economic Review, 95*(2), 158–165. doi:10.1257/000282805774670446

Egalite, A. J., & Kisida, B. (2018). The effects of teacher match on children's academic perceptions and attitudes. *Educational Evaluation and Policy Analysis, 40*(1), 59–81. doi:10.3102/0162373717714056

Egalite, A. J., Kisida, B., & Winters, M. A. (2015). Representation in the classroom: The effect of own-race/ethnicity teachers on children achievement. *Economics of Education Review, 45*, 44–52. doi:10.1016/ j.econedurev.2015.01.007

Ertl, M. M., Mann-Saumier, M., Martin, R. A., Graves, D. F., & Altarriba, J. (2019). The impossibility of client-therapist "match": Implications and future directions for multicultural competency. *Journal of Mental Health Counseling, 41*(4), 312–326. doi:10. Ill44\mehc.41.4.03

Gay, G. (2002). Culturally responsive teaching in special education for ethnically diverse students: Setting the stage. *International Journal of Qualitative Studies in Education, 15*(6), 613–629. doi:10.1080/09518390220000014349

Goldenberg, B. M. (2014). White teachers in urban classrooms: Embracing non-white students' cultural capital for better teaching and learning. *Urban Education, 49*(1), 111–144. doi:10.1177/0042085912472510

Griner, D., & Smith, T. B. (2006). Culturally adapted mental health interventions: A meta-analytic review. *Psychotherapy: Theory, Research, Practice, Training, 43*(4), 531–548.

Hayes, S. C., & Taormino, D. (1995). If behavioral principles are generally applicable, why is it necessary to understand cultural diversity? *Behavior Therapist, 18*, 21–23.

Ingraham, C. L., & Oka, E. R. (2006). Multicultural issues in evidence-based interventions. *Journal of Applied School Psychology, 22*(2), 127–149. doi:10.1300/J370v22n02_07

Ladson-Billings, G. (1994). *The dreamkeepers: Successful teachers of African American children.* San Francisco, CA: Jossey-Bass.

La Salle, T. P., Wang, C., Wu, C., & Neves, J. R. (2020). Racial mismatch among minoritized students and white teachers: Implications and recommendations for moving forward. *Journal of Educational and Psychological Consultation, 30*(3), 314–343. doi:10.1080/10474412.2019.1673759

Lopez, S. J., Edwards, L., Pedrotti, J. T., Ito, A., & Rasmussen, H. N. (2002). Culture counts: Examinations of recent applications of the Penn Resiliency Program, or, toward a rubric for examining cultural appropriateness of prevention programming. *Prevention & Treatment, 5*(1), 12. doi:10.1037/1522-3736.5.1.512c

Losen, D. J., & Skiba, R. J. (2010). Suspended education: Urban middle schools in crisis. *The Civil Rights Project.* Retrieved from http://escholarship.org/uc/item/8fh0s5dv

McIntosh, K., Moniz, C., Craft, C. B., Golby, R., & Steinwand-Deschambeault, T. (2014). Implementing school-wide positive behavioral interventions and supports to better meet the needs of Indigenous students. *Canadian Journal of School Psychology, 29*(3), 236–257. doi:10.1177/0829573514542217

Murphey, T. (1998). Motivating with near peer role models. In B. Visgatis (Ed.), *On JALT'97: Trends & Transitions* (pp. 205–209). Tokyo, Japan: JALT.

Rasheed, D. S., Brown, J. L., Doyle, S. L., & Jennings, P. A. (2020). The effect of teacher-child race/ethnicity matching and classroom diversity on children's socioemotional and academic skills. *Child Development, 91*(3), e597–e618. doi:10.1111/cdev.13275

Richards, L. C., Heathfield, L. T., & Jenson, W. R. (2010). A classwide peer-modeling intervention package to increase on-task behavior. *Psychology in the Schools, 47*(6), 551–566. doi:10.1002/pits.20490

Shriberg, D., Bonner, M., Sarr, B. J., Walker, A. M., Hyland, M., & Chester, C. (2008). Social justice through a school psychology lens: Definitions and applications. *School Psychology Review, 37*(4), 453–468.

Peer-Mediated Academic Interventions

## 4

Peer-Mediated Academic Interventions

SHOBANA MUSTI-RAO AND MICHELE M. NOBEL ■

Teachers face the challenge of teaching not just to the middle of the class, but to differentiate instruction to meet the needs of students with varying abilities. Federal mandates like the Individuals with Disabilities Education Act (IDEA, 2004) require that students with disabilities be educated in the least restrictive environment to the maximum extent possible. With the growing diversity in classrooms, it is important that teachers not only use instructional approaches that have strong evidence of effectiveness, but also have the capacity to actively engage all students in the learning process. One such approach with long-standing effectiveness in academic, behavior, and social areas is peer-mediated interventions (PMIs; Ryan, Reid, & Epstein, 2004). As the name suggests, PMIs include a variety of strategies in which students are responsible to deliver instruction to other students in an organized and structured manner.

In their review of peer-mediated academic interventions (PMAIs), Ryan and colleagues (2004) identified eight types, including Classwide Peer Tutoring (CWPT), Cooperative Learning, Cross-Age Tutoring, Peer Tutoring, Cross-Age Tutoring, Peer Tutoring, Peer-Assisted Learning Strategies (PALS), Peer Assessment, Peer Modeling, and Peer Reinforcement. Although their review was specific to the effects of peer-mediated strategies on the academic outcomes of students with emotional and behavioral disorders, the results of the 2004 review and a more recent review by Dunn, Shelnut, Ryan, and Katsiyannis (2017) collectively indicate that PMAIs were successful across academic subject areas and grade levels. A research synthesis of 14 studies reporting the effects of PMAIs with English learners (ELs) in kindergarten through Grade 12 revealed that the interventions brought about medium to large effects on measures of comprehension, vocabulary, and phonemic awareness when compared to teacher-mediated comparison conditions (Pyle, Pyle, Lignugaris/Kraft, Duran, & Akers, 2017). In this chapter, we will focus on introducing four specific types of PMAIs and will provide evidence of their effectiveness in classrooms. The four types are Peer Tutoring, PALS, Game-Based Cooperative Learning, and Peer-Mediated Writing Interventions. The PMAIs vary in the extent to which they are structured to include a balance between competition and cooperation among students. Some common features across these four types include students assuming and alternating specific roles (e.g., tutor–tutee, coach–player), a highly structured tutoring format, multiple opportunities to respond, a built-in error correction procedure, practice sessions, and a game-like format (Conderman, Bresnahan, & Hedin, 2012). Before discussing the research supporting the use of each of these PMAIs, it would be helpful to identify some of the strengths and challenges when implementing PMAIs in classrooms.

STRENGTHS AND CHALLENGES RELATED TO PMAIS

PMAIs have a long-standing history of effectiveness as supplementary reading or math intervention at the elementary level (e.g., Fuchs, Fuchs, Mathes, & Simmons, 1997; Fuchs, Fuchs, Hamlett, Phillips, & Karns, 1995; Greenwood, Delquadri, & Carta, 1988; Klingner & Vaughn, 1996). Although the research at the secondary level is not as vast, PMAIs have been effective with the middle and high school populations (Calhoon & Fuchs, 2003; Mastropieri et al., 2001; Mastropieri, Scruggs, Spencer, & Fontana, 2003; Veerkamp, Kamps, & Cooper, 2007). Due to the extensive research that exists for using PMAIs, researchers have been able to identify some common strengths and challenges when using PMAIs in the classroom.

Strengths. Some of the strengths commonly cited in the literature are that PMAIs (a) incorporate empirically-supported components of effective instruction, (b) allow for differentiation and individualization of instruction, (c) help alleviate workload demands, and (d) positively impact classroom climate and social behaviors.

Incorporate components of effective instruction. The different types of PMAIs incorporate established components of effective instruction such as academic engagement time, providing students with relevant practice, informed feedback, motivational strategies, and frequent progress evaluation (Ysseldyke, 2007). Students are trained to provide ongoing corrective feedback in a timely manner and provide increased opportunities to respond and practice the skill with peers (Hattie & Timperley, 2007; Wexler, Reed, Pyle, Mitchell, & Barton, 2015). The increased opportunities to respond serves as an antecedent for increased students' responses, which in turn results in teachers' feedback for correct or incorrect responses. The motivation strategies include point systems and public posting of students' individual and/or team performance (Calhoon & Fuchs, 2003). The use of curriculum-based measures is a critical assessment component of PMAIs such as CWPT and PALS and allows both the students and teachers to collect data on ongoing instruction. The training protocols require teachers and students to interpret scores and graphs to evaluate progress on a continuous basis (Baker, Gersten, Dimino, & Griffiths, 2004).

Allow for differentiation and individualization of instruction. The grouping practices adopted by the different types of PMAIs account for the academic diversity present in today's classrooms (Fuchs, Fuchs, Yazdian, & Powell, 2002). The grouping methods used in the various PMAIs ensure that all students are included and are accountable for each other's learning. The heterogeneous grouping method combined with the competitive element in the cooperative learning strategies ensures that all students (high-, average- and low-performing) work together to learn the academic material. In CWPT and PALS, teachers have the ability to *differentiate* instruction for their students by varying the difficulty of the instructional materials for some dyads or by varying the pace with which the student dyads progress through the peer tutoring session (Fuchs & Fuchs, 2005). By the same token, teachers can also *individualize* instruction on a classwide basis by providing students with specific materials to practice and master during the tutoring sessions (Utley, Mortweet, & Greenwood, 1997).

Help alleviate workload demands. Given the diverse needs of students in general education classrooms, PMAIs can be used effectively to help alleviate workload demands on teachers to provide individualized support by using the best resource they have in their classrooms: their students. Research has shown that peers can be effective intervention agents by providing feedback, modeling, and tutoring (Utley et al. 1997; Maheady, Mallette, & Harper 2006). PMAIs significantly lower the instructor to student ratio from 1:25–30 to 1:1. PMAIs free up the teacher to take on more of an administrative role in the classroom to ensure smooth implementation and monitor student progress (Maheady, Harper, & Mallette, 2001). The testing and evaluation component in many forms of PMAIs free teachers of the burden of individually testing students (Okilwa & Shelby, 2010). Because students are involved in data collection and charting of data as part of the process, teachers have data readily available to make instructional decisions.

Positively impact classroom climate and social behaviors. In addition to the academic benefits, PMAIs have the power to positively impact classroom climate and improve social behaviors among students with and without disabilities. Studies on peer tutoring have demonstrated improvements in social and conversational skills (Gumpel & Frank, 1999; Prater, Serna, & Nakamura, 1999), positive effects on classroom behavior (Sutherland & Snyder, 2007), and enhanced interview skills for students transitioning from school to work (Bobroff & Sax, 2010). Maheady, Harper, and Mallette (2001) contend that some forms of cooperative learning strategies allow students "to write and talk about academic content, and to debate, describe, defend, and challenge what they and their classmates are learning" (p.10) and as a result practice important interpersonal skills.

Challenges. Although teachers report high levels of social validity when engaged in PMAIs, which increases the likelihood that they will utilize PMAIs in their classrooms, there are a few challenges for implementing PMAIs noted in the literature. Some of these challenges may also contribute to the limited implementation of PMAIs in a systematic and structured manner in general education classrooms.

Teacher training and support. There is an apparent research to practice gap in the implementation and continuous use of PMAIs in classrooms. One of the strengths of the PALS research is that the studies were conducted in close collaboration with classroom teachers to ensure that PALS was implemented with a high degree of fidelity (Fuchs, Fuchs, Yazdian, & Powell, 2002; Fuchs, Fuchs, Mathes, & Martinez, 2002). The teachers, however, in these studies received on-site technical support in addition to the initial training. Baker and colleagues (2004) contend that the two ingredients to implementation and sustainability of any practice is to have administrative mandate and user commitment. Rohrbeck, Ginsburg-Block, Fantuzzo, and Miller (2003) recommend that the training be part of teacher training curriculums. Therefore, administrators should consider teacher training beyond in-service workshops to include on-going technical support and coaching for sustainable use of PMAIs.

PMAIs with students with low achievement. Wexler et al. (2015) conducted a synthesis of 13 studies that used PMAIs for reading and/or math. Their exploration of social validity data for these studies indicated that teachers in three of the studies (Mastropieri et al., 2001; Mastropieri, Scruggs, Spencer, & Fontana, 2003; Spencer, Scruggs, & Mastropieri, 2003) reported difficultly using PMAIs with students with extremely low achievement. Although research indicates that PMAIs are effective for most students, there have been a small percentage of students including some students at the secondary level who can be considered nonresponders, for example, to the PALS intervention (Calhoon & Fuchs, 2003). More research is needed to understand the conditions in which PMAIs can be effective for these students. This is especially true as educators conceptualize PMAIs as a Tier 1 or Tier 2 intervention in classrooms. Teachers need to use progress monitoring data to determine whether PMAIs are effective in bringing about academic gains (McMaster, Fuchs, & Fuchs, 2007).

EFFECTIVENESS AND EFFICACY OF PMAIS

In this section, we will provide a brief overview of four types of PMAIs (peer tutoring, PALS, game-based cooperative learning strategies, and peer-mediated writing interventions), along with research evidence to demonstrate their effectiveness and efficacy in improving academic outcomes. Each of the PMAIs have their origins with extensive research and development completed in universities from different parts of the United States of the America.

Peer tutoring. With over 40 years of research, PT has emerged as an effective PMAI, with applications across grade levels, content areas, settings (e.g., school, home), socioeconomic status, and student demographics (e.g., disability status, at-risk, EL). PT can be informal, such as when a teacher asks two students to "pair up and review together"; however, PT appears to produce the most effective results when it follows a systems approach (Heron, Villareal, Yao, Christianson, & Heron, 2006).

What constitutes a PT system? PT systems have (a) component parts and procedures such as explicit training to mastery criterion for each component of the system, (b) structured procedures that involve direct instruction with corrective feedback, (c) use of behavioral principles, and (d) a process for data collection and analysis. Since the 1980s, research on the effectiveness of PT systems has been sustained by several research centers (Gardner, Nobel, Hessler, Yawn, & Heron, 2007), each with slight variations on the design and implementation of their subsequent systems. The systems with the most extensive research are CWPT (Delquadri, Greenwood, Stratton, & Hall, 1983), START Tutoring (Heron, Heward, Cooke, & Hill, 1983; Miller, Barbetta, & Heron, 1994), PALS (Fuchs, Fuchs, Mathes, & Simmons, 1997), and Classwide Student Tutoring Teams (CSTT; Maheady, Sacca, & Harper, 1987). For brevity, this section of the chapter will address CWPT and START Tutoring research specifically. PALS and CSTT are discussed later in this chapter. For additional comparisons of these tutoring systems, see Maheady, Mallette, and Harper (2006).

Upon thorough review of PT systems literature, there is broad evidence regarding the effectiveness of tutoring systems. CWPT and START tutoring research spans from the 1980s (e.g., Heron et al., 1983) to recently published studies (e.g., Greene, McTiernan, & Holloway, 2018). Research lines for these systems have a lengthy history of systematic and replicated studies using single-subject research designs to demonstrate a functional relationship between tutoring and dependent variables (Cooper, Heron, & Heward, 2007) and group designs that seek to determine statistical significance and/or effect size (ES) with respect to tutoring applications.

Academic content. PT systems have been used to teach academic content and/or skills to students. Research indicates that PT has been used effectively to teach reading (Barbetta & Heron, 1991; Cooke, Heron, & Heward, 1983; Ezell, Kohler, & Strain, 1994; Oddo, Barnett, Hawkins, & Musti-Rao, 2010), math (Allsopp, 1997; Arreaga-Mayer, 1998; Greene et al., 2018; Harper, Mallette, Maheady, Bentley, & Moore, 1995; Hawkins, Musti-Rao, Hughes, Berry, & McGuire, 2009; Miller, Barbetta, Drevno, Martz, & Heron, 1996; Schloss, Kobza, & Alper, 1997), spelling (Delquadri et al., 1983; Hashimoto, Utley, Greenwood, & Pitchlyn, 2007), social studies/history (Lo & Cartledge, 2004; Mastropieri, Scruggs, Spencer, & Fontana, 2003), science (Bowman-Perrott, Greenwood, & Tapia, 2007; Nobel, 2005) and a variety of specialized content (Heron, Welsch, & Goddard, 2003). In addition to traditional delivery methods of PT, researchers have studied the effects of low tech (Wood, Mackiewicz, Van Norman, & Cooke, 2007) and computer-assisted technologies (Greenwood, Arreaga-Mayer, Utley, Gavin, & Terry, 2001; Wood, Mustian, & Lo, 2013) to enhance the effects of PT. Results of these studies indicate technology can be integrated successfully and effectively into PT systems.

Diverse learners. Over the past 40 years, PT systems have been used across many demographic categories. PT systems have shown promise when addressing the needs of students at-risk for failure (Green, Alderman, & Liechy, 2004; Gumpel & Frank, 1999; Nobel, 2005), ELs (Arreaga-Mayer, Greenwood, & Utley, 1994; Bowman-Perrott, deMartin, Mahadevan, & Etchells, 2016; Houghton & Bain, 1993), students with high incidence disabilities (Harper & Maheady, 2007; Hughes & Fredrick, 2006; Spencer, 2006), and students with low incidence disabilities (Herring-Harrison, Gardner, & Lovelace, 2007; McDonnell, Mathot-Buckner, Thorson, & Fister, 2001; Ward & Ayvazo, 2006).

Diverse settings. PT systems have also been utilized successfully in a variety of diverse instructional settings and grade levels including inclusive general education classrooms (Lo & Cartledge, 2004), self-contained classrooms (Sutherland & Snyder, 2007), resource rooms (Maheady, Sacca, & Harper, 1988), after-school settings (Gardner, Cartledge, Siedl, Woolsey et al., 2001; Heron et al., 1983; Mortweet, 1995), home (Miller et al., 1994), alternative placements (Bowman-Perrott et al., 2007), and group homes (Mayfield & Vollmer, 2007). Likewise, PT systems have been used successfully with students in preschool (Tabacek, McLaughlin, & Howard, 1994), elementary school (Taylor & Alber, 2003), middle school (Kamps, Greenwood, Arreaga-Mayer, Veerkamp, et al., 2008; Okilwa & Shelby, 2010), high school (Mastropieri et al., 2003), and postsecondary settings (Sansone, Ligorio, & Buglass, 2018).

Longitudinal effects. Effects of PT systems have been shown to be long-lasting. Greenwood (1991) presented longitudinal data demonstrating the effects of CWPT across multiple years and found that CWPT increased academic engagement and achievement of at-risk elementary students who continued to benefit academically in middle school (Greenwood, Terry, Utley, Montagna, & Walker, 1993) and were less likely to drop out of high school (Greenwood & Delquadri, 1995).

Recent directions in PT research. More recently, emphasis has been placed on conducting research with added measures of ES to supplement the robust single-subject and group design evidence gathered to date. A meta-analysis conducted by Bowman-Perrott and colleagues (2013) examined effects of PT across 26 single-case research experiments for 938 students in Grades 1–12. Researchers reported an overall ES of 0.75 with a confidence interval of 0.71 to 0.78, which indicates that moderate to large academic benefits can be attributed to PT. In addition, they examined five potential moderators of these effects: dosage (i.e., duration, intensity, number of sessions), grade level, reward, disability status, and content area. Their findings suggest that PT is an effective intervention regardless of dosage, grade level, or disability status. Effect size for PT studies that utilized a reward were statistically significant as compared to those that did not. Effect size varied across content areas with vocabulary having the largest ES (0.92; 95% confidence interval $[CI_{95}] = 0.77–1.0$), followed by math (ES = 0.86; $CI_{95} = 0.78–0.94$), reading (ES = 0.77; $CI_{95} = 0.71–0.82$), spelling (ES = 0.74; $CI_{95} = 0.62–0.85$), and social studies (ES = 0.57; $CI_{95} = 0.50–0.65$). Research such as this study confirming the moderate to large ES of PT intervention provides an additional level of confidence in the effectiveness of PT systems to positively affect student achievement.

Peer-Assisted Learning Strategies

PALS is a peer-mediated instructional approach that originated from work by researchers in the Peabody School of Education at Vanderbilt University. Modeled after the CWPT discussed earlier, PALS has shown positive outcomes for students with a broad range of instructional needs using large-scale rigorous experimental research. The student population in these studies ranged from urban to suburban, including students from high-poverty schools, students with disabilities, and students considered ELs. Students who received PALS significantly outperformed students in the no-PALS control condition in measures of fluency and comprehension at the elementary level (Fuchs et al., 1997), students showed gains in reading comprehension at the high-school level (Fuchs, Fuchs, & Kazdan, 1999), and showed improvements in beginning reading and phonemic awareness at the kindergarten and first-grade levels (Fuchs, Fuchs, Thompson, Al Otaiba et al., 2001; Fuchs et al., 2002). Math PALS has also shown to be effective in increasing the computational abilities of students with and without disabilities (Fuchs, Fuchs, Hamlett, Phillips, & Bentz, 1994), at the first-grade level (Fuchs, Fuchs, Yazdian, & Powell, 2002) and at the high school level (Calhoon & Fuchs, 2003).

One of the greatest strengths of the PALS body of research is the close collaboration between researchers and teachers in its implementation to ensure that the methods are feasible and effective in the classroom. In all of the randomized trial studies, teachers served as the intervention agents. The initial teacher training and on-site technical support ensures that teachers are able to implement the procedures with a high degree of fidelity (Fuchs, Fuchs, Yazdian, & Powell, 2002). In a study aimed to evaluate the sustainability of PALS among eight teachers, Baker and colleagues (2004) found that all eight teachers sustained the use of PALS in their classrooms four years after the research study. Although there are variations to the structure and activities of PALS for different age groups across reading and math, some common and critical features that contribute to its success are role reciprocity, opportunities to respond with immediate feedback and error correction, and the structured activities that serve as a supplement to the core curriculum (McMaster, Fuchs, & Fuchs, 2007).

Game-based Cooperative Learning

Cooperative learning as an instructional strategy has been around for over four decades, encompassing several types with variations. In general, cooperative learning refers to a learning environment created to allow students to engage in academic tasks in small, heterogeneous groups. Watson (1992) listed four elements that are needed to maximize achievement using cooperative learning. The first is the concept of cooperative task structure in which students work together toward completing a given task. The task can be structured such that there is division of labor and each member of the group is responsible for a unique part of the activity (i.e., task specialization) or all members of the group study together and become equally familiar with the task (i.e., group study). The second element is the cooperative incentive structure wherein there is a group reward based on individual learning or performance of the group as a whole. The third element is individual accountability that evaluated the learning of each individual in the group. The fourth and final element of cooperative learning is the heterogeneous grouping structures. The groupings can be done based on academic performance of students as high- and low-performing students or based on demographic characteristics such as gender, race, and ethnicity or based on attitudes and leadership abilities. Game-based cooperative learning includes strategies that combine cooperation with competition. Much of the work on game-based cooperative learning originated from research at the Center for the Study of Social Organization of Schools at Johns Hopkins University. Some examples include Jigsaw II (Slavin, 1986), Student Teams-Achievement Divisions (Slavin, 1978), and Teams-Games-Tournaments (TGT; DeVries & Slavin, 1978). Each of these strategies vary slightly from each other but share the basic elements of cooperative learning.

There is strong evidence to show the effectiveness of TGT with elementary (Devries, Mescon, & Slackman, 1975) and secondary populations (DeVries, Edwards, & Wells (1974) across both academic (e.g., reading vocabulary, verbal analogy, mathematics) and social domains. In a more recent study, Salam, Hossain, and Rahman (2015) studied the effects of TGT with 86 students from two eighth-grade classrooms and found that TGT resulted in higher learning in math and more positive attitude toward TGT in comparison to a control condition. Despite evidence for the effectiveness of these models, there have been very few studies with rigor conducted using TGT in the classroom in a structured, systematic manner.

Another game-based cooperative learning strategy that has elements of CWPT and TGT approaches is Classwide Student Tutoring Teams (CSTT; Maheady, Sacca, & Harper, 1987). Maheady, Sacca, and Harper (1987) studied the effects of CSTT with 91 students in ninth and tenth grades. Included in this population were students with mild disabilities. Using multiple baseline design in one classroom and ABAB design in another classroom, the data showed an immediate and systematic increase in weekly math test scores for all students. Harper, Mallette, Maheady, and Bresnan (1993) studied the combined effects of CSTT with direct instruction to teach math word problem-solving with a group of second-grade students. This exploratory study yielded mixed results on the students' short-term and long-term retention on how to solve word problems.

Along the same lines of game-based cooperative learning is a teacher questioning strategy that requires students to work collaboratively and cooperatively to answer questions posed by the teacher called Numbered Heads Together (NHT; Kagan & Kagan, 2009). NHT has shown to be effective in improving students' daily quiz scores, general knowledge, and curriculum based-measures in science and social studies (Maheady et al. 1991; Maheady, Michielli-Pendl, Harper, & Mallette, 2006). NHT can be used to encourage students to work together to solve problems, compare and contrast information, and analyze or summarize information (Hunter,

Maheady, Jasper, Williamson et al., 2015) and for learning that requires critical thinking (Lince, 2016). NHT can be used at the beginning of a lesson to serve as a "hook" during a lesson to maintain active student responding, or at the end of a lesson as a way to check for understanding. Maheady, Michielli-Pendl, Harper, and Mallette (2006) found that a behavioral incentive package added to the implementation of NHT was more effective than NHT alone in increasing the scores of lowest performing students in a general education science class. Use of an incentive package in combination with NHT resulted in higher on-task behaviors in a third-grade social studies classroom with a corresponding increase in quiz scores (Maheady et al., 1991). Using an alternative treatments design, Hunter and Haydon (2013) evaluated the effects of NHT with and without a behavior package on the math quiz scores and on-task behavior of four students with emotional and behavioral disorders in a self-contained classroom. Results indicated that students showed the highest rates of on-task behavior and increase in quiz scores when NHT was combined with a behavioral incentive. Students preferred use of NHT with and without behavioral incentive to existing classroom practices.

Peer-Mediated Writing Interventions

It is common practice for teachers to ask students to switch papers and peer edit, especially in secondary classrooms. Peer-mediated writing interventions extend these informal collaborative activities even further by providing explicit training and structured procedures for students to engage in more intentional peer feedback. As with other peer-mediated instructional strategies, peer-mediated writing strategies show great promise to improve the writing skills of students who struggle with written expression.

It is well documented that students who struggle significantly with writing are at a disadvantage academically (Graham & Harris, 2011; Harris & Graham, 2013). When students enter the upper elementary grades, writing becomes an essential tool for learning and demonstrating what they know. Harris and Graham (2013) note "lack of competence in writing puts students at risk for school failure, and the consequences extend beyond the school years" (p. 66). These challenges may be exacerbated for students of color and students living in poverty.

Deficits in written expression extend into all genres of writing. Applebee, Langer, Mullis, Latham, and Gentile (1994) indicate that students demonstrate significant difficulties with narrative, expository, and persuasive genres of writing. In addition, Applebee, Langer, and Mullis (1986) note that as students progress through the upper grades, they frequently demonstrate a deteriorating attitude toward writing, even though most children begin school with a positive attitude toward composition tasks.

Peer-mediated writing interventions have demonstrated effectiveness for students with learning or related disabilities (Maheady et al., 2001), as well as primary students (Graham & Harris, 2005), adolescents (Graham & Perin, 2007), and college students (Cho, Schunn, & Wilson, 2006) who struggle with writing.

Additional supporting evidence for peer-mediated writing interventions is expanding. In 2007, Graham and Perin conducted a meta-analysis of 123 studies to examine effective writing instruction techniques. They found peer assistance—working together with peers to plan, draft, and/or revise writing—had an average weighted ES of 0.75, suggesting that working with peers on writing tasks may serve as an effective tool to improve students' overall writing abilities.

Strategy instruction. Strategy instruction has been noted as one of the most impactful evidence-based instructional strategies for increasing academic performance (Graham & Perin, 2007; Harris & Graham, 2013; Schumaker & Deshler, 2003). Specifically, Self-Regulated Strategy Development (SRSD), which leverages peer modeling and peer collaboration within the six procedural stages has shown positive effects when used to improve writing skills. These elements of peer-mediated instruction are important to the instructional and motivational aspects of SRSD (Harris & Graham, 2013) and provide additional support for use of peer-mediated writing interventions to improve the quality of students' written expression.

Basic writing skills. The range of research involving peer-mediated writing instruction stretches from remediating basic skill deficits (e.g., punctuation) to enhancing all aspects of the writing process (i.e., planning, drafting, revising). One example of skill-based research was conducted by Campbell, Brady, and Linehan (1991). These researchers investigated the effects of peer-mediated instruction on the acquisition and generalization of capitalization skills for students with learning disabilities. Results indicated that all target students were able to increase their ability to identify capitals when writing to tutors and other peers. Response generalization results were mixed as some tutors increased their own capitalization skills when tutoring, yet others did not.

Writing fluency. Writers who struggle may not have deficits in basic skills, but rather may be challenged by a lack of fluency when writing. Poor fluency may cause students to spend their cognitive resources on the basics of writing rather than higher-level writing components such as planning their composition and making purposeful connections to content (Graham, Berninger, Abbott, Abbott, & Whitaker, 1997) Likewise, deficits in fluency may limit students ability to produce enough writing to convey their thoughts adequately, especially on high-stakes achievement tests required by the Every Student Succeeds Act (P.L. 114-95).

A writing fluency study conducted by Alitto, Malecki, Coyle, and Santuzzi (2016) explored the effects of peer-delivered feedback and goal setting on the writing production of 106 fifth-grade students. Students engaged in several peer-mediated tasks during this intervention including peer scoring and recording data from Curriculum-Based Measurement-Written Expression probes, discussion of progress toward meeting goals, and establishing new goals. Goal setting was not limited to increasing total words written on probes, but also involved discussion regarding quality of the written product. Alitto et al. (2016) found that peer feedback combined with goal setting produced significantly more student writing and a faster learning rate as compared to a practice-only control group that did not receive the peer feedback and goal setting intervention. The ES for production-dependent writing indices was small (range = 0.12–0.28) indicating that established evidence-based strategies such as performance feedback and goal setting may be further enhanced by using peers to score, analyze, and discuss students' quality and quantity when writing. In addition, students and teachers reported high satisfaction with the intervention, which may indicate that teachers and students would be inclined to use this intervention in the future.

Writing process. Researchers are expanding peer-mediated intervention research into aspects of the writing process, including investigating writing with peer response. According to Hoogeveen and van Gelderen (2018), writing with peer response has been defined as cooperation between students during different stages of the writing process (i.e., planning, formulation, and revision) and many studies have demonstrated peer response to be effective for improving students' writing (Graham, McKeown, Kiuhara, & Harris, 2012; Graham & Perin, 2007; Hoogeveen & van Gelderen, 2013). Hoogeveen and van Gelderen (2018) aimed to improve the general approach of writing with peer response by using different types of genre knowledge directed at improving text coherence. This study was conducted in the Netherlands with 11- to 13 year-olds using a posttest only experimental design with students randomly assigned to experimental conditions (specific genre knowledge [SGK], general aspects of communicative writing, and control). Peer writing conferences took place during planning and revising writing stages. Researchers noted strong effects for the condition in which peer response was supported by SGK as compared to the students in the general aspects of communicative writing and control groups. Students in the SGK group made significantly more functional revisions of meaning and form than students in each of the other two conditions (Hoogeveen & van Gelderen, 2018). Furthermore, researchers noted generalized effects when students in SGK condition were able to effectively revise their writing in the absence of peer feedback. The authors noted instruction about linguistic features combined with peer feedback is a promising approach to improving writing quality and proficiency of writers in primary and secondary education (Hoogeveen & van Gelderen, 2018).

Limitations. Even with the wealth of research indicating that peer-mediated writing interventions have great potential to improve the quality and quantity of students' written expression, there are some clear limitations for writing with peer response. It appears that peer response does not always lead to productive comments for the improvement of writing. Students can be preoccupied with editing tasks, such as spelling and grammar, rather than complexity of the material (MacArthur, Graham, & Schwartz, 1991). Students may be using the wrong criteria for judging text quality (Zammuner, 1995) such as misunderstanding rubric progressions, or could be observed giving general commentary as opposed to specific feedback (Goldberg, Roswell, & Michaels, 1996). Likewise, research on maintenance and generalization appears to be limited (Alitto, et al., 2016; Heir & Eckert, 2014; Hoogeveen & van Gelderen, 2018).

CONCLUSION

There is a wealth of research to support the use of different types of PMAIs with a wide range of learners in inclusive classrooms. Despite the overwhelming evidence of effectiveness, there is an apparent gap where these interventions may not make their way into today's classrooms in a systematic manner. This is particularly true of secondary school settings with limited evidence of effectiveness. As identified for Baker et al. (2004), in addition to an administrative mandate, teachers' commitment to using the interventions with a high degree of fidelity is important to the sustainability of the practice. The next four chapters in this section will include practical guidelines for the implementation of each of the four types of PMAIs discussed in this chapter. Students are the most underutilized resource and, when used effectively with training and guidance, can contribute to improving the academic outcomes for themselves and their peers.

REFERENCES

Alitto, J., Malecki, C. K., Coyle, S., & Santuzzi, A. (2016). Examining the effects of adult and peer mediated goal setting and feedback interventions for writing: Two studies. *Journal of School Psychology, 56*, 89–109.

Allsopp, D. H. (1997). Using classwide peer tutoring to teach beginning algebra problem-solving skills in heterogeneous classrooms. *Remedial and Special Education, 18*, 367–379.

Applebee, A., Langer, J., & Mullis, I. (1986). *The writing report card: Writing achievement in American schools*. Princeton, NJ: Educational Testing Service.

Applebee, A., Langer, J., Mullis, I., Latham, A., & Gentile, C. (1994). *NAEP 1992: Writing report card*. Washington, DC: US Government Printing Office.

Arreaga-Mayer, C. (1998). Increasing active student responding and improving academic performance through classwide peer tutoring. *Intervention in School and Clinic, 3*, 89–94, 117.

Arreaga-Mayer, C., Greenwood, C. R., & Utley, C. (1994). *Promoting literacy through ecobehavioral assessment and classwide peer tutoring for racial=ethnic limited English proficient minority students with disabilities* (OSEP grant CFDS No. 84.023C). Lawrence, KS: University of Kansas, Juniper Gardens Children's Project.

Baker, S., Gersten, R., Dimino, J. A., Griffiths, R. (2004). The sustained use of research-based instructional practice: A case study of Peer-Assisted Learning Strategies in mathematics. *Remedial and Special Education, 25*(1), 5–24.

Barbetta, P., & Heron, T. E. (1991). Project SHINE: Summer home instruction and evaluation. *Intervention in School and Clinic, 26*, 276–281.

Bobroff, S. & Sax, C. L. (2010). The effects of peer tutoring interview skills training with transition-age youth with disabilities. *Journal of Vocational Rehabilitation, 33*, 143–157.

Bowman-Perrott, L. J., Davis, H., Vannest, K., Williams, L., Greenwood, C. R., & Parker, R. (2013). Academic benefits of tutoring: A meta-analytic review of single-case research. *School Psychology Review, 42*(1), 39–55.

Bowman-Perrott, L. J., deMartin, S., Mahadevan, L., & Etchells, M. (2016). Assessing the academic, social, and language production outcomes of English language learners engaged in peer tutoring: A systematic review. *Education and Treatment of Children, 39*(3), 359–388.

Bowman-Perrott, L. J., Greenwood, C. R., & Tapia, Y. (2007). The efficacy of peer tutoring used in secondary alternative school classrooms with small teacher/pupil ratios and students with emotional and behavioral disorders. *Education and Treatment of Children, 50*(3), 65–87.

Calhoon, M. B., & Fuchs, L. S. (2003). The effects of Peer-Assisted Learning Strategies and curriculum-based measurement on the mathematics performance of secondary students with disabilities. *Remedial and Special Education, 24,* 235–245.

Campbell, B. J., Brady, M. P., & Linehan, S. (1991). Effects of peer-mediated instruction on the acquisition and generalization of written capitalization skills. *Journal of Learning Disabilities, 24*(1), 6–14.

Cho, K., Schunn, C. D., & Wilson, R. W. (2006). Validity and reliability of scaffolded peer assessment of writing from instructor and student perspectives. *Journal of Educational Psychology, 98*(4), 891–901. doi:10.1037/0022-0663.98.4.891

Conderman, G., Bresnahan, V., & Hedin, L. (2012). Promoting active involvement in classrooms. *The Education Digest, 77*(6), 33–39.

Cooke, N. L., Heron, T. E., & Heward, W. L. (1983). *Peer tutoring: Implementing classwide programs in the primary grades.* Columbus, OH: Special Press.

Cooper, J. O., Heron, T. E., & Heward, W. L. (2007). *Applied behavior analysis* (2nd ed.). Upper Saddle River, NJ: Prentice Hall.

Delquadri, J., Greenwood, C. R., Stretton, K., & Hall, R. V. (1983). The peer tutoring game: A classroom procedure for increasing opportunity to respond and spelling performance. *Education and Treatment of Children, 6,* 225–239.

DeVries, D. L., Edwards, K. J., & Wells, E. H. (1974). *Teams-games-tournament in the social studies classroom: Effects on academic achievement, student attitudes, cognitive beliefs and classroom climate* (Report number 173; ERIC No. ED 093884). Baltimore, MD: Johns Hopkins University.

DeVries, D. L., Mescon, I. T., & Slackman, S. L. (1975). *Teams–games–tournament (TGT) effects on reading skills in the elementary grades* (Report number 200; ERIC No: ED 109662. Baltimore, MD: Johns Hopkins University.

DeVries, D., & Slavin, R. (1978). Teams-games-tournaments (TGT): Review of ten classroom experiments. *Journal of Research and Development in Education, 12,* 28–38.

Dunn, M. E., Shelnut, J., Ryan, J. B., & Katsiyannis, A. (2017). A systematic review of peer-mediated interventions on the academic achievement of students with emotional/behavioral disorders. *Education and Treatment of Children, 40*(4), 497–524.

Ezell, H. K., Kohler, R. W., & Strain, P. (1994). A program description of evaluation of academic peer tutoring for reading skills of children with special needs. *Education and Treatment of Children, 17,* 52–67.

Fuchs, D., & Fuchs, L. S. (2005). Peer-Assisted Learning Strategies: Promoting word recognition, fluency, and reading comprehension in young children. *Journal of Special Education, 39*(1), 34–44.

Fuchs, D., Fuchs, L. S., Mathes, P. G., & Martinez, E. (2002). Preliminary evidence on the social standing of students with learning disabilities in PALS and no-PALS classrooms. *Learning Disabilities Research and Practice, 17*(4), 205–215.

Fuchs, D., Fuchs, L. S., Mathes, P. G., & Simmons, D. C. (1997). Peer-Assisted Learning Strategies: Making classrooms more responsive to diversity. *American Educational Research Journal, 34*, 174–206.

Fuchs, D., Fuchs, L., Thompson, A., Al Otaiba, S., Yen, L., Yang, N., Braun, M., & O'Connor, R. (2001). Is reading important in reading-readiness programs? A randomized field trial with teachers as program implementers. *Journal of Educational Psychology, 93,* 251–267.

Fuchs, L. S., Fuchs, D., Hamlett, C. L., Phillips, N. B., & Bentz, J. (1994). Classwide curriculum-based measurement: Helping general educators meet the challenge of student diversity. *Exceptional Children, 60*, 518–537.

Fuchs, L. S., Fuchs, D., Hamlett, C. L., Phillips, N. B., & Karns, K. (1995). General educators' specialized adaptation for students with learning disabilities. *Exceptional Children, 61*, 440–459. doi:10.2307/1511370

Fuchs. L. S., Fuchs, D., & Kazdan, S. (1999). Effects of Peer-Assisted Learning Strategies on high school students with serious reading problems. *Remedial and Special Education, 20*(5), 309–318.

Fuchs, L. S., Fuchs, D., Yazdian, L., & Powell, S. R. (2002). Enhancing first-grade children's mathematical development with Peer-Assisted Learning Strategies. *School Psychology Review, 31*, 569–583.

Gardner, R., III, Cartledge, G., Siedl, B., Woolsey, L. M., Schley, G. S., & Utley, C. (2001). Mt. Olivet after-school program: Peer-mediated interventions for at-risk students. *Remedial and Special Education, 22*(1), 22–33.

Gardner, R., III, Nobel, M. M., Hessler, T., Yawn, C. D., & Heron, T. E. (2007). Tutoring system innovations: Past practice and future prototypes. *Intervention in School and Clinic, 43*, 71–81.

Goldberg, G., Roswell, B., & Michaels, H. (1996). Can assessment mirror instruction? A look at peer response and revision in a large-scale writing test. *Educational Assessment, 3*, 287–314.

Graham, S., Berninger, V. W., Abbott, R. D., Abbott, S. P., & Whitaker, D. (1997). Role of mechanics in composing of elementary school students: A new methodological approach. *Journal of Educational Psychology, 89*, 170–182. doi:10.1037/0022-0663.89.1.170

Graham, S., & Harris, K. R. (2005). *Writing better: Effective strategies for teaching students with learning difficulties.* Baltimore, MD: Brookes.

Graham, S., & Harris, K. R. (2011). Writing and students with disabilities. In L. Lloyd, J. Kauffman, & D. Hallahan (Eds.). *Handbook of special education* (pp. 422–433). London, England: Routledge.

Graham, S., McKeown, D., Kiuhara, S., & Harris, K. R. (2012). A meta-analysis of writing instruction for students in the elementary grades. *Journal of Educational Psychology, 104*, 879–896. doi:10.1037/a0029185

Graham, S., & Perin, D. (2007). A meta-analysis of writing instruction for adolescent students. *Journal of Educational Psychology, 99*, 445–476.

Green, S. K., Alderman, G., & Liechy, A. (2004). Peer tutoring, individualized intervention, and progress monitoring with at-risk second grade readers. *Preventing School Failure, 49*(1), 11–17.

Greene, I., McTiernan, A., & Holloway, J. (2018). Cross-age peer tutoring and fluency-based instruction to achieve fluency with mathematics computation skills: A randomized controlled trial. *Journal of Behavioral Education, 27,* 145–171. doi:10.1007/s10864-018-9291-1

Greenwood, C. R. (1991). Longitudinal analysis of time, engagement, and achievement in at-risk versus non-risk students. *Exceptional Children, 57,* 521–535.

Greenwood, C. R., Arreaga-Mayer, C., Utley, C. A., Gavin, K. M., & Terry, B. J. (2001). Classwide peer tutoring learning management system. *Remedial and Special Education, 22,* 34–47.

Greenwood, C. R., & Delquadri, J. (1995). Classwide peer tutoring and the prevention of school failure. *Preventing School Failure, 39*(4), 21–25.

Greenwood, C. R., Delquadri, J., & Carta, J. J. (1988). *Classwide peer tutoring.* Seattle, WA: Educational Achievement Systems.

Greenwood, C. R., Terry, B.J., Utley, C. A., Montagna, D., & Walker, D. (1993). Achievement, placement, and service: Middle school benefits of classwide peer tutoring used at the elementary school. *School Psychology Review, 22*(3), 497–516.

Gumpel, T. P., & Frank, R. (1999). An expansion of the peer tutoring paradigm: Cross-age peer tutoring of social skills among socially rejected boys. *Journal of Applied Behavior Analysis, 32,* 115–118.

Harper, G. F., & Maheady, L. (2007). Peer-mediated teaching and students with learning disabilities. *Intervention in School and Clinic, 43*(2), 101–107.

Harper, G. F., Mallette, B., Maheady, L., Bentley, A. E., & Moore, J. (1995). Retention and treatment failure in classwide peer tutoring: Implications for further research. *Journal of Behavioral Education, 5,* 399–414.

Harper, G. F., Mallette, B., Maheady, L., & Brennan, G. (1993). Classwide student tutoring teams and direction instruction as a combined instructional program to teach generalizable strategies for mathematics word problems. *Education and Treatment of Children, 16,* 115–134.

Harris, K. R., & Graham, S. (2013). "An adjective is a word hanging down from a noun": Learning to write and students with disabilities. *Annals of Dyslexia, 63,* 65–79.

Hashimoto, K., Utley, C. A., Greenwood, C. R., & Pitchlyn, C. L. (2007). The effects of modified classwide peer tutoring procedures on the generalization of spelling skills of urban third-grade elementary students. *Learning Disabilities: A Contemporary Journal, 5*(2), 1–29.

Hattie, J., & Timperley, H. (2007). The power of feedback. *Review of Educational Research, 77,* 81–112. doi:10.3102/003465430298487

Hawkins, R. O., Musti-Rao, S., Hughes, C., Berry, L., & McGuire, S. (2009). Applying a randomized interdependent group contingency component to classwide peer tutoring for multiplication fact fluency. *Journal of Behavioral Education, 18,* 300–318.

Heron, T. E., Heward, W. L., Cooke, N. L., & Hill, D. S. (1983). Evaluation of a classwide peer tutoring system: First graders teach each other sight words. *Education and Treatment of Children, 6,* 137–152.

Heron, T. E., Villareal, D. M., Yao, M., Christianson, R. J., & Heron, K. M. (2006). Peer tutoring systems: Applications in classroom and specialized environments, *Reading & Writing Quarterly, 22* (1), 27–45. doi:10.1080/10573560500203517

Heron, T. E., Welsch, R. G., & Goddard, Y. (2003). Applications of tutoring systems in specialized subject areas: An analysis of skills, methodology, and results. *Remedial and Special Education, 24*(5), 288–300.

Herring-Harrison, T. J., Gardner, R., III, & Lovelace, T. S. (2007). Adapting peer tutoring for learners who are deaf of hard of hearing. *Intervention in School and Clinic, 43*(2), 82–87.

Hier, B. O., & Eckert, T. L. (2014). Evaluating elementary-aged students' abilities to generalize and maintain fluency gains of a performance feedback writing intervention. *School Psychology Quarterly, 29*(4), 488–502.

Hoogeveen, M., & van Gelderen, A. (2013). What works in writing with peer response? A review of intervention studies with children and adolescents. *Educational Psychology Review, 25*, 473–502. doi:10.1007/s10648-013-9229-z

Hoogeveen, M., & van Gelderen, A. (2018). Writing with peer response using different types of genre knowledge: Effects on linguistic features and revisions of sixth-grade writers. *Journal of Educational Research, 111*(1), 66–80. doi:10.1080/00220671.2016.1190913

Houghton, S., & Bain, A. (1993). Peer tutoring with ESL and below-average readers. *Journal of Behavioral Education, 3*(2), 125–142.

Hughes, T. A., & Fredrick, L. D. (2006). Teaching vocabulary with students with learning disabilities using classwide PT and constant time delay. *Journal of Behavioral Education, 15*, 1–23.

Hunter, W., & Haydon, T. (2013). Examining the effectiveness of numbered heads together for students with emotional and behavioral disorders. *Beyond Behavior, 22*(3), 40–45.

Hunter, W. C., Maheady, L., Jasper, A. D., Williamson, R. L., Murley, R. C., & Stratton, E. (2015). Numbered heads together as a tier 1 instructional strategy in multitiered systems of support. *Education and Treatment of Children, 38*(3), 345–362.

Kagan. S., & Kagan, M. (2009). *Kagan cooperative learning.* San Clemente, CA: Kagan.

Kamps, D. M., Greenwood, C, Arreaga-Mayer, C, . . . Bannister, H. (2008). The efficacy of classwide peer tutoring in middle schools. *Education and Treatment of Children, 31*, 119–152.

Klingner, J. K., & Vaughn, S. (1996). Reciprocal teaching of reading comprehension strategies for students with learning disabilities who use English as a second language. *Elementary School Journal, 96*, 275–293.

Lince, R. (2016). Creative thinking ability to increase student mathematical of junior high school applying models numbered heads together. *Journal of Education and Practice, 7*(6), 206–212.

Lo, Y., & Cartledge, G. (2004). Total class peer tutoring and interdependent group oriented contingency: Improving the academic and task related behaviors of fourth-grade urban students. *Education and Treatment of Children, 27*, 235–262.

MacArthur, C. A., Graham, S., & Schwartz, S. (1991). Knowledge of revision and revising behavior among students with learning disabilities. *Learning Disability Quarterly, 14*, 61–73.

Maheady, L., Harper, G. F., & Mallette, B. (1991). Peer-mediated instruction: A review of potential applications for special education. *Reading, Writing, and Learning Disabilities, 7*, 73–103.

Maheady, L., Harper, G. F., & Mallette, B. (2001). Peer-mediated instruction and interventions and students with mild disabilities. *Remedial and Special Education, 22*(1), 4–14.

Maheady, L., Mallette, B., & Harper, G. F. (2006). Four classwide peer tutoring models: Similarities, differences, and implications for research and practice. *Reading & Writing Quarterly, 22*(1), 65–89.

Maheady, L., Michielli-Pendl, J., Harper, G. F., & Mallette, B. (2006). The effects of numbered heads together with and without an incentive package on the science test performance of a diverse group of sixth graders. *Journal of Behavioral Education, 15*(1), 25–39.

Maheady, L., Sacca, M. K., & Harper, G. F. (1987). Classwide peer tutoring teams: Effects on the academic performance of secondary students. *Journal of Special Education, 21*(3), 107–121.

Maheady, L., Sacca, M. K., & Harper, G. F. (1988). Classwide peer tutoring with mildly handicapped high school students. *Exceptional Children, 55*, 52–59.

Mastropieri, M. A., Scruggs, T. E., Mohler, L., Beranek, M., Spencer, V., Boon, R. T., & Talbott, E. (2001). Can middle school students with serious reading difficulties help each other learn anything? *Learning Disabilities Research and Practice, 16*, 18–27.

Mastropieri, M. A., Scruggs, T. E., Spencer, V., & Fontana, J. (2003). Promoting success in high school world history: Peer tutoring versus guided notes. *Learning Disabilities Research & Practice, 18*(1), 52–65.

Mayfield, K. H., & Vollmer, T. R. (2007). Teaching math skills to at-risk students using home-based peer tutoring. *Journal of Applied Behavior Analysis, 40*, 223–237.

McDonnell, J., Mathot-Buckner, C., Thorson, N., & Fister, S. (2001). Supporting the inclusion of students with moderate and severe disabilities in junior high school general education classes: The effects of classwide peer tutoring, multi-element curriculum, and accommodations. *Education and Treatment of Children, 24*(2), 141–160.

McMaster, K. L., Fuchs, D., & Fuchs, L. S. (2007). Promises and limitations of peer-Assisted Learning Strategies in reading. *Learning Disabilities: A Contemporary Journal, 5*(2), 97–112.

Miller, A. D., Barbetta, P. M., Drevno, G. E., Martz, S. A., & Heron, T. E. (1996). Math peer tutoring for students with specific learning disabilities. *Learning Disability Forum, 21*(3), 21–28.

Miller, A. D., Barbetta, P. M., & Heron, T. E. (1994). Start tutoring: Designing, training, implementing, and adapting tutoring programs for school and home settings. In R. Gardner III, D. Sainato, J. O. Cooper, T. E. Heron, W. L. Heward, J. Eshleman, & T. A. Grossi (Eds.), *Behavioral analysis in education: Focus on measurably superior instruction* (pp. 265–282). Monterey, CA: Brooks-Cole.

Mortweet, S. (1995). *Classwide peer tutoring effects on the social interactions of students with mild disabilities and their typical peers across multiple settings* (Unpublished doctoral dissertation). University of Kansas, Lawrence, KS.

Nobel, M. M. (2005). *Effects of classwide peer tutoring on the acquisition, maintenance, and generalization of science vocabulary words for seventh grade students with learning disabilities and/or low achievement* (Unpublished doctoral dissertation). Ohio State University, Columbus. Retrieved from http://rave.ohiolink.edu/etdc/view?acc_num=osu1124116860

Oddo, M., Barnett, D. W., Hawkins, R. O., & Musti-Rao, S. (2010). Reciprocal peer tutoring and repeated reading: Increasing practicality using student groups. *Psychology in the Schools, 47*(8), 842–858.

Okilwa, N. S. A., & Shelby, L. (2010). The effects of peer tutoring on academic performance of students with disabilities in grades 6 through 12: A synthesis of the literature. *Remedial and Special Education, 31*, 450–463.

Prater, M. A., Serna, L., & Nakamura, K. K. (1999). Impact of peer teaching on the acquisition of social skills by adolescents with learning disabilities. *Education and Treatment of Children, 22*, 19–35.

Pyle, D., Pyle, N., Lignugaris/Kraftm B., Duran, L., & Akers, J. (2017). Academic effects of peer-mediated interventions with English language learners: A research synthesis. *Review of Education Research, 87*(1), 103–133.

Rohrbeck, C. A., Ginsburg-Block, M. D., Fantuzzo, J. W., & Miller, T. R. (2003). Peer-assisted learning interventions with elementary school students: A meta-analytic review. *Journal of Educational Psychology, 95*, 240–257. doi:10.1037/0022-0663.95.2.240

Ryan, J. B., Reid, R., & Epstein, M. H. (2004). Peer-mediated intervention studies on academic achievement for students with EBD: A review. *Remedial and Special Education, 25*(6), 330–341.

Salam, A., Hossain, A., & Rahman, S. (2015). Teams games tournaments (TGT) cooperative technique for learning mathematics in secondary schools in Bangladesh. *Journal of Research in Mathematics Education, 4*(3), 271–287. doi:10.4471/redimat.2015.1519

Sansone, N., Ligorio, M. B., & Buglass, S. L. (2018). Peer eTutoring: effects on students' participation and interaction style in online courses, *Innovations in Education and Teaching International, 55*(1), 13–22. doi:10.1080/14703297.2016.1190296

Schloss, P. J., Kobza, S. A., & Alper, S. (1997). The use of peer tutoring for the acquisition of functional math skills among students with moderate retardation. *Education and Treatment of Children, 20*, 189–208.

Shumaker, J. B., & Deshler, D. D. (2003). Can students with LD become competent writers? *Learning Disabilities Quarterly, 26*, 129–141.

Slavin, R. (1978). Student teams and achievement divisions. *Journal of Research and Development in Education, 12*, 39–49.

Slavin, R. (1986). *Using Student Team Learning* (3rd ed.). Baltimore, MD: Johns Hopkins University Press.

Spencer, V. G. (2006). Peer tutoring and students with emotional or behavioral disorders: A review of the literature. *Behavioral Disorders, 31*(2), 204–222.

Spencer, V. G., Scruggs, T. E., & Mastropieri, M. A. (2003). Content area learning in middle school social studies classrooms and students with emotional or behavioral disorders: A comparison of strategies. *Behavioral Disorders, 28*, 77–93.

Sutherland, K. S., & Snyder, A. (2007). Effects of reciprocal peer tutoring and self-graphing on reading fluency and classroom behavior of middle school students with emotional or behavioral disorders. *Journal of Emotional and Behavioral Disorders, 15*, 103–118.

Tabacek, D., McLaughlin, T. F., & Howard, V. F. (1994). Teaching preschool children with disabilities tutoring skills: Effects on preacademic behaviors. *Child & Family Behavior Therapy, 16*(2), 43–63.

Taylor, L. K., & Alber, S. R. (2003). The effects of classwide peer tutoring on the spelling achievement of first graders with learning disabilities. *Behavior Analyst Today, 4*(2), 183–201.

Utley, C. A., Mortweet, S. L., & Greenwood, C. R. (1997). Peer-mediated instruction and interventions. *Focus on Exceptional Children, 29*(5), 1–23.

Veerkamp, M. B., Kamps, D. M., & Cooper, L. (2007). The effects of classwide peer tutoring on the reading achievement of urban middle school students. *Education and Treatment of Children, 30*(2), 21–51. doi:10.1353/etc.2007.0010

Ward, P., & Ayvazo, S. (2006). Classwide peer tutoring in physical education: Assessing its effects with kindergartners with autism. *Adapted Physical Activity Quarterly, 23*, 233–244.

Watson, S. B. (1992). The essential elements of cooperative learning. *The American Biology Teacher, 54*(2), 84–86.

Wexler, J., Reed, D. K., Pyle, N., Mitchell, M., & Barton, E. E. (2015). A synthesis of peer-mediated academic interventions for secondary struggling learners. *Journal of Learning Disabilities, 48*(5), 451–470.

Wood, C. L., Mackiewicz, S. M., Van Norman, R. K., & Cooke, N. L. (2007). Tutoring with technology. *Intervention in School and Clinic, 43*(2), 108–115.

Wood, C. L., Mustian, A. L., & Lo, Y. (2013). Effects of supplemental computer-assisted reciprocal peer tutoring on kindergarteners' phoneme segmentation fluency. *Education and Treatment of Children, 36*(1) 33–48.

Ysseldyke, J. (2007). Effect of technology-enhanced continuous progress monitoring on math achievement. *School Psychology Review, 36*(3), 453–467.

Zammuner, V. L. (1995). Individual and cooperative computer-writing and revising: Who gets the best results? *Learning and Instruction, 5*, 101–124.

## 5

Peer Tutoring

DAVID A. KLINGBEIL, STACY-ANN A. JANUARY,
AND LANAE R. DRACHSLIN ■

Peer tutoring is a widely used and well-studied intervention in which students are trained to work together on academic content (Utley & Mortweet, 1997). This chapter focuses on two types of peer tutoring programs: classwide peer tutoring (CWPT) and nonreciprocal individual peer tutoring (IPT). Reciprocal peer tutoring programs, such as Peer-Assisted Learning Strategies, are discussed in Chapter 6. There is a great deal of research supporting CWPT and nonreciprocal peer tutoring (Leung, 2015; Moeyaert, Klingbeil, Rodabaugh, & Turan, 2019; Talbott, Trzaska, & Zurheide, 2017). Broadly, researchers have studied the use of peer tutoring programs as a method to supplement Tier 1 instruction and increase students' academic engagement during their practice of important academic skills (Utley & Mortweet, 1997). The focus of this chapter will be on the procedures for implementing both types of peer tutoring interventions as well as considerations for training students, teachers, and arranging the classroom environment prior to their use. The chapter is divided into three main sections. The first two sections focus on CWPT and nonreciprocal IPT, respectively. The chapter concludes with a discussion of how both types of peer tutoring can support students from diverse backgrounds to improve their academic achievement.

CLASSWIDE PEER TUTORING

CWPT is a specific peer tutoring intervention in which pairs of students work together in a whole class model. Originally developed by Charles Greenwood and colleagues (Delquadri et al., 1986; Greenwood, Delquadri, & Carta, 1997), CWPT is a form of reciprocal peer tutoring adapted to involve all students in the class simultaneously. CWPT is an instructional strategy that allows students increased opportunity to respond to academic instruction (Delquadri et al., 1986). In this model, teachers select student dyads of relative academic levels to work together on practice and assessment activities. Teachers organize activities to allow tutor pairs to practice relevant skills in content areas such as reading, math, science, and spelling. Essential to the effectiveness of this intervention is the students' ability to (a) alternate working as the tutor and tutee, (b) engage in error correction, and (c) earn points for collaboration (Talbott et al., 2017). The following pages will review teacher and student preparation for implementing CWPT. For further detailed assistance in implementing this intervention readers should consult the original CWPT manual (Greenwood et al., 1997). Published guides with example lessons or teacher scripts also exist (Arreaga-Mayer, 1998; Fulk & King, 2001; Maheady & Gard, 2010).

Recommendations for Implementation

Role of the teacher. Teachers play a critical role in setting up and monitoring the ongoing implementation of CWPT. As summarized by Greenwood (1997), these tasks are required of the teacher: (a) introducing and reviewing material that will be the focus within the peer tutoring sessions; (b) assigning and re-assigning pairs of students; (c) training students to conduct the reciprocal tutoring and error correction activities; and (d) assigning points to students, posting team scores, and providing contingent reinforcement based on team performance. Despite the number of tasks required, by all accounts, CWPT is a relatively straightforward intervention to implement (Arreaga-Mayer, 1998; Maheady & Gard, 2010). For example, Maheady et al. (1991) found that teachers reached a high implementation standard after approximately 90 minutes of initial training on the delivery of CWPT, and they continued to implement the intervention without consultative assistance. Similar findings were found for preservice teachers, although approximately one hr of posttraining consultation was needed (Maheady, Harper, Mallette, & Kearns, 2004).

Selecting academic content. CWPT is a flexible intervention that has been studied in general, special, and alternative education settings with kindergarten to high school students. In early studies of CWPT, researchers evaluated the use of the intervention to improve students spelling and reading skills; however, CWPT has also been used to improve students' performance in math, social studies, and science (Talbott et al., 2017). For optimal results, the developers of CWPT suggested that teachers select previously taught content that requires drill and memorization (U.S. Department of Education, 2007). Individuals interested in implementing CWPT should select an academic area in which its key components—(a) reciprocity of tutor–tutee roles, (b) error corrections, and (c) collaboration—can be executed successfully.

Materials. Once an academic content is selected, teachers should prepare materials and structure the tutoring unit. CWPT can target academic behaviors and skills such as oral reading of connected text, answering comprehension questions, spelling list practice, math facts, and vocabulary words (Delquadri et al., 1986). These skills can be addressed in various teacher-created or commercially prepared activities (e.g., flashcards), assignments (e.g., comprehension worksheets), and practice assessments (e.g., unit reviews).

Organization and structure. The original program requires CWPT takes place four times per week with each student in the dyad receiving 10 minutes of tutoring each day (Greenwood et al., 1992). Organizing daily and weekly units before implementation can facilitate maintenance of the intervention over an extended period of time. At the end of each week, students are assessed on the prior week's material and pretested on the next week's material (Arreaga-Mayer, 1998).

In addition to preparing physical materials for students, it is important to assign tutor and tutee pairs strategically. Pairs can have similar academic skills. Alternatively, when correct answers are pregenerated for tutors (i.e., the correct answers are visible to the tutor on the back of a flashcard), teachers can pair academically higher-achieving students with academically lower-achieving students. Although it is possible to pair students randomly, researchers suggest that teachers should take into account varying social relationships between students. To foster new social and teaching skills, as well as to keep students motivated, tutor pairs should be reassigned on a weekly basis (Greenwood, 1997).

As noted earlier, a key component of CWPT is the reciprocity of tutor–tutee roles and collaboration. Within a single tutoring session, tutor pairs alternate roles so that both students serve as the tutor and tutee. Both students in the tutor dyad work together to earn points for effective collaboration. Tutors earn points for following procedures and tutees earn points for correct responding. In addition, because all students are engaged in peer tutoring at the same time, the teacher can actively supervise ongoing instruction and award bonus points for appropriate tutoring behaviors such as the appropriate presentation of materials, accurate use of error correction procedures, or providing positive feedback to the tutee (Arreaga-Mayer, 1998; Greenwood, 1997; Maheady & Gard, 2010). Although there is no competition between tutor and tutee, whole-class competition is often included. At the end of the tutoring block, individual and group points are tallied and recorded publicly. Teachers may also post totaled daily and weekly points for each tutor pair.

Student training. In addition to alternating tutor–tutee roles and awarding points for collaboration, effective CWPT involves peer-delivered feedback and error corrections. Training students in the roles of tutor and tutee require specific instruction and modeling. Teachers begin by providing students with the rationale and purpose of CWPT. Teachers introduce the point system as a way to invest tutor pairs in collaborative effort instead of competition within the dyad. This can be accomplished by emphasizing, and awarding points for, effort and cooperative behavior as well as correct responses (Fulk & King, 2001).

Next, teachers explicitly model and discuss providing constructive corrective feedback. This provides students with an opportunity to see effective and positive methods to interact with peers while providing feedback and error corrections. The error correction procedure requires (a) providing the correct answer (modeling), (b) requiring the tutee to write and say the correct answer three times, and (c) awarding one point to the tutee for the corrections (Arreaga-Mayer, 1998).

Standardizing error corrections can increase tutees' opportunity to respond and practice concepts while receiving immediate corrective feedback. In the example of spelling tutoring, tutors say a word from the spelling list while the tutee writes it down. The tutee spells the word aloud. If spelled correctly, the tutor provides reinforcement by saying "Correct, give yourself two points." If the word was spelled incorrectly, the tutor first models the correct spelling by pointing to, pronouncing, and spelling the word orally to the tutee. The tutee is required to write the word with correct spelling three times to receive one point and move on to the next word. If the tutee does not get the word correct three times, the tutor moves on to the next word and no points are given. This procedure allows the tutee the opportunity to practice the word correctly multiple times before moving on the next word (Delquadri et al., 1983).

INDIVIDUAL PEER TUTORING

Unlike CWPT or reciprocal peer tutoring (which includes Peer-Assisted Learning Strategies), nonreciprocal IPT pertains to situations where there is a dedicated tutor (or tutors) assigned to a tutee (Talbott et al., 2017). Our focus in this section is on key considerations for implementing nonreciprocal IPT in school settings, drawing on the relatively large body of evidence supporting the use of nonreciprocal IPT to improve students' academic skills in several subjects (e.g., Leung, 2015; Moeyaert et al., 2019).

Recommendations for Implementation

Types of interventions. Researchers have used nonreciprocal IPT to improve tutees' reading, writing, spelling, and math skills in elementary and secondary grade levels (Leung, 2015). One critical aspect of any peer tutoring intervention is that the tutoring sessions are structured (Utley & Mortweet, 1997), in addition to the intervention having adequate empirical support. Results from a meta-analysis of reciprocal and nonreciprocal peer tutoring programs ($k = 72$) targeting academic skills indicated that structured sessions were associated with larger effect sizes ($g = 0.53$) than unstructured sessions ($g = 0.33$; Leung, 2015). For educators considering the use of IPT, identifying an intervention that peers can deliver with fidelity is also important.

At the broadest level, tutors should be trained to implement interventions that provide tutees with structured opportunities to practice academic skills. If the intervention requires that tutors provide instruction, then that instruction should be explicit, using materials at the appropriate instructional level for the task. Depending on the tutee's baseline academic skills, the intervention could incorporate empirically validated instructional practices that facilitate acquisition (e.g., modeling, immediate corrective feedback), fluency (e.g., increased opportunities to respond, delayed corrective feedback), or generalization (Daly et al., 1996;

Rivera & Bryant, 1992). Empirical evidence suggests that peers can effectively implement single interventions such as repeated reading, collaborative strategic reading, and incremental rehearsal (Klingbeil et al., 2017; Vaughn et al., 2000), as well as multicomponent intervention packages. For example, Dufrene et al. (2010) trained students to implement a tutoring package that included listening passage preview, repeated reading, performance feedback, and contingent reinforcement. Interventions that have been successfully included as part of CWPT or reciprocal peer-tutoring strategies are also promising interventions for use within non- reciprocal IPT.

Selecting and training peer tutors. After the intervention is selected, educators should select an appropriate tutor. Based on the results of several meta-analytic reviews (Elbaum et al., 1999; Leung, 2015; Zeneli et al., 2016), there is evidence supporting the effectiveness of peer tutoring when tutors are the same age as the tutee with higher or similar skill levels. Research also supports cross-age (i.e., older students tutoring younger students) tutoring, although perhaps not when the tutees have disabilities (Elbaum et al., 1999). Moreover, students with disabilities can be effective tutors for tutees with *and* without disabilities. This includes students with autism spectrum disorders (e.g., Kamps, Dugan, Potucek, & Collins, 1999), students with learning disabilities (Campbell, Brady, & Linehan, 1991), and students with emotional-behavioral disabilities (e.g., Franca et al., 1990; Tournaki & Criscitiello, 2003; Watts, Bryant, & Roberts, 2019) who may not typically be thought of as candidates to be tutors. Another consideration is that there is stronger empirical support for nonreciprocal IPT when the peer tutoring uses same gender tutoring dyads compared to mixed gender tutoring dyads (Leung, 2015; Zeneli et al., 2016). Researchers have also suggested teachers consider personal characteristics of the potential tutors and tutees when considering the implementation of peer tutoring. For example, Haisley et al. (1981) and Tournaki and Criscitiello (2003) purposefully matched more assertive tutors with tutees with more behavioral concerns.

After educators identify tutors, the next step is to train tutors in the intervention procedures. Tutor training is an essential ingredient to ensure that peer tutoring results in the desired outcomes (Utley & Mortweet, 1997). According to Stenhoff and Lignugaris/Kraft (2007), teachers should meet with the tutors to establish expectations for the tutoring sessions, model the components of the intervention, provided tutors with opportunities to practice all of the relevant instructional components, and practice problem-solving skills that may be necessary. In published studies (e.g., Dufrene et al., 2010; Franca et al., 1990), tutor training often occurred in multiple sessions.

In our previous work (Klingbeil et al., 2017), we used the following training procedures to teach peer tutors to implement incremental rehearsal to teach high-frequency words. First, we asked third-grade teachers to identify tutors who (a) would likely enjoy being a tutor to younger students, (b) would be able to deliver the flash-card intervention, and (c) had high attendance. Peer tutors were trained in three or four 20-min sessions (training session duration matched the amount of time tutors would deliver interventions). During the first session, we introduced the purpose of the intervention and discussed the general steps. Next, we modeled the intervention while the tutor observed and again while the tutor played the role of the tutee. In the second session, we modeled each of the core components (e.g., introducing a new word, presenting unknown items interspersed with known items, and providing corrective feedback). Tutors practiced each of these components in isolation. During the third and fourth sessions, the tutors practiced delivering the intervention to the researchers while another researcher observed and provided corrective feedback. Tutors were given detailed scripts with blanks for each of the unknown words that would be taught as well as a 3 × 5 index card that clearly stated the corrective feedback procedure (see the appendix to this chapter). Tutors began teaching the tutees after they administered the intervention to a researcher with 100% fidelity. Requiring 100% fidelity prior to implementing the intervention is a common standard in studies of nonreciprocal IPT (e.g., Dufrene et al., 2010), suggesting it would be an appropriate benchmark for educators implementing peer-tutoring in schools.

Monitoring implementation and student progress. Once tutors have been selected and trained, it is time to begin implementing the peer-tutoring intervention. To ensure consistent implementation, it is important for educators to monitor the instruction being provided by the tutor and the responses provided by the tutee (Fulk & King, 2001; Sterhoff & Kraft/Ling). Without these types of data, it is difficult to know why a tutee may not be responding to the intervention (i.e., whether the intervention is not working or if the intervention is not being implemented with fidelity). We provide an example direct rating form for evaluating peer tutors' implementation of incremental rehearsal in the appendix. Researchers also commonly recommend that teachers regularly meet with tutors after an intervention session to provide feedback on implementation and provide problem-solving support (e.g., Fulk & King, 2001; Jenkins & Jenkins, 1987).

Finally, the academic progress of the tutee should be monitored frequently. Researchers who studied nonreciprocal IPT often monitor student progress before or during each session. In fact, Dufrene et al. (2010) trained the peer tutors to collect progress monitoring data using curriculum-based measures of reading. The required frequency of progress monitoring data in applied contexts will likely be determined by the purposes of those data. Evaluating permanent products to determine the number of items completed during sessions may give educators a sense of the time spent on task or the tutee's acquisition of the skills that were practiced within that session. Collecting data weekly or every two weeks, perhaps using curriculum-based measures, regarding the tutee's progress toward longer-term goals in the academic skill would provide an estimate of the overall effectiveness of the peer-tutoring procedure (Shapiro, 2011).

CONSIDERATIONS OF DIVERSITY AND EQUITY

Peer-tutoring programs such as CWPT and nonreciprocal IPT are evidence-based methods with evidence supporting their use with students with disabilities,

English learners, students from diverse racial and ethnic backgrounds, and students from low-income households (Leung, 2015; Pyle, Pyle, Lignugaris/Kraft, Duran, & Akers, 2017; Talbott et al., 2017). Using CWPT is a promising method that could be used as part of broader efforts to facilitate responsible inclusion practices (Vaughn & Schumm, 1995) by allowing educators to meet the needs of all students in the class including those with disabilities. More specifically, CWPT practices promote the academic engagement of students with disabilities, can be used to individualize instruction and promote social interactions among students. Indeed, implementation of CWPT in general education classrooms has led to increased academic achievement for students with disabilities and their peers without disabilities (Bell, Young, Blair, & Nelson, 1990; Kamps, Barbetta, Leonard, & Delquandri, 1994; Mortweet et al., 1999).

Although the benefits of peer tutoring to the tutors in nonreciprocal IPT were not the focus of this chapter, there is evidence that peer-tutoring can have indirect effects on the tutors' academic and social-behavioral outcomes as well (e.g., Franca et al., 1990; Tournaki & Criscitiello, 2003). There is also evidence that students with disabilities, such as emotional-behavioral disorders, can effectively serve as peer tutors (Watts, Bryant, & Carroll, 2019). Therefore, educators could consider selecting students with disabilities to serve as tutors for younger students. This type of "reverse-role" tutoring provides both members of the dyad with opportunities to practice foundational academic skills. Allowing students with disabilities to serve as peer tutors in nonreciprocal IPT also provides a structured method to increase the social interaction between students with disabilities and students in general education.

As discussed by Collins et al. (Chapter 3, this volume), the use of peers as change agents is also a promising approach to increase the cultural responsiveness of instruction. CWPT and nonreciprocal IPT are comprised of empirically sound instructional practices—such as explicit instruction, increasing students' opportunities to respond, and providing immediate performance feedback— that are consistent with culturally responsive instruction (see Cartledge & Kourea, 2008). According to Ladson-Billings (1995), culturally relevant teaching encourages students to learn collaboratively, with a focus on developing a community of learners. CWPT emphasizes collaboration over competition within each peer dyad and student pairs can be reassigned frequently (Greenwood, 1997). Thus, the use of CWPT may be helpful as part of broader efforts to support the development of a community of learners within classrooms.

When implemented with fidelity, peer-tutoring is a low-cost, low-resource method that can be used to provide additional opportunities for students to practice foundational academic skills in a structured manner. There is substantial evidence that students can be trained (relatively quickly) to deliver academic interventions that incorporate effective instructional practices to their peers. Teachers and other educators play a critical role in the implementation of peer tutoring interventions. Tasks required of the teacher across the CWPT and nonreciprocal IPT studies we reviewed included selecting the intervention, organizing materials, training peer tutors, providing ongoing monitoring and support to the tutors, and monitoring the progress of tutees. Given the evidence supporting the effectiveness of CWPT and nonreciprocal IPT, we suspect readers of this chapter will find those investments worthwhile.

REFERENCES

Arreaga-Mayer, C. (1998). Increasing active student responding and improving academic performance through classwide peer tutoring. *Intervention in School and Clinic, 34*, 89–94. doi:10.1177/105345129803400204

Bell, K., Young, K. R., Blair, M., & Nelson, R. (1990). Facilitating mainstreaming of students with behavioral disorders using classwide peer tutoring. *School Psychology Review, 19*, 564–573.

Campbell, B. J., Brady, M. P., & Linehan, S. (1991). Effects of peer-mediated instruction on the acquisition and generalization of written capitalization skills. *Journal of Learning Disabilities, 24*, 6–14. doi:10.1177/002221949102400103

Cartledge, G., & Kourea, L. (2008). Culturally responsive classrooms for culturally diverse students with and at risk for disabilities. *Exceptional Children, 74*, 351–371. doi:10.1177/001440290807400305

Daly, E. J., III, Lentz, F. E., & Boyer, J. (1996). The instructional hierarchy: A conceptual model for understanding the effective components of reading interventions. *School Psychology Quarterly, 11*, 369–386. doi:10.1037/h0088941

Delquadri, J. C., Greenwood, C. R., Stretton, K., & Hall, R. V. (1983). The peer tutoring spelling game: A classroom procedure for increasing opportunity to respond and spelling performance. *Education and Treatment of Children, 6*, 225–239. doi:10.1177/001440298605200606

Delquadri, J. C., Greenwood, C. R., Whorton, D., Carta, J. J., & Hall, R. V. (1986). Classwide peer tutoring. *Exceptional Children, 52*, 535–542. doi:10.1177/001440298605200606

Dufrene, B. A., Reisener, C. D., Olmi, D. J., Zoder-Martell, K., McNutt, M. R., & Horn, D. R. (2010). Peer tutoring for reading fluency as a feasible and effective alternative in response to intervention systems. *Journal of Behavioral Education, 19*, 239–256. doi:10.1007/s10864-010-9111-8

Elbaum, B., Vaughn, S., Hughes, M., & Moody, S. W. (1999). Grouping practices and reading outcomes for students with disabilities. *Exceptional Children, 65*, 399–415. doi:10.1177/001440299906500309

Franca, V. M., Kerr, M. M., Reitz, A. L., & Lambert, D. (1990). Peer tutoring among behaviorally disordered students: Academic and social benefits to the tutor and tutee. *Education and Treatment of Children, 13*, 109–128.

Fulk, B. M., & King, K. (2001). Classwide peer tutoring at work. *Teaching Exceptional Children, 34*, 49–53. doi:10.1177/004005990103400207

Greenwood, C. R., Terry, B., Arreaga-Mayer, C., & Finney, R. (1992). The classwide peer tutoring program: Implementation factors moderating students' achievement. *Journal of Applied Behavior Analysis, 25*, 101–116. doi:10.1901/jaba.1992.25-101

Greenwood, C. (1997). Classwide peer tutoring. *Behavior and Social Issues, 7*, 53–57. doi:10.5210/bsi.v7i1.299

Greenwood, C. R., Delquadri, J., & Carta, I. I. (1997). *Together we can! Classwide peer tutoring to improve basic academic skills.* Longmont, CO: Sopris West.

Haisley, F. B., Tell, C. A., & Andrews, J. (1981). Peers as tutors in the mainstream: Trained "teachers" of handicapped adolescents. *Journal of Learning Disabilities, 14*, 224–238. doi:10.1177/002221948101400412,

Jenkins, J. R., & Jenkins, J. M. (1987). Making peer tutoring work. *Educational Leadership, 44*, 64–69.

Kamps, D. M., Barbetta, P. M., Leonard, B. R., & Delquadri, J. (1994). Classwide peer tutoring: An integration strategy to improve reading skills and promote peer interactions among students with Autism and general education peers. *Journal of Applied Behavior Analysis, 27*, 49–61. doi:10.1901/jaba.1994.27-49

Kamps, D. M., Dugan, E., Potucek, J., & Collins, A. (1999). Effects of cross-age peer tutoring networks among students with autism and general education students. *Journal of Behavioral Education, 9*(2), 97-115.

Klingbeil, D. A., Moeyaert, M., Archer, C. T., Chimboza, T. M., & Zwolski, S. A. (2017). Efficacy of peer mediated incremental rehearsal for English language learners. *School Psychology Review, 46*, 122–140. doi:10.17105/SPR46-1.122-140

Ladson-Billings, G. (1995). Toward a theory of culturally relevant pedagogy. *American Education Research Journal, 32*, 465–491. doi:10.3102/00028312032003465

Leung, K. C. (2015). Preliminary empirical model of crucial determinants of best practices or peer tutoring on academic achievement. *Journal of Educational Psychology, 107*, 558–579. doi:10.1037/a0037698

Maheady, L., & Gard, J. (2010). Classwide peer tutoring: Practice, theory, research, and personal narrative. *Intervention in School and Clinic, 46*, 71–78. doi:10.1177/1053451210376359

Maheady, L., Harper, G. F., Mallette, B., & Karnes, M. (2004). Preparing preservice teachers to implement class wide peer tutoring. *Teacher Education and Special Education, 27, 408*–418. doi:10.1177/088840640402700408

Maheady, L., Harper, G. F., Mallette, B., & Winstanley, N. (1991). Training and implementation requirements associated with the use of a classwide peer tutoring system. *Education and Treatment of Children, 14*, 177-198.

Medcalf, J., Glynn, T., & Moore, D. (2004). Peer tutoring in writing: A school systems approach. *Educational Psychology in Practice, 20*, 157–178. doi:10.1080/02667360410001691071

Mortweet, S. L., Utley, C. A., Walker, D., Dawson, H. L., Delquadri, J. C., Reddy, S. S., ... Ledford, D. (1999). Classwide peer tutoring: Teaching students with mild mental retardation in inclusive classrooms. *Exceptional Children, 65*, 524–536. doi:10.1177/001440299906500407

Moeyaert, M., Klingbeil, D. A., Rodabaugh, E., & Turan, M. (2019). Three-level meta-analysis of single-case data regarding the effects of peer tutoring on academic and social- behavioral outcomes for at-risk students and students with disabilities. *Remedial and Special Education*. Advance online publication. doi:10.1177/0741932519855079

Pyle, D., Pyle, N., Lignugaris/Kraft, B., Duran, L., & Akers, J. (2017). Academic effects of peer-mediated interventions with English language learners: A research synthesis. *Review of Educational Research, 87*, 103–133. doi:10.3102/0034654316653663

Rivera, D. M., & Bryant, B. R. (1992). Math instruction for students with special needs. *Intervention in School and Clinic, 28*, 71–86.

Shapiro, E. S. (2011). *Academic skills problems* (4th ed.). New York, NY: Guilford.

Stenhoff, D. M., & Lignugaris/Kraft, B. (2007). A review of the effects of peer tutoring on students with mild disabilities in secondary settings. *Exceptional Children, 74*, 8–30. doi:10.1177/001440290707400101

Talbott, E., Trzaska, A., & Zurheide, J. L. (2017). A systematic review of peer tutoring interventions for students with disabilities. In M. T. Hughes & E. Talbott (Eds.), *The Wiley handbook of diversity in special education* (pp. 319–356). Hoboken, NJ: Wiley.

Tournaki, N., & Criscitiello, E. (2003). Using peer tutoring as a successful part of behavior management. *Teaching Exceptional Children, 36*(2), 21–25.

U.S. Department of Education. (2007). What Works Clearing House: Beginning reading classwide peer tutoring. Retrieved from https://ies.ed.gov/ncee/wwc/Docs/InterventionReports/WWC_CWPT_070907.pdf

Utley, C. A., & Mortweet, S. L. (1997). Peer-mediated instruction and interventions. *Focus on Exceptional Children, 29*, 1–23.

Vaughn, S., Chard, D. J., Bryant, D. P., Coleman, M., Tyler, B., Linan-Thompson, S. . . . Kouzekanani, K. (2000). Fluency and comprehension interventions for third-grade students. *Remedial and Special Education, 21*, 325–335. doi:10.1177/074193250002100602

Vaughn, S., & Schumm, J. S. (1995). Responsible inclusion for students with learning disabilities. *Journal of Learning Disabilities, 28*, 264–270. doi:10.1177/002221949502800502

Watts, G. W., Bryant, D. P., & Carroll, M. L. (2019). Students with emotional-behavioral disorders as cross-age tutors: A synthesis of the literature. *Behavioral Disorders, 44*, 131–147. doi:10.1177/0198742918771914

Watts, G. W., Bryant, D. P., & Roberts, G. J. (2019). Effects of cross-age tutors with EBD for kindergarteners at risk of mathematics difficulties. *Journal of Emotional and Behavioral Disorders*. Advance online publication. doi:10.1177/1063426619884271

Zeneli, M., Thurston, A., & Roseth, C. (2016). The influence of experimental design on the magnitude of the effect size -peer tutoring for elementary, middle and high school settings: A meta-analysis. *International Journal of Educational Research, 76*, 211–223. doi:10.1016/j.ijer.2015.11.010

APPENDIX
INCREMENTAL REHEARSAL PEER TUTOR PROTOCOL

This intervention requires the tutor to present words written on flashcards and prompt a response. To facilitate accurate presentation of the known and unknown words, we wrote the unknown words on the back of the flashcard (the side that faced the tutor) with darker shading, and the known words with lighter shading.

1. Present the first unknown word ①
2. Say: This word is _____
3. Ask: What word is this? (show ①)
4. Say: Good, this word is _____.
   a. If wrong say: This word is _____
   b. Ask: What word is this?
   c. Say: Good, this word is _____
5. Say: Ok, let's begin.
6. Ask: What word is this? (show ①)

Continued on next page

7. Get rid of ⑦
8. Add ② to front of deck
9. Show ② and say: This word is _____
10. What word is this?
11. Good. This word is _____
12. Let's begin. What word is this?

(2) (1)
(2) (1) (1)
(2) (1) (1) (2)
(2) (1) (1) (2) (3)
(2) (1) (1) (2) (3) (4)
(2) (1) (1) (2) (3) (4) (5)
(2) (1) (1) (2) (3) (4) (5) (6)

13. Get rid of (6)
14. Add (3) to front of deck
15. Show (3) This word is _____
16. What word is this?
17. Good this word is _____
18. Let's begin. What word is this?

(3) (2)
(3) (2) (1)
(3) (2) (1) (1)
(3) (2) (1) (1) (2)
(3) (2) (1) (1) (2) (3)
(3) (2) (1) (1) (2) (3) (4)
(3) (2) (1) (1) (2) (3) (4) (5)

Error Correction Prompt

If a classmate says any word wrong:
1. This word is _____
2. What word is this?
3. Good, this word is _____

Tutor Integrity Form

PEER TUTORING WITH IR		
Briefly explained procedure	Yes	No
Correctly introduced the first unknown word	Yes	No
Completed the 1st IR procedure correctly	Yes	No
Correctly introduced the second unknown word	Yes	No
Completed the 2nd IR procedure correctly	Yes	No
Correctly introduced the 3rd unknown word	Yes	No
Completed the 3rd IR procedure correctly	Yes	No
Used error correction procedure verbatim each time target student made an error on an unknown word	Yes	No
Total Yes (%)		

## 6

Peer-Assisted Learning Strategies

DEVIN M. KEARNS, SARAH R. POWELL,
DOUGLAS FUCHS, AND LYNN S. FUCHS ■

Peer-Assisted Learning Strategies (PALS) is a peer-mediated academic intervention (PMAI) available in the areas of reading and mathematics. Developed at Vanderbilt University by Doug Fuchs and Lynn Fuchs, PALS is currently available in reading from kindergarten through high school and in mathematics from kindergarten through sixth grade. PALS is designed for use in general education settings with virtually all students, including many students with disabilities, and research supports the use of both Reading PALS and Math PALS (see Chapter 4 of this volume). PALS is supported by data indicating that peer support benefits many levels of students because working with a peer provides extensive practice with feedback (Fuchs et al., 1997). Although peers lack the expertise of teachers, students benefit from the opportunity to receive immediate feedback and engage in discussions using peer-to-peer language and ideas.

PALS PROCEDURES

Reading and Math PALS share several essential components designed to maximize achievement by increasing students' learning time (Archer & Hughes, 2010).

1. Each PALS lesson includes a set of activities designed to address critical grade-level skills.
2. Peers do almost all activities in pairs, a feature that distinguishes it from some other types of cooperative learning.
3. Students are cross-ability paired, meaning that one student in the pair has higher academic achievement than the other. This feature has the effect of increasing the skills of both students. Lower-performing

students benefit from the fluent models and corrections provided by their higher-performing peers, and high-performing students benefit from the opportunity to teach their peers. PALS data indicate that both types of students benefit.

4. The students are designated as the Coach or the Reader (Reading PALS)/ Player (Math PALS). Both students get to perform both jobs; that is, both students get to be the Coach regardless of their academic level.

5. There are very specific instructions for the peers to follow for each activity. The Coach gives the Reader/Player the instructions for each activity, and the Reader/Player follows the Coach's directions. The Coach also follows specific correction instructions when the Reader/Player makes a mistake or needs help. Figure 6.1 shows the Coach giving the Reader instructions and correcting a mistake for the Saying Sounds activity in First Grade PALS.

6. The lessons involve a reinforcement system to increase students' academic learning time. For example, in First Grade Reading PALS, students mark happy faces on their lesson sheets. Figure 6.1 shows the happy faces for the Saying Sounds activity in the lower right-hand corner of the lesson sheet. In First Grade Reading PALS, each happy face is worth 5 points. After the Reader finishes the activity, the Coach marks 5 points on the pair's point sheet (and they switch jobs). The students earn

Figure 6.1. A Coach (the bear) telling the Reader (the sheep) the instructions for the Saying Sounds activity. The Reader makes a mistake on the second sound-spelling (b = /b/), and the Coach follows the instructions for correcting mistakes.

points for each activity they complete and add them to the point sheet. There are somewhat different point-earning systems in each level, but point-earning is a component of all levels.

As a result of these features, students practice extensively in PALS—with minimal time off task. The fact that students spend the entirety of each PALS lesson practicing in a focused way with immediate support is one reason PALS has been shown to have positive effects on academic achievement.

READING PALS

Overview of Reading PALS Levels

There are four versions of Reading PALS: Kindergarten PALS (KPALS), First Grade PALS, PALS for Grades 2–6, and High School PALS. The four versions differ in their instructional foci based on the skills students learn in these grades. Table 6.1 shows the skills covered in each level. KPALS and First Grade PALS cover foundational phonological awareness skills (practice detecting and manipulating sound units in words) and phonics skills (identifying sound-spellings, reading high-frequency [sight] words, decoding using a blending strategy, and reading connected texts). Grades 2–6 and High School PALS focus on comprehension skills supported by strong empirical evidence, namely, reading for fluency, retelling

Table 6.1. PALS Programs, Skills, and Activities

Program	Skills	Activities
Kindergarten PALS (KPALS)	Phonological awareness, grapheme-phoneme (sound-spelling or letter-sound) correspondences, decoding (phonics), sight word reading, reading fluency	Sound Play,[†] What Sound? Sight Words, Sound Boxes, Sentences, Partner Reading
First Grade PALS	Grapheme-phoneme correspondence, decoding (phonics), sight word reading, reading fluency	Hearing Sounds and Sounding Out,[†] Saying Sounds, Sounding Out, Sight Words, Stories, Speed Game, Partner Reading
PALS for Grades 2–6 and High School PALS	Reading fluency, reading comprehension (summarizing, retelling, predicting)	Partner Reading, Retell, Paragraph Shrinking, Prediction Relay

Note: PALS = Peer-Assisted Learning Strategies Programs.

[†]This activity is only led by teachers. It is not part of peer-mediated instruction.

passages, identifying main ideas, and making predictions in a way that promotes inferencing (National Institute of Child Health & Human Development, 2000).

Students improve these skills through focused reading activities that constitute much of a given PALS program. For example, KPALS includes Sound Play activities that are designed to improve phonological awareness. Students listen and perform tasks that involve identifying sounds represented by pictures without using letters (e.g., showing a picture of a cat, the teacher asks, "What is the first sound in cat?"). Both KPALS and First Grade PALS include components to practice decoding via blending (i.e., Sound Boxes in KPALS and Hearing Sounds and Sounding Out [teacher-led] and Sounding Out [peer-mediated] in First Grade PALS).

Most of the activities are completed in student pairs, but the teacher plays an important role in several respects. First, the teacher leads a series of training lessons to introduce students to the activities. The training lessons are scripted but are designed to allow teachers to use them in a way that matches their teaching style. These lessons are essential for teaching students how to complete all activities correctly. Second, the teacher leads parts of lessons every day in KPALS and First Grade PALS and conducts short mini-lessons in Grades 2–6 PALS to reinforce key PALS concepts. The teacher's third critical role is to monitor students; provide specific, positive, and corrective feedback; model activities for pairs experiencing difficulty with them; and take notes on student strengths and weaknesses to support later additional instruction.

KPALS and First Grade PALS

KPALS and First Grade PALS are different in important ways. Notably, only KPALS includes a specific phonological awareness lesson (Sound Play), and only First Grade PALS includes teacher-led decoding practice (Hearing Sounds and Sounding Out) and an activity to build fluency called the Speed Game. Figure 6.2 shows the KPALS Sound Play activity, and Figure 6.3 shows the First Grade PALS Hearing Sounds and Sounding Out lessons.

However, in most other respects the two reading programs are very similar. The pairs practice identifying sound-spellings (also known as grapheme–phoneme correspondences) with the activity shown in Figure 6.1. They practice decoding with an activity similar to that in Figure 6.3 (except for Steps 1 and 2). They read high-frequency words with an activity called Sight Words. Figures 6.4 and 6.5 show the Sight Word activities for both grades.

The images show parts of daily decoding lesson sheets, printed one per pair; each lesson (there are more than 70) has a different sheet with new and more advanced word recognition skills. In KPALS and First Grade Reading PALS, students conduct activities involving a combination of new skills and review of previously presented skills, and they provide practice with carefully controlled texts, that is, texts containing only taught sound-spellings and sight words. To generalize skills and link these activities to experiences with more authentic literature, KPALS and First Grade PALS contain a story reading activity. In this activity, students

Figure 6.2. KPALS Sound Play activity.

Figure 6.3. First Grade PALS Hearing Sounds and Sounding Out activity.

				What word?
is	and	was	the	
and	on	the	and	
		☺ ☺	☺ ☺	

Figure 6.4. Sight Words activity and coach question to the reader (right side of vertical line) in KPALS.

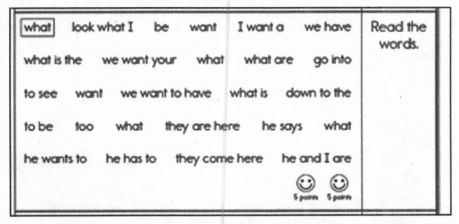

Figure 6.5. Sight Words activity and coach instructions in First Grade PALS. The words are organized in phrases to promote fluency.

read texts selected by the teacher—ones at the instructional level of the lower-performing reader.

Grades 2–6 PALS and High School PALS

The activities in these two versions of PALS for older students are the same, although there are some subtle differences in Coach instructions and corrections. Figure 6.6 lists each of the activities, their purposes, the time required for each student to complete the activity, and the instructions the Coach gives the Reader in Grades 2–6 PALS. In both Grades 2–6 and High School PALS, there is no lesson sheet. Rather, the students read texts at the instructional level of the lower-performing reader and conduct the PALS activities with these appropriately leveled texts. Coaches have an Activity Card to give Readers instructions and a Correction Card that reminds them how to help the Reader with mistakes (a correction is shown in Figure 6.6 in the Partner Reading box).

For the first activity, Partner Reading, the higher-performing reader does the Reader job first, providing a model of fluent reading for the lower-performing reader. Second is the Retell activity. Although both students do most activities, only the lower-performing reader does the Retell. The goal is to provide additional practice with a foundational skill. The next activity, Paragraph Shrinking, addresses a high-value comprehension strategy, identifying the main idea. It is similar to Getting the Gist in Collaborative Strategic Reading (Klingner, Vaughn, & Schumm, 1998). Paragraph Shrinking is powerful because it provides extensive practice extracting the main idea for manageable units of text (Graesser, 2007).

Prediction Relay is somewhat unique. It clearly provides practice making predictions. However, the structure of the activity also makes it a form of inference. Rather than predicting what will happen in the entire text, the Coach asks the

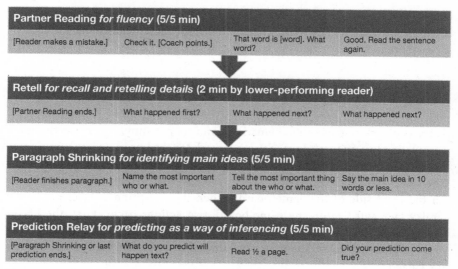

Partner Reading *for fluency* (5/5 min)			
[Reader makes a mistake.]	Check it. [Coach points.]	That word is [word]. What word?	Good. Read the sentence again.

Retell *for recall and retelling details* (2 min by lower-performing reader)			
[Partner Reading ends.]	What happened first?	What happened next?	What happened next?

Paragraph Shrinking *for identifying main ideas* (5/5 min)			
[Reader finishes paragraph.]	Name the most important who or what.	Tell the most important thing about the who or what.	Say the main idea in 10 words or less.

Prediction Relay *for predicting as a way of inferencing* (5/5 min)			
[Paragraph Shrinking or last prediction ends.]	What do you predict will happen text?	Read ½ a page.	Did your prediction come true?

Figure 6.6. The Grades 2–6 and High School PALS activities. The Partner Reading box includes the correction using when Readers mispronounce words in Grades 2–6 PALS. The other three boxes contain the instructions the Coach gives to the Reader for that activity in Grades 2–6 PALS.

Reader, "What do you predict will happen next?" and instructs the Reader, "Read half a page." This means that the reader must consider carefully the events (in a narrative) that have just occurred and consider their immediate effect. This will lead to more specific predictions (i.e., text-based inferences) than do predictions for an entire text, chapter, or section. Predicting events is only possible with narrative text, but the procedure works for expository texts with a slight modification. The Coach asks, "What do you predict you will learn next." In this way, Prediction Relay addresses the important skill of inferencing. Across all four activities, the Grades 2–6 and High School PALS activities address important reading comprehension skills.

MATH PALS

Typical Math PALS Components

Students work in pairs to solve different types of mathematics problems. One student starts as the Coach and the other acts as a Player; students switch roles throughout the lesson to ensure each student gets an opportunity to act as the Coach and the Player. In Kindergarten and Grade 1, pairs work on topics such as numbers, comparison, addition, subtraction, and place value. In Grades 2 through 6, pairs work on grade-specific mathematics skills related to computation (e.g., addition, subtraction, multiplication, division) or applications (e.g., charts and graphs, decimals, fractions, measurement, money, ratios, variables, word problems). See Powell and Fuchs (2015) for more detail about the content of each program.

Kindergarten and First Grade

Pairs work on a specific mathematics lesson (e.g., comparison) for the week completing two or three days of partner work for the lesson. Pairs share a game board (see Figure 6.7). On the left of the game board are the Coach's prompts. The Coach asks each prompt for every problem. The Player works the problems on the right side of the game board. When the Coach and Player get to the smiley face and flag on the game board, two actions occur. First, the Player shades in a smiley face on a Smiley Sheet shared by the pair. Second, the Coach and Player switch roles: The Coach becomes the Player, and the Player becomes the Coach.

Kindergarten and Grade 1 teachers conduct a brief class-wide demonstration when pairs start using a new game board. The teacher uses this demonstration to introduce or review the Coach's prompts and describe and practice the Player's actions. After the demonstration, students break into pairs and complete the game board as the teacher monitors pairs and provides feedback, when necessary. For many lessons, pairs use additional materials to show the mathematical concepts or procedures on the game board. For example, the activity in Figure 6.7 uses a counting manipulative (e.g., bears, clips, blocks) to understand subtraction as taking away. To keep costs minimal, teachers can use materials from the classroom (e.g., number lines, counters, place value blocks) or use templates provided within the Math PALS manuals.

In Grades 2 through 6, pairs work on a specific mathematics lesson for two weeks, completing two days of work during the first week and two days of work during the second week. In this way, pairs work on a single mathematics skill over

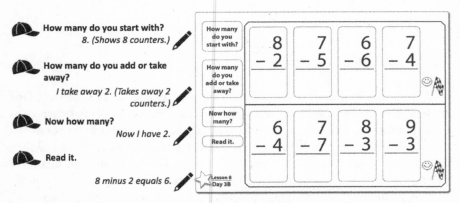

Figure 6.7. Sample dialogue between Coach (cap) and Player (pencil) at first grade.

a two-week period. During every day of Math PALS, the Coach and Player complete two activities: Coaching and Practice.

Coaching engages the Coach and Player to work through a series of mathematics problems. The Coach reads prompts off of a Coach's Question Sheet to engage the Player in dialogue about each problem (see Figure 6.8). The Player responds to the Coach's prompts for the first few problems. When the Coach and Player get to the stop sign, the Coach stops asking the prompts to the Player, and the Player engages in self-talk. During self-talk, the Player reflects upon the Coach's prompts as a guide and talks aloud about every step the problem. When the Coach and Player reach the flag, they switch roles: The Coach becomes the Player, and the Player become the Coach.

During Coaching, the Coach checks the Player's work by checking each digit that the Player writes. The Coach circles a digit answered correctly. If a digit is incorrect, the Coach helps the Player correct the mistake and then triangles the corrected digit. After each problem is solved, the Coach draws a circle around problems without any mistakes. This marking strategy allows Players to provide Coach feedback as the Player works through each problem. The marking strategy also provides clues to the classroom teacher about which errors a Player makes.

Practice allows the Coach and Player to practice independently what they just worked on as a pair. A Practice Sheet contains lesson-specific problems (e.g., problems about charts and graphs) plus a computation review. After five minutes, partners switch Practice Sheets and check one another's work. Students

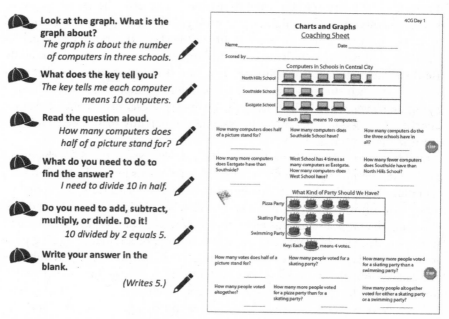

Figure 6.8. Sample dialogue between Coach (cap) and Player (pencil) at fourth grade.

earn points for correctly answered problems and mark points on a pair-shared Point Sheet.

In Math PALS at Grades 2 through 6, the teacher provides a demonstration of the Coaching and Practice activities at the beginning of PALS implementation. This demonstration typically lasts four days, with each day lasting 25 to 30 minutes. After the demonstration lessons, students begin each Math PALS day with Coaching followed by Practice. All mathematics instruction occurs at the peer level with teachers providing feedback as warranted.

RECOMMENDATIONS FOR IMPLEMENTATION

Pairing Students

To begin implementation of PALS, teachers must first decide how to pair their students. The goal is to pair students so that one student is higher-performing than the other but also so the gap in abilities is not too large. Pairing students is not an exact science.

Pairing is a three-step process. First, the students need to rank students by their reading skills, as shown in Figure 6.9. Teachers use a variety of data sources to decide students' academic performance levels, especially the first time they make pairs. Sources include standards assessments, progress monitoring (also called curriculum-based measurement) assessments, unit assessments, and teacher-made tests. The students do not have to be ranked exactly (Figure 6.7 shows that Ms. B was not sure about some students' levels). The second step is to match students so that the highest-performing and lowest-performing students are paired with peers at the average ability of the class. This prevents the gap in academic skill between students being so large that the students cannot easily use the same materials. The third step is to adjust the pairs to assure that each pair includes two students capable of cooperating. Partners who have difficulty getting along will make PALS time challenging for themselves and often the other students. As a result, pairs might be organized differently than their exact academic levels might indicate.

Students work with their partners for four to six weeks. The pairs change to give the teacher the opportunity to better match students by need—based on co-operation and academic level. Changing the pairs also gives students an opportunity to work with different peers and build relationships with other students. Changing the pairs also affords an opportunity to correct mistakes, that is, separate pairs that clearly struggle to cooperate. It is important that struggling pairs are not immediately reassigned because immediately responding to pair difficulty often makes other pairs worse: If one partner gets to change immediately, other students then often believe they should be able to change partners. The general rule is to give partners one week to get along and change them if this does not produce improvements.

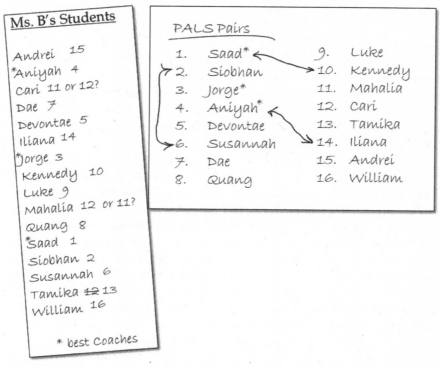

Figure 6.9. Example of how a Grade 4 teacher, Ms. B, makes pairs for Math PALS. She lists her students alphabetically and orders them by mathematics ability using data from progress monitoring assessments and last year's state standards assessment. The figure shows she was not certain about the rankings for Cari, Mahalia, and Tamika, but she does not worry because she knows she will adjust the pairs later. On the right, she has put the students in two columns and plans to match across, with the highest high-performing student (Saad) matched with the highest low-performing student (Luke, ninth in academic skill). She has also adjusted the pairings based on what she knows about her students and their ability to cooperate. For example, she has matched Saad with Kennedy because Siobhan and Kennedy have difficulty getting along. She has matched Aniyah with Iliana because she knows Iliana needs a very strong coach to keep her focused during lessons. She has matched Siobhan and Susannah even though they are more similar in ability than the students in many of the other pairs. However, pairing is not an exact science, and this pair still meets the expectations that one Player (Siobhan) is stronger and they will likely get along. Ms. B thinks they will both benefit from working together.

One additional consideration for pairing is that classrooms do not always have an even number of students. In this case, the teacher creates a triad, a group of three students. These three students divide the activities differently, following the teacher's instructions. Each manual gives specific instructions how to create triads for the given version of PALS. In all cases, triads should not include the most struggling students in the class. In addition, students who work in a triad for a four- to six-week period should change triads for the next period.

Supporting Student Success with PALS

Successful PALS implementation begins with strong initial lessons. All levels of PALS include introductory lessons, and these are important to conduct carefully. Students need to learn the procedures correctly, so much so that they can recite the instructions and corrections verbatim. This is important to standardize the way students do the PALS activities. This assures consistency across pairs and classrooms. If all students follow the exact same procedures, they will be able to work with a new partner easily immediately.

Another important factor for assuring PALS success is to provide supplemental support during PALS lessons, as needed. Occasionally, students will have difficulty with games and activities despite clear initial instructions. In these cases, it is appropriate to do additional short lessons to further help the students. One activity that often requires review lessons is Paragraph Shrinking in Grades 2–6 and High School PALS—an activity that involves the essential but complex and effort-intensive skill of identifying the main idea. As a result, teachers frequently conduct supplemental mini-lessons to assist students further. The manual for Grades 2–6 PALS includes optional mini-lessons for this purpose. Teachers can also increase implementation by giving successful pairs opportunities to model their PALS practice for their class. Model pairs find this reinforcing, and it provides other pairs with ideas how to improve their work together.

Another key factor for PALS success is to make sure that students maintain motivation throughout the school year. Students are almost always excited by the novelty of PALS when they first begin. However, once PALS becomes de rigueur, motivation can flag. Teachers can use several strategies to prevent this. One strategy is to make sure students get new partners every month or so. Another is to create group contingencies where students all get a reward that the entire class will find reinforcing (e.g., 10 mins of free play or additional recess after 10 consecutive PALS lessons where all pairs showed high levels of on-task behavior). Teachers can also prevent disinterest by maintaining their own excitement about PALS: Student behaviors often follow those of their teachers.

Successful implementation also occurs when teachers use PALS lesson time to monitor pairs carefully. PALS is an exciting part of the day for teachers because they can be confident that all students are engaged in academic learning and can focus on individual student needs without fearing that other students are not learning. Teachers can provide support to each pair as need, provide specific praise (e.g., saying, "Coach, you are doing a great job watching your Reader and correcting mistakes), or simply observe students and take notes. The notes can provide clues about student difficulties and allow teachers to provide supplemental instruction during non-PALS small group time (e.g., during individualized reading group time).

A final important point is that teachers must do enough PALS. PALS is designed to take between 20 and 45 mins, depending on the level. The lessons should be done about three times a week. Teachers can implement Reading and Math PALS by alternating days (Math, Reading, Math, Reading, Math in Week 1 of a cycle and Reading, Math, Reading, Math, Reading in Week 2). If students do not get enough PALS practice, the benefits may not obtain.

CONSIDERATIONS OF DIVERSITY AND EQUITY

The creators of the PALS programs designed PALS for use in the general education classroom to meet the needs of virtually all students with the expectation that higher-performing students would benefit from work in a pair through teaching and explaining, whereas lower-performing students would benefit from their teammate because of the individual attention and feedback (Fuchs et al., 2002). The explicit nature of the PALS programs, in which students work together in pairs through a series of problems with designated roles for the Coach and Reader/Player, reduces the cognitive load and working memory for many students (Martin, 2016).

Students who need language support may also benefit from the structure of each lesson and the consistent language in the prompts. Students may also benefit from the opportunity to learn from a peer using student-level language that teachers do not always know. This may be especially helpful for students with language processing difficulties and students in learning English. In the latter case, peers likely understand each other's language capabilities at a finer-grained level than their teachers, owing to their time playing and working together throughout the day. This is one reason PALS may be effective for English learners, as multiple studies have shown (McMaster, Kung, Han, & Cao, 2008; Sáenz, Fuchs, & Fuchs, 2005).

In experimental studies, researchers have also demonstrated significant gains for students with diverse needs, including students with disabilities (Rafdal, McMaster, McConnell, Fuchs, & Fuchs, 2011) and students at-risk for disabilities (Mattatall, 2017). Importantly, students with disabilities or students without many friends benefited from the structured social experiences provided through Reading PALS or Math PALS (Fuchs, Fuchs, Mathes, & Martinez, 2002; Dion, Fuchs, & Fuchs, 2005).

Teachers should consider the following for implementation of PALS with diverse students. First, teachers should select reading and mathematics activities reflective of diverse learners (King Thorius & Graff, 2018). For example, reading selections should be culturally and linguistically appropriate, and mathematics selections should respect varied approaches to solving the same problem. Second, teachers should follow guidelines in the PALS manuals for establishing a positive relationship between students in a pair and demonstrate how to work with a partner who is not a best friend. In a study about Reading PALS, students without a classroom friend developed friendships during the course of PALS (Dion et al., 2005), so teachers need to provide a safe classroom environment to allow friendships to flourish (Kroeger & Kouche, 2006). Teachers may need to discuss patience, if a partner works faster or slower than expected, and how to explain something in a kind and helpful way (i.e., not only telling a partner the correct answer). Third, teachers may want to incorporate goal setting to encourage students to focus on mathematics learning across the school year (Codding, Chan, Iannetta, Ferreira, & Volpe, 2011). Finally, not every student may benefit from PALS (Mattatall, 2017). Therefore, teachers need to continually measure the reading and mathematics performance of students and provide supplemental support to students when necessary.

CONCLUSION

Reading PALS and Math PALS provide teachers with a structured program to encourage peer-to-peer interaction and learning in the classroom. This chapter provided a general introduction to the PALS programs in reading and mathematics, and we hope this introduction encourages teachers to seek more information about the PALS programs.

ACKNOWLEDGMENTS

We gratefully acknowledge the following individuals (listed alphabetically) who, as faculty, staff, master's and doctoral students, and postdoctoral associates at Vanderbilt University, contributed ideas, developed curricula, wrote scripts, guided program implementation in hundreds of public schools, helped test thousands of children to evaluate program efficacy, contributed to data analysis and to the write-ups of published papers, and shared their enthusiasm and "can-do" spirit: Shelly Allen, Rose Allinder, Jill Allor, Stephanie Al Otaiba, Johnell Benz, Madeline Blanton, Judy Bowers, Mary Braun, Pam Burish, Eric Dion, Sue Dutka, Pam Fernstrom-Chaney, Alene Harris, Carol Hamlett, Sally Hewlett, Janie Pate Hodge, Kathy Karns, Michelle Katzaroff, Sarah Kazdan, Carol Ann Lloyd, Chris Lemons, Liz Martinez, Patricia Mathes, Kristen McMaster, Norris Phillips, Karen Prentice, Peggy Reeder, Holley Roberts, Laura Sáenz, Pamela Seethaler, Debbie Simmons, Pam Stecker, Ebba Svenson, Anneke Thompson, Keith Whinnery, Nancy Yang, Laura Yazdian, Loulee Yen Haga, and Caresa Young. We are also grateful to the many teachers who invited us into their classrooms and participated in PALS research studies, and we want to acknowledge the children who worked hard in PALS to improve their academic skills and relationships with their peers.

REFERENCES

Archer, A. L., & Hughes, C. A. (2010). *Explicit instruction: Effective and efficient teaching.* Guilford Press.

Codding, R. S., Chan-Iannetta, L., George, S., Ferreira, K., & Volpe, R. (2011). Early number skills: Examining the effects of class-wide interventions on kindergarten performance. *School Psychology Quarterly, 26,* 85–96. doi:10.1037/a0022661

Dion, E., Fuchs, D., & Fuchs, L. S. (2005). Differential effects of peer-assisted learning strategies on students' social preference and friendship making. *Behavioral Disorders, 30*, 421–429. doi:10.1177/019874290503000404

Fuchs, D., Fuchs, L. S., Mathes, P. G., & Martinez, E. A. (2002). Preliminary evidence on the social standing of students with learning disabilities in PALS and no-PALS classrooms. *Learning Disabilities Research and Practice, 17*, 205–215. doi:10.1111/1540-5826.00046

Fuchs, D., Fuchs, L. S., Mathes, P. G., & Simmons, D. C. (1997). Peer-Assisted Learning Strategies: Making classrooms more responsive to diversity. *American Educational Research Journal, 34*, 174–206.

Graesser, A. C. (2007). An introduction to strategic reading comprehension. In D. McNamara (Ed.), *Reading comprehension strategies: Theories, interventions, and technologies* (pp. 3–26). Mahwah, NJ: Erlbaum.

King Thorius, K. A., & Graff, C. S. (2018). Extending peer-assisted learning strategies for racially, linguistically, and ability diverse learners. *Intervention in School and Clinic, 53*, 163–170. doi:10.1177/1053451217702113

Klingner, J. K., Vaughn, S., & Schumm, J. S. (1998). Collaborative strategic reading during social studies in heterogeneous fourth-grade classrooms. *Elementary School Journal, 99*, 3–22. doi:10.1177/1053451217702113

Kroeger, S. D., & Kouche, N. (2006). Using peer-assisted learning strategies to increase response to intervention in inclusive middle math settings. *Teaching Exceptional Children, 38*(5), 6–13. doi:10.1177/004005990603800501

Martin, A. J. (2016). *Using Load Reduction Instruction (LRI) to boost motivation and engagement.* Leicester, England: British Psychological Society.

Mattatall, C. A. (2017). Using peer-assisted learning strategies for boys, Aboriginal learners, and at-risk populations. *Reading and Writing Quarterly, 33*, 155–170. doi:10.1080/10573569.2016.1142914

McMaster, K. L., Kung, S.-H., Han, I., & Cao, M. (2008). peer-assisted learning strategies: A "Tier 1" approach to promoting English learners' response to intervention. *Exceptional Children, 74*, 194–214. doi:10.1177/001440290807400204

National Institute of Child Health and Human Development. (2000). *Report of the National Reading Panel: Teaching children to read: An evidence-based assessment of the scientific research literature on reading and its implications for reading instruction: Reports of the subgroups* (NIH Publication No. 00-4754). Washington, DC: U.S. Government Printing Office.

Powell, S. R., & Fuchs, L. S. (2015). Peer-assisted learning strategies in mathematics. In K. R. Harris & L. Meltzer (Eds.), *The power of peers: Enhancing learning and social skills* (pp. 188–223). New York, NY: Guilford Press.

Rafdal, B. H., McMaster, K. L., McConnell, S. R., Fuchs, D., & Fuchs, L. S. (2011). The effectiveness of kindergarten peer-assisted learning strategies for students with disabilities. *Exceptional Children, 77*, 299–316. doi:10.1177/001440291107700303

Sáenz, L. M., Fuchs, L. S., & Fuchs, D. (2005). Peer-assisted learning strategies for English language learners with learning disabilities. *Exceptional Children, 71*, 231–247. doi:10.1177/001440290507100302

## 7

Game-Based
Cooperative Learning

ELIZABETH B. MCCALLUM, JAMIE LEIGH YARBROUGH,
AND ARA J. SCHMITT ■

Cooperative learning methods involving game-based mechanics can be fun, engaging ways of using peer-mediated academic intervention (PMAI) to increase student performance. They have been used to improve academic achievement, student attitudes toward each other and toward academic material, and classroom management for decades (Devries et al., 1975). Teams–Games–Tournaments (TGT) is perhaps the most commonly used of these structures, with the largest evidence base demonstrating its effectiveness across academic subject areas, populations, and age ranges (Slavin, 1995). This cooperative learning method relies on both within-team cooperation and between-team competition to maximize learning and student relationships. To be successful in TGT, students must rely on their team members to review important academic content and fill any gaps in their knowledge. They then go compete against students from other teams in academic tournaments to bring back points to their home teams. It is the teams that work the most cooperatively in preparing all students for success in the tournaments that earn the most points.

As the name implies, TGT consists of three components: teams, games, and tournaments. Teams are designed to create maximum heterogeneity in terms of dimensions such as academic achievement level, race, and sex. Importantly, teams should be planned so that each team within a classroom has a similar distribution of high, middle, and low achievers. A simple way to accomplish this is to assign high achievers and low achievers evenly across the groups, and then assign the middle achievers randomly. Approximately four or five students per team is typically recommended. Teams remain together over time to foster group cohesion and cooperation, and teachers can seat team members together in the classroom, and frequently assign group work sessions to further facilitate team building.

The games component of TGT involves a series of instructional games in which students compete with each other by answering true–false or multiple choice questions regarding the curricular material. The tournament component typically occurs weekly or biweekly and involves students of similar achievement levels competing against one another in small groups for tournament points, assigned based on individual performance in the tournament. When these tournaments are completed, the top, middle, and low scorer of each tournament are assigned points accordingly, and they return to their home teams, and team scores are tallied and a winning team is declared.

TGT has been successfully used since the 1970s to increase academic performance, student relationships, and student perceptions toward academic material (Devries et al., 1975; Devries, Edwards, & Slavin, 1978; Ke, 2008). Several explanations potentially account for TGT's success. First, the team score leads to a sense of interdependence among team members, which can be highly motivating. Additionally, there is individual accountability for each team member's own performance in the form of individually earned tournament points. Individual accountability has been demonstrated to be crucial for successful cooperative learning procedures (Slavin, 1995). Another unique element of TGT is the point-earning scoring model within the tournaments. Unlike traditional grading methods in which low achievers almost always earn lower scores than high achievers, because students of similar achievement levels compete against one another and scores are awarded for place rather than total points earned, TGT's scoring model is designed to allow all students the potential to earn similar scores. This scoring system is thought to be highly motivating, particularly for low-achieving students, who do not often experience academic success.

RECOMMENDATIONS FOR IMPLEMENTATION

The following steps should be taken in implementing TGT in the classroom setting. Keep in mind that TGT can be used with a wide variety of curricular material, and these procedures can be modified as necessary. Following this section, a detailed example of the strategy in action will be provided.

1. *Assign student home teams.* Four to five students per team is optimal, making sure students of all achievement levels and demographics are represented on each team.
2. *Prepare tournament question cards and answer sheets.* These should consist of short answer and/or multiple choice questions.
3. *Give student teams time to prepare for tournaments.* Visit each group to ensure students are on task.
4. *Assign tournament teams.* Unlike home teams, tournament "teams" are composed of students of similar achievement levels.
5. *Explain tournament rules and student roles within tournaments.* The tournament rules are somewhat complex and may be best understood

in the context of an example. Please see the following section for a full description of rules and student roles within the tournaments.

6. *Collect tournament points and ensure accuracy.* Do a quick check to make sure students have scored and awarded points accurately.

7. *Tally team scores and share tournament results!* If possible, find a simple way to celebrate group and individual successes that is acceptable to all.

TGT: A Practical Example

John Smith is a seventh-grade geography teacher using TGT to help his students master the content of a unit on European geography and culture. First, Mr. Smith divides his class of 16 students into four "home" teams of four students each. Each team contains one high achiever, two average achievers, and one low achiever. Next, Mr. Smith prepares the tournament materials, which include a study guide, a practice worksheet and corresponding answer sheet, four identical decks of question cards (see Table 7.1), answer sheets that correspond to the question cards (see Table 7.2), blank answer sheets, scoring sheets, and written copies of the tournament rules.

After presenting the unit material on Monday, Mr. Smith describes TGT to the class. He explains that he has divided students into home teams and that each team will be tasked with preparing its members to compete in a weekly tournament, which will be held the day before the unit exam. During the tournament, students will represent their team to earn points for their home teams. He provides a study guide to each student to review for homework Monday night.

On Tuesday, students gather with their team members. Each team chooses a team name. Next, Mr. Smith provides instructions and materials for team practice. He gives each team two copies of a practice worksheet and answer sheet and encourages students to work collaboratively rather than individually. He tells them to work together to review the content and prepare each team member for the tournament. Mr. Smith circulates the classroom to answer questions and ensure that each team remains on task. A second practice session takes place on Wednesday.

At the end of Wednesday's practice session, Mr. Smith explains the tournament rules to the class via a demonstration tournament using four volunteers, one from each team. After the four volunteers are seated at a table, Mr. Smith puts a stack of question cards in the center of the table. Each card has a number on one side and a question on the other side. Each student is given a blank answer sheet. One answer key and a game score sheet (see Table 7.3) are also provided.

First, Mr. Smith asks each player to randomly pick a card. The student with the highest number goes first and is the first reader. The game proceeds clockwise, such that the person to the left of the reader will be the first challenger, followed by the second challenger. The fourth student (to the right of the reader) is the checker.

Table 7.1. Sample of Tournament Question Cards

Europe Geography Question Cards

1. What is the capital of Sweden?
2. What mountain range divides Europe and Asia?
3. Which country borders Portugal?
4. What four countries are part of the United Kingdom?
5. What is the body of water that separates Europe from Africa?
6. What is the capital of Hungary?
7. What is the name of the smallest country in Europe?
8. What is the name of the peninsula that contains the countries of Spain and Portugal?
9. What is the name of the longest river in Europe?
10. What is the largest mountain range in Europe?
11. What country is surrounded by France, Belgium, and Germany?
12. What is the name of the waterway that separates the United Kingdom from the European continent?

Europe Landmark and Culture Question Cards

13. Name the four official languages spoken in Switzerland.
14. What country is the Leaning Tower of Pisa located in?
15. If you wanted to visit Stonehenge, what country would you have to travel to?
16. Within what city is the Vatican City situated?
17. What landmark is France most known for?
18. What are the three major religions of Europe?
19. Which Italian City has canals for roads?
20. What is the official language of Monaco?
21. How many time zones are in Europe?
22. How many countries are members of the European Union?
23. Name the three official languages of Belgium.
24. In what country is the Black Forest located?

Table 7.2. Sample Tournament Answer Sheet

Europe Geography Question Cards

1. Stockholm
2. The Ural Mountains
3. Spain
4. England, Scotland, Wales, and Northern Ireland
5. The Mediterranean Sea
6. Budapest
7. Vatican City
8. The Iberian Peninsula
9. The Volga River
10. The Alps
11. Luxembourg
12. The English Channel

Europe Landmark and Culture Question Cards

13. French, German, Italian, and Romansh
14. Italy
15. England
16. Rome
17. The Eiffel Tower
18. Judaism, Christianity, and Islam
19. Venice
20. French
21. Four
22. Twenty-eight
23. French, Dutch, and German
24. Germany

Table 7.3. Sample Game Score Sheet

Tournament Table # _____**Game Score Sheet**

Player	Team	Total # of Cards	Tournament Points
(Insert Player Name 1)	(Insert Team Name 1)		
(Insert Player Name 2)	(Insert Team Name 2)		
(Insert Player Name 3)	(Insert Team Name 3)		
(Insert Player Name 4)	(Insert Team Name 4)		

After returning the question cards to the deck, the reader shuffles the deck and places it in the center of the table. Then, the reader picks the top card, reads the number and question aloud, and places the card face up on the table. All four students write their answers on their blank answer key. The reader shares his or her answer with the others. Next, the first challenger decides whether or not she or he wants to challenge the reader's answer. If they opt to challenge, they provide an alternative answer. The checker reads the correct answer aloud. The player that answered correctly gets to keep the card. If the first challenger thinks the reader answered correctly, they may pass. The second challenger has the option of challenging or passing and the process is repeated. For subsequent question cards, play moves clockwise around the table such that each player has the opportunity to assume each role. The game continues until time runs out or each question card has been played.

On the day of the tournament, Mr. Smith sets up four tournament tables. One member from each team is sent to each table, with students of similar ability levels playing against each other in tournaments (see Figure 7.1). As a game is played at each table, Mr. Smith moves from group to group to ensure that students are playing correctly. At the end of the tournament, students count their cards and use the Game Score Sheet (Table 7.4) to record each player's raw score and tournament points. Mr. Smith collects the game score sheets and transfers the tournament points to a team summary sheet to determine the tournament champion home team. Certificates are awarded to all members of the winning team in recognition of their success.

CONSIDERATIONS OF DIVERSITY AND EQUITY

When Slavin introduced this intervention procedure in the 1970s, he clearly had notions of socially just, equitable classroom practices in mind. Evidence for this statement is provided by the deliberate procedures by which study teams and tournament teams, respectively, were formed. Possible is that Slavin's work was influenced by the emergence of social identity theory in that very time period (Tajfel & Turner, 1979). Social identity theory suggests that students, left to their own devices, may choose to form groups with similar characteristics to their own.

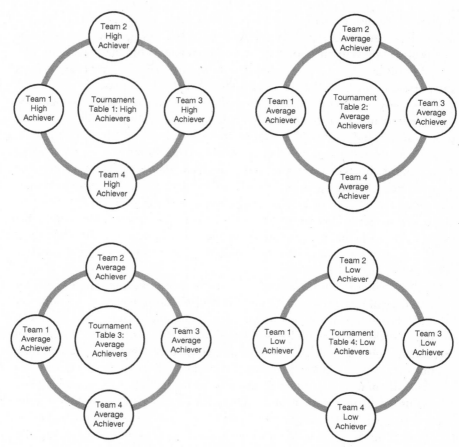

Figure 7.1. Depiction of how students are assigned to tournament tables.

Table 7.4. CALCULATING TOURNAMENT POINTS FOR A FOUR-PLAYER GAME

Player	No Ties	Tie for Top	Tie for Middle	Tie for Low	3-Way Tie for Top	3-Way Tie for Low	4-Way Tie	Tie for Low and High
Top Scorer	6 points	5	6	6	5	6	4	5
High Middle Scorer	4 points	5	4	4	5	3	4	5
Low Middle Scorer	3 points	3	4	3	5	3	4	3
Low Scorer	2 points	2	2	3	2	3	4	3

If students are allowed to form their own groups, groups could possibly be formed according to gender, race, perceived academic ability, language status, social status, or any other in-group/out-group distinction pertinent within that classroom. This would result in a socially segregated classroom. However, TGT procedures from their first appearance in the literature would not permit this to occur.

TGT study teams are carefully formed by first understanding the "groups" that are present within the classroom and then distributing members of those groups across study teams. This requires members of study teams who might not otherwise interact with each other to work together toward the common goals of helping each other learn and win cross-team tournaments. We argue that interactions with heterogeneous study team members do not just simply promote cooperation among students who might be perceived as different from oneself. Study group interactions may also facilitate increased awareness of the similarities between group members and afford group members the opportunity to talk about differences between group members. This might contribute to group cohesion identified in the TGT literature.

Students with disabilities might also particularly benefit from the composition of students within study teams. By the very nature of study teams being comprised of students of different ability levels, in addition to other characteristics, students with disabilities are inherently "included" within TGT procedures. The learning benefits are obvious. Increased opportunities to learn from more academically competent peers is afforded to students with disabilities. Likewise, if part of the student's disability, a student could also learn other skills, like age-appropriate social skills, from other study team members. We can imagine a multitude of other situations in which the learning from other team members might extend beyond the content that is the focus of the games and tournaments (e.g., English language skills if an English learner, age-related social norms if an immigrant from another country, etc.).

The composition of tournament teams is also indicative of equitable educational practices. Imagine if a student with a significant learning disability were placed in a tournament team with only high-achieving members of the other study groups. The social consequences for a poor performance for the child with a disability could be severe and difficult to repair. Likewise, the academic self-concept of the student, already likely to be low, could further suffer. Fortunately, TGT procedures guard against these circumstances as well. As described earlier, tournament team membership is assigned according to level of achievement—high, average, and low-achievement groups. This results in some assurance that each member of the tournament team has a similar chance of answering any given question and ultimately "bringing back points" to the home team. This would also serve to bolster the academic self-concept of the student.

Finally, members of the low-achievement group are further protected by TGT procedures that award points based on "place" within each tournament group rather than total number of questions correctly answered. High-, average-, and low-achieving students can each bring back the same number of points to the study team within a tournament. For example, first-place high-achievement study team members bring back the same number of points to the group as the first-place low-achievement group members. The same would be true of last place tournament performance within groups. This procedure for awarding points results in study team members bringing back similar amounts of points, regardless of ability level, making each team member equally valuable to the group.

CONCLUSION

In sum, TGT as a peer-mediated intervention is deliberate in its creation of equitable procedures for students of different groups. This may be particularly true for students with disabilities in inclusive settings and for students of groups that are not socially integrated within the classroom. By nature of the purposeful distribution of students across study teams and the grouping of tournament teams by ability level, TGT takes care to support the learning and social standing of all students within a classroom. TGT creates a learning community of students in its truest sense, understandably leading to the improved academic performance, student perceptions toward academic material, and social relationships identified in the extant literature.

REFERENCES

DeVries, D. L., Edwards, K. J., & Slavin, R. E. (1978). Biracial learning teams and race relations in the classroom: Four field experiments using teams-games-tournament. *Journal of Educational Psychology, 70*, 356–362.

DeVries, D. L., Mescon, I. T., & Shackman, S. L. (1975). Teams-Games-Tournament in the elementary classroom: A replication (Report No. 190). *Johns Hopkins University Center for the Study of Social Organization of Schools*. Retrieved from https://files.eric.ed.gov/fulltext/ED110885.pdf

Ke, F. (2008). Alternative goal structures for computer game-based learning. *International Journal of Computer-Supported Collaborative Learning, 3*, 429–445.

Slavin, R. E. (1995). *Cooperative learning: Theory, research, and practice* (2nd ed.). Boston, MA: Allyn & Bacon.

Tajfel, H., & Turner, J. C. (1979). An integrative theory of intergroup conflict. In W. G. Austin & S. Worchel (Eds.), *Social psychology of intergroup relations* (pp. 33–47). Monterey, CA: Brooks/Cole.

## 8

Peer-Mediated
Writing Interventions

CHRISTINE K. MALECKI AND SAMANTHA COYLE ■

In the academic area of writing, peer-mediated academic interventions (PMAIs) hold a great deal of promise and are ideally suited to be an excellent method of intervention delivery for a variety of reasons. Writing is a cognitively taxing and student-driven process that requires effort, motivation, and self-regulated, or active, learning (Graham & Harris, 1997). Therefore, it is important that interventions in writing promote the use of unique strategies to incorporate these processes as part of the intervention (Graham & Harris, 1997). Peer-mediated intervention approaches are an effective mechanism to accomplish these goals by motivating students and increasing student engagement, increasing opportunities to respond, gain frequent and immediate corrective feedback, and increase the maintenance and generalization of student knowledge and use of strategies/skills (Hoogeveen & Van Gelderen, 2013). In addition, writing products themselves tend to be lengthy to score and take time to provide detailed and meaningful feedback; by incorporating peers into this process, students are able to free up some of the teachers' time and obtain more immediate feedback. This allows teachers to allocate their resources efficiently and offer their support to meet the needs of those who require more intensive or individualized instruction.

Peer-mediated writing interventions can be developed and implemented at every grade level. For example, explicit and objective feedback can be used to promote fluency in young writers (e.g., counting the number of total words written by each peer), whereas with older students, more advanced writing feedback can be provided (e.g., identifying the key points or ideas conveyed and asking questions about clarity). Writing interventions can also be provided at various stages within the writing process including planning, drafting, reviewing, and editing. The additional benefit of this intervention is that data on students' writing progress is collected throughout the intervention, and teachers can use this information to make informed, data-based decisions on how to allocate their time and resources in the classroom.

RECOMMENDATIONS FOR IMPLEMENTATION

The following are recommendations that can be applied to any peer-mediated writing intervention implemented in the classroom including (a) identifying and planning for the purpose and aspect of the writing process for which the intervention will be used, (b) creating an appropriate structure and routine for implementation, and (c) implementing and monitoring fidelity of intervention procedures. One specific, evidence-based performance feedback and goal-setting intervention is explained in further detail to provide a concrete and specific example of a peer-mediated intervention for writing later in this section (Alitto, Malecki, Coyle, & Santuzzi, 2016).

Selecting the Targets for Writing Intervention

As mentioned, peer-mediated interventions in writing can be helpful resources at various stages of the writing process (Hoogeveen & van Gelderen, 2013). See Table 8.1 for a variety of ideas and suggestions regarding where peers can assist.

Develop a Structure and Process for the Intervention

Peer-mediated writing interventions can be done with students paired (one on one) or in small groups. Each method of grouping students has its own advantages and disadvantages, with small groups obtaining a larger range and quantity of feedback, as well as potentially less management for the teacher. However, the intervention presented here will focus on pairing students in groups of two (one-on-one interventions). Prior to the intervention, the teachers should organize the materials needed (what materials are required to carry out the intervention), plan the schedule (when the intervention will happen), introduce and practice rules surrounding the intervention, and create a routine so that students know how to efficiently transition into the intervention with the least instructional time lost. It is important that the students are well trained and the routine is explicitly taught so that students are able to understand what is expected of them each week and reduce any possibility for confusion. This is especially important given that students are the agents of change in this intervention. See Box 8.1 for a detailed list of steps for developing the intervention.

Table 8.1. PLACES IN THE WRITING PROCESS WHERE PEERS CAN SUPPORT
INTERVENTION

Process	Activities/Suggestions
Planning	• Practice vocabulary
	• Help choose topics
	• Brainstorm ideas and elaborate on thinking
	• Remind partners of the writing purpose
	• Help determine audience and message
	• Review and practice learning strategies used
Drafting	• Spend time writing together
	• Set fluency goals
Reviewing	• Point out things done well
	• Provide specific feedback.
	o use sentence starter prompts (e.g., "This part confused me because . . ." "I was very interested in this part because . . .")
	• Provide suggestions
	o content, word choice, details, organization, voice/tone, sentences, topic, content,
Editing	• Correct spelling errors
	• Correct grammar
	• Correct punctuation
	• Correct sentence structure

Box 8.1

A PROCESS CHECKLIST FOR DEVELOPING THE INTERVENTION

- ☑ Describe the purpose of the intervention to students
- ☑ Teach rules
- ☑ Teach the routine
- ☑ Model
- ☑ Practice
- ☑ Give feedback/adjust
- ☑ Obtain Baseline data
- ☑ Set goals
- ☑ Launch Intervention
- ☑ Give feedback/adjust periodically
- ☑ Progress monitor fidelity and acceptability
- ☑ Progress monitor outcomes

Monitor Treatment Integrity and Acceptability

Treatment integrity refers to whether an intervention is being delivered as intended or planned (Gresham, 1989). Treatment integrity is important because it is difficult to draw conclusions on the relationship between an intervention and the response if there has not been consistency in how the intervention was delivered (Wilkinson, 2007). As a result, it is recommended that any school-based intervention include some method of monitoring the intervention to ensure that all components are being implemented correctly. Included in Appendix A is one example of an intervention integrity form that can allow educators to monitor the consistency of the intervention delivery for the particular intervention discussed in this chapter. In addition to assessing intervention fidelity, it is also important to assess the acceptability of the interventions by students and teachers. Interventions that are not accepted are unlikely to be implemented with fidelity and may interfere with the effectiveness of the intervention (Eckert & Hintze, 2000; Martens, Witt, Elliott, & Darveaux, 1985). Checking in with students and teachers on how the intervention is going and whether it is manageable/acceptable is important throughout implementation.

Fluency and Quality Peer-Assisted Learning Strategy: A Detailed Example

One intervention that has been found to be effective in promoting student writing fluency and writing quality is described here as a model (Alitto et al., 2016). This intervention can be used across many grade levels starting at about third grade.

Step 1: Pair students. Before implementing the intervention, teachers should carefully group students into dyads. To facilitate this process, it may be helpful for teachers to list students in order of skill in overall writing (fluency and quality). Using teacher perceptions for these purposes is acceptable provided the teacher is familiar with the students writing quality. However, if the students are new to the teacher or if more information may be needed, a curriculum based measure (CBM) writing sample could be administered and used to do this ranking (see Alitto et al., 2016, for more details on CBM-Written Expression; CBM-WE). Teachers would then split the list in half. The top student in the second half would be paired with the top student in the first half; the second with the second, and so on.

Step 2: Create materials. Students are provided with individualized packets that are prepared prior to the intervention containing a number of items. First, students are provided with a probe packet, containing lined pieces of paper with a story starter at the top of the worksheet (Appendix B). The writing probes are the products that will be evaluated by peers in the intervention; a new probe will be provided during each intervention session creating a "packet" of probes. In addition to a probe packet, students are provided with a scoring sheet each week, to be completed by the student's partner and then reviewed by the student themselves (Appendix C). The scoring sheet is used to provide feedback on each student's writing sample and includes several components: a space for the partner to tally the total number of words written (TWW) by the student that week, a space to add one to that number to indicate their new goal for the next session, a space to write three things the student did well on the writing probe, and a space to include three things that their partner can improve on for the next time. Each student is also provided with a progress-monitoring folder to help them keep track of their goals and progress that includes a goal sheet (Appendix D) and a piece of graph paper (Appendix E). On the goal sheet, the student transcribes the TWW that week and the new goal established from the scoring sheet completed by their partner (Appendix C) to their progress monitoring sheet (Appendix D). They also indicate whether or not they had met their goal from the week before. The goal sheets have several rows for students to record a running record of biweekly performance. Lastly, the students are provided with a graph sheet to graph their TWW and their goals, as a way for them to visualize their progress in response to the intervention and focus their attention on their performance and goals.

Step 3: First administration. On the first day of the intervention, teachers provide students with one CBM-WE writing probe to establish a baseline of students writing fluency and explicitly teach and establish the routine. Teachers distribute their probe packets to each student and read the following directions aloud:

> You are going to write a story. First, I will read the story starter at the top of your page and you will write a story about it. You will have one minute to think about what you will write and three minutes to write your story. Remember to do your best work. If you don't know how to spell a word, you should guess. Are there any questions? (Pause—respond to questions.) Put your pencils down and listen. For the next minute, think about. . . . (Insert story starter and let the students think for one minute.) Now please begin writing. (Students write for three minutes.) Please stop and put your pencils down.

After completing their writing probes, students are prompted to meet with their assigned partner for the second part of the writing activity. Once gathered in their pairs, the students are asked to switch papers with their partner and complete the scoring sheet (Appendix C); specifically, students are instructed to count the TWW and record that number on their partner's scoring sheet. Teachers then use the following script to provide these instructions:

> You have been put together to share your writing with your classmates. Please exchange papers with your partner. (Pause and allow students to exchange papers.) Now you need to grade your classmate's writing. You will begin by counting the number of words your classmate wrote. You will write the number of words your classmate wrote on the scoring sheet attached to

your classmates' essay. (Pause and show scoring sheet.) Go ahead and start counting now.

After the students count the number of words written, they are asked to create new performance goals for their peers. Research has supported the use of two words per week as an ambitious but attainable goal for improvement in students (Alitto et al., 2016). If the intervention will be provided biweekly, that means that students would add one to their TWW score for the next administration. Some students may not increase their total number of words written; in those instances, the goal from the previous administration would remain their goal for the next probe. To facilitate this process, teachers read the following directions aloud:

Now I want you to set a goal for your classmate for next time. Most kids can write one extra word each time they write a new story. Add one to the number of words your classmate wrote and record it here. (Point to TWW goal blank.) If no improvement was made, the goal can stay the same as last time.

After providing quantitative feedback on their TWW, students are asked to provide three pieces of qualitative feedback including three things that their partner did well and one to three things that their partner can improve upon. Students are prompted to focus on punctuation, capitalization, spelling, and grammar when providing the feedback. Teachers instruct students to provide written feedback by reading the following directions aloud:

Now I want you to read the story again. After you finish reading the story write three things you think your partner did well when writing their story and one to three things you think they could do better next time. Things to think about are punctuation, capitalization, spelling and grammar.

Following these tasks, students return their written feedback (scoring sheets) to their partner and review their scores, goals, and written feedback. After reviewing the feedback, students are instructed to make one correction to their work that was identified by their peer as an area for improvement, record their performance goals and scores on their goal sheets, and graph this information on the progress monitoring graphs using the following instructions:

Now I want you to give the graded papers back to their owners. (Pause and allow students to exchange papers.). Look at your scores. Look at your goal for next week. Now I want you to take out your folders and write down your score and your goal for next week on your goal sheet. (Pause and allow students to record their scores.) I would also like you to graph the number of words you wrote and your goal on your chart. (Pause and allow students to graph.) Now I want you to take a look at what your classmate said you did well and what your classmate said you could improve on. Please fix one mistake you made on your story. (Pause and allow students to fix errors.).

Teachers should provide assistance throughout the intervention and give support/feedback to ensure that all students understand the task. After collecting the student packets, teachers should check the initial administration scoring and feedback for accuracy and provide individualized support and additional training to any students who may have had difficulty with the task until it is clear that they fully understand the task and are able to competently carry out the intervention with their partners.

Step 4: Subsequent administrations. After the initial intervention session, subsequent administration procedures follow a very similar format, and as will be evident, the instructions and procedures remain as consistent as possible to provide students with a clear and explicit routine and expectations. Instructions for subsequent administrations are slightly modified to first prime or remind students about their performance goals for the week by directing student attention to their progress monitoring folders and review their goal sheets. The following directions should be read at the beginning of all the remaining probe administrations:

Please open your writing folders and look at your score from last time. Please also take a look at your goal. This number is how many words you should write this time. (Pause and allow students to look at information.) Now you will write another story. Please open your packets to the first page. First, I will read the story starter at the top of your page and then you will write a story about it. You will have one minute to think about what you will write and three minutes to write your story. Remember to do your best work. If you don't know how to spell a word, you should guess. Are there any questions? (Pause—respond to questions.). Put your pencils down and listen. For the next minute, think about. . . . (Insert story starter and let the students think for one minute.) Now please begin writing. (Students write for three minutes.) Please stop and put your pencils down.

After completing their writing probes, students are prompted to meet with their assigned partner for the second part of the writing activity. Once gathered in their groups, the students are asked to provide explicit feedback to their partners, count the TWW, and record that number on their partners scoring sheet. After students complete this activity, they are then asked to create new performance goals for their peers, keeping the goal the same if no improvements were made, and provide written feedback on three things that can be improved and one thing that their partner did well. For these aspects of the intervention, teachers use the same script as outlined in Step 3.

Following these tasks, students return their written feedback to their partner and review their own scores, goals, and written feedback. After reviewing the feedback, students are instructed to make one correction to their work that was identified by their peer as an area for improvement, record their performance goals and scores on their goal sheets, and graph this information on the progress monitoring graphs using the following instructions. These instructions are slightly modified from the initial administration to have students note whether or not they met their goal for that week:

> Now I want you to give the graded papers back to their owners. (Pause and allow students to exchange papers.) Take a look at your scores (Pause.) Now I want you to take out your folders and look at your goal from last time. Compare it with your score. Did you meet your goal? Circle *yes* or *no* on your goal sheet. (Pause and allow students to record information.) Now I want you to write down your score from this time and your goal for next session on the goal sheet. (Pause and allow students to record their scores.) I would also like you to graph your goal and the number of words you wrote on your chart. (Pause and allow students to graph.) Now I want you to take a look at what your classmate said you did well and what your classmate said you could improve on. Please fix one mistake you made on your story. (Pause and allow students to fix errors.)

After completing the graphing activity, teachers collect the packets and progress monitoring folders. The intervention can be implemented once or twice a week, depending on scheduling and typically occurs over a period of 8 to 10 weeks, typically coinciding with a marking period. Teachers should make sure to review students' progress throughout the intervention and make any adjustments accordingly.

Barriers and Cautions in Implementation

As with any intervention in school-based settings, several barriers or cautions should be considered when planning or implementing peer-mediated interventions in writing.

Resistance by the learner. Given the significant cognitive demand involved and the fact that motivation plays a primary role in writing, it is not surprising that many struggling writers avoid writing activities. In fact, even when working with peers is involved, which might incentivize some students, others may still show resistance (Yarrow & Topping, 2001). Peer feedback increases the social pressure to perform well, and the potential for embarrassment is greater when it is a peer that is giving the feedback as opposed to a teacher, who is regularly reviewing the students' work (Gielen, Peeters, Dochy, Onghena, & Struyven, 2010). While some students may respond positively to increased social pressures, others may not, and it may be important to consider individual dispositions when using peers as a mechanism to provide feedback. In addition, some studies have found that youth were less likely to incorporate peer feedback into their writing products as opposed to teacher feedback (Yang, Badger, & Yu, 2006). This was attributed to the fact that youth felt their teachers were more experienced and trustworthy and valued teacher feedback more than peer feedback (Yang et al., 2006). However, others have argued that peer feedback may trigger youth to take more initiative toward improving their writing product for this reason, encouraging the student to reflect on the feedback and check to make sure it correct, rather than accepting feedback at face value (Gielen et al., 2010). In other words, teacher feedback may reduce the likelihood of self-regulated learning, given the notion of "expertise" by the teacher.

Reluctance by the peer. Youth may be reluctant to provide substantial or honest feedback to their peers, particularly if they worry that their peer may become upset or find their feedback to be overly critical. Some youth may find that providing feedback may be confrontational and avoid providing honest feedback to avoid the discomfort of criticizing the work of someone else. One potential mechanism to overcome this challenge is to provide specific and clear expectations about what is to be provided as feedback. For example, specifying precise and targeted revisions (e.g., "Make five corrections to your peers writing sample"; "What is being explained in this paper?") rather than open-ended or subjective judgements about their peer's work (e.g., "How good do you think this paper was?"). To decrease both peer and student reluctance, teachers may consider using positive reinforcement systems to reward effort and positive behavior during the intervention.

Incorrect feedback by the peer. Given that peer partners are students themselves, it is often a concern that students may provide each other with incorrect feedback. However, as Gibbs and Simpson (2004) have described, "imperfect feedback from a fellow student provided almost immediately may have much more impact than more perfect feedback from a tutor four weeks later" (p. 19). In other words, even feedback that is of lower quality than feedback that may be provided by a teacher can still be valuable given the immediacy of the feedback. Considering that youth are available to provide immediate feedback, whereas teacher feedback is often time-delayed, the use of peers, even if of lesser quality, may still have significant benefits. By utilizing peers in the classroom, peer feedback can occur more regularly rather than at the end of the learning process and provide students with more opportunities to respond in the classroom, two important elements of effective instruction (Gielen et al., 2010). However, to reduce the likelihood of incorrect feedback, it is important that students are provided with *specific* and *clear roles/instructions* in what is expected and how the task is supposed to be carried out. Providing explicit instruction, modeling, and guided practice is critical to ensure that students are well trained in the procedures of the intervention (Hoogeveen & Van Gelderen, 2013).

Levels of skill matching. Sometimes peers are grouped based on their skills, whereas other times students are paired with tutors or students who are more competent/knowledgeable on the topic. Some researchers have suggested that same-ability pairs may be especially helpful when reinforcing knowledge, whereas cross-ability pairs may be more effective in establishing or learning new material (Daiute & Dalton, 1993). The benefits of paired writing appear to extend beyond simply increasing writing products, but to increasing student's perceptions of their writing skills. For example, one study that examined the benefits of peer feedback with older tutors and younger tutees found that both the tutor and the tutee experienced gains in their writing, as well as gains in their perceptions of their writing skills (Yarrow & Topping, 2001). In other words, there appears to be benefits in grouping students of different abilities in both their response to interventions as well as in feelings of their self-efficacy in written expression, which may help students become more motivated and willing to engage in writing activities.

Behavior management. When students are working in groups or pairs, it is important that the behavioral expectations are made clear to avoid potential behavior challenges. Incentivizing positive student behavior during the intervention can be one method of handling any challenges of students working in pairs. Providing students with clear behavioral expectations before each intervention session and explicitly modeling, teaching and reminding students of what positive behavior during the intervention looks like may help clarify the expectations and reduce the likelihood that behavioral challenges might arise.

CONSIDERATIONS OF DIVERSITY AND EQUITY

Peer-mediated interventions, such as the one previously described in detail, are ideal interventions for students from diverse backgrounds and those with learning challenges in that the intervention incorporates the evidence-based elements of effective instruction from which all students benefit. For example, increasing student opportunities to obtain and respond to immediate feedback and providing students with clear and explicit goals that are specific to their own performance are essential in promoting success for *all learners*.

Writing instruction for students from diverse backgrounds and struggling learners may be especially important as part of a larger literacy program. Specifically, vocabulary is a key component of instruction for English learners (ELs) and academic vocabulary, or words used within an academic environment, is linked with stronger reading and writing performance (Fenner & Snyder, 2017). Using writing interventions to supplement vocabulary instruction may be an effective way to increase exposure and practice with vocabulary words and provide varied opportunities to practice vocabulary in different instructional formats (Baker et al., 2014; Calderón, Slavin & Sanchez, 2011). In addition, integrating oral and written language instruction into specific content areas is also considered best practice in working with diverse learners (Baker et al., 2014). Following this recommendation, teachers may consider selecting specific writing prompts relevant to content that students are working on in class and allow students more opportunities to apply what they are learning in their writing. Teachers may also consider using writing probes that include new vocabulary words to help support this process. Importantly, this particular intervention is consistent with the recommendation by Baker and colleagues (2014) to provide diverse learners with regular and structured opportunities to practice written language skills.

Importantly, it is essential that classroom and school environments are respectful of individual and cultural diversity and allow students from varied backgrounds to interact with one another regularly. Cooperative learning activities are helpful in promoting engagement and growth in diverse learners and fostering a classroom climate that prioritizes respect for individual diversity and promotes peer social support. A culturally responsive classroom emphasizes student strengths, encourages the exchange of diverse experiences and perspectives, and supports student learning (Fenner & Snyder, 2017). Providing students with the opportunity to learn from each other, rather than from the teacher only, communicates a message of cooperation, respect, and value to students, creating a student-centered learning environment ideal for academic and social growth (Fenner & Snyder, 2017). In addition, some work has suggested that providing students with opportunities to work in small groups provides students with a more comfortable and relaxed environment to practice and learn from their peers (Calderón, Sanchez, & Slavin, 2011) and provide ELs with more opportunities for active learning and development of academic language than larger whole class contexts (Cole, 2014). In fact, a meta-analysis investigating peer-mediated interventions to promote literacy in EL students has found support for the use of peer-mediated strategies in improving both reading and writing in diverse populations (Cole, 2014). In sum, facilitating peer interactions can be an effective method to create a culturally responsive classroom, while supporting the development and growth of all learners, including those from diverse backgrounds and students with disabilities.

CONCLUSION

Peer-mediated writing interventions are an efficient and effective method used to improve students writing in the classroom. By capitalizing on students as the agents of change, teachers can provide more frequent and immediate feedback to students and allocate their time more efficiently. The current chapter described one specific peer-mediated intervention that has been found to be effective in promoting the writing fluency of elementary-aged youth. Barriers often encountered when implementing peer mediated interventions such as reluctance of students, incorrect feedback and behavioral challenges were reviewed. Importantly, the benefits of peer-mediated writing interventions for diverse learners are noted, as students from diverse backgrounds benefit from opportunities to increase engagement, receive immediate corrective feedback, and support vocabulary development. All of these elements can be explicitly incorporated into peer-mediated writing interventions and promote literacy in *all learners.*

REFERENCES

Alitto, J., Malecki, C. K., Coyle, S., & Santuzzi, A. (2016). Examining the effects of adult and peer mediated goal setting and feedback interventions for writing: Two studies. *Journal of School Psychology, 56*, 89–109.

Baker, S., Lesaux, N., Jayanthi, M., Dimino, J., Proctor, C. P., Morris, J., . . . Newman-Gonchar, R. (2014). Teaching academic content and literacy to English learners in elementary and middle school (NCEE 2014-4012). *National Center for Education Evaluation and Regional Assistance, Institute of Education Sciences, U.S. Department of Education*. Retrieved from http://ies.ed.gov/ncee/wwc/publications_reviews.aspx

Calderón, M., Slavin, R., & Sánchez, M. (2011). Effective instruction for English learners. *Future of Children, 21*(1), 103–127.

Cole, M. W. (2014). Speaking to read: Meta-analysis of peer-mediated learning for English language learners. *Journal of Literacy Research, 46*(3), 358–382.

Daiute, C., & Dalton, B. (1993). Collaboration between children learning to write: Can novices be masters? *Cognition and instruction, 10*(4), 281–333.

Eckert, T. L., & Hintze, J. M. (2000). Behavioral conceptions and applications of acceptability: Issues related to service delivery and research methodology. *School Psychology Quarterly, 15*(2), 123.

Fenner, D. S., & Snyder, S. (2017). *Unlocking English learners' potential: Strategies for making content accessible*. Thousand Oaks, CA: Corwin Press.

Gibbs, G., & Simpson, C. (2004). Does your assessment support your students' learning. *Journal of Teaching and Learning in Higher Education, 1*, 1–30.

Gielen, S., Peeters, E., Dochy, F., Onghena, P., & Struyven, K. (2010). Improving the effectiveness of peer feedback for learning. *Learning and Instruction, 20*(4), 304–315.

Graham, S., & Harris, K. R. (1997). Self-regulation and writing: Where do we go from here? *Contemporary Educational Psychology, 22*, 102–114.

Gresham, F. M. (1989). Assessment of treatment integrity in school consultation and prereferral intervention. *School Psychology Review, 18*, 37–50.

Hoogeveen, M., & van Gelderen, A. (2013). What works in writing with peer response? A review of intervention studies with children and adolescents. *Educational Psychology Review, 25*(4), 473–502.

Martens, B. K., Witt, J. C., Elliott, S. N., & Darveaux, D. X. (1985). Teacher judgements concerning the acceptability of school-based interventions. *Professional Psychology: Research and Practice, 16*(2), 191–198.

Wilkinson, L. A. (2007). Assessing treatment integrity in behavioral consultation. *International Journal of Behavioral Consultation and Therapy, 3*(3), 420.

Yang, M., Badger, R., & Yu, Z. (2006). A comparative study of peer and teacher feedback in a Chinese EFL writing class. *Journal of Second Language Writing, 15*(3), 179–200.

Yarrow, F., & Topping, K. J. (2001). Collaborative writing: The effects of metacognitive prompting and structured peer interaction. *British Journal of Educational Psychology, 71*(2), 261–282.

APPENDIX A
PROCEDURAL INTEGRITY FORM

Procedural Integrity Form for Writing Intervention

Complete this form at least once a week as a helpful tool to ensure that intervention procedures are being followed.

> ➤ Teacher Name: _____

> ➤ Time: _____

> ➤ Date: _____

> ➤ Probe Given (story starter): _____

> ➤ Students' exchanged papers: YES   NO

> ➤ Students' provided feedback and set goals: YES   NO

> ➤ Students' Graphed Data: YES   NO

> ➤ Any extraordinary circumstances? If so, please note:
> _____
> _____
> _____

> ➤ Amount of time spent on the intervention today:
> _____

APPENDIX B
EXAMPLE WEEKLY WRITING PROBE

Name: _____

Weekly Writing Probe

One day I went for an airplane ride and....

_____

_____

_____

_____

_____

_____

_____

_____

_____

_____

_____

_____

_____

_____

_____

_____

_____

_____._......THE END!

APPENDIX C
SCORINGSHEET

Scoring Sheet

My Partner's Name is: _____

Things to think about!

- Spelling
- Capitalization
- Grammar
- Punctuation

# of words your partner wrote last week   =   _____

Add 1 to their score   +1

# of words your partner will write next week   =   _____

List three things you think your partner did well when writing their story

1. _____
   _____

2. _____
   _____

3. _____
   _____

List one to three things your partner could do better next time

1. _____
   _____

2. _____
   _____

3. _____
   _____

APPENDIX D

JOHNNY'S GOAL SHEET FOR WRITING

TIME ONE

# of words Johnny wrote this week = _____

+ 1

# of words Johnny will write next time = _____

TIME TWO

# of words Johnny wrote this week = _____

+ 1

# of words Johnny will write next time = _____

Did Johnny meet his goal?

YES ☐

NO ☐

TIME THREE

# of words Johnny wrote this week = _____

+ 1

# of words Johnny will write next time = _____

Did Johnny meet his goal?

YES ☐

NO ☐

APPENDIX E
GRAPHING SHEET

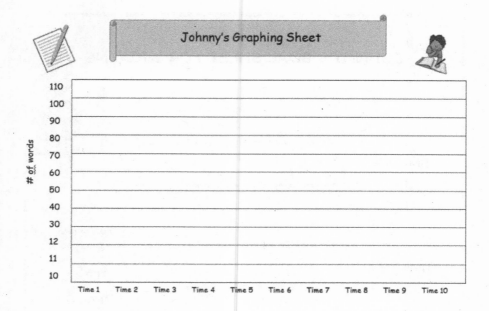

Johnny's Graphing Sheet

# of words

110
100
90
80
70
60
50
40
30
12
11
10

Time 1   Time 2   Time 3   Time 4   Time 5   Time 6   Time 7   Time 8   Time 9   Time 10

Peer-Mediated Behavioral Interventions

## 9

Peer-Mediated Behavioral Interventions

KEITH C. RADLEY ■

Teachers are tasked with multiple demands while in the classroom. Primary demands often center on academic achievement of students, with teachers providing group and individualized instruction to students. Equally important, teachers must manage the behavior of students within the classroom—as disruptive behavior of one or several students is likely to impact the learning of all within the classroom (e.g., Higgins, Williams, & McLaughlin, 2001). For many teachers, balancing these demands is challenging—with disruptive classroom behaviors being the leading referral concern (Rose & Gallup, 2005). Resolving problem behaviors though services of additional trained personnel, be they direct or indirect, may effectively resolve the concerns identified. However, in some cases, a lack of personnel resources may prohibit such a solution. For example, a behavior specialist, paraprofessional, or other support personnel may not be able to effectively respond to all requests for assistance. As an alternative to relying on additional support from school personnel, schools may instead look to leverage their greatest resource—students—as a means of implementing behavioral interventions within classrooms and other school contexts.

Peer-mediated behavioral interventions (PMBIs) is a term that may be used to describe a broad class of interventions in which peers (i.e., students) implement an intervention within a school setting. Although many variations of PMBIs have been developed, all procedures share some commonalities. First, PMBIs are facilitated in some way by a peer of a student or group of students. The level of facilitation may vary broadly across intervention strategies. In some strategies, a peer may be responsible for all facets of intervention implementation. For example, a peer may implement a Check-In/Check-Out (CICO) procedure in which they meet with another student in the morning, review a daily behavior report (DBR) at the end of the day, determine whether a reinforcement criterion has been met, and, if so, provide access to reinforcement (Sanchez, Miltenberger, Kincaid, & Blair, 2015). In other cases, the peer's role may be circumscribed to one particular element of an intervention. For instance, a peer may provide reinforcement to another student contingent upon demonstration of a target behavior (e.g., Lewis & Sugai, 1996). Second, PMBIs have non-academic behavior of students as their primary intervention target. This differs from procedures previously described in this book that have targeted academic behaviors of students. Although the target behaviors of PMBIs differ from those of peer-mediated academic interventions, the overarching goal of the procedures is the same—promote socially meaningful behavior change through peer-implemented intervention.

PMBIs have long been proposed as a solution to the limited resources available to school personnel with respect to implementation of behavioral interventions. As strategies such as peer-mediated instruction became increasingly researched throughout the 1970s (e.g., Rosenbaum, 1973). Researchers began to evaluate the utility of these procedures applied to non-academic behaviors of students. For example, Strain, Shores, and Timm (1977) found that training peers to engage with students with disabilities resulted in greater rates of initiations and responses of those same students. From initial research on utilizing peers to address the social isolation experienced by students with disabilities (Nordquist, 1978), researchers increasingly began to evaluate the effects of peer-mediated interventions on other student behaviors, such as disruptive behavior (e.g., Smith & Fowler, 1984) and obscene language (Salend & Meddaugh, 1985). From these beginnings, PMBIs have been applied to a wide variety of student behaviors within school settings— garnering substantial support both in terms of intervention effectiveness and efficiency.

Since initial research evaluating PMBIs, the literature supporting the use of such procedures has continued to grow. Recent meta-analyses provide a contemporary view of the utility of PMBIs within school settings. Dart, Collins, Klingbeil, and McKinley (2014) conducted a meta-analysis of PMBIs, evaluating procedures in which peers implemented strategies to address social skills, classroom behavior, and communication of other students. Across all outcomes, Dart and colleagues found peers to be moderately effective in promoting behavior change. Although these interventions were implemented least frequently with students without an identified disability, they were found to have the largest effect for this population. Findings of the meta-analysis also highlighted that peers who received relatively more training produced effects that were larger than peer interventionists who received less training in intervention implementation. Other findings of the meta-analysis included greater effects when peers were not matched by gender, when peers shared a class, and when intervention dosage was less than 200 minutes.

It is important to note that the majority of studies in Dart and colleagues' (2014) meta-analysis targeted children and adolescents with autism spectrum disorder (ASD) and social skills deficits. Inclusion of peers in social skills training for individuals with ASD is often recommended (e.g., Battaglia & Radley, 2014)— a suggestion that is not only supported by Dart and colleagues, but also other meta-analyses of social skills interventions for individuals with ASD. For example, Whalon, Conroy, Martinez, and Werch (2015) found peer-mediated social skills interventions to procedure large intervention effects—a finding supported by an earlier meta-analysis of social skills interventions for children with ASD (Wang, Cui, & Parrila, 2011). Although substantial research has been devoted to PMBIs for students with ASD, meta-analyses of these interventions have also indicated their utility for students with emotional and behavioral disorders (Dunn, Shelnut, Ryan, & Katsiyannis, 2017) and Attention-Deficit/Hyperactivity Disorder (ADHD; Cordier, Vilaysack, Doma, Wilkes-Gillan, & Speyer, 2018).

Beyond their effectiveness, PMBIs are associated with a number of other benefits. Perhaps most salient of all benefits is the multiplication of interventionists within a school setting. Providing an example of the efficiency of PMBIs, Dart et al. (2015) suggest that it would take one adult CICO mentor approximately 80 minutes each day to implement the intervention with 20 students. If four peers were to be trained to serve as CICO mentors under the supervision of an adult, time for implementation would be reduced to approximately 20 minutes—allowing the adult to reallocate their time to providing services elsewhere. Although training peers to implement an intervention represents an initial investment in time, multiplying the number of available interventionists ultimately increases the efficiency with which the intervention is implemented—potentially augmenting the number of students who may be served by school personnel.

Other benefits are also associated with peer-mediated interventions. By utilizing peers as behavior-change agents, this may remove the need for school personnel to fill an authoritarian role (Barbetta, 1990). Thus, instead of expending time and energy to manage the behavior or a student or group of students, a teacher may instead focus on teaching academic content and rely for behavior management to be provided by peers. Shifting the role of school personnel may have an impact on school climate. Whereas teachers have been found to provide far more reprimands and redirections than praise statements (e.g., Sutherland, Lewis-Palmer, Stitcher, & Morgan, 2008; White, 1975), a move away from an authoritarian position may result in greater teacher recognition of expectation-following behavior—creating an atmosphere of time-in within the classroom (e.g., Mandal, Olmi, Edwards, Tingstrom, & Benoit, 2000).

Finally, PMBIs fit within the developmental trajectory of students in schools. Although adult influence is initially high during early childhood, peer influence becomes increasingly more potent as children mature and enter into adolescence (Nathanson, 2001; Youniss & Haynie, 1992). Given that behavior problems in school typically increase during adolescence (Langberg et al., 2011), the increasing peer influence during this state of development suggests that PMBIs may be particularly applicable as children and adolescents mature.

Despite the potential benefits of PMBIs, some potential limitations must also be considered. First, training peers to implement an intervention requires an initial investment in time. Once trained, peers require continued monitoring to ensure that interventions are implemented with integrity. Thus, depending on the intensity and planned duration of the intervention, the time required for training and supervision may exceed that of an intervention implemented entirely by school personnel. Second, peers who implement peer-mediated intervention may be unable to make rapid changes to intervention adaptations (Maheady, Harper, & Mallette, 1991). Whereas skilled school personnel may be able to rapidly identify the need for intervention adaptation to suit the needs of a student, such changes may occur more slowly in PMBI due to the indirect nature of intervention. Third, the maintenance of confidentiality may be challenging when implementing PMBIs. As such, use of these procedures requires that threats to confidentiality be considered and addressed a priori (e.g., Guevremont, MacMillan, Shawchuck, & Hansen, 1989).

Although several considerations should be made prior to implementation of PMBIs, they have generally been found to be effective and efficient in addressing a wide range of behaviors in children and adolescents. As previously described, a variety of modalities of PMBIs have been empirically evaluated. In the remainder of this chapter, several distinct types of PMBIs will be introduced and their empirical support discussed. The remaining chapters in this section will provide a further, more detailed, description of implementation and considerations of the strategies described. Specific attention will be paid to the following seven types of PMBIs: peer management, peer-mediated social skills training, peer support arrangements, peer-mediated pivotal response training, peer modeling interventions, peer-mediated play interventions, and restorative and conflict resolution interventions.

Peer Management Interventions

Peer management interventions may be conceptualized as a type of PMBI in which the peer of a child or adolescent is responsible for management of some or all of a behavior intervention plan. Substantial research has found peers to be able to implement peer management interventions with integrity (e.g., Watkins et al., 2015), with results generally indicating the utility of peer management procedures (e.g., Dart et al., 2014). Within peer management interventions, peers may assume a variety of roles. Commonly, peer interventionists are tasked with one or more of the following: providing prompts, monitoring behavior, evaluating responding, and providing consequences.

In an example of a peer management procedure in which peers provided prompts, Sainato, Strain, Lefebvre, and Rapp (1987) trained peers to provide prompts for movement to children with ASD. Peers were trained to provide antecedent prompts (i.e., ringing a bell) and physical prompts (i.e., taking a peer by the hand) as part of the intervention—with both procedures resulting in increases in movement of children with ASD. In a more recent example, Tan and Alant (2018) trained a peer to prompt a student with ASD to use a speech-generating device during mathematics activities. Results of the study indicated that implementation of peer prompting increased spontaneous communication and overall communication by the student with ASD.

Peer management procedures may also involve peer monitoring, which utilizes a peer to collect data regarding the behavior or another child or adolescent. Peers may engage in either direct (e.g., observation) or indirect (e.g., rating scale) monitoring of behavior. In one example, Fowler (1986) trained peers to engage in direct observation of the behavior of classmates. Students in the classroom recorded their participation in various classroom activities. At the end of transition periods, the students in the classroom reported their participation to a classroom captain, who determined whether the self-report of the students concurred with his or her independent assessment of student behavior. Implementation of the peer monitoring procedure was associated with increases in participation as well as decreases in inappropriate classroom behavior. In another example, Smith and Fowler (1984) found that a peer-monitored token system was effective in reducing disruptive behavior of students with behavioral disorders. Further, Smith and Fowler found peers to accurately provide tokens contingent upon student behavior—suggesting that peers may validly collect behavioral data once provided with training.

Peer management interventions may also entail evaluative components, in which a peer is tasked with determining whether a criterion has been met. One example of training peers to evaluate the behavior of other students may be found in Collins, Gresham, and Dart (2016). Collins and colleagues trained peers to serve as CICO mentors for students determined to be socially neglected. As part of the intervention, peers were responsible for reviewing daily behavior report cards (DBRCs) completed by the teachers of socially neglected students. During evaluation, peers compared points earned on the DBRC to a previously determined daily criterion. Peers were found to implement the intervention with 100% integrity, suggesting that peers may accurately evaluate the behavior of other students and that this may be utilized as a means of promoting behavior change.

Finally, peers may be trained to provide or withhold reinforcement. Peers may be responsible only for providing reinforcement or may also assume roles of monitoring and evaluating behavior in addition to providing reinforcement. Flood, Wilder, Flood, and Masuda (2002) trained peers to provide reinforcement for on-task behavior of students with ADHD. Peers provided continuous reinforcement when the student with ADHD demonstrated on-task behavior and redirection when off-task—demonstrating monitoring, evaluation, and reinforcement. Implementation of the intervention resulted in large and immediate decreases in off-task behavior of students with ADHD.

Whereas some researchers have focused only on one element of peer management interventions, others have tasked peers with prompting, monitoring, evaluating, and providing reinforcement. Dart, Radley, Furlow, and Murphy (2017) trained peers to facilitate discrete trial training for students with ASD. Behaviors targeted included vacuuming, putting on a helmet, removing shoes, and sorting coins. Following training, peers were assessed on their appropriate provision of prompts, correct recording of student responses, correct evaluation of accuracy of responses, and delivery of an appropriate reinforcer. As with the peer management interventions previously described, peer interventionists were found to be capable of implementing the intervention with a high level of accuracy—suggesting the ability of peers to implement even complex behavioral interventions.

Peer-Mediated Social Skills Training

Social skills training is a widely implemented intervention class for students with and without identified disabilities. Despite the frequency with which it is implemented, particularly for students with ASD (Hess, Morrier, Heflin, & Ivey, 2008), social skills training has often been criticized for failing to produce generalized intervention effects. In other words, social skills training may result in behavior change in the training setting but not in non-training settings. A variety of strategies may be considered to improve generalized effects of interventions (Stokes & Baer, 1977), one of which consists of incorporating common stimuli into social skills training. Including peers in social skills training provides participants with an opportunity to practice new skills with naturalistic social skills partners and enables peers to serve as discriminative stimuli for social skill use once participants return to non-training settings (e.g., classroom, recess).

Peer-mediated social skills training has garnered substantial support as an empirically supported intervention. As previously stated, Dart and colleagues (2014) found social skills to be the most common target of PMBI research. Although no meta-analysis has been conducted for peer-mediated social skills training across disability categories, those conducted specific to individuals with ASD indicate the efficacy of the strategy. For example, Whalon and colleagues (2015) found peer-mediated social skills training for individuals with ASD to produce strong intervention effects—a finding supported by previous meta-analyses (e.g., Wang et al., 2011; Zhang & Wheeler, 2011). Data from meta-analyses also indicate that peer-mediated social skills interventions are generally implemented with participants with ASD aged 10 or younger, with limited data evaluating the utility of the procedure with older participants.

In one of the studies with older individuals, Bambara, Cole, Kunsch, Tsai, and Ayad (2016) utilized high school-age peers to address conversational skills of students with ASD. Peers were trained in strategies to promote conversation, initiations, and follow-up questions. Peers were also taught to use cue cards for starting a question and continuing a conversation. Following introduction of the peer-mediated intervention, conversational acts, initiations, and follow-up questions increased in participants with ASD. Further, conversations between individuals with ASD and their peers were longer in duration. One noteworthy finding was that improvements in conversational skills were maintained over time—suggesting that peer-mediated social skills training was capable of promoting durable behavior change.

Although much of the peer-mediated social skills training literature has focused on individuals with ASD, research also supports the utility of the approach with other populations. For example, Blake, Wang, Cartledge, and Gardner (2000) investigated the effect of students with serious emotional disturbances to facilitate a social skills group for other students with serious emotional disturbances. Following termination of social skills instruction provided by a researcher, social skills group members assumed responsibility of reteaching all the social skills lessons. During student-facilitated social skills lessons, the group member who had demonstrated the most positive social initiations up until that point was selected to facilitate the intervention. This student was subsequently responsible for introducing the target skill, providing step-by-step instructions for completing the skill, and directing practice of the skill. Upon the introduction of peer-mediated social skills training, the number of positive initiations, positive statements, and positive terminations made by group members increased. In a follow-up study, peers directed all of a social skills group without previous instruction by a researcher. Results indicated that students with serious emotional disturbances increased the number of supportive behaviors and decreased the number of abusive behaviors directed toward peers. Together, these findings suggest that peer-mediated social skills interventions may be useful for improving the social behaviors of both the peers mediating instruction and those receiving instruction. Further, this study highlights the fact that peers with disabilities may serve effectively in the role of a peer interventionist.

Peer Support Arrangements

Peer support arrangements, sometimes referred to as peer support interventions and peer buddy interventions, are a type of PMBI in which peers are trained to provide behavioral support to another student. Peer support arrangements differ from peer-mediated social skills training in that peers are not responsible for teaching or otherwise facilitating social skills training. Instead, peers are taught strategies that may support participation in school activities and routines. In this framework, a peer is assigned to be a tutor or buddy to a particular student. Once assigned to this role, the peer may be encouraged to talk to their buddy, play with them, support them in the classroom, or otherwise create opportunities for interactions between themselves and the buddy. Whereas peer-mediated social skills interventions are typically highlighted by direct learning and instruction, the mechanism of peer support arrangements is more indirect. That is, new skills and behaviors are promoted not through instruction, but through incidental learning and increased opportunities to interact with peers.

No meta-analyses have evaluated peer support arrangements as a separate class of PMBIs. However, the utility of the approach has been repeatedly documented across decades of research. In an early example of a peer support arrangement, Ragland, Kerr, and Strain (1978) trained a peer to initiate social interactions with students with ASD. Specifically, the peer was instructed to try his best to get the students with ASD to play with him, and he practiced strategies for engaging peers during role plays with researchers. During baseline, the students with ASD rarely demonstrated positive social behaviors. However, once the peer support arrangement was implemented, positive social behavior increased rapidly and dramatically.

Since initial evaluations of peer support arrangements, evaluations of such procedures have consistently demonstrated the efficacy of the approach for a range of students. Research has continued to demonstrate the efficacy of peer support arrangements for students with ASD across developmental levels (e.g., Laushey & Heflin, 2000). Others have found the procedure to be useful for other populations. For example, Tzani-Pepelasi, Ioannou, Synnott, and McDonnell (2019) found a peer support arrangement to potentially be useful as a strategy for preventing and intervening for school bullying. In addition to behavior change observed across target students, peer buddy groups are also beneficial for peers tasked with being a buddy. Positive outcomes associated with being a peer buddy increased positive attitudes toward persons with severe disabilities and a greater sense of civic responsibility (Hughes et al., 2001).

Peer-Mediated Pivotal Response Treatment .

Pivotal Response Treatment (PRT) is an intervention methodology that applies principles of behavior analysis to promote learning of individuals with ASD. Behaviors targeted within PRT include motivation, responding to multiple cues, self-management, and self-initiations. These four skills are identified as pivotal skills—skills that, when acquired, will result in the acquisition and generalization of other new skills. PRT emphasizes child-led intervention that occurs in naturalistic contexts. Whereas the emphasis on instruction in child-led, naturalistic settings may differ from other behavior analytic interventions (e.g., discrete trial training), it is consistent with other behavioral approaches in its application of reinforcement as a means of promoting behavior change.

A large body of literature supports the use of PRT with individuals with ASD. A review of empirical support for various intervention strategies for individuals with ASD identified PRT as 1 of 27 evidence-based practices for individuals with ASD (Wong et al., 2014). Although not differentiated in the review by Wong and colleagues, several studies assessed peer-mediated PRT—a procedure in which peers are trained to facilitate PRT. Peer-mediated PRT has been proposed as being a particularly appropriate intervention strategy, as it promotes social skill development and interaction between students with ASD and typically developing peers (Boudreau, Corkum, Meko, & Smith, 2015).

In the earliest evaluation of peer-mediated PRT, Pierce and Schriebman (1995) taught peers to implement PRT using behavioral skills training (i.e., instruction, modeling, role play, feedback). Trained peers were then tasked with implementing PRT with two students with ASD in the absence of direct adult supervision. Following implementation of intervention, students with ASD increased the percentage of intervals of initiations and maintained interaction. The number of words spoken and teacher ratings of social behavior also increased following introduction of intervention.

Since initial positive findings, additional researchers have evaluated the efficacy of peer-mediated PRT in promoting acquisition of new behaviors in individuals with ASD. A review of peer-mediated PRT identified a total of five empirical evaluations of the strategy (Boudreau, Corkum, Meko, & Smith, 2015), including the initial study by Pierce and Schreibman (1995). Similar to Pierce and Schreibman, other evaluations of peer-mediated PRT generally indicated positive outcomes for individuals with ASD. Although outcomes were favorable, Boudreau and colleagues (2015) indicated that peer-mediated PRT could not yet be identified as an evidence-based practice due to the small number of extant studies. Since the publication of Boudreau and colleagues' review, researchers have continued to evaluate peer-mediated PRT and documented improvements in behaviors such as peer interaction and appropriate play (e.g., Brock, Dueker, & Barczak, 2018).

Peer Modeling Interventions

Peer modeling interventions describe procedures in which a target student views a peer demonstrate a behavior that is to be learned or demonstrated with greater frequency. Peer modeling may occur in vivo with peers who are in close physical proximity to the student. Alternatively, peer modeling may occur via video—a procedure in which a student watches peers, either known or unknown, demonstrate a behavior.

Peer modeling interventions have been utilized to address a wide range of behaviors. In an early example of an in vivo modeling intervention, Brown and Pearce (1970) trained students with emotional and behavioral disorders in an envelope-filing task. Once trained, they then served as models for three students with an intellectual disability—resulting in an increase in task completion of students with an intellectual disability. Other behaviors targeted through peer modeling include, but are not limited to, conversation (Charlop & Milstein, 1989), on-task behavior (King, Radley, Jenson, Clark, & O'Neill, 2014; Richards, Tuesday-Healthfield, & Jenson, 2010), eye contact (O'Handley, Radley, & Whipple, 2015), and consumption of fruits and vegetables (Laureati, Bergmaschi, & Pagliarini, 2014).

Although a substantial number of studies have evaluated peer modeling interventions, no recent meta-analyses or systematic reviews have evaluated the effects of peer modeling interventions across target behaviors and populations. Although not recent, Schunk (1987) evaluated 29 evaluations of peer modeling interventions, concluding that learning is likely to occur regardless of model age or sex, but noted that these factors may influence the performance of a newly learned behavior. Interventions that provided multiple models were also determined to be more effective than interventions in which a single model was provided.

Whereas Schunk (1987) provides the most recent broad summary of the peer modeling intervention literature, other researchers have provided more narrow summaries of peer modeling interventions. For example, Zhang and Wheeler

(2011) found peer modeling interventions to be the most effective of all peer-mediated interventions for individuals with ASD. Mason, Ganz, Parker, Burke, and Camargo (2012) found video modeling interventions to be highly effective for individuals with ASD and moderately effective for those with developmental disabilities. Of age groups evaluated, effects of video modeling were largest among elementary-age students and for play behaviors.

Peer-Mediated Play Interventions

Peer-mediated play interventions describe interventions in peers are taught strategies for interacting during play. These interventions are similar to peer support arrangements, in which a peer is trained in strategies for increasing opportunities for interaction between themselves and another student. Whereas the focus of peer support arrangements may be broad, peer-mediated play interventions exclusively focus on interactions during game or play settings. Interventions targeting play skills may be particularly important for students with developmental disabilities, as they are often lack skills to benefit from unstructured play periods (e.g., recess; Cappadocia & Weiss, 2011) and interact with fewer peers than their classmates (Anderson, Moore, Godfrey, & Fletcher-Flinn, 2004).

Kasari, Rotheram-Fuller, Locke, and Fulsrud (2012) provide a model for a peer-mediated play intervention, in which peers of students with ASD were trained to identify isolated students and utilize strategies to engage them in play. Results indicated that the peer-mediated play intervention was effective in reducing isolation and increasing joint engagement than a child-specific intervention. Similarly, Kretzman, Shih, and Kasari (2015) provided training to peers training in identifying and engaging students with ASD during recess periods. As in Kasari and colleagues' (2012) study, students with ASD increased peer engagement following implementation of the intervention. These studies stand in support of other research indicating that training peers to interact with students with identified disabilities is an effective means of facilitating interactions and play between peers and target students (e.g., Knapczuk, 1989; Licciardello, Harchik, & Luiselli, 2008). Although a myriad of studies indicate support for peer-mediated play interventions, no systematic reviews or meta-analyses are available to describe the overall research evaluating the procedure.

Restorative and Conflict Resolution Interventions

Restorative and conflict resolutions describe approaches to school discipline, both proactive and reactive, that focus on building and maintaining social relationships. Instead of focusing on punishment of rule violations, restorative and conflict resolution interventions focus on taking responsibility, learning, and mutual support. At their core, restorative and conflict resolution interventions propose that individuals are able to be think about how their behavior impacts themselves and those around them and that the responsibility of the peer community is to support responsible decision-making and accountability. Ultimately, the goal of restorative and conflict resolution interventions is to both repair harm and encourage reintegration of offenders into the social community (Suvall, 2009). Given the central role of peers in supporting the behavior of other students in restorative and conflict resolution interventions, these interventions may considered a PMBI.

Although these types of interventions have an extensive literature base in areas outside of schools (e.g., Latimer, Dowden, & Muise, 2005), the research evaluating school-based implementation is limited (Noltemeyer, Ward, & Mcloughlin, 2015). In one review of school-based restorative procedures in educational settings, Anfara, Evans, and Lester (2013) identified five peer-reviewed articles describing these procedures. Of those articles described, findings included reduced disciplinary issues (Karp & Breslin, 2001) and greater teacher willingness to reflect on interactions with students and colleagues (e.g., McCluskey, Lloyd, Kane, Riddell, Stead, & Weedon, 2008). Despite promising findings, most articles reviewed described evaluation reports instead of empirical evaluation of interventions—thus, caution is required in interpreting outcomes.

Since Anfara and colleagues' (2013) review, additional peer-reviewed articles have evaluated the topic. However, a limited number have been empirical in nature. In one of the few extant examples, Gregory et al. (2018) examined the effect of a restorative intervention on out-of-school suspensions. Results of the study found implementation to reduce the rate of out-of-school suspensions, but disparities in suspensions between Black and White students were not strongly impacted by the intervention. Although studies such as that conducted by Gregory and colleagues provide important information regarding the utility of restorative interventions, there continues to be a clear need for additional research to address the gap between popular interest and empirical support of these procedures.

SUMMARY

PMBIs have been repeatedly found to be effective strategies for addressing child and adolescent behavior within school settings. Although some of the strategies introduced in this chapter have been more regularly evaluated than others, all procedures have been found to be promising in their ability to effect socially meaningful behavior change within educational settings. Although rarely quantified in the empirical literature, these procedures also leverage student resources to improve the efficiency of interventions and the number of students capable of being served by school personnel, all while engaging high influence peers. The remainder of this section will focus on the individual strategies described in this chapter, providing a detailed guide to implementation in applied contexts.

REFERENCES

Anderson, A., Moore, D., Godfrey, R., & Fletcher-Flinn, C. (2004). Social skills assessment of children with autism in free-play situations. *Autism, 8*, 369–385.

Bambara, L. M., Cole, C. L., Kunsch, C., Tsai, S. C., & Ayad, E. (2016). A peer-mediated intervention to improve the conversation skills of high school students with autism spectrum disorder. *Research in Autism Spectrum Disorders, 27*, 29–43.

Barbetta, P. M. (1990). GOALS: A group-oriented adapted levels system for children with behavior disorders. *Academic Therapy, 25*, 645–655.

Battaglia, A. A., & Radley, K. C. (2014). Peer-mediated social skills training for children with autism spectrum disorder. *Beyond Behavior, 23*, 4–13.

Blake, C., Wang, W., Cartledge, G., & Gardner, R. (2000). Middle school students with serious emotional disturbances serve as social skills trainers and reinforcers for peers with SED. *Behavioral Disorders, 25*, 280–298.

Boudreau, A. M., Corkum, P., Meko, K., & Smith, I. M. (2015). Peer-mediated pivotal response treatment for young children with autism spectrum disorders: A systematic review. *Canadian Journal of School Psychology, 30*, 218–235.

Brock, M. E., Dueker, S. A., & Barczak, M. A. (2018). Brief report: improving social outcomes for students with autism at recess through peer-mediated pivotal response training. *Journal of Autism and Developmental Disorders, 48*, 2224–2230.

Brown, L., & Pearce, E. (1970). Increasing the production rates of trainable retarded students in a public school simulated workshop. *Education and Training of the Mentally Retarded, 5*, 15–22.

Cappadocia, C., & Weiss, J. (2011). Review of social skills training groups for youth with Asperger syndrome and high functioning autism. *Research in Autism Spectrum Disorders, 5*, 70–78.

Charlop, M. H., & Milstein, J. P. (1989). Teaching autistic children conversational speech using video modeling. *Journal of Applied Behavior Analysis, 22*, 275–285.

Collins, T. A., Gresham, F. M., & Dart, E. H. (2016). The effects of peer-mediated check-in/check-out on the social skills of socially neglected students. *Behavior Modification, 40*, 568–588.

Cordier, R., Vilaysack, B., Doma, K., Wilkes-Gilan, S., & Speyer, R. (2018). Peer inclusion in interventions for children with ADHD: A systematic review and meta-analysis. *BioMed Research International, 2018*, 1–52.

Dart, E. H., Collins, T. A., Klingbeil, D. A., & McKinley, L. W. (2014). Peer management interventions: A meta-analytic review of single-case research. *School Psychology Review, 43*, 367–384.

Dart, E. H., Furlow, C. M., Collins, T. A., Brewer, E., Gresham, F. M., Chenier, K. H. (2015). Peer-mediated check-in/check-out for students at risk for internalizing disorders. *School Psychology Quarterly, 30*, 229–243.

Dart, E. H., Radley, K. C., Furlow, C. M., & Murphy, A. N. (2017). Using behavioral skills training to teach high school students to implement discrete trial training. *Behavior Analysis: Research and Practice, 17*, 237–249.

Dunn, M. E., Shelnut, J., Ryan, J. B., & Katsiyannis, A (2017). A systematic review of peer-mediated interventions on the academic achievement of students with emotional/behavioral disorders. *Education and Treatment of Children, 40*, 497–524.

Flood, W. A., Wilder, D. A., Flood, A. L., & Masuda, A., (2002). Peer-mediated reinforcement plus prompting as treatment for off-task behavior in children with attention deficit hyperactivity disorder. *Journal of Applied Behavior Analysis, 35*, 199–204.

Fowler, S. A., (1986). Peer-monitoring and self-monitoring: Alternatives to traditional teacher management. *Exceptional Children, 52*, 573–581.

Guevremont, D. C., MacMillan, V. M., Shawchuck, C. R., & Hansen, D. J. (1989). A peer-mediated inter4vention with clinic-referred socially isolated girls: Generalization, maintenance, and social validation. *Behavior Modification, 13*, 32–50.

Hess, K. L., Morrier, M. J., Heflin, L. J., & Ivey, M. L. (2008). Autism Treatment Survey: Services Received by Children with Autism Spectrum Disorders in Public School Classrooms. *Journal of Autism and Developmental Disorders, 38*, 961–971.

Higgins, J. W., Williams, R. L., & McLaughlin, T. F. (2001). The effects of a token economy employing instructional consequences for a third-grade student with learning disabilities: A data-based case study. *Education and Treatment of Children, 24*, 99–106.

Hughes, C., Copeland, S. R., Guth, C., Rung, L. L., Hwang, B., Kleeb, G., & Strong, M. (2001). General education students' perspectives on their involvement in a high school peer buddy program. *Education and Training in Mental Retardation and Developmental Disabilities, 36*, 343–356.

Karp, D. R., & Breslin, B. (2001). Restorative justice in school communities. *Youth & Society, 33*, 249–272.

Kasari, C., Rotheram-Fuller, E., Locke, J., & Gulsrud, A. (2012). Making the connection: Randomized controlled trial of social skills at school for children with autism spectrum disorders. *Journal of Child Psychology and Psychiatry, 53*, 431–439.

King, B., Radley, K. C., Jenson, W. R., Clark, E., & O'Neill, R. E. (2014). Utilization of video modeling combined with self-monitoring to increase rates of on-task behavior. *Behavioral Interventions, 29*, 125–144.

Knapczyk, D. R. (1989). Peer-mediated training of cooperative play between special and regular class students in integrated play settings. *Education and Training in Mental Retardation, 24*, 255–264.

Langberg, J. M., Molina, B. S. G., Arnold, L. E., Epstein, J. N., Altaye, M., Hinshaw, S. P., ... Hetchman, L. (2011). Patterns and predictors of adolescent academic achievement and performance in a sample of children with attention-deficit/hyperactivity disorder. *Journal of Clinical Child and Adolescent Psychology, 40*, 519–531.

Latimer, J., Dowden, C., & Muise, D. (2005). The effectiveness of restorative justice practices: A meta-analysis. *Prison Journal, 85*, 127–144.

Laureati, M., Bergamaschi, V., & Pagliarini, E. (2014). School-based intervention with children. Peer modeling, reward and repeated exposure reduce food neophobia and increase liking of fruits and vegetables. *Appetite, 83*, 26–32.

Laushey, K. M., & Heflin, L. J. (2000). Enhancing social skills of kindergarten children with autism through the training of multiple peers as tutors. *Journal of Autism and Developmental Disorders, 30*, 183–193.

Lewis, T. J., & Sugai, G. (1996). Descriptive and experimental analysis of teacher and peer attention and the use of assessment-based intervention to improve pro-social behavior. *Journal of Behavioral Education, 6*, 7–24.

Licciardello, C. C., Harchik, A. E., & Luiselli, J. K. (2008). Social skills intervention for children with autism during interactive play at a public elementary school. *Education and Treatment of Children, 31*, 27–37.

Maheady, L., Harper, G. F., & Mallette, B. (1991). Peer-mediated instruction: A review of potential applications for special education. *Journal of Reading, Writing, and Learning Disabilities, 7*, 75–103.

Mandal, R., Olmi, D. J., Edwards, R. P., Tingstrom, D. H., & Benoit, D. A. (2000). Effective instruction delivery and time-in: Positive procedures for achieving child compliance. *Child & Family Behavioral Therapy, 22*, 1–12.

McCluskey, G., Lloyd, G., Kane, J., Riddell, S., Stead, J., & Weedon, E. (2008). Can restorative practices in schools make a difference? *Educational Review, 60*, 405–417.

Nathanson, A. I. (2001). Parents versus peers: Exploring the significance of peer mediation of antisocial television. *Communication Research, 28*, 251–274.

Noltemeyer, A. L., Ward, R. M., & Mcloughlin, C. (2015). Relationship between school suspension and student outcomes: A meta-analysis. *School Psychology Review, 44*, 224–240.

Nordquist, V. M. (1978). A behavioral approach to the analysis of peer interactions. In M. J. Guralnick (Ed.), *Early intervention and the integration of handicapped and nonhandicapped children* (pp. 53–84). Baltimore, MD: University Park Press.

O'Handley, R. D., Radley, K. C., & Whipple, H. M. (2015). The relative effects of social stories and video modeling toward increasing eye contact of adolescents with autism spectrum disorder. *Research in Autism Spectrum Disorders, 11*, 101–111.

Pierce, K., & Schreibman, L. (1995). Increasing complex social behaviors in children with autism: Effects of peer-implemented pivotal response training. *Journal of Applied Behavior Analysis, 28*, 285–295.

Ragland, E. U., Kerr, M. M., & Strain, P. S. (1978). Behavior of withdrawn autistic children: Effects of peer social initiations. *Behavior Modification, 2*, 565–578.

Richards, L. C., Tuesday-Healthfield, L., & Jenson, W. R. (2010). A classwide peer-modeling intervention package to increase on-task behavior. *Psychology in the Schools, 47*(6), 551–566.

Rose, L. C., & Gallup, A. M. (2005). The 37th annual Phi Delta/Kappa/Gallup poll of the public's attitude toward the public schools. *Phi Delta Kappan, 87*, 41–57.

Rosenbaum, P. S. (1973). *Peer-mediated instruction*. New York, NY: Teachers College Press.

Sainato, D. M., Strain, P. S., Lefebvre, D., & Rapp, N. (1987). Facilitating transition times with handicapped preschool children: A comparison between peer-mediated and antecedent prompt procedures. *Journal of Applied Behavior Analysis, 20*, 285–291.

Salend, S. J., & Meddaugh, D. (1985). Using a peer-mediated extinction procedure to decrease obscene language. *The Pointer, 30*, 8–11.

Sanchez, S., Miltenberger, R. G., Kincaid, D., & Blair, K. S. C. (2015). Evaluating check-in check-out with peer tutors for children with attention maintained problem behaviors. *Child & Family Behavior Therapy, 37*, 285–302.

Schunk, D. H. (1987). Peer models and children's behavioral change. *Review of Education Research, 57*, 149–174.

Smith, L. J. C., & Forlwer, S. A. (1984). Positive peer pressure: The effects of peer monitoring on children's disruptive behavior. *Journal of Applied Behavior Analysis, 17*, 213–227.

Stokes, T. F., & Baer, D. M. (1977). An implicit technology of generalization. *Journal of Applied Behavior Analysis, 10*, 349–367.

Strain, P. S., Shores, R. E., & Timm, M. A. (1978). Effects of peer social initiations on the social behavior of withdrawn preschool children. *Journal of Applied Behavior Analysis, 10*, 289–298.

Sutherland, K. S., Lewis-Palmer, T., Stitcher, J., & Morgan, P. L. (2008). Examining the influence of teacher behavior and classroom context on the behavioral and academic outcomes for students with emotional or behavioral disorders. *Journal of Special Education, 4*, 223–233.

Suvall, C. (2009). Restorative justice in schools: learning for Jena High School. *Harvard Civil Rights-Civil Liberties Law Review, 44*, 547–569.

Tan, P., & Alant, E. (2018). Using peer-mediated instruction to support communication involving a student with autism during mathematics activities: A case study. *Assistive Technology, 30*, 9–15.

Tzani-Pepelasi, C., Ioannou, M., Synnott, J., & McDonnell, D. (2019). Peer support at schools: The buddy approach as a prevention and intervention strategy for school bullying. *International Journal of Bullying Prevention, 1*, 111–123.

Wang, S. Y., Cui, Y., & Carrila, R. (2011). Examining the effectiveness of peer-mediated and video-modeling social skills interventions for children with autism spectrum disorders: A meta-analysis in single-case research using HLM. *Research in Autism Spectrum Disorders, 5*, 562–569.

Watkins, L., O'Reilly, M., Kuhn, M., Gevarter, C., Lancioni, G. E., Sigafoos, J., & Lang, R. (2015). A review of peer-mediated social interaction interventions for students with autism in inclusive settings. *Journal of Autism and Developmental Disorders, 45*, 1070–1083.

Whalon, K. J., Conroy, M. A., Martinez, J. R., & Werch, B. L. (2015). School-based peer-related social competence interventions for children with autism spectrum disorder: A meta-analysis and descriptive review of single case research design studies. *Journal of Autism and Developmental Disorders, 45*, 1513–1531.

White, M. A. (1975). Natural rates of teacher approval and disapproval in the classroom. *Journal of Applied Behavior Analysis, 8*, 367–372.

Wong, C., Odom, S. L., Hume, K., Cox, A. W., Fetting, A., Kucharczyk, S., . . . Shultz, T. R. (2014). *Evidence-based practices for children, youth, and young adults with Autism Spectrum Disorder*. Chapel Hill, NC: University of North Carolina, Frank Porter Graham Child Development Institute, Autism Evidence-Based Practice Review Group.

Youniss, J., & Haynie, D. L. (1992). Friendship in adolescence. *Journal of Developmental and Behavioral Pediatrics, 13*, 59–66.

Zhang, J., & Wheeler, J. J. (2011). A meta-analysis of peer-mediated interventions for young children with autism spectrum disorders. *Education and Training in Autism and Developmental Disabilities, 46*, 62–77.

## 10

Peer Management Interventions

KATE A. HELBIG AND EVAN H. DART ■

Peer management interventions, a type of peer-mediated behavioral intervention (PMBI), were defined in the previous chapter as those strategies that recruit students to take on a managerial role in the implementation of a behavioral intervention. This chapter will extend the discussion of peer management interventions in a way that facilitates implementation with a threefold purpose. First, we will introduce and describe specific peer management interventions that can be used to address a variety of student behavior. Second, we will discuss practical recommendations that are relevant to establishing any peer management intervention. Finally, we will provide readers with several considerations related to the implementation context and how contextual factors may alter the effectiveness or practicality of peer management interventions.

Dart, Collins, Klingbeil, and McKinley (2014) conducted a meta-analysis of the peer management literature and found that these strategies were moderately effective (Tau-U = 0.78) in addressing a range of student behavior concerns. As part of the meta-analysis, three broad classes of peer management interventions were conceptualized, based not on the topography of the procedures but on the topography of the behavior they were designed to address. Although behavior function is often used to categorize behavior intervention strategies (Ingram, Lewis-Palmer, & Sugai, 2005), we focus on topography here for three reasons. First, the function of a student's behavior is often not considered within multitiered systems of support until the most intensive level of service delivery (Anderson & Borgmeier, 2010). At this stage, peer management interventions may no longer be appropriate due to the prolonged and severe nature of the behavioral concern unless they are included as one component within a more comprehensive treatment package. Second, when student behavior function is considered, it is often not effectively incorporated into the resulting behavior intervention plan (Scott, McIntyre, Liaupsin, Nelson, Conroy, & Paine, 2005). Third, many peer management strategies have not been modified to address a particular function of behavior, meaning we do not know if any are effective to address specific behavior functions (Dart et al., 2014). Thus, for practical purposes, the three categories of peer management interventions introduced will include those designed to address students' (a) appropriate and disruptive behaviors, (b) communication, and (c) social skills.

PEER MANAGEMENT INTERVENTION STRATEGIES

In this section, we will provide a brief overview of each category of peer management intervention as well as a thorough implementation guide for one exemplar strategy from each category. It is important to remember that the defining feature of peer management interventions is that the bulk of the implementation and management of the intervention plan is assigned to a student instead of a traditional adult interventionist. Thus, any extant behavior intervention strategy could be modified to be implemented as a peer management strategy. The following examples are meant to provide practitioners with a basic set of peer management strategies to address common referral concerns in the classroom setting.

Appropriate and Disruptive Behaviors

Peer management interventions addressing students' appropriate and disruptive behaviors seek to promote behaviors that facilitate learning and reduce behaviors that interfere with learning. One simple and effective strategy to do both simultaneously is through the use of differential reinforcement of alternative behavior (DRA; Petscher, Rey, & Bailey, 2009). Using DRA, appropriate behavior is reinforced when it is exhibited while a target problem behavior is placed on extinction. DRA essentially shifts the stream of reinforcement a student receives for engaging in problem behavior to a different, more appropriate, alternative behavior. Grauvogel-Macaleese and Wallace (2010) evaluated a peer-mediated DRA intervention to address the on-task behavior of elementary aged children with Attention-Deficit/Hyperactivity Disorder (ADHD) during an afterschool homework program. Student interventionists were trained to provide praise and helping statements to a target student whenever they exhibited on-task behavior in the presence of academic task demands. If the target student was off-task (i.e., not engaged in the academic task), the student interventionists were trained to withhold all attention until the target student re-engaged the academic task. The effect of this simple intervention was powerful, with all three target students exhibiting near zero levels of off-task behavior when the treatment was in place. Furthermore, replications of this treatment protocol in traditional classroom settings have been similarly effective (e.g., Helbig, 2017). See Appendix A for a step-by step guide to the implementation of an intervention similar to the one evaluated by Grauvogel-Macaleese and Wallace (2010).

Communication

Peer management interventions addressing students' communication skills seek to increase the frequency with which students interact with their peers, teachers, or other school staff members. These strategies are most common for students with developmental disabilities that inhibit appropriate social interaction such as Autism Spectrum Disorder (ASD; Dart et al., 2014). Lee, Odom, and Loftin (2007) trained pairs of typically developing third grade students to initiate social interactions with a peer with ASD. Five 20-min training sessions were conducted for each pair of student interventionists. During the training sessions, student interventionists were taught social behaviors such as sharing and suggesting play ideas before being given the opportunity to observe an adult model exhibit these behaviors, being asked to demonstrate the behavior themselves, and receiving feedback on their performance. Once the training was completed, the student interventionists were returned to structured play activities with the target students while social interactions were observed. Teachers were instructed to prompt social initiations if none were exhibited by the student interventionists in a 30-s period. The results of this study demonstrated increases in social interaction between the target students with ASD and their typically developing peers to levels previously unseen prior to treatment implementation. As an added benefit, the target students exhibited a decrease in stereotypic behavior while the treatment was in place and the results generalized in the presence of untrained peers. See Appendix B for a step-by step guide to the implementation of an intervention similar to the one evaluated by Lee and colleagues (2007).

Social Skills

Peer management interventions addressing social skills seek to teach students to exhibit behaviors that allow them to navigate social interactions successfully. Whereas peer management interventions targeting communication focus solely on the frequency or duration of interactions, social skills interventions place an emphasis on the quality of the interaction, making them a distinct category. However, similar to those interventions targeting communication, peer management social skills interventions are frequently implemented for students with developmental disabilities such as ASD and are also the most well-researched class of peer management interventions (Dart et al., 2014). Morrison, Garcia, and Parker (2001) targeted three social skills (i.e., requesting, commenting, sharing) using a peer management paradigm. Specifically, three target students with ASD (aged 10–13) were paired with a typically developing student interventionist. Although an adult interventionist was initially responsible for explicit instruction in each of the three social skills, the student interventionist was responsible for prompting and reinforcing the target student's continued use of each skill within the context of a game or activity. Results of the study indicate that the peer prompting and reinforcement resulted in a substantial increase in skill accuracy across all three target peers. Additionally, the intervention was eventually modified to a self-management arrangement whereby the target students were responsible for reinforcing their own skill accuracy, suggesting that the peer management procedure could be faded and more naturalistic contingencies might maintain the behavior change. See Appendix C for a step-by-step guide to the implementation of an intervention similar to the one evaluated by Morrison and colleagues (2001).

RECOMMENDATIONS FOR IMPLEMENTATION

The purpose of this section is to provide the reader with various recommendations and aspects to consider prior to and during the implementation of a peer-management interventions in school settings. The specific considerations noted in this section include the identification and selection of the student interventionist, informed consent for service delivery, training strategies, and social validity.

First and foremost, the identification of student interventionists is one of the most important tasks for which the adult coordinating the intervention is responsible. Although teacher nomination is the most simple and straightforward method for identifying student interventionists, there are several characteristics that can be used to describe the ideal student interventionists to teachers who are asked to make recommendations. High achievement is an example of a characteristic a teacher should be seeking in a student interventionist, as this student will be required to take on an additional task during instructional time. A student who is exhibiting academic difficulties may not be the best candidate to select as a peer interventionist, as it is not in the best interest of that student to increase their task demand and divert their attention and effort away from the academic material. Other characteristics commonly used to described ideal student interventionists include *motivated, responsible,* and *willingness to help* (Dart et al., 2014; Helbig, 2017); however, there are no data linking these characteristics with performance as a student interventionist.

Once students have been identified, the adult coordinating the intervention may consider obtaining objective data to verify the teachers' nomination of the student. This can be done through the assessment of universal screening data or discipline referral data. Another option is to conduct a direct observation of the student in the environment in which the intervention will be implemented. Some examples of behaviors to look for during the observation are academic engagement or interactions with peers. In either case, potential student interventionists should not be at risk for academic or behavioral failure.

With regard to ethical considerations associated with peer management interventions, informed consent should be addressed. If possible, it is encouraged to obtain consent from the parents of the student interventionist and consult the schools' procedures regarding consent for Tier 2 interventions. In no circumstance should a student be placed in an interventionist role without first obtaining consent from their parent or guardian. Consent forms for this role should appear similar to consent forms for the student receiving service. That is, the nature and scope of services should be fully detailed, the student's role should be described, and the possible risks and benefits should be explained. Additionally, and depending on the age of the student interventionist, assent from the student should be solicited, and the adult coordinator should be prepared to handle the student's refusal to perform in an interventionist role. Finally, it is important to clarify that the student interventionist should not be tasked with serving in an evaluative capacity (e.g., collecting data regarding the target student's behavioral performance), as this could lead to ethical concerns related to protecting the target student's privacy.

Another aspect to consider are the strategies that will be employed to train the student interventionist. Although it will be dependent upon the specific peer management intervention being employed, behavioral skills training is a general evidence-based procedure to train student interventionists (Dart et al., 2014; Helbig, 2017). This is a relatively efficient procedure that entails a didactic teaching component, modeling the intervention, role-playing the intervention, and providing performance feedback to the student (i.e., praise and corrective feedback). Dart and colleagues (2014) found that student interventionists undergoing 60 or more minutes of training produced greater treatment effects (Tau-U = 0.846) than those that received less than 60 minutes of training (Tau-U = 0.643). Although this finding might mean that more thoroughly trained students are more effective interventionists, it could also reflect a link between treatment complexity and effectiveness or treatment integrity and training time. Practitioners should ensure that student interventionists receive sufficient training to implement treatment components with fidelity and provide retraining when lapses in fidelity occur repeatedly. These training sessions should occur during non-academic periods, such as recess or elective classes. Although previous research suggests that student interventionists can implement interventions with fidelity (Collins et al., 2017; Dart et al., 2014), it is crucial that treatment integrity is assessed formatively for the duration of the implementation period as with any intervention effort.

Research has also suggested that social validity is an aspect to consider when implementing behavioral interventions (Miramontes, et al., 2016). Social validity refers to the degree to which intervention or treatment strategies are viewed as acceptable and feasible and whether the goals of the treatment are deemed appropriate and worthwhile in light of the required implementation effort. In relation to peer management interventions, there is preliminary evidence to suggest that peer-management interventions are viewed as socially valid by both the consumers (i.e., student receiving the intervention) and providers (i.e., student interventionist; Carter et al., 2011). Thus, practitioners may want to consider assessing the social validity of the peer management intervention. Student interventionist perceptions of social validity may be best assessed first during intervention training. Additionally, both student interventionists and students receiving the intervention could be asked to provide their perception of the strategy's social validity periodically throughout implementation.

CONSIDERATIONS OF DIVERSITY AND EQUITY

In addition to these implementation considerations, it is important to consider several contextual factors that could potentially impact the effectiveness of a peer management intervention. One of the most salient factors with practical implications is the contextual fit between characteristics of a target student and a student interventionist. For example, Dart and colleagues (2014) included gender-matching as a moderator of intervention effectiveness in their meta-analysis; however, because of strong homogeneity (i.e., nearly all studies did not match students on gender), it was difficult to determine whether this factor meaningfully impacted treatment effectiveness. Still, the idea of matching target students and student interventionists on gender, or any other demographic variable, is intuitively appealing. There is evidence in related literature, such as peer tutoring, to suggest that although matching on some variables may impact treatment effectiveness (e.g., ethnicity), matching on others (e.g., age) do not (Robinson, Schofield, & Steers-Wentzell, 2005). Unfortunately, similar data are not available for peer management paradigms. Thus, it may be best to allow target students to select a student interventionist from a pool of acceptable students, when possible.

Ethnicity is another variable to consider when selecting a student interventionist, as mentioned previously. However, it is important to note that there is minimal research that has been conducted on ethnicity matching between student interventionist and target student, and of the limited available research, most concerns peer tutoring interventions. One of the factors that may contribute to lack of research surrounding ethnicity-matching is the lack of reporting of ethnicity within the available research (Ryan, Reid, & Epstein, 2004); however, the available evidence indicates that ethnicity-matching increases perceived effectiveness of the tutoring (Fresko & Chen, 1989). Thus, it may be beneficial for peer management student interventionists and target students to be matched on ethnicity, when possible.

Finally, when training individuals with ASD, it may be important to consider selecting a typically developing peer interventionist who exhibits appropriate social skills, especially when the intervention emphasis is on promoting the generalization of skill acquisition. Previous research has indicated that when peers with typical language and social skills are implementing the intervention, there was a stronger likelihood of generalization and maintenance of trained skills (Watkins, et al., 2015). Several other contextual factors were examined by Dart and colleagues (2014), such as disability status of the target student (i.e., ASD or intellectual disability, ADHD or emotional and behavioral disorders, and no disability), the ratio of student interventionists to target students (i.e., >1:1 or ≤1:1), and whether the student interventionist and target student shared a classroom. However, none of these variables produced differential treatment outcomes. Thus, practitioners may establish peer management interventions with some degree of confidence that these contextual factors will not meaningfully impact effectiveness.

CONCLUSION

In conclusion, peer management interventions are empirically supported strategies to improve the appropriate, social, and communicative behavior of students in schools. Implementation considerations such as informed consent, interventionist identification, interventionist training, and social validity should be considered when establishing peer management strategies. Finally, although most contextual factors do not appear to impact the effectiveness of peer management strategies, interventionist training does appear to play a role, either by itself or through intervention complexity, as does ethnicity-matching of the student interventionist and target student.

REFERENCES

Anderson, C. M., & Borgmeier, C. (2010). Tier II interventions within the framework of school-wide positive behavior support: Essential features for design, implementation, and maintenance. *Behavior Analysis in Practice, 3*(1), 33–45.

Carter, E. W., Moss, C. K., Hoffman, A., Chung, Y., & Sisco, L. (2011). Efficacy and social validity of peer support arrangements for adolescents with disabilities. *Exceptional Children, 78*(1), 107.

Collins, T. A., Hawkins, R. O., & Flowers, E. M. (2017). Peer-mediated interventions: A practical guide to utilizing students as change agents. *Contemporary School Psychology, 18*(1), 1–7.

Dart, E. H., Collins, T. A., Klingbeil, D. A., & McKinley, L. E. (2014). Peer management interventions: A meta-analytic review of single-case research. *School Psychology Review, 43*(4), 367–384.

Fresko, B., & Chen, M. (1989). Ethnic similarity, tutor expertise, and tutor satisfaction in cross-age tutoring. *American Educational Research Journal, 26*, 122–140.

Grauvogel-MacAleese, A. N., & Wallace, M. D. (2010). Use of peer-mediated intervention in children with attention deficit hyperactivity disorder. *Journal of Applied Behavior Analysis, 43*(3), 547–551.

Helbig, K. A. (2017). *Effects of a function-based peer management intervention with middle-school students with ADHD* (Unpublished master's thesis). University of Southern Mississippi, Hattiesburg, MS.

Ingram, K., Lewis-Palmer, T., & Sugai, G. (2005). Function-based intervention planning: Comparing the effectiveness of FBA function-based and non–function-based intervention plans. *Journal of Positive Behavior Interventions, 7*(4), 224 - 236.

Lee, S., Odom, S. L., & Loftin, R. (2007). Social engagement with peers and stereotypic behavior of children with autism. *Journal of Positive Behavior Interventions, 9*(2), 67–79.

Miramontes, N. Y., Marchant, M., Heath, M. A., & Fischer, L. (2016). Social validity of a positive behavior interventions and support model. *Education and Treatment of Children, 34*(4), 445–468.

Morrison, L., Kamps, D., Garcia, J., & Parker, D. (2001). Peer mediation and monitoring strategies to improve initiations and social skills for students with autism. *Journal of Positive Behavior Interventions, 3*(4), 237–250.

Petscher, E. S., Rey, C., & Bailey, J. S. (2009). A review of empirical support for differential reinforcement of alternative behavior. *Research in Developmental Disabilities, 30*(3), 409–425.

Robinson, D. R., Schofield, J. W., & Steers-Wentzell, K. L. (2005). Peer and cross-age tutoring in math: Outcomes and their design implications. *Educational Psychology Review, 17*(4), 327–362.

Ryan, J. B., Reid, R., & Epstein, M. H. (2004). Peer-mediated intervention studies on academic achievement for students with EBD. *Remedial and Special Education, 25*(6), 330–341.

Scott, T. M., McIntyre, J., Liaupsin, C., Nelson, C. M., Conroy, M., & Payne, L. D. (2005). An examination of the relation between functional behavior assessment and selected intervention strategies with school-based teams. *Journal of Positive Behavior Interventions, 7*(4), 205–215.

Watkins, L., O'Reilly, M., Kuhn, M., Gevarter, C., Lancioni, G. E., Sigafoos, J., & Lang. R. (2015). A review of peer-mediated social interaction interventions for students with autism in inclusive settings. *Journal of Autism and Developmental Disorders, 45*, 1070–1083.

APPENDIX A
PEER-MEDIATED DRA INTERVENTION

Session Duration: 20 minutes
Setting: Classroom
Training Procedures:

1. Begin training by explaining student will be helping a classmate do better in class.
2. Explain DRA intervention: "When you see your buddy paying attention during class, your job is to say encouraging words to your buddy. You can say things like 'Great job working' or 'Awesome job listening to the teacher!'"
3. Explain the extinction component of the DRA intervention: "When you see your buddy is being disruptive or not paying attention in class, do not say anything to them, but instead just ignore their behavior."
4. Model the DRA intervention.
5. Student interventionist role plays implementing the DRA intervention to the adult.
6. Adult provides praise and/or corrective feedback to student interventionists during role play.
7. Student interventionists demonstrate mastery of implementation at a minimum of once per training session.

APPENDIX B
COMMUNICATIONINTERVENTION

Session Duration: 20 minutes
Setting: Play Time
Materials: Toys (e.g., blocks, dolls, cars)
Training Procedures:

1. Begin training by explaining student will be helping a classmate talk with their friends.
2. Explain the communication intervention: "When you see your buddy sitting by themselves, you should try to play with them. You can do this by sharing a toy with them" or asking them something like "Will you play blocks with me?"
3. Model the communication intervention.
4. Student interventionist role plays implementing the communication intervention to the adult.
5. Adult provides praise and/or corrective feedback to student interventionists during role play.
6. Student interventionists demonstrate mastery of implementation at a minimum of once per training session.

APPENDIX C
SOCIAL SKILLS INTERVENTION

Session Duration: 20 minutes
Setting: Recess
Materials: Reward (i.e. stickers, candy); preferred toys of the target student
Training Procedures:

1. Begin training by explaining student will be helping a classmate ask nicely for things they want to play with.
2. Explain the social skills intervention: "Each time you see your buddy ask nicely for a toy they want to play with, make a tally on your notecard. If your buddy gets three tallies during recess then you will give a sticker."
3. Model what "asking nicely" and "asking inappropriately" looks like.
4. Student interventionist role plays implementing the social skills intervention by accurately identifying "asking nicely" from "asking inappropriately" and delivering a reward for appropriate requesting.
5. Adult provides praise and/or corrective feedback to student interventionists during role play.
6. Student interventionists demonstrate mastery of implementation at a minimum of once per training session.

## 11

Peer-Mediated Social Skills Training

JESSICA N. SIMPSON AND TIMOTHY J. LEWIS ■

The need to build social competence among students with disabilities and those at risk has been well established (Gresham, Sugai, & Horner, 2001). Research continues to document the efficacy of instructional strategies in teaching children and youth key social skills (Spence, 2003). Social skills are defined as discrete behaviors individuals use within interactions with others that allow the individual to achieve a desired social outcome (Gresham, 2016). Social competence is the outcome of social skills used across a myriad of contexts that others view as appropriate as defined by the groups' shared values (Gresham, 2016). Social skills instruction, like other effective instruction, typically follows a tell-show-practice format (Lewis, Jorgenson, Simpson, & Guffey, 2020). First, teachers define and explain the skill and under what context it should be used (tell). Second, teachers demonstrate a range of examples and nonexamples of what the skill looks like (show). Finally, students practice the skill through prompted role plays.

An additional key component of effective instruction is matching instruction to prior student learning history and current patterns of appropriate and inappropriate social skill use. Challenging behavior, or the lack of appropriate social skill use, falls into one of two categories. First, the student displays a social skill deficit defined simply as the student does not know how or when to perform a social skill (Sugai & Lewis, 1996). Social skill deficits are typically common among students with moderate to severe intellectual disabilities and students with moderate to severe autism. Second, the student displays a performance problem whereby the student knows what the appropriate social skill is given the context and can display the skill when prompted. Through a functional lens, the problem behavior, or the inappropriate social skill, is more efficient or effective in achieving the desired outcome from the student's perspective. By understanding the type of social skill

challenge, instruction can be matched to increase the likelihood of skill use (i.e.,
teach and practice deficit problems to fluency, teach a replacement behavior that
achieves the same or similar outcome for performance problems).

While the improved use of social skills following instruction has been well
documented (Lewis et al., 2020), maintaining and generalizing social skill use
beyond the instructional context is a well-documented challenge (Gresham
et al., 2001). Generalization refers to the ability of a student to use social skills
in settings beyond where they are learned, and maintenance refers to the continued use of a skill over time, particularly following targeted interventions. To
promote generalization, it is recommended that social skills training (SST) be
implemented across multiple settings, trainers, and peer groups. As social behavior varies by context and social skills can be complex within and across each
setting, the more a skill is practiced across different contexts and settings, the
greater the likelihood that the skill will generalize and maintain. However, the
need to promote generalized responding, especially among student peer groups,
over time continues to be a challenge for educators (Gresham et al., 2001). One
strategy to promote generalized responding that has strong empirical support
is the use of peers within the instructional process. Peer-mediated behavioral
interventions (PMBIs) are typically used with young students or students with
disabilities (Trembath, Balandin, Togher, & Stancliffe, 2009). PMBIs have been
found to increase the rate of social interaction in students with disabilities by
reinforcing and prompting typically developing peers to initiate interactions to
shape the social responding of students with disabilities (Odom & Strain, 1986;
Odom, Hoyson, Jamieson, & Strain, 1985).

PMBIs involve the training of typically developing peers to model and reinforce
social interactions for students with social skill deficits through SST interventions.
The use of typically developing peers as change agents provide target students
with opportunities to practice and apply social skills in natural contexts and are
optimal for use in school settings. Using peers as intervention agents can help
to increase intervention access and promote generalized responding (Chan et al.,
2009). In PMBIs, adults monitor target students and peers but only directly intervene when necessary. Most studies have investigated the use of PMBIs on
children aged 13 years and younger (Chan et al., 2009); however, PMBIs can be
implemented with students of all ages. A major benefit of PMBIs is the increased
generalization of social skills as a result of the use of peers in natural learning
environments.

PEER-MEDIATED BEHAVIORAL INTERVENTION
PROCEDURES

There are a variety of ways that peers may be used in SST to improve student
social competence. The two most effective and commonly used PMBIs in SST
are prompting and reinforcing peer interactions and peer-initiated interventions.
Social network and proximity interventions may also be implemented utilizing

peers as change agents. In prompting interventions, a prompt is considered to be an instruction given by a peer directed to a target student. In prompting and reinforcing PMBIs, peers are used to help shape the desired and appropriate behaviors of target students. Peers are trained to prompt target students and to reinforce their appropriate responses (Odom & Strain, 1984). Peers can be trained to prompt different behaviors, such as play skills, motor skills, and communication. For example, a trained peer may prompt a target child by saying "Hey, let's play Legos." If the target student engages, the peer would then reinforce the target child's interaction by saying, "I have a lot of fun building Legos with you!" The purpose of the peer reinforcement is to increase the likelihood that the desired behavior displayed by the target student will occur again in the future. Peers are taught to offer praise when the target student makes any attempt at reciprocal play (Harper, Symon, & Frea, 2008). Some PMBIs include both prompting and reinforcement, while others include only one or the other. Prompting plus initiation is the most commonly used PMBI strategy to date (Watkins et al., 2015).

In peer initiation interventions, peers are trained to initiate play or conversation with target students. Peers are also provided training on how to appropriately respond to the target student if they initiate social interactions (Odom & Strain, 1984). Peers are instructed to naturally reinforce initiations by responding to target students in conversation and engaging in reciprocal play. Additionally, peers are trained to attempt to maintain successful interactions and respond to attempts to communicate made by a target student. To maintain interactions, peers are taught to repeat and expand on statements made by the target student (Sainato, Goldstein, & Strain, 1992). For example, if a peer initiates play by handing the target student his favorite toy and the target student takes the toy and moves away from the peer, to maintain the interaction the peer may say, "Can we play with that toy together?" Peers can also be trained to make requests of the target student (Sasso, Mundschenk, Melloy, & Casey, 1998). For example, a peer may ask a target student to hand them a specific toy and then attempt to maintain the interaction. Peer initiation interventions are often combined with prompting and reinforcement strategies.

Social network interventions are another variation of PMBIs. Social networks can help students integrate more fully into the school experience by increasing participation, awareness, and acceptance by peers. Social networks involve training multiple typically developing peers to interact with a target student. Social networks are able to enhance SST, as many natural social interactions take place in group settings. Most SST and peer interventions involve the work of a pair of students or a student and an adult. In contrast, social networks provide opportunities for target students to practice skills in groups which are more likely to resemble typical socialization situations in schools. Being able to practice social skills across a network of peers can help students with skill deficits more effectively generalize skills, as they are receiving increased levels of practice and reinforcement across multiple individuals in natural contexts. For example, Haring and Breen (1992) implemented a social network strategy in a secondary school setting in which peers were given different schedules of interactions, based on the proximity of the target student and peers during transition periods. Each peer was responsible for interacting with the target student for one transition period per day. Peers also ate lunch with target students either daily or on a rotating schedule. A unique aspect of this intervention involved peers being trained and agreeing to collect data to report and rate the quality of interactions with the target students.

Peer-mediated proximity interventions have also been used in SST. In proximity interventions, peers and target students are placed near each other in locations like lunch tables, playground equipment, social clubs and other unstructured free play settings (Odom & Strain, 1984). The purpose of this type of intervention is to place target students near typically developing students who model appropriate social behaviors in hopes that the target student will observe and perform the appropriate behaviors. In proximity interventions, no direct training is provided for peers, which may limit its effectiveness with students who have difficulty reading social cues. In this format, SST would rely on natural social interactions. Peer-mediated proximity interventions have produced the least favorable results in the social skills literature including poor generalization and maintenance of skills (Odom & Strain, 1984). The lack of generalization of proximity interventions could be due to the absence of training, prompting, and socially responsive reinforcement by peers. A recent review found that when used alone or packaged together, initiation, prompting, and reinforcement promoted generalization of skills across settings and maintenance over time, while proximity PMBIs alone did not (Watkins et al., 2015).

RECOMMENDATIONS FOR IMPLEMENTATION

Step 1: Assess Social Skills and Collect Present Level Data

Prior to implementing PMBIs, it is important to distinguish between acquisition and performance deficits to ensure the intervention is matched to student need. Acquisition deficits are understood as skills that the student "can't do," meaning the child lacks the knowledge of how to perform the skill. A performance deficit, or a "won't do" skill, occurs when students have acquired the knowledge of how to perform a skill, but they do not use the skill regularly and fluently when it is appropriate to do so.

Assessment of social skills in target students aids in planning, designing, and evaluating PMBIs. Assessment can take the form of direct behavioral observation, teacher rating sales, self-report measures, behavioral role plays, interviewing, and sociometric ratings. The optimal assessment strategy is through direct behavioral observations and behavioral rating scales. Elliot and Gresham (1987) recommend analyzing student behavior in natural settings to ensure the most valid assessment. Unstructured times like recess, lunch, and periods of free play are ideal for direct behavior observation of social skills since these settings allow students to socially interact at high rates. Merrell (2001) recommends observing students during free play over a period of at least 15 minutes. Data may be collected on constructs related to social skills, such as social engagement, participation, parallel play, initiations, exclusion, or the frequency of peer initiations and responses.

Step 2: Peer Selection

The next step in the PMBI SST process is to select peers who will be part of the intervention. Strain and Fox (1981) suggest the following as key traits of peer change agents: (a) comply with adult requests, (b) express a willingness to participate, (c) no history of negative social interactions with peers, and (d) be able to perform related verbal and motor behaviors. In addition to the peer selection guidelines provided by Strain and Fox, other researchers have advised selecting peers who have regular attendance, be approximately the same age as the target student, and are able to participate in the entire length of the intervention (Kerr & Nelson, 1983; Odom & Strain, 1984). Peer participants may also be recruited based on previous volunteering and interactions with target students (Hughes et al., 2013).

Step 3: Train and Support Participating Peers

Trainings typically begin with a discussion about similarities and differences. The purpose of this activity is to promote awareness of differences between individuals. Next, the trainer should explain to peers the logic of interacting with students with disabilities and those at risk and the targeted outcome of the intervention, as well as the behavioral expectations of peers delivering the intervention.

Over extended interventions, peers have been found to engage less in the peer-mediated process (Odom & Strain, 1984). To reduce fatigue effects, peers should be incentivized or reinforced for their participation (Lord, 1984). Odom, Stein, and Jenkins (1983) suggest using play and social activities as incentives for participation for younger children. Verbal prompts provided by teachers can be equally effective to earned consequences (e.g., Odom, Chandler, Ostrosky, McConell, & Reaney, 1992).

Step 4: Implement Intervention

Once the trainer determines that peers are ready, peers implement the intervention with the target student in a structured teaching session. For young students, structured teaching sessions are typically five to eight minutes. Next, the intervention should be implemented in the targeted settings. If necessary, adults can prompt peers to use a certain strategy. Prompting can be provided to peers through explicit instructions (e.g., "Try asking him to play Legos with you"), indirect verbal instructions (e.g., "Try again"), or through non-verbal signals (e.g., use a hand to motion the peer to move in front of the target student). If the peer does not respond after 10 seconds, the adult should provide another prompt and physical assistance. Environmental adjustments can also be made to include the target students preferred interests (Koegel, Koegel, & Schwartzman, 2013).

Step 5: Promote Generalization and Maintenance of Skill

Generalization has been found to be enhanced when peers are provided training and include direct instruction, coaching, reinforcing, and modeling (Strain & Odom, 1986). Additionally, to promote generalization, target students should practice skills across different natural social situations and settings (e.g., lunch period, free play in the classroom, and recess). Furthermore, to promote maintenance, after the intervention has ended, the target skill should be revisited with the target student by providing explicit opportunities to practice over time. Periodic checks and possible "booster" PMBI sessions may be necessary to promote skill generalization and maintenance.

CONSIDERATIONS OF EQUITY AND DIVERSITY

The U.S. Census Bureau (2008) estimates that groups who are currently considered to be ethnic minorities will make up more than 50% of the population by 2050. As the number of individuals representing different cultures continues to increase, it is especially important to ensure that instruction, including peer-mediated instruction, is culturally relevant and responsive. Culturally responsive instruction is "using the cultural characteristics, experiences, and perspectives of ethnically diverse students as conduits for teaching them more effectively . . . [and making sure that] academic knowledge and skills are situated within the lived experiences and frames of reference of students" (Ford, 2012, p. 106). To create culturally responsive social skills interventions, the following characteristics should be considered of both the target student and the peer implementers: (a) learning histories, (b) cultural norms, and (c) values of family, school, and neighborhood communities (Sugai, O'Keefe, & Fallon, 2012). To ensure culturally responsive practices are considered, simply ask families, educators, peers, and community members for input during the planning and designing phases of PMBIs. Cultural differences such as levels of touch, gestures, personal space, facial expressions, posture, and voice levels and tone should be factored into instructional examples.

Inclusive Practices

A central tenant of the Individuals with Disabilities Education Act is to maximize the opportunities for students with disabilities to learn alongside their peers across school settings. It is important to understand that simply placing students with disabilities into contexts where there is proximity to typically developing peers is not sufficient to promote social interaction and/or improved social functioning. Rather, a systematic approach is necessary to increase student learning and social engagement to provide equal opportunities in the classroom, including strategies such as PMBIs. Educators should purposefully find ways to integrate students with disabilities into learning opportunities and to encourage meaningful interactions between peers. Using peers as change agents through peer-medicated social skill instruction is an appropriate way to promote inclusion and foster relationships between peers and students with disabilities to improve student outcomes.

To date, PMBIs have been used with a range of children, and the empirical support for PMBIs is especially strong with students with autism (Neitzel, Boyd, Odom, & Edmondson Pretzel, 2008). As social interactions with peers are typically very challenging for students with autism, intervention for social skills deficits remain a priority (Lang, Regester, Rispoli, Pimentel, & Carmago, 2010). Children with autism may display deficits in initiating interactions, responding to interactions from peers, engaging in reciprocal conversations, and maintaining social engagement (Koegel, Koegel, Fredeen, & Gengoux, 2008; White, Keonig, & Scahill, 2007). Students with autism also have fewer reciprocal friendships (Bauminger et al., 2008), have been found to be unengaged with peers on the playground (Frankel, Goropse, Chang, & Sugar, 2011) and have smaller social networks (Locke, Kasari, Rotheram-Fuller, & Jacobs, 2013). Shattuck, Wagner, Narendorf, Sterzing, and Hensley (2011) reported that about half of adolescents with autism are never called by friends, do not see friends outside of school, and are rarely invited to social engagements, and their overall level of social participation is much lower than that of students with other disabilities. As a result of the lack of social interactions with peers and noted social skills deficits, students with autism experience loneliness (Bauminger, Shulman, & Agam, 2003), exclusion (Frankel et al., 2011), bullying (Kloosterman, Kelley, Craig, Parker, & Javier, 2013), anxiety and depression (Strang et al., 2012), and suicidal ideation (Mayes, Gorman, Hillwig-Garcia, & Syed, 2013). Using PMBIs to encourage friendships and social networks for adolescents with autism may serve as a protective factor against these negative outcomes (Bradley, 2016).

CONCLUSION

Research suggests that PMBIs can be implemented to help teach social skills and aid in the generalized responding across student peer groups. These interventions can help shape the social responding of students with disabilities and can be designed with cultural responsivity in mind to improve outcomes. Using peers as change agents to model and reinforce social interactions for students with social skills deficits helps students practice and apply social skills in natural contexts.

ACKNOWLEDGMENTS

This chapter was supported in part by a grant through the Office of Special Education Programs (OSEP) of the U.S. Department of Education (H325D110012). The views expressed herein do not necessarily represent the positions or policies of the U.S. Department of Education. No official endorsement by the U.S. Department of Education of any product, commodity, or enterprise mentioned in this document is intended or should be inferred.

REFERENCES

Bauminger, N., Shulman, C., & Agam, G. (2003). Peer interaction and loneliness in high-functioning children with autism. *Journal of Autism and Developmental Disorders, 33*(5), 489–507.

Bauminger, N., Solomon, M., Aviezer, A., Heung, K., Gazit, L., Brown, J., & Rogers, S. J. (2008). Children with autism and their friends: A multidimensional study of friendship in high-functioning autism spectrum disorder. *Journal of Abnormal Child Psychology, 36*(2), 135–150.

Bradley, R. (2016). "Why single me out?" Peer mentoring, autism and inclusion in mainstream secondary schools. *British Journal of Special Education, 43*(3), 272–288.

Chan, J. M., Lang, R., Rispoli, M., O'Reilly, M., Sigafoos, J., & Cole, H. (2009). Use of peer-mediated interventions in the treatment of autism spectrum disorders: A systematic review. *Research in Autism Spectrum Disorders, 3*(4), 876–889.

Elliott, S. N., & Gresham, F. M. (1987). Children's social skills: Assessment and classification practices. *Journal of Counseling and Development, 66*, 96–99.

Frankel, F. D., Gorospe, C. M., Chang, Y. C., & Sugar, C. A. (2011). Mothers' reports of play dates and observation of school playground behavior of children having high-functioning autism spectrum disorders. *Journal of Child Psychology and Psychiatry, 52*(5), 571–579.

Ford, D. Y. (2012). Culturally different students in special education: Looking backward to move forward. *Exceptional Children, 78*, 391–405.

Gresham, F. M. (2016). Evidence-based interventions for social skill deficits in children and adolescents. In L. A. Theodore (Ed.), *Handbook of Evidence-Based Interventions for Children and Adolescents* (pp. 365–376). New York, NY: Springer.

Gresham, F. M., Sugai, G., & Horner, R. H. (2001). Interpreting outcomes of social skills training for students with high-incidence disabilities. *Exceptional Children, 67*(3), 331–344.

Haring, T. G., & Breen, C. G. (1992). A peer-mediated social network intervention to enhance the social integration of persons with moderate and severe disabilities. *Journal of Applied Behavior Analysis, 25*(2), 319–333.

Harper, C. B., Symon, J. B. G., & Frea, W. D. (2008). Recess is time-in: Using peers to improve social skills of children with autism. *Journal of Autism and Developmental Disorders, 38*, 815–826.

Hughes, C., Harvey, M., Cosgriff, J., Reilly, C., Heilingoetter, J., Brigham, N., ... Bernstein, R. (2013). A peer-delivered social interaction intervention for high school students with autism. *Research & Practice for Persons with Severe Disabilities, 38*, 1–16.

Kerr, M. M., & Nelson, C. M. (1983). *Strategies for managing behavior problems in the classroom*. Columbus, OH: Merrill.

Kloosterman, P. H., Kelley, E. A., Craig, W. M, Parker, J. D., & Javier, C. (2013). Types and experiences of bullying in adolescents with an autism spectrum disorder. *Research in Autism Spectrum Disorders, 7*, 824–832.

Koegel, R., Kim, S., Koegel, L., & Schwartzman, B. (2013). Improving socialization for high school students with ASD by using their preferred interests. *Journal of Autism and Developmental Disorders, 43*, 2121–2134.

Koegel, L. K., Koegel, R. L., Fredeen, R. M., & Gengoux, G. W. (2008). Naturalistic behavioral approaches to treatment. In K. Chawarska, A. Klin, & F. R. Volkmar (Eds.), *Autism Spectrum Disorders in infants and toddlers: Diagnosis, assessment, and treatment*. New York: The Guilford Press.

Lang, R., Regester, A., Rispoli, M., Pimentel, S., & Camargo, S. H. (2010). Rehabilitation issues for children with autism spectrum disorders. *Developmental Neurorehabilitation, 13*, 153–155.

Lewis, T. J., Jorgenson, C., Simpson, J., & Guffey, T. (2020). Effective practices for teaching social skills. *Oxford Research Encyclopedia of Education*. Retrieved from https://oxfordre.com/education

Locke, J., Kasari, C., Rotheram-Fuller, M., & Jacobs, J. (2013). Social network changes over the school year among elementary school-aged children with and without an autism spectrum disorder. *School Mental Health, 5*(1), 38–47.

Lord, C. (1984). The development of peer relations in children with autism. *Applied Developmental Psychology, 1*, 165–230.

Mayes, S. D., Gorman, A. A., Hillwig-Garcia, J., & Syed, E. (2013). Suicide ideation and attempts in children with autism. *Research in Autism Spectrum Disorders, 7*(1), 109–119.

Merrell, K. W. (2001). Assessment of children's social skills: Recent developments, best practices, and new directions. *Exceptionality, 9*(1–2), 3–18.

Neitzel, J., Boyd, B., Odom, S. L., & Edmondson Pretzel, R. (2008). Peer-mediated instruction and intervention for children and youth with autism spectrum disorders: Online training module (Chapel Hill: UNC-Chapel Hill, National Professional Development Center on Autism Spectrum Disorders, FPG Child Development Institute). *Ohio Center for Autism and Low Incidence (OCALI), Autism Internet Modules*. Retrieved from http://www.autisminternetmodules.org

Odom, S. L., Chandler, L. K., Ostrosky, M., McConnell, S. R., & Reaney, S. (1992). Fading teacher prompts from peer-initiation interventions for young children with disabilities. *Journal of Applied Behavior Analysis, 25*(2), 307–317.

Odom, S. L., Hoyson, M., Jamieson, B., & Strain, P. S. (1985). Increasing handicapped preschoolers social interactions: Cross-setting and component analysis. *Journal of Applied Behavior Analysis, 18*(1), 3–16.

Odom, S. L., Stein, M., & Jenkins, J. R. (1983, May). *Peer-initiation and individual contingency interventions for promoting social interaction of handicapped preschool children*. Paper presented to the Association for Behavior Analysis. Milwaukee, WI.

Odom, S. L., & Strain, P. S. (1984). Peer-mediated approaches to promoting children's social interaction: A review. *American Journal of Orthopsychiatry, 54*(4), 544–557.

Odom, S. L., & Strain, P. S. (1986). A comparison of peer-initiation and teacher-antecedent interventions for promoting reciprocal social interaction of autistic preschoolers. *Journal of Applied Behavior Analysis, 19*(1), 59–71.

Sainato, D. M., Goldstein, H., & Strain, P. S. (1992). Effects of self-evaluation on pre-school children's use of social interaction strategies with their classmates with autism. *Journal of Applied Behavior Analysis, 25*(1), 127–141.

Sasso, G. M., Mundschenk, N. A., Melloy, K. J., & Casey, S. D. (1998). A comparison of the effects of organismic and setting variables on the social interaction behavior of children with developmental disabilities and autism. *Focus on Autism and Other Developmental Disabilities, 13*(1), 2–16.

Shattuck, P. T., Wagner, M., Narendorf, S., Sterzing, P., & Hensley, M. (2011). Post-high school service use among young adults with an autism spectrum disorder. *Archives of Pediatrics & Adolescent Medicine, 165*(2), 141–146.

Spence, S. H. (2003). Social skills training with children and young people: Theory, evidence and practice. *Child and Adolescent Mental Health, 8*(2), 84–96.

Strain, P. S., & Fox, J. J. (1981). Peers as behavior change agents for withdrawn classmates. In B. B. Lahey & A. E. Kazdin (Eds.), *Advances in Clinical Child Psychology* (pp. 167–198). Boston, MA: Springer.

Strain, P. S., & Odom, S. L. (1986). Peer social initiations: Effective intervention for social skills development of exceptional children. *Exceptional Children, 52*(6), 543–551.

Strang, J. F., Kenworthy, L., Daniolos, P., Case, L., Wills, M. C., Martin, A., & Wallace, G. L. (2012). Depression and anxiety symptoms in children and adolescents with autism spectrum disorders without intellectual disability. *Research in Autism Spectrum Disorders, 6*(1), 406–412.

Sugai, G., Fallon, L., & O'Keefe, B. (2012, November 2). SWPBS: Reconceptualizing & studying culture. *Center for Behavioral Education & Research*. Retrieved from https://www.mayinstitute.org/pdfs/presentations/PBIS2012%20Sugai%202.pdf

Sugai, G., & Lewis, T. J. (1996). Preferred and promising practices for social skills instruction. *Focus on Exceptional Children, 29*(4), 1–16.

Trembath, D., Balandin, S., Togher, L., & Stancliffe, R. J. (2009). Peer-mediated teaching and augmentative and alternative communication for preschool-aged children with autism. *Journal of Intellectual and Developmental Disability, 34*(2), 173–186.

U.S. Census Bureau. (2008). Percent of the projected population by race and Hispanic origin for the United States: 2010 to 2050 (NP2008-T6). Retrieved from http://www.census.gov/population/www/projections/summarytables.html.

Watkins, L., O'Reilly, M., Kuhn, M., Gevarter, C., Lancioni, G. E., Sigafoos, J., & Lang, R. (2015). A review of peer-mediated social interaction interventions for students with autism in inclusive settings. *Journal of Autism and Developmental Disorders, 45*(4), 1070–1083.

White, S. W., Keonig, K., & Scahill, L. (2007). Social skills development in children with autism spectrum disorders: A review of the intervention research. *Journal of Autism and Developmental Disorders, 37*(10), 1858–1868.

## 12

Peer Support Interventions in Inclusive Classrooms

ERIK W. CARTER ■

Most schools provide a rich array of social and learning opportunities to their students. Across a wide range of courses, students encounter rigorous instruction, learn relevant knowledge and skills, and develop relationships with their peers and teachers. Yet many students with severe disabilities still miss out on these important opportunities. Despite decades of policy and research advances, involvement in inclusive classes remains limited, access to the general education curriculum is inconsistently supported, and the friendships that can make school so enjoyable remain elusive (Carter, 2018; Kurth, Morningstar, & Kozleski, 2015). A constellation of barriers—including the expectations of educators, the attitudes of peers, the characteristics of students, the presence of paraprofessionals, and the service delivery models of schools—often coalesce to limited access to inclusive education. Indeed, students with autism, intellectual disability, and multiple disabilities regularly remain on the peripheries of everyday school life. How might educators ensure students with severe disabilities participate fully and meaningfully in the array of academic and social opportunities taking place throughout their schools?

INTERVENTION OVERVIEW

Peer support arrangements are an evidence-based approach for promoting school inclusion for children and youth with severe disabilities. This individualized intervention involves equipping one or more same-age peers to provide ongoing academic, social, and/or behavioral support to their classmate with severe disabilities, all while receiving ongoing guidance from a paraprofessional or teacher (Carter, Cushing, & Kennedy, 2009; Carter et al., 2015). A core planning team begins by identifying the supports and resources a student will need to participate in the various social and learning opportunities that comprise a particular inclusive class. In addition, they determine which of these supports might come from peers, which come from the general educator, and which come from special educators, paraprofessionals, or related service providers. Peers without disabilities who are enrolled in the same inclusive classroom are then invited to participate in the intervention as "peer partners." These peer partners participate in an initial orientation session addressing their roles and responsibilities related to working alongside their classmate. Likewise, the paraprofessional who will be assisting the students is taught how to facilitate the intervention in ways that attend to both fidelity and flexibility.

As the students begin working together throughout the semester, peer partners provide a variety of supports in ways that reflect the role of a classmate rather than a tutor. For example, peer partners might share their materials, collaborate on specific assignments, restate a key idea in a more understandable way, demonstrate how to complete an activity, or write down an answer the student shared through her augmentative and alternative communication (AAC) device. Socially, peer partners might encourage the student to contribute to group or class discussions, converse about shared interests while waiting for class to start, introduce the student to other classmates, reinforce appropriate use of an AAC device, model how to respond to a question, or walk to the next class together. These types of individualized supports are outlined in a peer support plan developed by the planning team and addressed during the initial orientation meeting (see Box 12.1). However, the paraprofessional is initially nearby to model or prompt those supports, to provide feedback to the students, to facilitate interactions, and to offer encouragement. As the students gain confidence working together, the paraprofessional gradually fades back her direct support and close proximity. Instead, she adopts a broader support role within a classroom by assisting the general education teacher as needed.

One attractive aspect of this intervention has been its impact on the outcomes of participating students. Nearly two dozen studies have evaluated these interventions across a wide range of classes (e.g., core academic, career and technical education, related arts, electives) and school levels (i.e., elementary, middle, and high school). For students with severe disabilities, participation in peer support arrangements have a host of social and academic benefits relative to receiving most or all of their support from an individually assigned paraprofessional or special educator (see reviews by Brock & Huber, 2017; Carter, 2017). Socially, students substantially increase their interactions with peers during class activities, which includes conversations about both their schoolwork (task-related interactions) and noninstructional topics (social-related interactions) such as afterschool events, friends, sports, and popular culture. Such interactions take place both with peer partners as well as with other classmates who are not formally involved in the intervention. Other social improvements have included increases in conversational initiations, reciprocity, and quality; greater use of

Box 12.1

Example Peer Support Arrangement Plan

Peer Support plan

Stephen is a fun and imaginative young man. Earth Science is a great class for him to work on some of his goals such as choice making, initiating and responding to peers, and improving his writing skills. Stephen loves to write with markers, use the computer, spell, and talk about food processing.

At the beginning of class . . .

STEPHEN COULD . . .	PEERS COULD . . .	THE FACILITATOR COULD . . .
• Get out materials for taking notes form the board • Converse with peers about a social topic • Say hello to peers	• Prompt Stephen to get out his notebook and copy down information; remind him we do this once every day • If he arrives late, let stephen copy down the board information from your notebook • Ask Stephen about his day, his hobbies, or his latest culinary adventures • Make sure to greet him when he arrives to class	• Encourage peers to engage Stephen in conversation and provide some conversation starts if peers are uncertain • Offer peers ideas for Stephen's participation and answers any questions peers may have • Look through class materials to see if any adaptations or modifications may be needed.

When there are lectures or whole instruction . . .

STEPHEN COULD . . .	PEERS COULD . . .	THE FACILITATOR COULD . . .
• Highlight key words and ideas in the PowerPoint handout • Write those key points in his notebook • Periodically compare his notes with those of his peers • Attend to the teacher as he presents information and leads discussion	• Prompt Stephen to highlights relevant information on the handout • Occasionally summarize key points to make sure Stephen is following along • Prompt Stephen to pay attention if he seems distracted	• Make sure Stephen and his peers have the handouts • Watch for body language Stephen is stressed • Check in to review the accuracy of Stephen's note • Work with the general educator or special educator to identify any needed adaptations or modifications for Stephen

(*continued*)

When there are small group or Lab activities . . .

STEPHEN COULD . . .	PEERS COULD . . .	THE FACILITATOR COULD . . .
• Listen and follow directions • Ask questions of specific peers who are sitting at his table • Make a choice about which parts of the lab activity he would like to take the lead on • Record all required subject matter in calendar of planner	• Involve stephen as much as possible in the lab by modeling key steps, checking for understanding, and asking for his input • Provide Stephen with choices about which aspects of the activity he will take the lead on • Ask Stephen directly to do something specific	• Observe to make sure Stephen remains involved in and contributes to his group • Redirect Stephen's questions to one of his peer partners. • Offer suggestions to the peers in Stephen's group if they are uncertain what he can do • Look for signs Stephen may engage in challenging behaviour, particularly if he is unsure of what is coming up next

Reprinted from Carter, E. W., Moss, C. K., Asmus, J., Fesperman, E., Cooney, M., Brock, M. E., . . . Vincent, L. (2015). Promoting inclusion, social connections, and learning through peer support arrangements. *Teaching Exceptional Children, 48*(1), 9–18.

AAC systems; access to new forms of social support; development of new social skills; and the emergence of new friendships. Academically, students with severe disabilities tend to maintain or actually increase their engagement in class as a result of working with peers. A few studies have even documented greater access to academic support, acquisition of individualized learning goals, and mastery of core curricular content.

The impact of peer support arrangements extends beyond students with severe disabilities. Peer partners also appear to benefit substantially from their involvement. Rather than falling behind in their learning, academically strong peers tend to maintain their already high levels of engagement and grades. In contrast, peers who are themselves struggling academically tend to become more engaged and improve their grades when serving as a peer partner (e.g., Cushing & Kennedy, 1997; Shukla et al., 1998, 1999). Moreover, peers often talk about internal transformations that can be more difficult to capture through direct observations. For example, peers have reported developing more positive attitudes toward individuals with disabilities, deepening their commitment to diversity, advocating more strongly for inclusion, experiencing personal growth (e.g., becoming more caring, confident, or self-aware), sharpening their advocacy skills, and making lasting friendships.

For educators, the peer support arrangements are attractive for their feasibility and flexibility (Carter, Dykstra Steinbrenner, & Hall, 2019). In a number of studies, general educators, special educators, paraprofessionals, and related service providers have indicated that the time and resource requirements for this intervention are reasonable, the implementation steps are understandable, and the fit with their classroom is strong. Moreover, they are motivated to use the approach with other students, and they affirm that participating students benefit from the intervention. Peer support arrangements are individualized interventions that can be adapted to meet the particular needs of a student within a particular general education classroom. This flexibility allows educators to adapt the intervention in ways that make sense for the student, fit within the classroom, and align with the curriculum being covered.

RECOMMENDATIONS FOR IMPLEMENTATION

Although peer support arrangements can be implemented in various ways, they draw upon common set of components. Each is described in the following text and detailed in Box 12.2.

Collaborating on Intervention Design

Best practices in inclusive education emphasize the importance of collaborative teaming. Implementing peer support arrangements should be established on the same strong foundation. Drawing upon the experience and perspectives of general educators, special educators, paraprofessionals, related service providers, and families can strengthen the design of the intervention, as well as ensure all aspects of inclusion are implemented well. For example, Biggs, Carter, and Gustafson (2017) formed intervention planning teams comprised of special educators, speech/language pathologists, paraprofessionals, and parents. The team worked together to (a) craft communication profiles for students with complex communication needs, (b) determine intervention goals, (c) identify the ways in which peer partners could support those goals, (d) develop a written peer support plan, and (e) identify strategies for ensuring students and peers would be successful.

Equipping Paraprofessionals to Facilitate the Intervention

Although general and special educators can facilitate peer support arrangements, this responsibility usually goes to paraprofessionals who are accompanying students with severe disabilities to general education classes. Therefore, it is essential that these staff receive sufficient training and guidance to carry out this responsibility effectively and confidently. Although the nature of this professional development will vary based on the prior experience of paraprofessionals and the settings in which they provide support, several topics may be valuable to address (Brock & Carter, 2016). These include (a) the rationale for establishing

Box 12.2

EXAMPLE PROCEDURAL FIDELITY CHECKLIST. Core Intervention Components Are Bolded. Flexible Components Are Listed Underneath Without Bold

☐ **Educational team collaboratively develops a written peer support plan**
☐ **Between 1–3 peers are recruited from within the same classroom**
☐ **Facilitators are taught how to support intervention delivery**
☐ **Facilitator addresses all relevant topics at the initial orientation meeting (e.g., rationale, background about student, support strategies)**
☐ **Facilitator supports peer partners and students as they work collaboratively**
  ☐ Facilitates interactions during class when appropriate
  ☐ Provides reminders/feedback to peer partners during and/or outside of class
  ☐ Provides praise and feedback to students with severe disabilities during or outside of class

☐ **Peer partners sit in close proximity to focus student throughout class**
  ☐ Students sit next to each other, when appropriate
  ☐ Students remain in close proximity to each other during out-of-seat activities
  ☐ During small-group and lab activities, students join the same group

☐ **Peer partners interact with the student throughout the class period**
  ☐ Peer partners exchange social amenities with the student (e.g., "Hi" or "See you later")
  ☐ Peer partners involve the student in interactions with other classmates

☐ **Peer partners assist the student academically throughout the class**
  ☐ Peer partners help the student participate in class activities
  ☐ Peer partners repeat or rephrase instructions for student
  ☐ Peer partners appropriately prompt the student
  ☐ Peer partners provide appropriate feedback to the student
  ☐ Students work together on classroom activities
  ☐ Students share class materials

☐ **Facilitators collect and teams review data addressing social and academic participation**

peer support arrangements, (b) the implementation steps, and (c) examples of strategies for facilitating peer interactions and academic support. This training generally takes two to three hours and may be enhanced by incorporating role play and follow-up coaching in the classroom.

Crafting Peer Support Plans

A written plan should be developed to delineate the ways in which students and their peer partners will work together throughout the semester, as well as the ways in which the paraprofessional can support this cooperative arrangement. A variety of planning tools have been described in the literature (e.g., Biggs et al., 2017; Carter et al., 2009). However, most tools encourage teams to consider (a) the different instructional formats used within the class (e.g., whole-group discussion, lectures, small-group projects, labs, independent work, downtime), (b) the ways in which the student with a severe disability will participate in each of these activities throughout the semester, (c) the social and academic supports peer partners will provide during each of these activities, and (d) the ways in which the general educator and paraprofessional will assist the students. Box 12.1 displays a completed example. Such plans are especially helpful for paraprofessionals, who often receive limited guidance on how best to support general education inclusion. Of course, the initial written plan can be updated and adapted throughout the semester as new ideas are shared and the curriculum changes.

Selecting Peer Partners

The selection of peer partners is a critical aspect of intervention planning and likely shapes the outcomes and enjoyment students experience. Teams will have to decide on the number of participating peers, the attributes these peers should possess, and the ways in which they will extend invitations. Researchers recommended involving two or three peers (Carter, 2017). Involving just one can leave a peer feeling overwhelmed and involving more than three can be disruptive or distracting. When deciding which peers from a particular class to invite, qualities to consider include the extent to which peers work well with others, would serve as a positive model, exhibit appropriate social skills, have shown interest in the student they would be supporting, would benefit socially or academically from serving in this role, has prior experience, and has good attendance (Brock & Huber, 2017). Another consideration is whether the peers share interests or experiences that might set the stage for a new friendship.

Invitations to peers can be extended in a variety of ways. For example, educators can identify and personally invite students whom they anticipate would be effective in this role. This approach often leads to subgroups of students (e.g., females, high-achieving students). In contrast, teachers can make general announcements about the availability of opportunities to serve in a support role in the class, accompanied by an invitation to learn more by talking with the teacher after class. This approach enables students to volunteer who educators might not initially have considered. Finally, some educators have adopted peer-mediated approaches for all students in their class (e.g., classwide peer tutoring) or rotated who serves as a peer partner over the course of the semester. These latter approaches increase the number of peers who have the opportunity to get to know and work closely with the student with severe disabilities.

Orienting Peer Partners

Once selected, peers attend an initial orientation designed to prepare them for their roles and responsibilities. The orientation session typically is led by a special educator and/or the paraprofessional and takes about one hour. These meetings can be held before or after school, during a study hall or advisory period, or over lunch. Often, peers may not know well (or know at all) the student with whom they will soon be working. A well-planned session should clarify the goals of peer support arrangements, provide peers with relevant information about their class-mate, address expectations related to this role, and guide them in which types of support that should and should not provide (Carter, Asmus, & Moss, 2014). A list of topics typically addressed in studies is displayed in Box 12.3. However, the emphasis is on teaching peer partners strategies for supporting the communi-cation, social participation, and/or academic engagement of their classmate. For example, peers may be shown how to elicit initiations, prompt use of an AAC de-vice, extend conversational turns, redirect inappropriate conversations, reinforce conversation attempts, or model particular social skills. Likewise, they may learn strategies for promoting academic engagement through systematic instruction, providing feedback, reviewing class content, highlighting key concepts, or mod-eling self-management strategies. The written peer support plan guides much of this discussion and ideas generated by peers can be added.

Facilitating Shared Work and Interactions

Throughout the semester, the student with severe disabilities sits next to her peer partners and works collaboratively with them on various class activities, as delineated in the written plan and approved by the general educator. During the first couple of weeks, the paraprofessional might remain nearby the students, modeling the strategies outlined on the plan, answering questions of peers, and encouraging the group as they work together. Gradually, the peers assume a more prominent and independent role in assisting the student academically and so-cially, as they might any other classmate. As the group gains experience working together and becomes more familiar with one another, the paraprofessional sys-tematically fades back her close proximity and support of the students. Rather than serving as the primary or exclusive source of support to the student with

Box 12.3

EXAMPLE PEER SUPPORT ORIENTATION TOPICS

- Reasons for involving peers in supporting their classmate with severe disabilities
- Specific goals associated with a peer support arrangement (e.g., increasing the number of peers with whom the student interacts, developing new friendships, increasing independence and involvement in class, acquiring particular skills or knowledge)
- Information about the strengths, interests, talents, and school involvement of their partner with severe disabilities
- The educational goals of the student they are supporting, described generally in ways that do not breach confidentiality
- The importance of maintaining privacy and using respectful language
- Basic instructional and support strategies (e.g., modeling, reinforcing, prompting, and constructive feedback)
- Strategies for interacting with someone who uses assistive technology or an AAC system
- Ideas for motivating and encouraging their partner
- Ideas for increasing interactions between the student and other classmates
- Guidance on when to seek assistance from educators or paraprofessionals
- Any other responsibilities and expectations specific to their roles in a particular classroom including stated emphasis on attending to and completing their own classroom work

severe disabilities—a widely used approach in contemporary schools—she shifts to a more facilitative role. This might involve modeling ways of interacting with someone who has complex communication challenges, calling attention to things students have in common, redirecting questions back to students, teaching needed social skills, or interpreting unusual or idiosyncratic behaviors (Carter et al., 2015). Even as she shifts to a broader support role within the classroom, the paraprofessional keeps an eye on the social and academic participation of all participating students. She also collects information on the fidelity with which the intervention is being implementing (see Box 12.2).

Evaluating the Impact

Ongoing evaluation enables the planning team to determine whether peer support arrangements are working as intended or require further refinement. A data-driven approach that incorporates both summative and formative data can provide valuable insights into the implementation and impact of peer support arrangements (Huber & Carter, 2016). Observations are the most objective approach for capturing the impact on students with severe disabilities. Data can be collected by paraprofessionals on the students' social interactions (e.g., frequency, appropriateness, reciprocity, quality), communication device use, social skills, academic engagement, class participation, and individualized goal progress. In addition, feedback should be sought from adults, peers, and students involved in the intervention. Educators and paraprofessionals can be asked about (a) the ways in which peer support arrangements are impacting students and peers, (b) the extent to which the intervention fits well within the classroom, and (c) their ideas for better supporting the student in class. Peer partners can be asked about (a) the nature of their relationship with their classmate, (b) the strategies they feel are and are not working well, (c) the ways they are personally benefiting from their involvement, and (d) any additional information or assistance they would consider helpful. Students with disabilities can be asked (a) about their experiences receiving support from their peers, (b) whether they enjoy spending time with these classmates, and (c) if they would like to continue receiving support from peers. This information can be gathered through interviews or surveys.

CONSIDERATIONS OF DIVERSITY AND EQUITY

Peer support arrangements were initially developed as a pathway for addressing the persistence of segregated educational placements for students with severe disabilities (Carter & Kennedy, 2006). Students with intellectual disability, autism, and multiple disabilities have long had limited involvement in regular education courses alongside their peers without disabilities (Kurth et al., 2015). By supporting meaningful access to the general education curriculum right alongside other students in neighborhood schools, peer support interventions challenge prevailing expectations about what students with severe disabilities can achieve and create a more effective learning environment for these students. Indeed, this intervention approach is now widely advocated as an important pathway for advancing inclusive education in primary and secondary schools (Carter, 2018; Olson, Leko, & Roberts, 2016).

The influence of these interventions on peers without disabilities is also important to consider. Perhaps more than any other factor, current attitudes are shaped by prior experiences (Scior & Werner, 2016). Peers who have the opportunity to meet, learn alongside, and develop relationships with their classmates who have severe disabilities often leave these experiences with substantially different views and expectations about individuals with disabilities. As future coworkers, employers, community leaders, and neighbors, these early encounters with inclusion can shape their later encounters in adulthood. Efforts to create a more just and equitable society for individuals with severe disabilities may have some of their origins in the classrooms and schools of today.

As the demographic profiles of schools across the country continue to change, however, it is essential that practices recommended in the literature work well for the diversity of students with and without disabilities who attend these schools. Peer support arrangements have been evaluated in schools that vary widely with regards to both community type (e.g., rural, suburban, urban) and locale (e.g., California, Kansas, Hawaii, North Carolina, Ohio, Tennessee, Texas, Wisconsin). Moreover, the students with severe disabilities involved in this research have reflected a breadth of racial/ethnic backgrounds. Yet continued research is needed to further expand the diversity of students involved in this research and deepen the field's understanding of how best to individualize these interventions in ways that attend to the cultural and contextual needs of students.

Peer support arrangements offer a powerful approach for helping students with severe disabilities access the myriad social and learning opportunities available within inclusive classrooms. Moreover, these very practical interventions can positively shape the attitudes, expectations, and learning of those peers without disabilities who participate. Along with other peer-mediated interventions described in this book, peer support arrangements can help advance the goals of inclusion and equity for a group of students who so often are excluded from everyday educational experiences in their schools. However, adopting these interventions in widespread ways will require strong investments in preservice training and ongoing professional development.

CONCLUSION

Expanding access to inclusive education has been a long-standing focus of legislative, research, and advocacy initiatives. Peer support arrangements provide an effective and feasible pathway for advancing this goal in elementary and secondary schools. By equipping and engaging peers to support the academic and social participation of their classmates, students with severe disabilities participate more fully and meaningfully in the rich social and learning opportunities available throughout their schools. Moreover, the perspectives and personal attributes of peers can be positive impacted by their ongoing involvement.

REFERENCES

Biggs, E. E., Carter, E. W., & Gustafson, J. R. (2017). Efficacy of collaborative planning and peer support arrangements to increase peer interaction and AAC use in inclusive classrooms. *American Journal on Intellectual and Developmental Disabilities, 122*, 25–48.

Brock, M. E., & Carter, E. W. (2016). Efficacy of teachers training paraprofessionals to implement peer support arrangements. *Exceptional Children, 82*, 354–371.

Brock, M. E., & Huber, H. B. (2017). Are peer support arrangements an evidence-based practice? A systematic review. *Journal of Special Education, 51*, 150–163.

Carter, E. W. (2017). The promise and practice of peer support arrangements for students with intellectual and developmental disabilities. *International Review of Research in Developmental Disabilities, 52*, 141–174.

Carter, E. W. (2018). Supporting the social lives of secondary students with severe disabilities: Critical elements for effective intervention. *Journal of Emotional and Behavioral Disorders, 26*, 52–61.

Carter, E. W., Asmus, J. M., & Moss, C. K. (2014). Peer support interventions to support inclusive education. In J. McLeskey, N. Waldron, F. Spooner, & B. Algozzone (Eds.), *Handbook of research and practice for effective inclusive schools* (pp. 377–394). New York, NY: Routledge.

Carter, E. W., Asmus, J., Moss, C. K., Amirault, K. A., Biggs, E. E., Bolt, D., . . . Wier, K. (2016). Randomized evaluation of peer supports arrangements to support the inclusion of high school students with severe disabilities. *Exceptional Children, 82*, 209–233.

Carter, E. W., Cushing, L. S., & Kennedy, C. H. (2009). *Peer support strategies for improving all students' social lives and learning.* Baltimore, MD: Paul H. Brookes.

Carter, E. W., Dykstra Steinbrenner, J. R., & Hall, L. J. (2019). Exploring feasibility and fit: Peer-mediated interventions for high school students with autism spectrum disorder. *School Psychology Review, 48*, 157–169.

Carter, E. W., & Kennedy, C. H. (2006). Promoting access to the general curriculum using peer support strategies. *Research and Practice for Persons with Severe Disabilities, 31*(4), 284–292.

Carter, E. W., Moss, C. K., Asmus, J., Fesperman, E., Cooney, M., Brock, M. E., . . . Vincent, L. (2015). Promoting inclusion, social connections, and learning through peer support arrangements. *Teaching Exceptional Children, 48*(1), 9–18.

Cushing, L. S., & Kennedy, C. H. (1997). Academic effects on students without disabilities who serve as peer supports for students with disabilities in general education classrooms. *Journal of Applied Behavior Analysis, 30*, 139-152.

Huber, H. B., & Carter, E. W. (2016). Data-driven individualization in peer-mediated interventions for students with ASD: A literature review. *Review Journal of Autism and Developmental Disorders, 3*, 239–253.

Kurth, J. A., Morningstar, M. E., & Kozleski, E. B. (2015). The persistence of highly restrictive special education placements for students with low-incidence disabilities. *Research and Practice for Persons with Severe Disabilities, 39*, 227–239.

Olson, A., Leko, M. M., Roberts, C. A. (2016). Providing students with severe disabilities access to the general education curriculum. *Research and Practice for Persons with Severe Disabilities, 41*, 143–157.

Scior, K., & Werner, S. (Eds.). (2016). *Intellectual disability and stigma: Stepping out from the margins.* London, England: Palgrave McMillan.

Shukla, S., Kennedy, C. H., & Cushing, L. S. (1998). Adult influence on the participation of peers without disabilities in peer support programs. *Journal of Behavioral Education, 8*, 397–413.

Shukla, S., Kennedy, C. H., & Cushing, L. S. (1999). Intermediate school students with severe disabilities: Supporting their social participation in general education classrooms. *Journal of Positive Behavior Interventions, 1*, 130–140.

## 13

Peer-Mediated Pivotal Response Training

DACIA M. MCCOY, CHELSEA RITTER,
AND J. MEREDITH MURPHY ■

Teachers and parents are increasingly aware of the deficits in social competencies of individuals diagnosed with developmental disabilities, including autism spectrum disorder (ASD), which may become barriers to interacting with same-aged peers. Significant time and resources are allocated to providing early intervention and evidence-based instruction, but social behaviors are complex to teach and often fail to generalize (McGee, Almeida, Sulzer-Azaroff, & Feldman, 1992). The educational system and community are becoming increasingly integrated, allowing for the implementation of interventions that are designed to explicitly teach and reinforce the skills necessary for positive social behaviors in natural settings, thus promoting generalization of skills and allowing all members to engage in meaningful peer interactions.

OVERVIEW OF PIVOTAL RESPONSE TRAINING

Pivotal Response Training (PRT) is an evidence-based, naturalistic, behavioral approach designed to teach critical skills to individuals with ASD and other pervasive developmental disorders. PRT targets core, underlying areas called pivotal behaviors, which generalize and trigger improvements in many other target behaviors that are common in individuals with ASD. The keystone pivotal behavior of PRT is motivation. Early PRT research showed more efficient behavior change and greater client social acceptability of interventions when motivational components were incorporated in treatment (Koegel & Mentis, 1985). In addition to motivation, PRT is being used today to target pivotal behaviors such as responsivity to multiple cues, self-management, and social initiations.

By targeting these pivotal areas, a growing body of evidence supports a PRT approach in targeting several language functions, social skills, academic skills, and problem behaviors.

The PRT approach is comprised of a number of different components that are evidence-based in both isolation and combination. Some core components of PRT include clear and appropriate prompts, child choice, contingent reinforcement, turn-taking, and multiple cues. Characteristically, PRT strategies are implemented during existing routines and in everyday settings in order to facilitate the generalization of positive behaviors to new environments, tasks, and people. This natural implementation makes PRT feasible for parents, siblings, and peers to implement, thus allowing for frequent practice opportunities without requiring the same intensive, structured environment that may be necessary for other effective interventions (e.g., Discrete Trial Training; Koegel & Koegel, 2012). Given this naturalistic approach and that children spend most of the day at school, PRT is well suited to take place in a school environment.

Peer-mediated PRT (PM-PRT) is the variation of PRT in which a typically developing peer serves as the interventionist. PM-PRT is more naturalistic and more cost-effective, and promotes greater generalization than if adults were implementing the same procedures (Harper, Symon, & Frea, 2008; Pierce & Schreibman, 1995). The approach is typically used to improve language, attending skills, play behaviors, and social skills in individuals with ASD. PM-PRT has the added benefit of fostering inclusion practices among typically developing classmates.

RECOMMENDATIONS FOR IMPLEMENTATION

This section will expand on the four key steps of PM-PRT: (a) information gathering and baseline data collection, (b) selecting and training typically developing peer interventionists, (c) intervention implementation and data collection, and (d) supporting intervention procedures over time. This structure allows you to tailor the intervention based on the strategies that are most relevant for the identified target behaviors and skills.

Step 1: Information Gathering and Baseline Data Collection

The first step is gathering information that will lay the groundwork for intervention implementation. Interviewing stakeholders such as parents and teachers can help to identify the behaviors that will be targeted with PM-PRT. Commonly selected general target behaviors include language, play behavior, social skills, or joint attention. The identified behavior should then be narrowed to a specific skill that is observable and measurable, such as initiates assistance-seeking phrases. This interview can also include prioritizing behaviors from most to least important and is a good time to discuss goals for PM-PRT and stakeholder availability to collaborate with intervention implementation. In addition to asking the target child his or her preferences, stakeholders are a good resource to help determine the target child's favorite toys, activities, and topics of conversation. It will also be important to directly observe the target child in the environment selected to determine feasibility of PM-PRT and to notice what happens before and after the behaviors to guide the selection of effective strategies. You will note what toys are available, the size of the environment, and if the space is conducive to play behavior.

The next step is collecting baseline data on the behavior(s) that will be targeted during PM-PRT. Selection of a proper measurement system at this point is key, as the same measurement system will be used during baseline and intervention to record student progress. Once the target behavior, goals, and baseline data have been gathered, the strategies that will be used during PM-PRT should be selected. A menu of common strategies utilized in PM-PRT is listed in Table 13.1; however, it is not necessary to utilize each strategy during intervention implementation. Peer interventionists can be used to implement one or two strategies, or peers can implement comprehensive treatment packages (Gonzalez-Lopez & Kamps, 1997). Rather than utilizing every PM-PRT strategy, it is more important that strategies are selected based upon student goals. "Take turns" and "model appropriate behavior" would be important strategies to prioritize when the goal is to develop play behavior, whereas "providing a clear opportunity to respond" and "encourage and extend conversation" would be more appropriate when the goal is the development of language. "Follow target student choice of tasks" and "direct reinforcement" are two key components of PM-PRT designed to enhance motivation that should be among the selected strategies in almost every case.

In addition to selecting strategies based on goals, strategies should be selected based upon feasibility of implementation and likelihood of success. Age and developmental level of the target child and peer interventionist will play a key part in determining which strategy is feasible. An older or advanced peer interventionist would be better suited to implement more complex strategies such as "vary task difficulty" and "provide multiple cues." While appropriate training can help a peer learn to speak in such a way that is easiest for the target student to understand, "narrate play" or "encouraging conversation" may not be the best strategies to be implemented by a peer interventionist who speaks rapidly, in long sentences, or uses metaphors frequently.

Step 2: Selecting and Training Peer Interventionists

Some settings may naturally incorporate "buddies" such as classrooms or camps while others may require more planning. Regardless of the setting, identifying peers that are likely to be successful and supporting the pairs or triads throughout the process are critical components of intervention planning. Peers may be selected based on teacher recommendation of students who are cooperative and friendly (Pierce & Schreibman, 1995) or by asking the target student about

Table 13.1. DESCRIPTIONS AND EXAMPLES OF STRATEGIES COMMONLY USED
IN PM-PRT

Strategy	Description	Example(s)
Gain attention	Peer gains attention of target student. Eyes of target student should be looking at peer or at current activity. This step ensures the target student is practicing attending skills and is ready for prompts by peer interventionist.	"Hey, Ben! Watch me."
Model appropriate behavior	Peer engages in developmentally appropriate social skills and play behavior when interacting with target student.	Peer models play language: "I'll use the green car. Jess likes yellow, so she can play with the school bus." Peer interventionist acts out a scripted or unscripted puppet show.
Take turns	Peer manages a socially appropriate give and take interaction with target student. This strategy promotes sharing and appropriate play behavior.	"I will play with it for 30 seconds, and then you play with it for 30 seconds." "Let's spin the wheel to see who goes first!" "My turn." "Your turn."
Narrate play	Peer verbally describes what is happening as he or she is playing to provide target student with exposure to language	Peer describes how to build a Lego castle as she is building it. Peer discusses the color of the Lego, the number of dots on top of the Lego, where the piece fits, what it will help build, etc. "I am jumping."
Provide a clear opportunity to respond	Target student is provided with a clear opportunity to respond to a developmentally appropriate question or a cue from the peer interventionist. Each opportunity to respond is a learning opportunity for the target student. Also, clear cues from the peer helps data collectors to measure and monitor the target student's responsivity to cues/prompts.	"Your turn, Timothy." "What puzzle piece fits here?" "Wow! Look at that big fish!"

Table 13.1. CONTINUED

Strategy	Description	Example(s)
Encourage and extend conversation	When target student is engaging in conversation, peer continues conversation with questions and nonverbal body language (e.g., nodding, smiling). To encourage conversation, peer withholds an object from target student until student emits verbal response related to that object or activity. Peer can begin conversation by describing tangible items in the environment.	"Your favorite movie is *The Incredibles*? I like that movie too! Which character is your favorite?" "Tell me which action figure you want, and then I will give it to you." "Good job saying 'ba'. Here is the ball." "This black rock looks like a heart to me. What do you think?"
Follow target student choice of tasks	Peer must follow activities initiated by the target student. Play items and tasks must be varied frequently. Engaging in various activities the target student finds interesting keeps motivation to take part in social activities high. *Note:* It would be beneficial to conduct a preference assessment of the target student's favorite items for environmental planning and to promote play.	Peer interventionist can ask, "What would you like to play with today?" for a target student with more advanced play skills. For most target students, the peer should provide 2–3 toys or activities preferred by the target student: "Do you want to play on the swing set or on the monkey bars?"
Vary task difficulty	Prompts, activities, and play should vary from easy to difficult. This strategy helps students acquire new skills and build fluency and mastery of acquired skills.	"We finished this 10 piece puzzle, how about trying a 20 piece puzzle together? Would you like the Minnie Mouse or Donald Duck puzzle?" "We worked so hard to finish that worksheet. Do you want to color?"
Provide multiple cues	Peer provides two or more aspects of a toy or activity to teach object properties and promote language. When possible, peer provides prompts that require the target student to talk about object properties.	"Let's go sit under the *cool, shaded oak* tree." "Do you think she hid the treasure *under* the *wooden desk*, or on *top* of the *white shelf*?" "*Green* dino, or *red* dino?"

(continued)

Table 13.1. Continued

Strategy	Description	Example(s)
Provide direct reinforcement of attempts contingent on child's behavior	Peer verbally reinforces target student for responding or attempting to respond to a cue, question, or prompt. Reinforcement should be natural, contingent on target student behavior, and immediately administered after the positive behavior. Reinforcement increases the likelihood that the positive behavior of the target student will occur in the future.	"I like the colors you used in your picture." "Thanks for sharing." "I like your idea of taking the dolls to the grocery store. Let's go!" "Good job asking nicely for this toy. Here you go!"

preferred classmates (Brock, Dueker, & Barczak, 2018). Additional criteria such as regular attendance, proficiency in English, strong social and communication skills, and eagerness to volunteer to support or assist others should also be considered (Harper et al., 2008). Allowing typically developing peers to self-select by volunteering to participate as a buddy is also an option depending on the age of the peers (Suhrheinrich, 2011).

Training multiple peers to serve as alternates in case the peer is absent or not available is advised and has demonstrated the promotion of skill generalization (McGee et al., 1992). A ratio of two peers to one target student is recommended. The use of triads allows for increased modeling of typical peer interactions, including small group activities. Triads also allow for multiple peers to share responsibility for strategy implementation, allowing them to work together to engage the target child (Harper et al., 2008). Working in pairs or groups may also increase the peers' ability to socialize and learn from other peers' techniques (Pierce & Schreibman, 1995).

After strategies have been determined, the teacher should meet individually with peer interventionists to begin training. The teacher should select an appropriate environment for peer training to occur, with an ideal setting that has minimal distractions. Over time, the peer should be trained and supported in the natural setting (e.g., the playground) where the intervention will occur (Pierce & Schreibman, 2007). The amount of time it will take to train peers may vary, but it is recommended that peers attempt the strategies with the target student following training on basic intervention concepts (Pierce & Schreibman, 2007).

An important first step is to discuss the goal of the intervention. The teacher can share with the student why they have been chosen to be part of the intervention, (e.g., they are a role model in the classroom), and how they can help a friend in the classroom learn new skills by playing and making friends (Pierce & Schreibman, 2007). Additionally, discussion of confidentiality, appropriate language the peer should use with the target student, the role of the teacher, and how they will support the peer should be included (Brock et al., 2018). The teacher can then begin the process of instructing the peer on PRT strategies and implementation guidelines. An example of a training session can be found in the intervention training script (Appendix A). The script can be altered to include strategies specific to the needs of the target student and feasibility for the peer and teacher. Pierce and Schreibman (2007) make note that some target students may display excessive preoccupation with specific toys or objects and consideration of whether or not to include these items into the environment is necessary. It is recommended to leave highly preferred items out of the environment if it may be too distracting. In contrast, access to these items may be a successful strategy to begin the interaction so the target student associates the peer trainer with a preferred item or activity.

Training sessions vary in frequency and duration, ranging from one 45-min session (Brock et al., 2018) to seven 20-min sessions across seven school days (Harper et al., 2008). A typical training session includes four key steps to train the peer on antecedent strategies (e.g., gaining target student's attention) and consequence strategies (e.g., providing reinforcement to target student): instruction, modeling, role play, and cue cards (see example in Appendix A). Instruction includes reviewing the skill with the peer. For gaining attention, the teacher can verbally explain that the peer will need to gain target student's attention by making eye contact and saying the target student's name. Then, the teacher will model the skill with the peer.

Next, the peer will practice the skill of gaining attention, with the teacher role-playing as the target student. This is a good opportunity to provide examples and nonexamples to allow the peer practice opportunities on how to handle various situations. For instance, if the student says the teacher's name, the teacher could intentionally not make eye contact as this is a situation they may encounter during the actual intervention. Lastly, the teacher should review the cue card(s) with the peer. Cue cards are used to remind the peer about each strategy and can be written statements or in picture format. An example cue card is provided in Appendix A. Additional examples of cue cards can be found in the "How to Be a Great Friend: Peer Manual" developed by Pierce and Schreibman (2007). The teacher should repeat the previous steps for each strategy that is covered during the training session(s). Pierce and Schreibman developed a PM-PRT training manual that has additional examples and explanations related to implementation.

One additional strategy to consider is training peers to handle potentially difficult behaviors. Teachers can review behaviors that the peer trainer may encounter, such as aggression, and train the student to back away and ask for help from an adult (Harper et al., 2008); however, it is ideal to have an adult nearby during intervention implementation to assist with intervention steps or possibly mediate any negative interactions.

Step 3: Intervention Implementation and Data Collection

After completion of peer training, the intervention can be implemented. Each target student should be introduced to their assigned peer trainer(s). Every day before intervention implementation, the teacher should provide the peer with the cue cards and review the strategies to be implemented with the target student (Pierce & Schreibman, 1995). It is recommended to have a teacher or another adult interventionist observe the PM-PRT implementation process each time it is implemented to collect data on target student behavior change, to note implementation adherence, to manage potentially negative interactions, and to provide feedback and praise to the peer trainers (Pierce & Schreibman, 1995). An example adherence data collection form, which can be used to assist in providing feedback to the peer, can be found in Appendix B.

Step 4: Support Intervention Procedures Over Time

Even when the peer interventionist regularly engages in intervention procedures with success, teachers should provide ongoing coaching through continued discussion with peers about their role (Brock et al., 2018). Regular coaching meetings with peer trainers allows for continued modeling and review of cue cards or scripts prior to play sessions, provision of supplemental support, regular feedback, and intervention acceptability check-ins. Ongoing monitoring of intervention adherence supports high-quality intervention implementation and identifies areas to address during coaching meetings. Even peers that initially demonstrate a high level of adherence may drift over time and supplemental supports such as integration of new activities or the addition of a prompting device (e.g., vibrating timer) may be required.

Furthermore, incorporating reinforcement is a strategy that can be added to the PM-PRT intervention to increase motivation of the peer trainer to continue engagement in the intervention process. For example, a token economy system in which a peer earns a token or tally for intervention administration can later be turned in for predetermined reinforcers that can be used to award the peer for completing the intervention each day (Maggin, Chafouleas, Goddard, & Johnson, 2011). The reinforcers should be something the peer likes, such as access to a preferred activity, a homework pass, etc.

Ongoing data collection will indicate when the intervention may need to be faded or intensified. Often PM-PRT is used in combination with other interventions to support social skill development. It may be necessary to also provide direct instruction through a social skills training and incorporate additional strategies such as video modeling (Pierce & Schreibman, 2007). PRT is a naturalistic intervention conducive to generalization (Pierce & Schreibman, 1995), meaning that students will likely show improvements across various behaviors, settings, toys, people, etc. Due to this, support and coaching may be faded after the peer becomes more fluent in the skills or even begins engaging with the target student automatically, without intervention supports in place.

CONSIDERATIONS OF DIVERSITY AND EQUITY

PM-PRT is an intervention approach that uniquely addresses barriers and supports individuals from differing backgrounds and ranges of ability. Research has demonstrated the effectiveness of PRT strategies for students of all ages, genders, and ethnicities (Baker-Ericzen, Stahmer, & Burns, 2007) with a growing research base for PM-PRT (Boudreau, Corkum, Meko, & Smith, 2015). In the following text, considerations for implementation will be discussed.

Facilitates Inclusion

The implementation of PM-PRT integrates within an inclusion model of supports and offers a variety of benefits to the target child, peer interventionist, and teacher or parent. First, the intervention directly teaches and models targeted behaviors for development in significant areas such as initiating social interactions and verbal skills. The strategies are positive, expand on the target child's motivation, and support relationships with same-aged peers. Second, PM-PRT provides typically developing peers with training opportunities to learn more about the unique strengths and interests of the target child in addition to strategies to initiate friendships and interactions with individuals with different needs. The PM-PRT training and the strategies learned may generalize to other individuals, reduce fears or uncertainty, and model an inclusive approach for others. Finally, the peer trainer model produces minimal, if any, economic strain on a school budget and may be a viable and more socially appropriate alternative to individualized assistance from an adult, which can form prompt dependence and restrict natural peer interactions (Harper et al., 2008).

Extensions to Home Setting

Although this chapter has focused on peer implementation, environmental settings may impact PRT implementation. Research has indicated that training a child in their natural environment is a critical component of PRT and necessary for skill generalization (Koegel & Koegel, 2006). Additionally, training in multiple settings can positively impact generalization of learned skills (Pierce & Schriebman, 1995). Furthermore, positive outcomes and improvements in communication skills have been seen when PRT-trained parents implemented PRT strategies with their children (Coolican, Smith, & Bryson, 2010). To facilitate increased practice opportunities and support generalization, parents may teach these strategies to peers in naturally occurring or structured playgroups. Parents have a distinctive opportunity to support their child with ASD in gaining exposure to peer interactions that may lead to long-term positive social outcomes (Koegel & Koegel, 2006). Similarly, siblings typically spend even more time together than with their parents and, for some, may be the longest-lasting relationship (Kramer, Hall, Heller, 2013). Training siblings to use the PM-PRT strategies may provide social benefits for the sibling diagnosed with a disability and support overall sibling interactions.

Addressing Barrier of Language Deficits

Even though research demonstrates intervention effectiveness across a range of ability levels, research also suggests that students with limited verbal language in their repertoire (e.g., single words or speech approximations) may exhibit greater gains than students considered non-verbal (Pierce & Schreibman, 2007). This may be relevant when determining readiness for the intervention or may be a potential barrier to address. Furthermore, additional consideration may be necessary when training peers to interact with target students with limited verbal language, as verbal responses from the target student may facilitate the comfort level of peer interventionists and serve as reinforcement (Pierce & Schreibman, 2007).

Respect for Social Preference

As previously discussed, selecting appropriate peers is an important aspect to the success of the intervention. In addition to assessing the peer interventionists' willingness to serve as a peer, efforts should also be made to assess the target child's friend preference. This may be done through direct observation of dyad interactions. When observing, Pierce and Schreibman (2007) suggest asking the following questions: "a) Does the peer trainer seem interested in the target child, or does he/she wait for your instruction? b) Does the target child actively run away from the peer trainer? c) Does the target child allow the peer trainer to remain in proximity? d) Does the target child appear more anxious in the presence of the peer trainer?" (p. 4). It may also be appropriate to consider similar interests of peers, provide ongoing monitoring of peer dynamics, and provide choice to the target child regarding which peer he or she would like to play.

CONCLUSION

In conclusion, PM-PRT is an intervention that directly targets skills such as communication and motivation to initiate social interactions that are commonly critical areas of development for individuals diagnosed with ASD or other pervasive developmental disorders. Strategies implemented by peer interventionists provide opportunities for typical exchanges among same-aged peers that are guided by the target child's interests and strengths. The naturalistic approach is not only beneficial for the target students, but is also a valuable experience for the peer trainers and has been found to be an efficient and economical intervention across a variety of settings.

REFERENCES

Baker-Ericzen, M. J., Stahmer, A. C., & Burns, A. (2007). Child demographics associated with outcomes in a community-based pivotal response training program. *Journal of Positive Behavior Interventions, 9*(1), 52–60.

Boudreau, A. M., Corkum, P., Meko, K., & Smith, I. M. (2015). Peer mediated pivotal response treatment for young children with autism spectrum disorders: A systematic review. *Canadian Journal of School Psychology, 30*(3), 218–235.

Brock, M. E., Dueker, S. A., Barczak, M. A. (2018). Brief report: Improving social outcomes for students with autism at recess through peer-mediated pivotal response training. *Journal of Autism and Development, 48*, 2224–2230.

Coolican, J., Smith, I. M., & Bryson, S. E. (2010). Brief parent training in pivotal response treatment for preschoolers with autism. *Journal of Child Psychology and Psychiatry, 51*(12), 1321–1330.

Gonzalez-Lopez, A., & Kamps, D. M. (1997). Social skills training to increase social interactions between children with autism and their typical peers. *Focus on Autism and Other Developmental Disabilities, 12*(1), 2–14.

Harper, C. B., Symone, J. B. G., & Frea, W. D. (2008). Recess is time-in: Using peers to improve social skills of children with autism. *Journal of Autism Developmental Disorders, 38*, 815–826.

Koegel, R. L., & Mentis, M. (1985). Motivation in childhood autism: Can they or won't they? *Journal of Child Psychology and Psychiatry, 26*, 185–191.

Koegel, R. L., & Koegel, L. K. (2006). *Pivotal response treatments for autism: Communication, social, & academic development*. Baltimore, MD: Paul H. Brookes.

Koegel, R. L., & Koegel, L. K. (2012). *The PRT pocket guide: Pivotal response treatment for autism spectrum disorders*. Baltimore, MD: Paul H. Brookes.

Kramer, J., Hall, A., Heller, T. (2013). Reciprocity and social capital in sibling relationships of people with disabilities. *Intellectual and Developmental Disabilities, 51*(6), 482–495.

Maggin, D. M., Chafouleas, S. M., Goddard, K. M., Johnson, A. H. (2011). A systematic evaluation of token economies as a classroom management tool for students with challenging behavior. *Journal of School Psychology, 49*, 529–554.

McGee, G., Almeida, C., Sulzer-Azaroff, B., Feldman, R. S. (1992). Promoting reciprocal interactions via peer incidental teaching. *Journal of Applied Behavior Analysis, 25*, 117–126.

Pierce, K., & Schriebman, L. (1995). Increasing complex social behavior in children with autism: Effects of peer-implemented pivotal response training. *Journal of Applied Behavior Analysis, 28*, 285–295.

Pierce, K., & Schreibman, L. (2007). Kids helping kids: Teaching typical children to enhance play and social skills of their friends with autism and other PDDs: A manual. Retrieved from https://medschool.ucsd.edu/som/neurosciences/centers/autism/pages/default.aspx

Suhrheinrich, J. (2011). Training teachers to use pivotal response training with children with autism: Coaching as a critical component. *Teacher Education and Special Education, 34*(4), 339–349.

Suhrheinrich, J., Stahmer, A., Reed, S., Schreibman, L, Reisinger, E., & Mandell, D. (2013). Implementation challenged in translating pivotal response training into community settings. *Journal of Autism and Developmental Disorders, 43*(12), 2970–2976.

APPENDIX A
PIVOTAL RESPONSE TRAINING—PEER TRAINING SCRIPT

Materials: cue cards, examples of activities the peer's friend may want to engage in **Steps:**

1. Discuss goal of PRT with peer. This can include information about why they have been selected to work with a friend and what their role will look like. For example, explain that they will have the chance to help another friend in the class/environment to learn to play/interact with others.
2. Components when training the student on each antecedent and consequence strategy:
   - Instruction
     - Trainer reviews each skill and provides an example
     - Peer provides explanation in their own words with an example
   - Modeling
     - Trainer models each skill
   - Role-Play
     - With and without target peer with feedback provided by trainer
     - In natural setting with typically available materials
   - Cue Cards
     - Peer has access to cards as a brief reminder (words and/or pictures) of each strategy that will be accessible during play sessions
     - Review cue cards prior to session
3. Example of training peer to *gain attention*
   - Instruction
     - Verbally tell the peer that prior to working with their friend, they must first gain their attention by saying the friend's name and making eye contact
   - Modeling
     - Show the peer this by saying the peer's name and making eye contact
     - Ask the peer to practice with you (trainer)
   - Role-Play
     - Continue practicing this in the environment with the peer by having them gain your attention. Provide examples and nonexample opportunities where the peer may have to say your name more than once to ensure they have your attention and times when you face them but do not make eye contact.
   - Cue Cards
     - Show the peer the cue card associated with Gaining Attention and tell the peer that they will have this when they play with their friend to help remind them what to do

4. Apply the steps from the example in step 3 to the following strategies/skills:

- **Model Appropriate Behavior**—the peer provides examples of how and when to engage in play situations
- **Narrate Play**—the peer describes play actions as they are doing them
- **Provide a Clear Opportunity to Respond**— the peer should provide clear statements and cues that are at or just above their friend's developmental level
- **Encourage and Extend Conversation**—the peer can ask the target student if they can play with an item or offer a toy to the target student and share that it is their turn now
- **Vary Task Difficulty**—this will likely be specific to each friend of the peer based on social goals. The peer should offer their friend different options to play (e.g., ask if they would like to play on the slide or in the sandbox while on the playground)
- **Follow Target Student Choice of Tasks**—peer to follow student's lead, provide choices of activities, and materials. This may vary based on social goals
- **Take Turns**—peer models and initiates taking turns with the student
- **Provide Multiple Cues**—instruction should include multiple components to increase learner's ability to be aware of multiple cues within the environment
- **Provide Direct Reinforcement of Attempts Contingent on Child's Behavior**—teach the peer to enthusiastically praise the learner for attempts at functional play

Example cue card:

Skill: <u>Gain Attention</u>

1. Say your friend's name
2. Make eye contact with your friend before you begin talking to them

First:

Then:

APPENDIX B
PEER PRT ADHERENCE CHECKLIST AND FEEDBACK FORM

PRT STRATEGY	DEFINITION	RATING AND EXAMPLE OF USE	MISSED OPPORTUNITY EXAMPLE
Example: Gaining Attention	Saying the target child's name and making eye contact before initiating conversation or asking a question	4—Used target child's name and moved in close proximity to gain attention before providing a choice	Asked student a question, but peer continued to look away and play with preferred toy

Rating Criteria:

1. Does not implement throughout session
2. Implements occasionally, but misses majority of opportunities
3. Implements up to half the time, but misses many opportunities
4. Implements a majority of the time, but misses some opportunities
5. Implements completely throughout the session

Rating scale adapted from Suhrheinrich et al. (2013).

## 14

Peer Modeling Interventions

HUNTER C. KING, AARON J. FISCHER,
HEATHER L. J. LEWIS, AND JULIO CESAR PAYAN ■

In school-based settings, a student's ability to demonstrate effective social skills and communicative behaviors can help them to maximize social reinforcement and minimize negative interactions (Gresham, 1986; Gresham & Elliot, 2008). Although a variety of evidence-supported learning strategies have shown to help students acquire new or strengthen existing skills, learning by observing others plays a key role in skill acquisition and performance enhancement (Braaksma, Rijlaarsdam, & van den Bergh, 2002). In school settings, applied researchers have capitalized on the known effects of observational learning through the use of peers as interventionists, which led to the concept of peers as change agents (Blake, Wang, Gartledge, & Gardner, 2000; Collins, Hawkins, & Flowers, 2018; Strain & Fox, 1981) and the development of corresponding peer-mediated interventions (PMIs). Peer modeling (PM), for example, is a peer-mediated behavioral intervention (PMBI) in which a selected peer is instructed to model a desired behavior for target student (i.e., learner), with the target student expected to imitate the behavior in a similar context (Katz & Girolametto, 2013). Furthermore, modeling refers to the behavioral, cognitive, and affective changes that result from directly observing peer models (Berger, 1977; Rosenthal & Bandura, 1978; Zimmerman, 1977).

Dating back over 40 years, PM has shown to be an effective learning strategy for various populations, including students diagnosed with autism spectrum disorders (ASD), emotional and behavioral disorders, and other developmental disabilities (Clinton, 2016; Gilmour, 2015; Markey & Miler, 2015). During this time, two general variations of PM resulted, which include (a) in vivo PM in which the learner is in close proximity to the peer model and (b) video PM (VPM), which uses video recordings rather than live scenarios for the learner to observe. The purpose of this chapter is to describe the treatment approach underlying each variation of PM and offer practical recommendations for their use in educational settings.

RECOMMENDATIONS FOR IMPLEMENTATION OF PEER MODELING

Generally, for modeling strategies to be effective, the learner (i.e., student) must be able to demonstrate requisite skills relative to the principles of observational learning. For example, the PM literature has shown that study outcomes were moderated by the student's ability to imitate others (Dart, McKinley, & Helbig, 2019) and process and comprehend visual information (Delano, 2007; Rayner, Denholm, & Sigafoos, 2009; Shukla-Mehta, et al., 2010). Specific to VPM, however, scholars have argued that effective imitation results from the learner's ability to see, hear, and sustain visual attention for approximately one min (Bellini & Akullian, 2007; Delano, 2007; Shukla-Mehta et al., 2010). Thus, to determine the appropriateness of a particular a modeling strategy (PM or VPM) for a student, one should collect and/or review student data from multiple forms of assessment.

Both a direct and indirect assessment of the learner's abilities are suggested, such as a review of benchmark performance goals listed on the learner's individualized education program (IEP), teacher or caregiver report, or obtained by directly observing the student during school-based activities in which they are expected to display a specific behavior. If the information from assessment procedures suggests that the learner would likely benefit from a PMBI, staff or school personnel should then aim to identify an appropriate target skill and peer model.

Assessing and Selecting an Appropriate Target Skill

A skill that is either emerging or can be evoked through prompting would serve as an appropriate target for change (Wilson, 2013). The chosen target skill should be determined on the basis of assessment procedures and consultation with the learner's team. For example, formal or informal communication (e.g., meetings, emails, conference calls) among school team members (e.g., caregivers, teachers, paraprofessionals, school administrators) may aid in in identifying a socially valid and meaningful target skill. Additionally, the use of various standardized instruments and procedures have been used to assess the presence and severity of specific skill deficits, such as the Children's Communication Checklist (Bishop, 2003) for all aspects of communication (e.g., pragmatic speech and language), the Social Responsive Scale (Constantino, 2005) for reciprocal social interaction communication, and the Social Language Development Test: Elementary or Adolescents (Bowers, Huisingh, & LoGuidice, 2008) for perspective taking and social inferences. In conjunction with indirect assessment procedures, directly observing the student cross various classroom-related activities would offer a more objective, contextual account of the learner's capabilities in settings in which they are expected to display certain behaviors. Important to note, and supported through social learning theory, learners are more likely to model nonambiguous, external behaviors (e.g., interactions, requests, and play), as opposed to internal behaviors (e.g., emotion and cognitive regulation, vocabulary comprehension), as they offer clearer examples and expectations.

Choosing a Peer Model

Once a target skill has been selected, the selection of an appropriate peer model is facilitated by the learner's school team. Specific to in vivo PM, peer models are expected to be imbedded within the same environment as the learner, making them well-suited to a model target behavior(s), as long as the peer model can easily demonstrate the chosen target skill (Mathur & Rutherford, 1991). Although the physical proximity between the learner and model is vital to in vivo PM, learning also depends on various, research-supported model characteristics.

The question of whether or not the model and learner share similar characteristics has received considerable attention from educators and applied researchers, as some have argued that increased perceived similarity between the two results in positive study outcomes (Kornhaber & Schroeder, 1975; Markey & Miller, 2015). This concept is best understood through the effects of model–observer similarity, which posits that perceived similarity between the learner and peer model moderates the effectiveness of observational learning strategies. Despite some agreement, scholars continue to debate the importance and impact of certain model characteristics on the learner's imitative behavior.

For example, although McCoy and Hermanesn (2007) and Markey and Miller (2015) recommended the model be the same gender as the learner, Dart, Collins, Klingbeil, and McKinley's (2014) meta-analysis revealed similar effects on study outcomes regardless of whether or not gender matched the learner. There is less debate over the model's age, as most research has shown that adult models were more effective and efficient than peer models (Hoogerheid, van Wermeskerken, Loyens, & van Gog, 2016). Hoogerheid and colleagues' findings echo Wilson's (2013) brief note on Bandura's (1965) work on behavior modeling by arguing that social factors (e.g., authority, popularity, perceived competence of the model) may increase the learner's attention to the model. Lastly, Dart and colleagues found that there was a slightly greater effect when studies utilized peer models from the same classroom as a learner. Thus, when considering who to use as a peer model, it may be beneficial to select a peer who (a) is in the same class as the learner regardless of gender; (b) is perceived as competent, an authority figure, popular, or confident; and/or (c) can model the selected target behavior with ease (for review of peer-characteristic moderator variables and study outcomes, see Dart et al., 2014).

RECOMMENDATIONS FOR IMPLEMENTATION OF VIDEO PEER MODELING

As noted earlier, VPM is a subset of PMBIs in which the learner observers an edited video recording of the peer model displaying a specific target skill. Similar to PM, VPM draws upon the learner's visual strengths as opposed to learning via a nonvisual stimulus (Markey & Miller, 2015). Additionally, VPM does not require in-person interaction between the learner and model, which makes this learning strategy particularly attractive for populations who have an aversion to eye contact, such as individuals diagnosed with ASD (Corbett & Addullah, 2005); however, the use of videos and corresponding technology may deter some from its use. In an effort to demystify ambulance or confusion, we offer a brief introduction into VPM procedures and practical considerations.

The "V" in Video Peer Modeling

Recent technological advancements have provided the field of education the means to address respective issues with greater access, efficiency, and effectiveness, for example, by offering students easy access open educational resources (Kinskey, King, & Miller, 2018) and permitting virtual face-to-face problem-solving consultation in school-based settings (Bice-Urbach, Kratochwill, & Fischer, 2018), to name a few. This is certainly the case for using VPM in classroom and educational settings (Charlop-Christy, Lee, & Freeman, 2000; Hume, Loftin, & Lantz, 2009; Wilson, 2013). In VPM, a video stimulus (i.e., permanent product) is developed that can be conveniently accessed by teachers and students and repeatedly viewed as needed (Markey & Miller, 2015); however, developing the video requires both a video recording device (e.g., smartphone, tablet, computer) and video editing software (e.g., iMovie, Adobe Premiere Pro, OpenShot). For a review on the specifics of video recording and editing, see Sigafoos, O'Reilly, and de la Cruz (2007) or Collier-Meek, Fallon, Johnson, Sanetti, and Delcampo (2012).

Recording environment. Video recording procedures necessitate careful attention to the selection of an appropriate setting for modeling and recording. Filming will ideally take place a setting in which the learner is expected to display the behavior. For example, if the student has a history of yelling to obtain adult attention in a classroom, filming a peer model raising their hand in a classroom setting would promote ecological validity. Moreover, Bellini, Peters, Benner, and Hopf (2007) conducted a meta-analysis of 55 VPM studies whose results showed that filming in natural settings (e.g., classroom, home, playground) produced greater study outcomes as well as higher levels of skill maintenance and generalization.

Video clip length. Video clip length is an important to aspect to consider due to concerns regarding the learner's attention span. Some students, for example, may become distracted or bored while viewing a particularly long video while, conversely, a short video may not offer the student sufficient time to view and comprehend the footage. Gardner and Wolfe (2013) conducted a meta-analysis of 13 video-modeling and video-prompting studies that examined many study variables, including video length, which revealed that video clip lengths ranged from 18 s (folding a shirt) to 2 min and 42 s (e.g., putting away groceries). With no specific guidelines, deciding on video length may be better approached on the basis of a task analysis of the target behavior (i.e., more complex behaviors merit longer videos). To illustrate, modeling hand-raising does not necessarily require a complex repertoire and, thus, can be modeled and recorded multiple times in different environments within a relatively short video clip. However, more complex behaviors, such as certain types of social skills (interacting/reciprocating) or learning to use an online library (Markey & Miller, 2015) involve a longer task analysis, possibly resulting in fewer recorded examples or multiple examples embedded within a longer video clip.

VPM in School Settings

Inherent to all behavioral interventions, caregiver consent must first be obtained to video record the target student. Once the video has been edited to display the modeled behavior in an environment the learner is expected to imitate, considerations must be made regarding the frequency, timing, and location of viewing. Regarding location, a private environment is preferable to mitigate unwanted attention from peers (Clare et al., 2000; Wilson, 2013). Collier-Meek and colleagues (2012) noted in their VSM procedural guide that students have been shown the video in a private place (Clarke, Bray, Kehle, & Truscott, 2001) as well as in the corner of a classroom (Buggey, 2005). Due to the efficiency of VPM, the student's caregiver can also have the learner view the video at home—if barriers to video viewing present at school. A private location is suggested for the purpose of encouraging sustained attention and focus during video viewing. However, a secluded and reliably private location may not always be feasible, and, in such cases, Wilson (2013) has recommended a hallway or empty classroom. Furthermore, when auditory distractions are of concern, and if resources permit, the learner should be given the option to wear headphones.

Video viewing. The timing of video viewing should be guided by intervention goals and learner characteristics. The video modeling (VM) literature, in general, reports that video viewing should occur shortly before the activity in which the target behavior is expected to be displayed, with multiple views occurring throughout the day (Bellini & Akullian, 2007; Wilson, 2013). For example, Adamo and colleagues (2015) successfully increased the physical activity of two children diagnosed with Down's syndrome by instructing the learner to view videos ranging from two to four times during one 10-min session, across a total of 27 sessions, while King, Radley, Jenson, Clark, and O'Neill (2014) instructed participants to view two peer-modeling videos and two self-monitoring videos each week (four videos total). In addition, Shukla-Meheta and colleagues' (2010) systematic review revealed that that repeated viewing (e.g., two to four times per session) of a video-recorded peer model can bolster intervention effects, especially for children with ASD.

The frequency of viewing should be considered on the basis of the chosen target skill. For example, Collier-Meek and colleagues (2012) have recommended that videos meant to promote skill acquisition be viewed at least once per day, while videos that are meant to increase the frequency of existing skills be viewed once or twice per week (Bellini & McConnel, 2010). Additionally, some scholars suggest that viewing occur at spaced intervals, which is based on the principle that increased learning results from intermittent exposure of an intervention, as opposed to a single use (Dempster, 1988).

Monitoring VPM effects. The collection of pre- and post-intervention data is a vital step in evaluating whether the VPM resulted in skill acquisition or an increase in skill performance (Collier-Meek et al., 2012). The selected recording procedure should be guided by the target skill, as different behaviors require different recording systems. For example, the use of a direct observation, such as a continuous recording procedure (e.g., duration recording) would be more appropriate for target skills that vary in length (e.g., in-seat behavior, on-task behavior, social interactions; Green et al., 2017), while a discontinuous procedure (e.g., partial interval recording) would capture a fairly accurate estimate of spontaneous responses (e.g., hand-raising; Kahng, Ingvarsson, Quigg, Seckinger, & Teichman, 2011). Although indirect methods tend to be less valid and require higher levels of inference, they do offer a viable alternative when direct assessment procedures are not feasible, which include (a) stakeholder self-report (e.g., teacher, caregiver, school team); (b) checklists and rating scales (e.g. Functional Assessment Checklist for Teachers as Staff; March et al., 2000; Child Behavioral Checklist; Achenback & Rescorla, 2000); and (c) and the number of office discipline referrals. If the intervention and data-collection procedures were implemented with adequate fidelity, the data will reveal whether or not the intervention is working relative to baseline responding, and, if the data suggest little to no effect, intervention components can be altered to increase appropriate responding.

Video Self-Modeling

In some instances, identifying an appropriate peer model simply may not be feasible when certain barriers present, such as small class sizes or when schools have a high prevalence of students with severe skill deficits and or developmental and cognitive disabilities. In such cases, video self-modeling (VSM) can be a viable alternative. Formally defined, VSM involves "the observation of images of oneself engaged in adaptive behavior" (Dorwick, 1999, p. 23) and has shown to be a useful intervention to promote skill acquisition, strengthen skill performance, and reduce problem behaviors (Bellini & McConnel, 2010). This section offers a brief discussion into the parameters of learning by observing oneself.

Learning from oneself. The specific nature and severity of a student's developmental disability may impede their ability to display socially appropriate classroom behaviors (e.g., raising a hand). If a school team concludes that the behavioral deficits of a student are to be listed on and addressed through the learner's IEP, it would seem improbable that the target student could learn to demonstrate an appropriate replacement behavior if they have never before displayed the behavior. To verify this, it would be beneficial to confer with stakeholders (caregiver or teacher report, the student's IEP, etc.) and directly observe the student across various school-related activities in which they would be expected to use such a behavior. In some cases, the student may spontaneously engage in the target behavior, which would hopefully be video recorded; the video would be edited to only display appropriate behaviors, with all instances of inappropriate behaviors edited out; however, if zero occurrences of target behavior are noted, a different method can be applied that involves physical prompts.

If direct and/or indirect assessment procedures conclude that "raising a hand," for example, does not fall within that student's repertoire but their ability to imitate others has been observed, the adult video recording the student can model (i.e., physically prompt) the target behavior in the hopes that the student's imitation, along with receiving teacher praise, will be captured in the video; this is also referred to as feedforward, in which a student is shown performing a behavior above their current capacity of performance (Hitchcock, Dowrick, & Prater, 2003). The student has now been video recorded demonstrating the exact behavior they have been struggling to exhibit on their own. The student is then directed to observe the video displaying themselves receiving verbal praise for appropriately seeking teacher attention. The video length, frequency of video viewing, and environment in which the video is observed are consistent with the VPM procedures previously discussed.

VSM in the schools. A number of applied VSM studies have supported its use in school-based settings for children and adolescents with ASD (Ayres & Langone, 2005; Buggey & Ogle, 2012; Mason et al., 2013), developmental disabilities (Hepting & Goldstein, 1996; Hitchcock et al., 2003) and for problem behaviors such as crying, difficulty, transitioning, off-task behavior (Coyle & Cole, 2004), and noncompliance (Sherr et al., 2001). Moreover, a series of meta-analyses have also examined the effects of VSM on study outcomes, with promising results. For example, Mason and colleagues (2016) reviewed 25 VSM studies in an effort to examine treatment effects on academics, challenging and socially appropriate behavior, independent living, and social communication. Improvement rate difference (IRD) effect sizes were calculated and varied, suggesting that VSM had the largest effect on combined behavior (IRD = 0.88; $n = 19$), followed by independent living (IRD = 0.84; $n = 7$), social communication (IRD = 0.76; $n = 22$), and academics (IRD = 0.25; $n = 9$). Previous meta-analyses (Bellini & Akullian, 2007; Mason et al., 2013) have also indicated that VSM to be an effective intervention for producing change in target outcomes.

ADVANTAGES OF PEER MODELING AND VIDEO PEER MODELING IN SCHOOL SETTINGS

The use of PM and VM interventions (e.g., VSM, VPM) in school-based settings offers many logistical and programmatic advantages to teachers and school personnel; for example, both are considered low-cost interventions as they capitalize on the availability of peers as models during the course of program development and implementation. Although the cost of implementing a PM intervention is essentially zero—as the intervention solely relies on the peer model demonstrating the selected target—there can be a higher financial cost associated with VM interventions due to the necessity of technology use, such as a video camera and editing software; however, recent advancements in technological innovation have led to the identification of less expensive and more accessible commodities that have video recording and editing capabilities, such as smartphones or tablet devices. Importantly, some VM interventions may not require the use of editing software when creating a video, as the peers that are selected are those who can demonstrate the appropriate behavior. In fact, there have been several VPM studies that did not require any editing before showing the video to the target student (Clare et al., 2000; McCurdy & Shapiro, 1988).

Another advantage of PM in schools is that there is an abundance of students who could act as interventionists in the classroom. Unlike many other school-based interventions that require an adult staff member to implement the intervention, the use of peer models allows for greater flexibility within and across school-related activities. Peer models can be selected on the basis of cited characteristics, some of which include how well they demonstrate the desired behavior or how well they get along with the target student. Importantly, however, the selected peer model(s) must be cooperative and willing to participate, which may pose a challenge during program development. In sum, PMIs place less strain on a teacher's time and energy as they play a minimal role during the intervention.

Lastly, the videos created for VM interventions can be reused for other students with similar skill deficits and throughout subsequent school years. Using multiple models has shown to be beneficial within the PM and VM literature, so it may be useful to create a bank of videos for desired behaviors by saving and reusing peer-modeling videos for later use. Furthermore, having several, different videos with a variety of models may lead to the target student being more attentive to the video and less distractible. Thus, despite the potential barriers to implementation, the advantages of utilizing both PM and VPM are abundant.

CONSIDERATIONS OF DIVERSITY AND EQUITY

In any situation striving for equity, individuals from all identities and backgrounds are provided access to requisite supports, opportunities, and resources needed for personal success. This is a particularly relevant topic in school-based settings in which the student demographics have become increasingly diverse over the past few decades (Acquah, Tandon, & Lempinen, 2016; Brown, Shriberg, & Wang, 2007; Miranda & Gutter, 2002). As such, the need for more culturally, ethnically, and linguistically diverse teachers is on the rise; however, given the increasing diversity of students in school-based settings, this issue can be conceptualized differently with regard to peer models and PMIs. Specifically, if student demographics are widening, then students are in a unique position to serve as peer models for students with similar backgrounds, experiences, or identities. This relates to the effects of the model–observer similarity where perceived similarities between the peer model and the target student moderate the effectiveness of the PMI (Kornhaber & Schroeder, 1975; Markey & Miller, 2015); however, as noted earlier in this chapter, scholars continue to report mixed findings regarding the importance of similarity of the peer model.

Research recommends that teachers grow in their cultural responsiveness (Bank & Mcgee, 2010) as more students from diverse backgrounds populate schools. Although this concept is inarguably tied to equity for diverse student populations and should be heavily considered by all educators, the effectiveness of PMIs is moderated through effective imitation and reinforcement within an appropriate context. Thus, although cultural awareness and responsiveness are necessary to match today's diverse student demographics, PMIs can easily be adapted to meet the specific needs of students—for example, students who are averse to peer interactions can receive a VM (self or peer) intervention, while students who prefer to work with adults can observe and imitate an adult model. Further, with contemporary animation technologies (e.g., Vyond; www.vyond. com) practitioners can quickly develop dynamic animated videos of avatars modeling various behaviors. Developers can customize the avatars along numerous dimensions, ultimately allowing for modeling interactions from diverse individuals, some who might not be accessible locally.

CONCLUSION

General guidelines and practical considerations regarding the use of PM and VM strategies in school-based settings are provided in this chapter. As discussed, a number of research-supported, programmatic considerations must be made for these strategies to be effective, such as model and learner characteristics, appropriate intervention environments, and the specifics to the use of videos (e.g., length of video, frequency of video viewing). The advantages of PMIs are well-documented within the educational literature, and, fortunately, such advantages make their implementation more feasible for school personnel.

REFERENCES

Acquah, E. O., Tandon, M., & Lempinen, S. (2016). Teacher diversity awareness in the context of changing demographics. *European Education Research Journal, 15*(2). 218–235.

Achenback, T. M., & Rescorla, L. A. (2000). *Child behavior checklist*. Burlington, VT: ASEBA.

Adamo, E. K., Wu, J., Wolery, M., Louise-Hemmeter, M. L., Ledford, J. R., & Barton, E. E. (2015). Using video modeling, prompting, and behavior specific praise to increase moderate-to-vigorous physical activity for young children with Down's syndrome. *Journal of Early Intervention, 37*(4), 270–285.

Ayres, K. M., & Langone, J. (2005). Intervention and instruction with video for students with autism: A review of the literature. *Education and Training in Developmental Disabilities, 40*, 183–196.

Bandura, A. (1965). Influences of models' reinforcement contingencies on the acquisition of imitative responses. *Journal of Personality and Social Psychology, 1*, 589–595.

Banks, J. A., & McGee Banks (Eds.). (2010). *Multicultural education: Issues and perspectives* (7th ed.). Hoboken, NJ: Jossey-Bass.

Bellini, S., & Akullian, J. (2007). A meta-analysis of video modeling and video self-modeling interventions for children and adolescents with autism spectrum disorders. *Exceptional Children, 73*(3), 264–287.Bellini, S., & McConnel, L. L. (2010). Strength-based educational programming for students with autism spectrum disorders: A case for video self-modeling. *Preventing School Failure, 54*, 220–227.

Bellini, S., Peters, J. K., Benner, L., & Hopf, A. (2007). A meta-analysis of school-based social skills interventions for children with autism spectrum disorders. *Remedial and Special Education, 28*, 153–162.

Berger, S. M. (1977). Social comparison, modeling, and perseverance. In J. M. Suls & R. L. Miller (Eds.), *Social comparison processes: Theoretical and empirical perspective* (pp. 209–234). Washington, DC: Hemisphere.

Bice-Urbach, B., Kratochwiill, T., & Fischer, A. J. (2018). Teleconsultation: An application to provision of consultation services for school consultants. *Journal of Educational and Psychological Consultation, 28*, 255–278.

Bishop, D. V. M. (2003). Development of the Children's Communication Checklist (CCC): A method for assessing qualitative aspects of communicative impairment in children. *Journal of Child Psychology and Psychiatry, 39*(6), 879–891.

Blake C., Wang, W., Cartledge, G., & Gardner, R. (2000). Middle school students with serious emotional disturbances serve as social skills trainers and reinforcers for peers with SED. *Behavioral Disorders, 25*(4), 280–298.

Bowers, L., Huisingh, R., & LoGuidice, C. (2008). *Social language development test elementary*. East Moline, IL: LinguiSystems.

Braaksma, M. A., Rijlaarsdam, G., & Van den Bergh, H. (2002). Observational learning and the effects of model-observer similarity. *Journal of Educational Psychology, 94*(2), 405–415.

Brown, S. L., Shriberg, D., & Wang, A. (2007). Diversity research literature on the rise? A review of school psychology journals from 2000 to 2003. *Psychology in the Schools, 44*(6), 639–650.

Buggey, T. (2005). Video self-modeling applications with students with autism spectrum disorder in a small private school setting. *Focus on Autism and Other Developmental Disabilities, 20*, 52–63.

Buggey, T., & Ogle, L. (2012). Video self-modeling. *Psychology in the Schools, 49*, 52–70.

Charlop-Christy, M. H., Le, L., & Freeman, K. A. (2000). A comparison of video modeling with in vivo modeling for teaching children with autism. *Journal of Autism and Developmental Disorders, 30*, 537–552.

Clare, S. K., Jenson, W. R., Kehle, T. J., & Bray, M. A. (2000). Self-modeling as a treatment for increasing on-task behavior. *Psychology in the Schools, 37*(6), 517–522.

Clarke, M. A., Bray, M. A., Kehle, T. J., & Truscott, S. D. (2001). A school-based intervention designed to reduce the frequency of tics in children with Tourette's syndrome. *School Psychology Review, 30*, 11–22.

Clinton, E. (2016). A meta-analysis of video modeling interventions for children and adolescents with emotional/behavioral disorders. *Education Research Quarterly, 40*(2), 67–86.

Collier-Meet, M. A., Fallon, L. M., Johnson, A. H., Sanetti, L. M. H., & Delcampo, M. A. (2012). Constructing self-modeling videos: Procedures and technology. *Psychology in the Schools, 49*, 3–14.

Collins, T. A., Hawkins, R. O., & Flowers, E. M. (2018). Peer-mediated interventions: A practical guide to utilizing students as change agents. *Contemporary School Psychology, 22*(3), 213–219.

Constantino, J. N. (2005). *The social responsiveness scale (SRS) manual*. Los Angeles, CA: Western Psychological Services.

Corbett, B. A., & Abdullah, M. (2005). Video modeling: Why does it work for children with autism. *Journal of Early and Intensive Behavior Intervention, 2*, 2–8.

Coyle, C., & Cole, P. (2004). A videotaped self-modeling and self-monitoring treatment program to decrease off-task behavior in children with autism. *Journal of Intellectual and Developmental Disabilities, 29*, 3–16.

Dart, E. H., Collins, T. A., Klingbeil, D. A., & McKinley, L. E. (2014). Peer management interventions: A meta-analytic review of single-case research. *School Psychology Review, 43*(4), 367–384.

Dart, E. H., Mckinley, L. E., & Helbig, K. A. (2019). Peer-mediated interventions. In. K. Radley & E. H. Dart (Eds.), *Handbook of behavioral interventions in school: Multitiered systems of support*. New York, NY: Oxford University Press.

Delano, M. E. (2007). Video modeling interventions for individuals with autism. *Remedial and Special Education, 28*, 33–42.

Dempster, F. N. (1988). The spacing effect: A case study in the failure to apply the results of psychological research. *American Psychologist, 43*(8), 627–634.

Dorwick, P. W. (1999). A review of self-modeling and related interventions. *Applied Preventive Psychology, 8*, 23–40.

Gardner, S., & Wolfe, P. (2013). Use of video modeling and video prompting interventions for teaching daily living sills to individual with autism spectrum disorders: A review. *Research and Practice for Persons with Severe Disabilities, 38*(2), 73–87.

Gilmore, F. G. (2015). Comparing the teaching efficacy of two video modeling programs delivered in a group format in special education classrooms to improve expressive language. *Journal of Special Education and Technology, 30*(2), 112–121.

Green, V. A., Prior, T., Smart, E., Boelema, T., Drysdale, T. B. H., Harcourt, S., . . . Waddington, H. (2017). The use of individualized video modeling to enhance positive peer interactions in three preschool children. *Education and Treatment of Children, 40*(3), 353–378.

Gresham, F. M. (1986). Conceptual and definitional issues in the assessment of children's social skills: Implications for classifications and training. *Journal of Clinical Child Psychology, 15*, 3–15.

Gresham, F. M., & Elliot, S. N. (2008). *Social Skills Improvement System Rating Scales manual*. Minneapolis, MN: NCS Pearson.

Hepting, N. H., & Goldstein, H. (1996). Requesting by preschoolers with developmental disabilities: Videotaped self-modeling and learning of new linguistic structures. *Topics in Early Childhood Special Education, 16*(3), 407–427.

Hitchcock, C. H., Dowrick, P. W., & Prater, M. A. (2003). Video self-modeling intervention in school-based settings: A review. *Remedial and Special Education, 24*, 36–46.

Hoogerheide, V., van Wermeskerken, M., Loyens, S. M. M., & van Gog, T. (2016). Learning from video modeling examples: Content kept equal, adults are more effective models than peers. *Learning and Instruction, 44*, 22–30. doi:10.1016/j.learninstruc.2016.02.004

Hume, K., Loftin, R., & Lantz, J. (2009). Increasing independence in autism spectrum disorders: A review of three focused interventions. *Journal of Autism and Developmental Disabilities, 39*(9), 1329–1338.

Kahng, S., Ingvarsson, E. T., Quigg, A. M., Seckinger, K. E., & Teichman, H. M. (2011). Defining and measuring behavior. In W. W. Fischer, C. C. Piazza, & H. S. Roane (Eds.), *Handbook of applied behavior analysis* (pp. 113–131), New York, NY: Guilford Press.

Katz, E., & Girolametto, L. (2013). Peer-mediated interventions for preschoolers with ASD implemented in early childhood education settings. *Topics of Early Childhood Special Education, 33*(3), 133–143.

King, B., Radley, K. C., Jenson, C., & O'Neill, R. E. (2014). Utilization of video modeling combined with self-monitoring to increase rates of on-task behavior. *Behavioral Interventions, 29*, 125–144.

Kinskey, C., King, H. C., & Miller, C. L. (2018). Open educational resources: An analysis of Minnesota state colleges and universities student preferences. *Journal of Open, Distance, and e-Learning, 33*(3), 190–202.

Kornhaber, R. C., & Schroeder, H. E. (1975). Importance of model similarity on extinction avoidance behavior in children. *Journal of Consulting and Clinical Psychology, 43*, 601–607.

March, R. E., Horner, R. H., Lewis-Palmer, T., Brown, D., Crone, D., & Todd, A. W. (2000). *Functional Assessment Checklist--Teachers and Staff (FACTS)*. Eugene, OR: Educational and Community Supports.

Markey, P. T., & Miller, M. L. (2015). Introducing an information-seeking skill in a school library to students with autism spectrum disorder: Using video modeling and least-to-most prompts. *School Library Research, 18*, 1–31.

Mason, R. A., Davis, H. S., Ayres, K., Davis, J. L., & Mason, B. A. (2016). Video self-modeling for individuals with disabilities: A best-evidence, single case meta-analysis. *Journal of Developmental and Physical Disabilities, 28*(4), 623–642.

Mason, R. A., Ganz, J. B., Parker, R. I., Boles, M. B., Davis, H. S., & Rispoli, M. J. (2013). Video-based modeling: Differential effects due to treatment protocol. *Research on Autism Spectrum Disorders, 7*, 120–131.

Mathur, S. R., & Rutherford, R. B. (1991). Peer-mediated interventions promoting social skills of children with behavioral disorders. *Education and Treatment of Children, 14*(3), 227–242.

McCoy, K., & Hermansen, E. (2007). Video modeling for individuals with autism: A review of model types and effects. *Education and Treatment of Children, 30*(4), 183–213.

McCurdy, B. L., & Shapiro, E. S. (1988). Self-observation and the reduction of inappropriate classroom behavior. *Journal of School Psychology, 26*(4), 371–378.

Miranda, A. H., & Gutter, P. B. (2002). Diversity research literature in school psychology: 1990–1999. *Psychology in the Schools, 39*(5), 597–604.

Rayner, C., Denholm, C., & Sigafoos, J. (2009). Video-based intervention to individuals with autism: Key questions that remain unanswered. *Research in Autism Spectrum Disorders, 3*, 291–303.

Rosenthal, T. L., & Bandura, A. (1978). Psychological modeling: Theory and practice. In S. L. Garfiel., & A. E. Begin (Eds.), *Handbook of psychotherapy and behavior change: An empirical analysis* (2nd ed., pp. 621–658). New York, NY: Wiley.

Seok, S., DaCosta, B., McHenry-Powell, M., Heitzman-Powell, L. S., & Ostmeyer, K. (2018). A systematic review of evidence-based video modeling for students with emotional and behavioral disorders. *Education Sciences, 8*, 170.

Sherer, M., Pierce, K., Paredes, S., Kisacky, K., Ingersol, B., & Schreibman, L. (2001). Enhancing conversation skills in children with autism via video technology: Which is better, "self" or "other" as model? *Behavior Modification, 25*, 140–158.

Shukla-Mehta, S., Miller, T., & Callahan, K. J. (2010). Evaluating the effectiveness of video instruction on social communication skills training for children with autism spectrum disorders: A review of the literature. *Focus on Autism and Other Developmental Disabilities, 25*, 23–46.

Sigafoos, J., O'Reilly, M., & de la Cruz, B. (2007). *How to use video modeling and video prompting.* Austin, TX: Pro-Ed.

Strain, P. S., & Fox, J. J. (1981). Peers as behavior change agents for withdrawn classmates. *Advances in Clinical and Child Psychology, 4*, 167–198.

Wilson, K. P. (2013). Incorporating video modeling into a school-based intervention for students with autism spectrum disorders. *Language, Speech, and Hearing Services in Schools, 44*, 105–117.

Zimmerman, B. J. (1977). Modeling. In H. Hom & P. Robinson (Eds.), *Psychological processes in children's early education* (pp. 37–70). New York, NY: Academic Press.

## 15

Peer-Mediated Play Interventions

LAURA A. NABORS ■

Play is central to the social development of children (Bass & Mulick, 2007; Pellegrini, 1987; Watkins et al., 2015). Social play typically involves another individual in an interaction and consists of three phases: (a) orienting or observing another child, (b) playing near another child, and (c) engaging in activities or interaction with a peer or peers (Bass & Mulick, 2007). Play skills involve asking a peer to play, sharing materials, taking turns, giving things to others, requesting things of others, showing things to others, coping with negative behavior appropriately, and explaining things to others (Bass & Mulick, 2007). Children with special needs, such as Autism Spectrum Disorders (ASD) and other types of special needs (e.g., developmental disabilities or mental health problems), may have difficulty engaging in reciprocal play with peers, which can limit opportunities to develop social skills, school success, emotional functioning, and cultural competence (Bass & Mulick, 2007; Watkins et al., 2015). Similarly, peer relationships are central to social skill development, success at school, and emotional development (Kasari, Rotheram-Fuller, Locke, & Gulsrud, 2012). Peer-mediated behavioral interventions (PMBIs) are one tool for improving social opportunities and building social skills of children with special needs (Bass & Mulick, 2007).

As mentioned throughout this book, PMBIs are interventions that allow children who are developing typically to initiate, reinforce, and prompt social interactions that may improve the play behaviors and interactions of children with special needs (Bass & Mulick, 2007). The primary focus of this chapter will be to review peer-mediated play interventions to improve the social and emotional functioning of children with ASD, since the literature search revealed a wealth of information in this area. However, some studies focus on children with other types of developmental disabilities (e.g., language delay, deficits in cognitive functioning) or mental health diagnoses. Children with ASD often cope with deficits in communication, social relatedness, reciprocal social interaction, and imagination that can make social play difficult (Yang, Wolfberg, Wu, & Hwu, 2003). Seminal work in the area of PMBI was developed by Strain, Odom, and their colleagues (e.g., Brown, Odom, & Conroy, 2001; Odom, Chandler, Ostrosky, McConnell, & Reaney, 1992; Odom & Strain, 1984, 1986; Strain & Odom, 1986). One model (Strain, 1987) uses peers to deliver initiation of social activities with peers who have ASD. Peers learn how to invite children to play, give assistance to involve children in play, and provide compliments to reinforce social play. Interactions are focused on specific materials and activities, and peers receive reinforcement until they acquire the skills to help their peers. After this, reinforcers are faded (Strain, 1987). Another study used posters to describe social skills (inviting a child to play) and behaviors (depicting ways to play together) to the peers, usually called confederates (Strain & Odom, 1986).

EXAMPLES OF PMBIS

This section of the chapter reviews literature describing interventions in the field. Odom et al. (1992) examined the effectiveness of peer interventionists in improving social play for six preschool children with disabilities (including intellectual disabilities and language delay). Peer interventionists were trained in five sessions where they learned five skills: (a) sharing, (b) how to make a sharing request, (c) how to organize play, (d) how to assist a child in playing with them, and (e) how to maintain play once it has started. One or two peer interventionists were paired with a child with a special need or a disability during play. At first the teacher specified different play activities in which the children could engage. Next, prompts for play activities were faded and teachers invited children to play, rather than telling them what to do, and rewards were given for social play. Results indicated that peer initiations with children with special needs increased significantly after they participated in training and remained even when teachers stopped prompting interactions.

Robertson, Green, Alper, Schloss, and Kohler (2003) used songs during regularly scheduled activities to improve the social skills of preschool-aged children with special needs in an inclusive preschool setting. Teachers trained peer interventionists to initiate social interaction with two peers with special needs by prompting sharing and other social behaviors. Peer interventionists were thanked for being "good helpers" when they worked with a classmate. Brown et al. (2001) described how preschool teachers can designate an area of the classroom, such as sociodramatic play, as a place for socialization for 5 to 15 mins. Teachers can limit activity to this space so that children are close to each other, allowing children with special needs to observe and learn from more socially competent children. Within the 5 to 15 mins, teachers can structure several activities, such as having a tea party, having a costume party, or going to a friend's house for dinner.

Trembath, Balandin, Togher, and Stancliffe (2009) also used peer interventionists to improve communication of children with ASD in inclusive preschool settings. Peer interventionists learned what to do through reading a story and then interacted with target peers (three children with ASD) using the "show, wait, and tell" procedure. Peers worked to show target children what they were doing or how they could play together, wait to see if they wanted to play, and provide the names of activities. The two target children in their study demonstrated increased communicative behaviors during generalization probes (usually at mealtimes). In a review of PMBIs for children with ASDs, Watkins et al. (2015) recommended several components of successful interventions. One was the use of scripts. Scripts for training the peer interventionist about how to interact with the target child (and these scripts can be presented in stories or songs) may assist with training. Scripts may also be presented with photographs or illustrations. They can be reviewed orally or be in writing. In addition, reviewing scripts, perhaps through social stories, to teach the target child skills he or she will need can set this child up for success when interacting with a peer interventionist. Additionally, Watkins et al. (2015) suggested using the target child's interests to develop ideas for interactions or even clubs where children can interact. Teachers need to prompt and monitor play to ensure the success of interactions, and after this, fading can occur. In the case of fading, continued assessment should be used to ensure social skills are maintained.

Siblings as peer interventionists may be an underutilized resource for play-based interventions to improve social development. Tsao and Odom (2006) used siblings as buddies to improve social skills of children with ASD. Siblings were between 4 and 11 years and target children (with ASD) were between 3 and 6 years of age. These researchers taught siblings to stay close with brothers or sisters with ASD and find conversation topics, often using key interests of siblings to begin conversations. They taught sharing and persisting, as persisting in play requests may be central to engaging children with ASD in play. They also taught siblings to create opportunities to share and take turns in play. They taught them how to compromise in play and understand the needs of children, like their brothers or sisters, who had ASD. They worked to teach siblings not to feel discouraged and understand that they might need to work steadily to slowly improve their brother's or sister's involvement in social play. They used generalization probes, where they would take the children to parks or playgrounds to observe unstructured play. Their results indicated that siblings increased their social behaviors. Children with ASD were attending more to their siblings' behaviors and thus could observe more positive social behaviors, although generalization probes did not show change in behaviors for children with ASD.

There are also interesting studies of peer-mediated play for older children. For example, Corbett et al. (2014) used a theater-based PMBI to improve social interactions and skills for children with ASD. Children with ASD were paired with peers who were developing typically. The peer interventionist provided support, and the children could interact together during a structured activity (theater). There were multiple opportunities to communicate and learn communication skills. Corbett et al. implemented the theater in a summer camp program. Children engaged in peer-tutored games involving mirroring another's actions, speaking lines from scripts, imaginative play (pretending to be animals), music games, and role-playing different scenes in plays. The use of the games faded after a day or so, and children concentrated on learning a play. Rehearsals involved role play and identifying how characters felt. The two-week camp ended with a presentation of a play. Peer interventionists learned about autism, how to use reinforcement, modeling appropriate behavior, shaping, redirection, and extinction. Corbett et al. found that children with ASD were engaging in more interactions with peers and showing greater ability to remember faces after participating in the intervention, although eye contact did not significantly change. Corbett et al. included assessment of implementation fidelity, which was a strength of their study. More research in this field needs to focus on implementation fidelity and then applying interventions in different settings (Chang & Locke, 2016).

McFadden, Kamps, and Heitzman-Powell (2014) developed a peer-mediated recess intervention for children with ASD, implementing their intervention in two elementary schools. They targeted recess skills such as playing together and having fun (e.g., during tag games), complimenting and encouraging friends (e.g., "You did it"; "Let's catch up with the group"), talking about what you are doing and giving ideas about what to do, and using the target child's name to get his or her attention. They provided lessons and "huddles" to review skills prior to recess. "Whistle stops" were used during recess to allow peers to gather with the teacher and see if they were implementing skills with target children. Adults taught peer interventionists to prompt, teach, and praise social behaviors. All four target children participating in this study showed increases in social communication. Another applied setting for social skills development is the lunchroom. Having a lunch buddy program, where peers engage in social conversation over lunch, may facilitate friendships for children with special needs (Bell & Carter, 2013). Peer interventionists can talk about social events with a child with a special need or perhaps can start of conversation in areas of interest, which may be especially helpful for children with ASDs (Smith, 2012).

PMBIs may be helpful for skill development of children with mental health issues. There are a few studies of PMBIs with children with Attention-Deficit/Hyperactivity Disorder. Grauvogel-MacAleese and Wallace (2010) reported that peer attention for appropriate behaviors improved academic performance of children with ADHD. Cordier, Bundy, Hocking, and Einfeld (2009) developed a model of play for children with ADHD that may improve their social behaviors and abilities to empathize with others. Another group where PMBI might show a positive impact is for children who have experienced maltreatment and experience subsequent social withdrawal. Peers can be used to encourage engagement and interactive play for these children (e.g., Fantuzzo, Manz, Atkins, & Meyers, 2005).

RECOMMENDATIONS FOR IMPLEMENTATION

A six-step process may assist in developing play-based PMBIs: (a) consider the skill and needs of the target child, (b) consider the play setting and materials, (c) consider the skills and strengths of the peer interventionist, (d) plan for how interactions will be initiated, (e) plan for how interactions will be maintained, and (f) develop ideas for generalization of skills in other applied settings. This sixth step is critical to skill development for the target child and is an area where knowledge and research is lacking (Chang & Locke, 2016). Applying these steps provides an example of how they might work. Let's consider an intervention for a child with limited social skills who has good motor skills especially on the playground. The target child engages in ongoing play but struggles to join a group (i.e., being an onlooker). The setting is recess/playground, and we know that the target child likes to run, has good motor skills, and has played chase with the student teacher. A game of tag then is a good area for skill development and might be a good skills area to use in the recess/playground setting. Materials needed are minimal: instructions for the child and the peer interventionist, which can be illustrated on picture cards. Each child can role-play to learn the skill. Next, the peer interventionist learns about being a buddy or helper. After this, the peer interventionist learns how to teach the target child, by walking with him or her to the group and asking if they both can play tag. The target child has reviewed the rules of tag and understands that the peer interventionist will help them prior to the game at recess (perhaps in a special huddle session with a teacher). The teacher will set up or prompt the initial game of tag. The peer interventionist will play alongside the target child. After a few days of coaching from the peer interventionist, it may be possible for peer coaching to fade, and after this, assessment of child involvement in play should occur. If the first intervention was successful, then a next step in generalization of skills training would be for the target child to ask to join in play on the swings or in other games on the playground.

Teachers may select play activities and materials, and this can facilitate interaction between children with and without special needs. Table 15.1 provides ideas for play activities and materials for use in PMBI.

Some ideas for play materials may be blocks, trucks, dramatic play materials (e.g., costumes), small figures, clay, and zoo animals. Teachers want to select activities and materials that encourage sharing and turn-taking in play. It is recommended that teachers develop scripts and use photographs or pictures to describe play to preschool and elementary students who will be peer interventionists.

The six-step process outlined earlier provides a general approach; however, there are many critical factors to consider when designing interventions. For example, when selecting a peer interventionist, it is important to select a child who has good language skills, is fairly well-liked by others in the class, has a positive

Table 15.1. IDEAS FOR PLAY ACTIVITIES AND MATERIAL FOR PEER-MEDIATED INTERVENTIONS

Low Physical Activity Play	Physically Active Play
Magazines, stories	Tire swing or swing set
Games	Tag
Share photo albums	Bikes
Play with dolls	Hot Potato
Coloring	Kickball
Clay	Slides

history of social interaction with the child with a special need, responds well to adult direction, wants to participate, and attends school regularly (Brown et al., 2001; Fettig, 2013; Strain & Odom, 1986). With regard to training, adults typically provide coaching to the peer interventionist, especially in skills areas that are areas for improvement for the child with a special need. Peer interventionists may receive training in a number of skill areas: sharing, turn-taking, instructions on how to stay with your buddy, ideas of what to talk with your buddy about, suggestions for use of praise and positive feedback to your buddy, ideas for helping the child with a special need participate in play (e.g., "This is how you show your buddy to kick a ball, play hide and seek, etc."), and respond to requests for help from the child (Texas Education Agency, 2015). After teaching the skills to the peer interventionist, teachers or adult coaches may practice the skills with them through role play. By learning scripts and routines for involving children with special needs in play, peer interventionists can be prepared when social opportunities arise. Odom and Strain (1984) also mentioned that it might be important to monitor fatigue effects for the peer interventionist and also to determine if they drift in terms of implementing the intervention (fidelity of implementation). Incentives can be used to counter fatigue effects. Finally, maintenance checks, where teachers measure social communication across settings, can be critical and provide information about whether booster sessions are needed to review social skills. Similarly, it is important to fade teacher prompts and reinforcers and measure social skills after fading (e.g., Corbett et al., 2014; Odom et al., 1992).

In addition to rehearsing skills for playing with peers, teachers could also help children with special needs review their roles through scripts and stories that describe the steps and social actions needed for the friendship activity. Teachers may also want to provide the child with a special need with scripts for understanding how to respond when the peer interventionist initiates an interaction. For example, a script for a positive response could be, "Thank you. I like to play." Teachers often may review several types of social skills with a child (e.g., how to say "I want to play" and how to make eye contact during conversations) and prompt the child to use them when a peer interventionist initiates a social interaction. At first, teachers often need to be very involved in the interactions, but this can fade after social interactions are occurring and running smoothly. Rewarding the child for initiating and engaging in interactions may facilitate child involvement, especially at the initial intervention stages.

Assessing the effectiveness of the intervention provides ideas about its impact and can provide ideas for improving it in the future. Trembath et al. (2009) and Tsao and Odom (2006) offered some good ideas for assessment of progress, such as assessing change in social communication, negative behaviors, attention of the child with a special need to social interactions, positive and negative social initiations, engagement or time in positive social interaction, joint attention, teaching by the peer interventionist, and stereotypic behaviors (by the target child). Bass and Mulick (2007) provided helpful suggestions for developing one's observational system, including observing positive behaviors, assistance of peers, affection, and negative behaviors. Importantly, Tsao and Odom (2006), Trembath et al. (2009), and McFadden et al. (2014) conducted generalization probes, assessing social behaviors in other settings, which can attest to the success of one's intervention.

Considerations of Diversity and Equity

Chang and Locke (2016) recommended understanding the impact of PMBIs with children with special needs exhibiting significant delays (e.g., significant cognitive or physical delays), children in underresourced settings, and children from culturally and linguistically diverse groups. It may be more difficult to use traditional PMBIs for children with significant delays or speech and language deficits, and in these cases, more teacher guidance may be needed to ensure PMBIs are successful. It will be critical to train teachers in underresourced settings through teacher workshops, so that they have abilities to disseminate these successful practices. Training parents about the success of these methods will be important as well, as they might not have heard of the success of PMBIs, especially those for facilitating play and social skills development. Researchers need to study how PMBIs work in diverse settings and what types of changes, if any, are needed for successful implementation in these settings. Understanding how to disseminate PMBIs in the aforementioned settings is important to ensure equity in social development opportunities.

CONCLUSION

This chapter reviewed ideas for PMBIs to facilitate play and thereby social and emotional skill development of children with special needs. A majority of interventions focused on children with ASD. Tips for success included training peer interventionists, developing scripts for peer interventionists and children with special needs, rehearsing skills, planning for skills generalization, using reinforcers, and monitoring the success of interventions. Social settings such as the playground and lunchroom, and social settings and activities in classrooms, afford opportunities to include children with special needs in play. Interventions with children with mental health problems and other types of developmental disabilities is a promising area for future research as is disseminating current interventions in understudied settings and with underresearched groups.

REFERENCES

Bass, J. D., & Mulick, J. A. (2007). Social play skill enhancement of children with autism using peers and siblings as therapists. *Psychology in the Schools, 44*(7), 727–735. doi:10.1002/pits.20261

Bell, L., & Carter, E. W. (2013). *Peer-mediated support strategies. Tennessee Department of Education.* Retrieved from https://vkc.mc.vanderbilt.edu/assets/files/resources/psiPeermedstrategies.pdf

Brown, W. H., Odom, S. L., & Conroy, M. A. (2001). An intervention hierarchy for promoting young children's peer interactions in natural environments. *Topics in Early Childhood Special Education, 21*(3), 162–175.

Chang, Y-C. & Locke, J. (2016). A systematic review of peer-mediated interventions for children with autism spectrum disorder. *Research in Autism Spectrum Disorders, 27,* 1–10. doi:10.1016/j.rasd.2016.03.010

Corbett, B. A., Swain, D. M., Coke, C., Simon, D., Newsom, C., Houchins-Juarez, N., . . . Song, Y. (2014). Improvement in social deficits in autism spectrum disorders using a theatre-based, peer-mediated intervention. *Autism Research, 7,* 4–16. doi:10.1002/aur.1341

Cordier, R., Bundy, A., Hocking, C., & Einfeld, S. (2009). A model for play-based intervention for children with ADHD. *Australian Occupational Therapy Journal, 56,* 332–340. doi:10.1111/j.1440-1630.2009.00796.x

Fantuzzo, J., Manz, P., Atkins, M., & Meyers, R. (2005). Peer-mediated treatment of socially withdrawn maltreated preschool children: Cultivating natural community resources. *Journal of Clinical Child and Adolescent Psychology, 34,* 320–325. doi:10.1027/s15374424jccp3402_11

Fettig, A. (2013). *Peer-mediated instruction and intervention (PMII) fact sheet.* Chapel Hill, NC: The University of North Carolina, Frank Porter Graham Child Development Institute, The National Professional Development Center on Autism Spectrum Disorders.

Grauvogel-MacAleese, A. N., & Wallace, M. D. (2010). Use of peer-mediated intervention in children with attention deficit hyperactivity disorder. *Journal of Applied Behavior Analysis, 43,* 547–551. doi:10.1901/jaba.2010.43-547

Kasari, C., Rotheram-Fuller, E., Locke, J., & Gulsrud, A. (2012). Making the connection: randomized controlled trial of social skills at school for children with autism spectrum disorders. *Journal of Child Psychology and Psychiatry, 53*(4), 431–439. doi:10.1111/j.1469-7610.2011.02493.x

McFadden, B., Kamps, D., & Heitzman-Powell, L. (2014). Social communication effects of peer-mediated recess intervention for children with autism. *Research in Autism Spectrum Disorders, 8,* 1699–1712. doi:10.1016/j.rasd.2014.08.105

Odom, S. L., Chandler, L. K., Ostrosky, M., McConnell, S. R., & Reaney, S. (1992). Fading teacher prompts from peer-initiation interventions for young children with disabilities. *Journal of Applied Behavior Analysis, 25,* 307–317.

Odom, S. L., & Strain, P. S. (1986). A comparison of peer-initiation and teacher-antecedent interventions for promoting reciprocal social interaction of autistic preschoolers. *Journal of Applied Behavior Analysis, 19,* 59–71.

Odom, S. L., & Strain, P. S. (1984). Peer-mediated approaches to promoting children's social interaction: A review. *American Journal of Orthopsychiatry, 54,* 544–557.

Pellegrini, A. D. (1987). Rough-and-tumble play: Developmental and educational significance. *Educational Psychologist, 22*(1), 23–43.

Robertson, J., Green, K., Alper, S., Schloss, P. J., & Kohler, F. (2003). Using a peer-mediated intervention to facilitate children's participation in inclusive childcare activities. *Education and Treatment of Children, 26,* 182–197.

Smith, T. (2012). *Making inclusion work for students with autism spectrum disorders: An evidence-based guide.* New York, NY: Guilford Press.

Strain, P. S. (1987). Comprehensive evaluation of intervention for young autistic children. *Topics in Early Childhood Special Education, 7,* 97–110.

Strain, P. S., & Odom, S. L. (1986). Peer social initiations: Effective intervention for the social skills development of exceptional children. *Exceptional Children, 52,* 543–551.

Texas Education Agency. (2015, August). Peer-mediated instruction and intervention (PMII). TSLAT. *Texas Statewide Leadership for Autism Training. Education Service Center of Texas Region 13.* Retrieved from http://txautism.net/assets/uploads/docs/EBP-PMII.pdf

Trembath, D., Balandin, S., Togher, L., & Stancliffe, R. J. (2009). Peer-mediated teaching and augmentative and alternative communication for preschool-age children with autism. *Journal of Intellectual and Developmental Disability, 34,* 173–186. doi:10.1080/13668250902845210

Tsao, L-L., & Odom, S. L. (2006). Sibling mediated social interaction for young children with autism. *Topics in Early Childhood Special Education, 26,* 106–123.

Watkins, L., O'Reilly, M., Kuhn, M., Gevarter, C., Lancioni, G. E., Sigafoos, J., & Lang, R. (2015). A review of peer-mediated social interaction interventions for students with autism in inclusive settings. *Journal of Autism and Developmental Disorders, 45,* 1070–1083. doi:10.1007/s10803-014-2264-x

Yang, T-R., Wolfberg, P. J., Wu, S-C., Hwu, P-Y. (2003). Supporting children on the autism spectrum in peer play at home and at school: Piloting integrated play groups model in Taiwan. *Autism, 7,* 437–453. doi:10.1177/1362361303007004009

Restorative and Conflict Resolution Interventions

RHONDA N. T. NESE, SARA C. MCDANIEL,
PAUL MICHAEL MENG, LISETTE FRANKLIN SPRAGGINS,
VICTORIA T. BABBS, AND ERIK J. GIRVAN ■

Humans, as social animals, have developed a broad spectrum of strategies for maintaining order. At one extreme are formal, institutionalized, and directive systems of externally imposed rules and punishments enforced by a small number of individuals delegated the authority to do so—approaches often associated with rigidly hierarchical or authoritarian organizations. At the other are relatively organic, decentralized, or even ad hoc efforts to establish community, facilitate the resolution of conflicts when they arise, repair the harms that precipitated or were caused by the conflicts, and ultimately reestablish community relations disrupted by them—strategies common in informal gatherings and egalitarian groups.

Even within the same building, school discipline policies and practices fall all along this spectrum. Administrators and teachers may endorse and establish relatively punitive or preventative approaches to creating and preserving a safe environment, with little consistency existing from classroom to classroom (Skiba & Rausch, 2006). Students may be automatically suspended or expelled for serious or trivial violations of zero-tolerance policies (Girvan, 2019), provided additional support and the opportunity to learn from their mistakes, or simply find the space and time to talk with each other, often with peer support, to raise concerns, make amends, and restore their own friendships (Morril & Musheno, 2018).

This chapter focuses on the application of peer-mediated behavioral interventions (PMBIs) that attempt to capture the relational emphasis of the latter part of the spectrum in formal discipline systems associated with the former: Those derived from conflict resolution theory and restorative practices. It begins with a brief definition of restorative practices, their contemporary history as deliberate school-discipline interventions, and a description of how they can operate in the context of multitiered systems of support. It then describes main lessons learned from practical application of the approaches in schools. Finally, the chapter concludes with a discussion of considerations of equity in implementation of restorative practices.

HISTORY AND DESCRIPTION OF RESTORATIVE APPROACHES IN SCHOOLS

Systems of restorative justice—those with a primary objective of responding to and repairing harm to individuals rather than exacting punishments for rule breaking—date back to antiquity (Braithwaite, 1999; Zehr, 2015). However, recognition of restorative justice as an innovative practice that could be incorporated into Western criminal justice systems did not occur until the mid-1970s and 1980s (Zehr, 2015). By 1989, for example, New Zealand had substantially transformed the core of its juvenile justice system to emphasize a restorative, rather than punitive philosophy (Blood & Thorsborne, 2005). Australia (Payne & Welch, 2015), the United Kingdom (Hopkins, 2002), and the United States (Gonzales, 2012) later made similar changes. For their part, schools began incorporating the principles of restorative justice in their discipline policies and practices in the 1990s and 2000s (Hopkins, 2002; Morrison, 2002) in response to increased concerns about issues like bullying and harassment, disengagement from school, and excessive and disproportionate applications of exclusionary discipline to racial and ethnic minoritized students (Kehoe, Bourke-Taylor, Broderick, 2018; Mansfield, Fowler, & Rainbolt, 2018; Nese et al., in press).

Restorative practices represent the transformation of restorative justice to the school system. By definition, restorative practices provide a framework for responding to unwanted behaviors through the process of building community, dialogue, and mutual respect among students and educators. Some common applications of restorative practices in schools include

> *Restorative circles.* A meeting of students and educators in a circle, to discuss group norms, concerns, and reflect on current issues or repair relationships and conflict. In general, the procedures for restorative circles include allowing one person to talk at a time with a "talking piece," and encouraging equal voice talk time.
>
> *Restorative chats.* Guided conversations with the individuals involved where the focus is on identifying the area that individuals are making amends over, what they learned about how it made them and others feel, what they will do in the future to prevent the same issue from occurring, and how they will handle it differently if it does occur.

Classroom agreements. A process of developing classwide expectations or norms for how students and educators will treat one another, how they will work together and problem-solve around issues and concerns, and what they expect from one another. These agreements are cooperatively developed *with* the students, to increase a sense of ownership over their classroom culture.

Table 16.1 provides a few more common examples of such practices in the context of an education model involving multi-tiered systems of supports. The examples are organized into major components of restorative practice implementations: Explicit initial and supplemental instruction in the theory behind and goals of restorative approaches and the skills necessary to enact them; specific efforts to build, maintain, and repair relationships; and informal and formal processes for taking collective responsibility for defining community expectations and redressing harm. The next section of this chapter focuses on the critical role that students play in the buy-in, implementation, and ownership of such restorative approaches in their school buildings.

Table 16.1. Restorative Practices in School Settings Across Multiple Systems of Support

Tiers of Support	Explicit Social-Emotional Learning	Relationship Building	Conflict Management and Resolution
Tier 1	Instruction regarding theories of social order, conflict, and processes used to manage them Teaching communication, mediation, and other conflict management skills	Greeting all students at the door by name Circles to discuss student and teacher reactions to current events	Creating space for informal student and peer management of conflict Circles to develop classroom agreements or discuss reoccurring violations of them
Tier 2	Augmented instruction of specific social skills	Small group personal interviews Joint problem-solving tasks	Restorative chats Responsive circles regarding particular incidents Peer-mediated self-management
Tier 3	Restitution activity aligned with function of unwanted behavior	One-on-one discussions and getting-to-know-you activities Re-entry planning	High-stakes restorative conferences Circles involving key community stakeholders

RECOMMENDATIONS FOR IMPLEMENTATION

Peer involvement is both a necessary and core component of restorative practices in schools (Wearmouth, McKinney, & Glynn, 2007). Research suggests that peers can effectively support the development of prosocial skills amongst their classmates, by helping other students engage more actively in instructional tasks through tutoring, attending more consistently to the classroom expectations via group contingencies, and making instruction more explicit via peer modeling and feedback (Fuchs, Fuchs, Mathes, & Simmons, 1997; Johnson & Street, 2012; Kohler & Strain, 1990; Simonsen et al., 2008). Peer-mediated strategies have been associated with positive changes in peer–peer relationships (relationship repair; Kehoe et al., 2018), student–teacher relationships (Gregory, Clawson, Davis, Gerewitz, 2014; Syrjalainen et al., 2015), school climate (connectedness; Gregory et al., 2014), and more general social skills needed to successfully navigate life beyond school (Kim & Mabourgne, 2003). Additionally, peer cooperation is required for successful restorative circles, restorative chats, and classroom agreements. Without students communicating and helping to mediate their own conflict, restorative practices will be less powerful and, thus, effective.

Implementing peer-mediated practices also presents its own challenges. Most students in schools with more traditional discipline systems are not familiar with restorative approaches and are unsure, or even distrusting, of them. Prior to students explaining, modeling, or using restorative practices or themselves facilitating formal processes such as circles (i.e., structured, formal, safe opportunities for sharing, discussion, and problem-solving), they need to develop the skills and confidence necessary to do so. Also, it is important to not *require* student/peer participation, which can quickly turn into a power struggle and can deteriorate relationships, rather than build them. Once these skills are taught, modeled and practiced by all students in relatively safe settings, such as proactive relationship building exercises, they can become more comfortable in the practices thus resulting in more confidence to take the lead and facilitate their own processes.

Take Implementation Slow

Decisions to adopt new processes are often met with excitement and determination to implement everything immediately school or district wide. This does not allow room for those teachers who, like some students, are resistant to implementation due lack of understanding, frustration with program overload, or initiative fatigue to have concerns addressed and buy into the process. Accordingly, full implementation seldom is as effective as a "slow-grow" implementation process.

Slow implementation involves selecting a pilot group of teachers who have expressed interest in the restorative practices and are willing and able to implement them (Fixsen, Naoom, Blase, Friedman, & Wallace, 2005). Selecting the pilot teachers across grade levels minimizes the criticism that the new systems are only for a certain grade level, provides some opportunity for continuity for students, and provides a way to learn about differences and adjustments that may be needed to match practices with student development (Fixsen et al., 2005). As the pilot teachers become proficient and comfortable with restorative practices, it is important to allow other teachers to participate in the practices. Once teachers have been exposed to the process and provided additional training, the school administrator can then decide to expand the work with another small cohort of teachers interested in implementing restorative practices. Over time, the administrator can layer on more teachers to implement every year until the entire school staff are implementing. The administrator may also decide to have the entire school staff implement after the first group of pilot teachers. Whatever is decided, the pilot teachers become the restorative practices coaches to support the school or district with expanding this work.

Develop Basic Skills and Common Language

Before jumping into formal restorative practices such as restorative circles, common language needs to be established among students and school staff. Instruction around important communication skills, such as affective statements, coupled with practice developing agreements and norms or expectations, is one way to start this. Affective statements, or "I" statements, are a specific format to communicate feelings that emphasize connections between specific behaviors and responses to them: "I felt happy when you told me I did a great job on my math test this morning." Staff members should not only teach the use of affective statements but also model their use consistently with parents, students, and colleagues. In doing so, they can send information regarding the use of affective statements home to assist in informing families regarding the use of various restorative discipline practices, as well as foster the use of strong relational skills across multiple settings.

Similarly, it is beneficial for teachers to work collaboratively with their students from the outset on developing classroom agreements. These are social contracts in which each class defines what they as a classroom community find valuable in developing and maintaining strong relationships (Clifford, 2015). The agreements will ultimately define the specifics of how all members of the classroom, including staff, will interact with each other. It is also vital that the norms developed by the class are aligned with the schoolwide behavioral norms and expectations to assist with generalization across different settings within their school (Clifford, 2015). Once norms are established, circles can be used proactively and routinely for low-stakes check-ins, relationship building, discussion, or even instruction to ensure that students and teachers understand how circles work before they are used for higher-stakes problem-solving and responses to particular incidents involving harm (Clifford, 2015).

Increasing Sustainability

Even teachers who have a strong desire to use restorative practices, including circles, in class feel the stress of "too much to do and not enough time to do it." The most successful models of implementation are those where administrators are driving this work and supportive of the use of restorative discipline practices. For administrators who want to increase and ensure the sustainability of restorative practices, (a) devoting resources such as circle starters (i.e., examples of successful circle topics); (b) creating time and space for using them, such as modifying the school schedule to allow for a "morning meeting" or providing a physical space for private restorative chats; and (c) expressing their support for use of the practices not only in classrooms but also team or staff meetings such as public acknowledgement notes or positive emails is imperative.

Let Peers Lead and Keep It Fun

Sustaining the implementation of restorative practices like circles also involves keeping the students interested and engaged. Like any activity for children and adolescents, if the practices are no longer fun, cause conflict or stress, or are too adult-driven, they will disengage or avoid the practice. In working with students to facilitate circles, providing structured, low-stakes lesson plans on topics they select and enjoy such as "My favorite song is . . ." can increase participation and help ease student concerns or discomfort (Ortega, Lyubansky, Nettles, & Espelage, 2016). Once students experience success in leading parts of circles, they will gain confidence and can progress to facilitate them on their own with adult supervision. Finally, when addressing serious topics, it is important that when the circle closes students feel heard and connected with the members of the circle. While serious topics such as "A time I had to let go of resentment was . . ." can be difficult, sharing with each other in the circle as a supportive environment builds stronger peer-to-peer and student-to-teacher connections.

CONSIDERATIONS OF DIVERSITY AND EQUITY

Some argue that to truly implement restorative practices (i.e., the broader set of proactive, relationship-oriented strategies), schools must move radically away from punitive authoritarian systems toward more egalitarian, democratic approaches to education (Bazemore & Schiff, 2010; Cremin, 2011). Instead of taking an "all or nothing" approach, it may be useful to take a slow grow approach and (a) shift to the use of restorative responses to less serious unwanted behavior such as using inappropriate language or (b) start pairing the typical punitive discipline responses with a restorative practice such as a restorative chat. While building momentum with these slow-grow restorative practice strategies, administrators and teachers may notice that students who have either received only a restorative response or those who received a paired restorative response are less likely to repeat the unwanted behavior and are able to use their newly developed conflict resolution skills as a replacement for disrespectful or aggressive behavior. Reducing overall exclusionary discipline by replacing it with restorative practices, or reducing the repetition of the unwanted behavior that results in exclusionary discipline improves equity and disrupts the school-to-prison pipeline that requires the persistent use of exclusionary disciplinary practices.

Diversity "includes all the ways in which people differ, and it encompasses all the different characteristics that make one individual or group of individuals different from another. It is all-inclusive and recognizes everyone and every group as part of the diversity that should be valued" (Racial Equity Tools, n.d.). In addition to race and ethnicity, diversity also includes culture, national origin, disability status, sexual orientation, socioeconomic status, religion, and language. Diversity also accounts for varying perspectives and values. All of these differences can and should be considered when planning and implementing restorative practices and conflict resolution in schools. To make adaptations with individual and group differences in mind, schools must first work to get to know their students well enough to identify and understand the specific differences.

There are three primary strategies for identifying and understanding diversity in schools, related to effective restorative practices and conflict resolution tools. First, educators should seek to establish and maintain strong relationships with students and their families. Many relationship building strategies including school activities, purposeful one-on-one time, and surveys or inventories could promote relationships across school and home. Second, schools could host diversity activities and celebrations allowing students to highlight and celebrate their diversity. Third, educators should seek to understand students and their families in the context of their communities by visiting and participating in local community events.

Once individual and group differences (diversity) are identified and understood, those differences can be incorporated into interventions to improve cultural responsiveness and effectiveness. Examples may include (a) providing material translation or primary language discussions to reduce language barriers; (b) identifying matched peer and adult mentors and facilitators who most closely resemble and therefore relate to students with identified needs; (c) explicit and frequent reminders regarding safe spaces for discussions and reframing language in circles and mediations that may be biased or hurtful; (d) choosing peer mediation, community circles, or individual circles based on values and perspectives; and (e) strategies for students to identify common differences across the two peers in conflict or across a peer and adult in conflict.

Social Justice

Building upon identified diversity across individuals or groups of students, educators can also utilize restorative practices and conflict resolution to teach and promote social justice. Social justice work centers on fairness, equity, and inclusivity in relation to diversity by understanding the effects of historical events, systemic structures, and privilege on individuals and groups in the minority and majority cultures. Social justice standards such as those provided by Teaching Tolerance (2016) can be taught explicitly and integrated into restorative practices and conflict resolution interventions. Specifically, students who are taught to be focused on actions and language that reflect inclusion, equity, and justice may have (a) longer, more in-depth circle discussions; (b) use inclusive, non-biased language; and (c) prevent and resolve conflict deeply rooted in differences when provided the tools to use social justice in issues of conflict. These skills must be proactively and explicitly taught for students to have the background knowledge and vocabulary to be able to analyze, understand, and identify issues of discrimination, bias, and unjust thoughts and actions underlying conflict when it arises.

Student and Home Input

Restorative practices and peer-mediated conflict resolution should include caregivers and students in the planning and teaching phases. Without student and caregiver input into the planning phase of implementation, educators alone may design ineffective or nonresponsive interventions. Students, specifically, are useful in the teaching phases of the new interventions with caregivers being helpful in reinforcing these strategies in the home such as encouraging caregivers to use the previously mentioned affective statements.

Strength-based Programming

Across all of these considerations, it is critical that educators, caregivers, and students use asset, or strength-based, practices and minimize working from deficit constructs. This also pertains to supporting students with disabilities and those from low socioeconomic backgrounds. While students with deficits may require additional supports, strengths should always be inventoried, and interventions should be built on strengths, matched to student interest and ability. Restorative practices should be strengths-driven, with a focus on the opportunity to build from what is present and focused on developing mindsets that support solving problems internally rather than depending on external factors to solve individual problems. It is important to facilitate restorative practices from a strengths approach and to help students see their peers and conflict from a strengths approach. This asset-based approach applied to restorative practices and conflict management will also help two students in conflict to shift their mindset from the conflict to identifying what is right and good between them and their communities or groups and building on that to develop a plan based on hope and future-oriented thinking where both individuals and their communities benefit.

CONCLUSION

The benefits of utilizing students as guides for improving the relationships within their school community are numerous. In addition to developing invaluable skills for avoiding as well as addressing conflict in prosocial and healthy ways, students get to shape the environment that they learn in by making it an inclusive place for themselves, their peers, and their teachers to learn and thrive. This is accomplished through peer mediation delivered within a restorative practices framework where everyone is supported through the process of making amends and repairing relationships when conflict arises. In contrast to harmful exclusionary discipline practices such as out-of-school suspensions, restorative practices allow students to be included in the problem-solving process while gaining vital social skills, without being excluded from the learning environment with no opportunity for skill development or relationship building. Although conflict will always be inevitable within our schools, communities, and homes, equipping students with the skills necessary for navigating such issues in their lives serves as an incredible opportunity for education systems to set students up for the greatest successes in their interpersonal relationships.

ACKNOWLEDGMENTS

Preparation of this chapter was supported by the Institute of Education Sciences, U.S. Department of Education, through Grant R305A180006 to University of Oregon. The opinions expressed are those of the authors and do not represent views of the Institute or the U.S. Department of Education.

REFERENCES

Bazemore, G., & Schiff, M. (2010, November). *No time to talk: A cautiously optimistic tale of restorative justice and related approaches to school discipline.* Paper presented at the American Society of Criminology meetings, San Francisco. CA.

Blood, P., & Thorsborne, M. (2005, March). *The challenge of culture change: Embedding restorative practice in schools.* Paper presented at the Sixth International Conference on Conferencing, Circles and other Restorative Practices: "Building a Global Alliance for Restorative Practices and Family Empowerment," Sydney, Australia.

Braithwaite, J. (1999). Restorative justice: Assessing optimistic and pessimistic accounts. *Crime and Justice, 25*, 1–127. doi:10.1086/449287

Chazin, K. T., & Ledford, J. R. (2016). Preference assessments. In *Evidence-based instructional practices for young children with autism and other disabilities.* Retrieved from http://vkc.mc.vanderbilt.edu/ebip/preference-assessments

Clifford, A. (2015). *Teaching restorative practices with classroom circles.* Santa Rosa, CA: Center for Restorative Process.

Cremin, H. (2011). Talking back to Bazemore and Schiff: A discussion of restorative justice interventions in schools. In R. Rosenfeld, K. Quinet, & C. Garcia (Eds.), *Contemporary Issues in Criminological Theory and Research* (pp. 107–114). Belmont, CA: Wadsworth.

Fixsen, D., Naoom, S., Blase, K., Friedman, R., & Wallace, F. (2005). *Implementation research: A synthesis of the literature.* Tampa, FL: University of South Florida, Louis de la Parte Florida Mental Health Institute, National Implementation Research Network.

Fuchs, D., Fuchs, L. S., Mathes, P. G., & Simmons, D. C. (1997). Peer-assisted learning strategies: Making classrooms more responsive to diversity. *American Educational Research Journal, 34*, 174–206. doi:10.3102/00028312034001174

Girvan, E. J. (2019). The law and social psychology of racial disparities in school discipline. In B. Bornstein & M. Miller (Eds.), *Advances in psychology & law* (Vol. 4, pp. 235–76). Cham, Switzerland: Springer International.

González, T. (2012). Keeping kids in schools: Restorative justice, punitive discipline, and the school to prison pipeline. *Journal of Law and Education, 41*(2), 281–335.

Gregory, A., Gerewitz, J., Clawson, K., Davis, A., & Korth, J. (2014). *RP-observe manual* (Unpublished manual). Rutgers University, New Brunswick, NJ.

Hopkins, B. (2002). Restorative justice in schools. *Support for Learning, 17*(3), 144–149.

Johnson, K., & Street, E. M. (2012). *Response to intervention and precision teaching: Creating synergy in the classroom.* New York, NY: Guilford Press.

Kehoe, M., Bourke-Taylor, H., & Broderick, D. (2018). Developing student social skills using restorative practices: A new framework called H.E.A.R.T. *Social Psychology of Education, 21*, 189–207. doi:10.1007/s11218-017-9402-1

Kim, W. C., & Mauborgne, R. (2003). Fair process: Managing in the knowledge economy. *Harvard Business Review, 81*, 127–136.

Kohler, F. W., & Strain, P. S. (1990). Peer-assisted interventions: Early promises, notable achievements, and future aspirations. *Clinical Psychology Review, 10*, 441–452. doi:10.1016/0272-7358(90)90047-E

Mansfield, K. C., Fowler, B., & Rainbolt, S. (2018). The potential of restorative practices to ameliorate discipline gaps: The story of one high school's leadership team. *Educational Administrative Quarterly, 54*, 303–323. doi:10.1177/0013161X17751178

Morrill, C., & Musheno, M. (2018). *Navigating conflict: How youth handle trouble in a high-poverty school.* Chicago, IL: University of Chicago Press.

Morrison, B. (2002). *Bullying and victimisation in schools: A restorative justice approach* (Vol. 219). Canberra, Australia: Australian Institute of Criminology.

Nese, R. N. T., Bastable, E., Gion, C., Massar, M., Nese, J. F. T., & McKroskey, C. (in press). Preliminary effects of an instructional alternative to exclusionary discipline on student and staff behaviors. *Journal of At-Risk Issues.* https://files.eric.ed.gov/fulltext/EJ1253864.pdf

Ortega, L., Lyubansky, M., Nettles, S., & Espelage, D. L. (2016). Outcomes of a restorative circles program in a high school setting. *Psychology of Violence, 6*(3), 459–468. doi:10.1037/vio0000048

Payne, A. A., & Welch, K. (2015). Restorative justice in schools: The influence of race on restorative discipline. *Youth and Society, 47*, 539–564. doi:10.1177/0044118X12473125

Racial Equity Tools. (n.d.). Diversity. Retrieved from https://www.racialequitytools.org/glossary#diversity. Accessed May 25, 2019.

Simonsen, B., Fairbanks, S., Briesch, A., Myers, D., & Sugai, G. (2008). Evidence-based practices in classroom management: Considerations for research to practice. *Education and Treatment of Children, 31*, 351–380.

Skiba, R. J., & Rausch, M. K. (2006). Zero tolerance, suspension, and expulsion: Questions of equity and effectiveness. In C. M. Evertson & C. S. Weinstein (Eds.), *Handbook of classroom management: Research, practice, and contemporary issues* (pp. 1063–1089). Mahwah, NJ: Erlbaum.

Syrjalainen, E., Jukarainen, P., Varri, V. M., & Kaupinmaki, S. (2015). Safe school day according to the young. *Young, 23*, 59–75. doi:10.1177/1103308814557399

Teaching Tolerance. (2016). Social justice standards the teaching tolerance anti-bias framework. Retrieved from https://www.tolerance.org/sites/default/files/2017-06/TT_Social_Justice_Standards_0.pdf.

Wearmouth, J., McKinney, R., & Glynn, T. (2007). Restorative justice in schools: A New Zealand example. *Educational Research, 49*, 37–49. doi:10.1080/00131880701200740

Wearmouth, J., McKinney, R., & Glynn, T. (2007). Restorative justice: Two examples from New Zealand schools. *British Journal of Special Education, 34*, 196–203. doi:10.1111/j1467-8578.2007.00479.x

Zehr, H. (Ed.). (2015). *The little book of restorative justice: Revised and updated.* New York, NY: Good books.

Peer-Mediated Group Supports

Peer-Mediated Group Supports

CHRISTOPHER H. SKINNER, TARA MOORE,
AND JESSICA F. ESHBAUGH ■

Extensive bodies of research have demonstrated positive academic and behavioral outcomes associated with using peer-mediated group supports in school and classroom settings. In contrast to peer-mediated behavioral interventions discussed in this book, peer-mediated group supports are designed to efficiently influence the behavior of large groups of students at the same time. Central to these approaches is an anticipation of typical problems in school settings that disrupt positive and productive school and classroom environments. In response, teachers and school professionals can then establish systems that prevent or lessen those problems by explicitly specifying criteria and expectations for learning and behavior (e.g., explicitly teaching behavioral expectations or setting goals for academic performance) and by rewarding desired appropriate behaviors (e.g., providing rewards to student who exhibit appropriate behavior or providing rewards for meeting academic performance goals).

In this chapter, we will introduce three broad systems used to establish peer-mediated approaches to support appropriate behavior and to prevent and reduce problem behaviors for large groups of students: School-Wide Positive Behavior Interventions and Supports, effective classroom management, and group contingencies. We will provide examples of peer-mediated systems and provide highlights from research conducted in school settings. The focus of this chapter, and in subsequent chapters in this section of this book, will be on peer-mediated group supports for establishing classroom and school environments where students work together to achieve common and individual goals and where peer influence is used in a positive way to promote appropriate, respectful, productive, and safe behaviors.

The goal for this section is to provide recommendations for teachers and professionals to thoughtfully select and implement supports to allow them to address behavior more efficiently and simultaneously for larger groups of students and for educators to purposefully and responsibly leverage peer influence to create school environments which are "reinforcing" for all students. By this, we mean that school environments should set up all students to be successful: each and every student should have many opportunities throughout the day to learn, to successfully engage in and complete academic tasks, to engage in positive and mutually rewarding interactions with their peers and adults, to meet behavioral and academic expectations, and to earn and receive positive feedback and acknowledgement for their good work and behavior. The recommendations provided in this section should supplement recommendations provided in previous sections to allow for a more comprehensive use of peer-mediated interventions for promoting appropriate behaviors and engagement within reinforcing school environments.

Structures and Reward Systems for Supporting Group Behavior

Kagan (1985) described cooperative learning environments where structures (e.g., tasks, expectations) and reward systems are in place to promote students' appropriate behaviors as they work with and alongside their peers. To this end, an important first step in creating effective and cooperative school environments is to establish structures for promoting appropriate student behaviors that we expect to see in schools such as active engagement and learning, positive interactions, and rule following. When talking about peer-mediated group supports, the focus should be on establishing structures to address behaviors of groups of students, rather than just on individual students. In schools and in classrooms, students work together and alongside each other in defined spaces, and in many ways, the success of one depends on the success of all.

There are several ways teachers and school professionals can establish structures for peer-mediated supports for effective school environments. Some of these strategies are focused on incorporating opportunities for cooperative or peer-mediated instructional activities and learning. For example, the peer-mediated academic interventions discussed in this volume are designed to explicitly and purposefully train peers to work together to increase specific academic outcomes. These and other effective instructional strategies are designed to ensure appropriately-matched supports are provided to all students in a classroom so that they can successfully engage in academic tasks.

Beyond these instructional strategies, teachers can establish structures for promoting group-level appropriate behaviors in additional ways. Notably, peer-mediated group supports share a common focus on identifying and providing explicit instruction about what teachers want students to do. This can include teaching students the behavioral expectations (i.e., rules) or academic expectations in school and classroom settings as well as other specific expectations or criteria, such as stating criteria for performance on academic tasks or providing prompts or reminders to pre-correct problem behaviors that typically occur in particular contexts (Moore et al., 2019). It is important for teachers and school staff to be explicit about their expectations: adults can provide examples and nonexamples and model desired behaviors for students. It is also important to provide frequent reminders of expectations (Fudge, Reece, Skinner, & Cowden, 2007) and ongoing opportunities for students to practice appropriate behaviors in the natural setting and to provide feedback to support students' learning. The group supports discussed in this section also focus on establishing classroom and school environments that are characterized as positive, respectful, productive, and safe. To this end, teachers and school staff establish behavioral expectations that are closely aligned with those goals (e.g., expectations for respectful interactions with others, working hard, being safe)and that can be applied across common, daily activities to ensure more productive and efficient use of time.

Peer-mediated group supports focus on providing feedback to students and using reward systems to reinforce, or build up, appropriate behaviors in school settings. These rewards can be used to reinforce appropriate academic and social behaviors for individual students like those discussed in the previous section. In addition, teachers frequently use rewards that are delivered or occur contingent upon (or because of) students' appropriate behaviors in an effort to reinforce appropriate behaviors across a group of students at the same time. Group-oriented contingencies, like those discussed in Chapters 21 and 22 of this volume, are designed to be efficient and easy to implement relative to implementing a number of different, highly individualized contingencies across several students at the same time. Most scholarly research, discussion, and recommendations on using group-oriented contingencies in schools focus on providing positive consequences contingent upon students' appropriate behaviors; however, group-oriented contingencies also include negative consequences for students' inappropriate behaviors.

PREVIEW OF PEER-MEDIATED GROUP SUPPORTS

School-Wide Positive Behavioral Interventions and Supports

Positive Behavioral Interventions and Supports (PBIS) represent an approach for selecting and implementing research-based strategies to cultivate "school environments that improve lifestyle results (personal, health, social, family, work, recreation, etc.) for all children and youth by making problem behavior less effective, efficient, and relevant and making desired behavior more functional" (Sugai et al., 2000, p. 134). When adopted and implemented with fidelity across a whole school (i.e., School-Wide PBIS [SWPBIS]), the focus is on establishing structures across all school settings to support more appropriate behaviors for all students. Sugai et al. (2000) outlined hallmarks of PBIS that make it an effective and efficient framework for preventing and reducing problem behaviors for large numbers of students at the same time. These hallmarks include a focus on principles and research from applied behavior analysis (e.g., behavior is learned and can be taught and changed, behavior is influenced by factors within the environments in which they occur); the selection of research-based interventions that can be readily implemented in natural environments; targeting socially, educationally, and culturally relevant outcomes that are useful and important across settings (i.e., in and out of school); and a focus on establishing systems to support installation and sustainability of continuums of effective behavioral supports over time, across settings, and across students (Sugai et al., 2000). Therefore, schoolwide applications of PBIS should focus on providing instruction to teach students to exhibit appropriate behaviors and behaviors to replace more problematic behaviors, improving classroom and school environments that support students' use of these more appropriate behaviors, altering contingencies in the natural environment to reinforce appropriate behaviors (i.e., making them more functional or useful), and reducing reinforcement for problem behaviors (i.e., making them less functional).

Sugai and Horner (2002) provided an overview of common practices associated with schoolwide approaches to preventing problem behaviors. First, school staff identify and define behavioral expectations for students across all settings of the school. Then they develop and implement procedures for teaching behavioral expectations, appropriate behaviors, and routines to all students in the school and across school settings. Next, they develop and install procedures for encouraging appropriate behaviors (i.e., systematic ways for providing multiple and varied types of rewards to students who exhibit desired behaviors). Finally, staff develop and install procedures for preventing and responding to problem behaviors (e.g., systematically applying consequences for problem behaviors or for not following expectations or removing or limiting things in the environment may actually reinforce students' inappropriate behaviors).

SWPBIS can be considered a peer-mediated group support for several reasons. First, at the prevention level, behavioral expectations and routines are defined for all students in the school. Second, systems for responding to appropriate behaviors and problem behaviors are developed and apply to all students. The focus is on developing effective and efficient school environments that are structured to promote and reinforce safe, respectful, and productive behaviors for all students and staff. SWPBIS allows for staff to draw again from what we know about effective individualized behavioral interventions and tweak supports to address the needs of smaller groups of students identified to be at risk of or exhibiting problem behaviors. In these instances, these more intensive interventions typically included more focused teaching, practice, feedback, and reinforcement to increase these students' use of more appropriate behaviors that are expected in school settings.

Researchers have established the effectiveness of SWPBIS practices and systems to improve behavioral outcomes for large groups of students. Positive outcomes have been demonstrated with both the school as the unit of analysis and with subgroups of students. Lewis, McIntosh, Simonsen, Mitchell, and Hatton (2017) reviewed the evidence of effectiveness and found a solid research base contributing evidence of positive school-level outcomes (e.g., improvements in social culture, school safety, and climate) and student-level outcomes (e.g., discipline rates, referral for counseling services, and bullying). Specific to positive whole-school outcomes, SWPBIS has led to large-scale improvements in school climate.

Horner et al. (2009) conducted an effectiveness analysis of school outcomes across two states that implemented SWPBIS in a large number of schools; results from a survey of perceived school safety (i.e., School Safety Survey; Sprague, Colvin, & Irvin, 1996) suggest that SWPBIS implementation fostered substantial improvements in staff perceptions of school safety and climate. Bradshaw, Koth, Thorton, and Leaf (2009) examined measures of school organizational health and found significant improvements in school climate during a large-scale, five-year implementation of SWPBIS. Waasdorp, Bradshaw, and Leaf (2012) found that SWPBIS significantly decreased teacher reports of student bullying and peer rejection, which suggest a broader impact on the schools' social-cultural climate.

There is also evidence that SWPBIS leads to improvements in student-level behavioral outcomes. A critical intention of SWPBIS practices and systems is to reduce problem behavior levels and, in doing so, lower school discipline rates (e.g., office discipline referrals [ODRs] and in- and out-of-school suspension rates). Muscott, Mann, and LeBrun (2008) examined a statewide scale-up initiative of SWPBIS; among 28 implementing schools, disciple data indicated that 83% of the schools were able to reduce the number of ODRs reported daily, and 77% of schools reported reductions in the total number of ODRs from year 1 to year 2 of implementation. In addition, Muscott et al. (2008) found that SWPBIS reduced rates of both in- and out-of-school suspension during the two-year implementation period with the most significant decreases in suspensions occurring in middle and high schools. Horner et al. (2009) also reported low rates of ODRs in schools using SWPBIS practices during a three-year period compared to schools not implementing SWPBIS. Bradshaw, Mitchell, and Leaf's (2010) examination of a five-year SWPBIS implementation found that schools applying SWPBIS practices and systems reported reductions in the number of ODRs per day during each year and rates of suspension declined significantly over time compared to schools not implementing SWPBIS.

Research has also been conducted to examine the impact SWPBIS on the behavior of students with serious behavior problems being served in an alternative school setting. Simonsen, Britton, and Young (2010) examined the effects of SWPBIS implementation at an alternative school over time; despite environmental challenges during the study (i.e., moving to a new school building during year 1 of trial), results indicated positive effects on student behavior evidenced by a reduction in the number of students using physical aggression that resulted in restraint from year 1 to year 2. Farkas et al. (2012) analyzed the impact of SWPBIS implementation in an alternative school setting for students with emotional disturbance and other serious behavior problems; there was an immediate reduction in the number of ODRs and a downward trend in ODR data throughout the year-long implementation. These findings provide evidence of the effectiveness of SWPBIS practices and features on discipline rates among subgroups of students (i.e., students with emotional or behavioral disorders). Chapter 18 of this book further discusses how to improve student outcomes by leveraging positive peer influence within the framework SWPBIS practices and systems.

Classroom Management

Effective classroom management requires teachers to provide structures and systems of rewards to prevent problem behaviors from occurring in the first place and to select and implement interventions to address the specific problems of the class as a whole, small groups of students in the class, or individual students. Good classroom management mirrors schoolwide approaches of providing PBIS to prevent and reduce problem behaviors and to promote more appropriate student behaviors. Again, the focus is on applying research-based strategies to establish effective classroom environments to support student behavior.

At the classroom level, the primary focus is on creating environments that promote student engagement and learning and encourage students and teachers to listen to, be respectful of, and learn from each other. In addition, good classroom management should limit disruptive behaviors and downtime while increasing the amount of time each student spends learning. Typical features of effective classrooms include appropriate instructional supports to ensure students are able to successfully engage in learning activities; clear instructions related to academic tasks, behavioral expectations, and criteria for performance; examples and models of academic and behavioral expectations; ongoing opportunities for students to practice academic and behavioral skills; ongoing monitoring and feedback related to students' academic and behavioral performance; and use of contingencies in the natural environment to reinforce appropriate behaviors and limit reinforcement for problem behaviors.

The research base on effective classroom management strategies draws heavily from principles and research from applied behavior analysis. Research teams have conducted reviews of original research to identify and summarize classroom management strategies that are supported by research, and these include strategies to prevent problems from occurring as well as intervention strategies to address specific problems. Reviews have been updated over time to include continued research on classroom management strategies. Taken as a whole and across decades, review teams examining original research have provided consistent summaries about classroom management strategies that are supported by research.

For example, Lewis, Hudson, Richter, and Johnson (2004) conducted a review of published research and identified sets of research-based practices that teachers and school staff can implement to support positive outcomes for students who typically exhibit problem behaviors. The review team identified basic prevention strategies, including providing teacher praise and other forms of rewards to reinforce students' appropriate behaviors, as well as providing high rates of opportunities for students to respond successfully to academic work. In addition, they identified intervention approaches including identifying and providing instruction to teach more appropriate behaviors or social skills designed to replace problem behaviors, as well as developing and implementing behavioral interventions designed to specifically address hypothesized function of problem behavior. For example, if a teacher hypothesized a student is exhibiting problem behavior to get attention from the teacher, the teacher could then use strategies to teach the student more appropriate behaviors and ways to solicit attention from her teacher in more appropriate ways. Then, the teacher could implement a focused intervention approach to provide more attention to the student when she exhibits appropriate behaviors and to limit or withhold attention when the student exhibits the problem behavior.

More recently, Simonsen, Fairbanks, Breisch, Myers, and Sugai (2008) conducted a similar review to identify research-based practices for classroom management in general. Strategies for preventing problem behaviors included providing classroom and instructional structure (i.e., structuring academic activities and physical arrangement to minimize distraction); posting, teaching, reviewing, monitoring, and reinforcing behavioral expectations; and engaging all students in learning activities (i.e., providing high rates of opportunities to respond, providing instructional supports, and monitoring student work). Simonsen et al. (2008) also identified strategies for intervening with specific classroom problems. Research-based interventions focused on strategies to acknowledge or reinforce appropriate behaviors (i.e., providing behavior-specific praise contingent on appropriate behavior, using group contingencies to reinforce behaviors for groups of students, using behavior contracts to specify and reinforce replacement behaviors, and using token economies). Further, they identified strategies used to respond to inappropriate behaviors: providing error corrections and specific feedback for academic and behavioral skills and increasing reinforcement for appropriate behaviors while limiting or withholding reinforcement for problem behaviors.

A review team from the Institute of Education Sciences (Epstein, Atkins, Cullinan, Kutash, & Weaver, 2008) reported similar findings about classroom strategies to reduce problem behaviors. This review team found strong evidence for broad strategies, including providing appropriate instructional supports and activities so that all students can successfully engage in learning and teaching and reinforcing classroom behavioral expectations. The team also reported research-based approaches to addressing problem behaviors once they occurred that involved using information and observation to identify factors that were prompting (or antecedents to) problem behavior and reinforcing (or building up) problem behaviors. For example, teachers could observe a student to determine under what circumstances a behavior is likely to occur and what is the likely function, or purpose, of the problem behavior (e.g., problem behaviors that are attention-seeking, problem behaviors that typically result in a student being able to escape or avoid aversive or nonpreferred tasks).

Building on Simonsen et al's (2008) review, Zaheer et al. (2019) recently outlined and updated research-based practices for managing classroom behaviors for students with and at risk for emotional or behavioral disorders. Zaheer and colleagues organized research-based practices into a broad strategy set that teachers can implement in their classrooms. For different practices, they provide a description of the practice, cite research studies where the practice has been evaluated, and summarize student outcomes reported by original researchers. The first broad research-based practices focus on creating structure and predictability to establish an efficient classroom environment (i.e., creating a physical environment to support learning and needs, establishing routines, and actively supervising and providing feedback for students' behavior and academic work). The second set of research-based practices focuses on strategies to promote and maintain an overall positive classroom environment. These include establishing classroom rules or behavioral expectations, providing behavior-specific praise to reinforce appropriate behaviors, using token economies to reinforce appropriate behaviors, and using noncontingent reinforcement (i.e., reinforcement, such as teacher attention, is provided often and throughout the class in an effort to reduce students' motivation to engage in attention-seeking problem behaviors). The final set of teacher-implemented research-based practices focus on providing effective instruction and instructional supports to increase students' social and academic skills. Specific research-based strategies in this set include using explicit instruction to teach academic or socials skills, providing high rates of opportunities to respond successfully to academic tasks or demands, and providing student with performance feedback to improve their academic or social skills. Chapter 19 of this book discusses common peer-mediated strategies in classroom management that effectively support appropriate behaviors and prevent and reduce problem behaviors for groups of students, and Chapter 20 outlines recommendations for incorporating technology into classroom management strategies.

Group Contingencies

Contingencies in the classroom describe if–then relationships between students' behaviors and classroom events. Group contingencies are effective in managing problem behaviors for a group of students as they allow the teacher to streamline management efforts toward a group or class criteria for behavior and away from numerous individual criteria (Theodore, Bray, & Kehle, 2004). Litow and Pumroy (1975) identified and described three different types of group-oriented contingencies including independent and interdependent group-oriented contingencies.

With *independent* group-oriented contingencies, rewards are available and delivered to each student contingent upon (or because of) their own behavior. The group-oriented aspect of an independent contingency is that the behavior and criteria required to obtain the reward is the same simultaneously for all members of the group, making it easier for the teacher and students to readily determine who has met the criteria set for all students (Litow & Pumroy, 1975). Most people are familiar with independent group-oriented contingencies as they are ubiquitous in our schools (e.g., grades delivered for academic performance and positive rewards for appropriate behaviors, such as teacher praise or stickers). Punitive consequences for inappropriate behaviors or for not meeting behavioral expectations or standards are also often applied schoolwide via independent group-oriented punishment. Because each student receives access to consequences based solely on their own behavior, independent group-oriented contingencies may not encourage collaboration to the same degree as the other types of group-oriented contingencies, including interdependent group-oriented contingencies.

When applying *interdependent* group-oriented contingencies, all members of a group receive access to the same consequence contingent upon some aspect of the group's behavior (Litow & Pumroy, 1975). With interdependent group contingencies, each student's access to a consequence is contingent upon not only their own behavior but also the behavior of other group members. In this way, interdependent group-oriented contingencies encourage students to do their best and help (e.g., encourage) their peers do their best. This is sometimes called positive interdependency. When interdependent group rewards are applied, this interdependency often results in two rewards, the reward they earned and the social rewards that frequently occur when a group (e.g., team or class) earns a reward or wins, which include social praise from adults and peers and celebratory behavior.

Interdependent group contingencies can leverage peer influence to affect group behavior. The fundamental purpose of interdependent group reinforcement is to prevent and manage behavioral problems and increase appropriate behaviors across groups of students through the use of three general procedures: establish classroom expectations, explicitly teach the expectations, and reinforce the expectations (Chow & Gilmour, 2016). Specifically, group contingency procedures establish behavioral criteria for a group (e.g., class average or small group average) and consequent meeting behavioral criteria with a group reward (Greenwood, Hops, Delquadri, & Guild, 1974). While various procedures for group-oriented rewards can be delineated, the overall function is the same: students access a reward based on the behavior of other individuals in the group (Greenwood et al.,1974; Speltz, Shimamura, & McReynolds, 1982).

The Good Behavior Game (GBG) is a prevalent and effective peer-mediated group support that relies on interdependent group rewards whereby peers in a team (e.g., a whole class or small groups within a class) positively influence the behavior of the group to accumulate points and earn rewards for low levels of inappropriate behavior (Barrish, Saunders, & Wolf, 1969). While the GBG was originally implemented in an elementary setting, this adaptable group structure has effectively increased appropriate behaviors in students aged preschool to adolescence, students at risk for learning and behavior problems, and students with disabilities (Bowman-Perrott, Burke, Zaini, Zhang, & Vannest, 2016; Tingstrom, Sterling-Turner, & Wilczynski, 2006). In addition to being effective in preventing problem behaviors, the GBG can be simple or complex by offering teachers flexibility in how the game is implemented and how points and rewards are earned (Tingstrom et al., 2006).

Researchers have applied interdependent group-oriented contingencies targeting academic behaviors (e.g., engagement) and performance (Skinner, Williams, & Neddenriep, 2004). The findings from this research suggest that supplementing typical classroom procedures with interdependent bonus rewards can cause meaningful increases in these behaviors (Skinner, Skinner, & Burton, 2009). Additionally, these additional rewards that are delivered to all member of a group or no member of a group enhance the amount of reinforcement all students receive at school, which can occasion many positive side effects, especially in students who rarely meet independent group-oriented criteria for earning a reward (Cashwell, Skinner, Dunn, & Lewis, 1998; Scott et al., 2017). Chapter 21 (this volume) outlines recommendations for using interdependent group contingencies while Chapter 22 (this volume) focuses on using interdependent and dependent group contingencies as peer-mediated groups supports.

STRENGTHS AND CHALLENGES

There are strengths and challenges associated with SWPBIS, classroom management, and group-oriented contingencies. While there are numerous strategies for conceptualizing these challenges, we will focus on the interaction of target behaviors and contingency. When focusing on preventing inappropriate behaviors via the application of punishment, there are several reasons why both schoolwide and classroom-wide strategies have primarily applied independent group oriented punishment procedures. First, having the same contingency for each student's behavior (independent) is easier to manage than multiple, different contingencies (e.g., different behaviors, criteria, and rewards) for each student in a group (Pumroy & McIntire, 1991). In our society, punishing someone for someone else's behavior is almost always unacceptable (Skinner, Skinner, Skinner, & Cashwell, 1999). Thus, interdependent or dependent group-oriented *punishment* should be avoided in most instances.

However, typical schoolwide or classwide independent punishment can be supplemented with interdependent group bonus rewards, which can both decrease the rate of individual students being punished and increase rewards delivered to all students. As previously mentioned, the GBG has been successful in applying interdependent group-oriented bonus rewards contingent upon lower rates of inappropriate behavior classwide or within subgroups with a class (Bowman-Perrott, et al., 2016; Tingstrom et al., 2006). With such contingencies, rather than encouraging classmates' to engage in undesired behaviors, students may encourage or support each other to avoid such behaviors.

One concern with applications of interdependent group-oriented contingencies applied to inappropriate behavior is that classmates may threaten or punish students who behave poorly, which results in the group failing to earn a reward (Romeo, 1998). There are several strategies that can be used to reduce these negative side effects when using interdependent group contingencies, including targeting behaviors that are not public (e.g., academic behaviors), randomly selecting target behaviors and criteria, and not informing students which target behavior was selected unless they earn their reward (Skinner et al, 2009). Other strategies include teaching students how to appropriately encourage each other on how to avoid misbehaving. Finally, because educators are providing supplemental *bonus* rewards to students, the group has nothing to lose with these additional strategies, and they can only access additional reward. Educators can monitor for such behaviors (e.g., threatening peers) and suspend the contingency when students behave inappropriately in an attempt to decrease classmates' inappropriate behaviors (McCurdy, Skinner, McClurg, Whitsitt, & Moore, 2020).

Also, educators can apply a variety of other classroom management strategies that can reduce inappropriate behaviors classwide but do not involve the application of structured contingencies. For example, rather than apply one set of behavior expectations for all class activities, researchers have developed multiple sets of clear rules, with some rules designed to set expectations for some activities (e.g., independent seat work) and other rules design to set expectation for other activities (e.g., listening to teacher as the next activity is introduced). Additionally, they should develop structured routines that can be consistently used to transition students from one set of rules to another as they transition from one set of activities to another (Skinner & Skinner, 2007). Findings suggest that these types of classroom management strategies reduce inappropriate classroom behavior even when no additional contingencies are applied (Kirk et al., 2010).

Of course, the goals of education are not merely to decrease undesired behaviors but to also enhance desired student behaviors. Again, general classroom management strategies can enhance students' desired behaviors and learning. Such procedures can also be supplemented with interdependent group-oriented bonus rewards delivered contingent upon students' academic performance (McCurdy et al., 2020), attending to instruction (Heering & Wilder, 2006), and desired prosocial behaviors (Wright, Skinner, Kirkpatrick, Daniels, & Moore, 2019). A recent review of research that focused on the impact of such supplemental rewards on students' mathematics performance (e.g., percentage correct on assignments, homework, exams) showed that such procedures enhance students' percentage correct classwide, frequently by 20% or more (McCurdy et al., 2020). An interesting finding from the math studies was that applying interdependent bonus rewards caused the largest increases in the lowest-performing students (e.g., Popkin & Skinner, 2003). The reason this may have occurred is that these students could not perform well enough to earn rewards that are typically delivered contingent upon all students meeting the same criteria. Thus, they may have stopped putting forth much effort. However, with interdependent bonus rewards, their improved performance lead to reinforcement when their group met their goal (Scott et al., 2017).

CONSIDERATIONS FOR IMPLEMENTATION

All of the peer-mediated group supports presented in this section focus on simultaneously establishing structures and providing rewards to promote appropriate behaviors for groups of students. To one degree or another, the strategies outlined in this section focus on one or more of the following: defining criteria for expectations (whether they be criteria for academic performance, for appropriate behavior, or for routines or procedures), explicitly teaching students what we expect them to do (e.g., providing explicit instruction, modeling, examples and nonexamples, opportunities to practice expected behaviors in the natural environment), and providing feedback and reinforcement for appropriate behaviors or to correct inappropriate behaviors. Much of the research on these peer-mediated group supports is grounded in principles and decades of research in applied behavior analysis, and findings from these extensive bodies of research provide evidence for the potential of these strategies to improve outcomes of students and across multiple behavioral and academic domains.

In subsequent chapters in this section, authors outline recommendations for how to implement these strategies. However, a broad outline of considerations related to implementing these peer-mediated strategies will be provided that are based primarily on our work with teachers (preservice and in-service) and school professionals. The focus is on potential challenges specific to defining criteria or expectations, explicitly teaching expectations to students, and providing reinforcement for appropriate behaviors and reduced problem behaviors.

With respect to identifying criteria and expectations, it is important to choose the most meaningful and important target behaviors that are functionally, socially, and culturally relevant. In particular, defined behavioral expectations should enable students to be successful across multiples settings, not only in schools but also in their homes, communities, and workplaces. Finally, behavioral expectations should be aligned with the overall goals of the context (e.g., a positive, productive, and safe classroom).

For some schools, it can be challenging to gain consensus across most teachers, staff, and students to identify a small set of behavioral expectations that are applicable and appropriate across multiple school settings. Moreover, some schools struggle with ensuring all adults in the school consistently apply these expectations. Inconsistencies in expectations can occur within a single classroom, too; sometimes teachers have rules or expectations that are not applied consistently. For example, a teacher has a rule that students must raise their hand before speaking, but the teacher does not always expect students to raise their hand, and in some cases, the teacher may actually reinforce a student when he calls out a correct answer.

Second, there are considerations for explicitly teaching expectations and, in particular, teaching expectations for student behavior. It is often recommended that schools and teachers build in sufficient time at the beginning of the year to teach expectations. But, in reality, students need frequent, ongoing reminders and reteaching of expectations throughout the school year. It is sometimes difficult for teachers to find time to devote to providing instruction focused on appropriate classroom and school behavior. Moreover, some teachers do not see the importance in teaching expected behaviors because they feel like students should already know how to behavior. Some teachers of older students in middle or high school settings are most reluctant to spend the time and effort on teaching behavioral expectations.

Finally, there are challenges associated with positive feedback and reinforcement. With respect to incidental inappropriate behaviors, typical schoolwide and classroom procedures focus on designing, installing, and maintaining preventive independent group-oriented punishment procedures. Thus, educators spend much of their time monitoring students for inappropriate behavior and punishing those behaviors (Skinner, Cashwell, & Skinner, 2000). Even though many educators would rather not spend so much time and energy applying these punishment systems, they may still find it difficult to simultaneously monitor and reward incidental desired or prosocial behaviors. It is critical that everyone supports educators' efforts to enhance their reinforcement for incidental, desired social behaviors, even when students are merely "doing what they should be doing." One solution may be to teach students to monitor, encourage, and reward each other's prosocial behaviors (Skinner, Neddenriep, Robinson, Ervin, & Jones, 2002).

CONCLUSION

We conclude this introductory chapter with a reminder that the peer-mediated group supports are aimed at establishing productive and efficient school environments where students and teachers feel safe, supported, and respected and where all students can learn and be successful. Schools and classrooms should be places where students want to be, and they should be places where students think good things can happen to them and their peers. As the peer group may be a critical potential behavior change agent (Greenwood & Hops, 1981), procedures that enhance the quality of peer interactions and support peers' efforts to encourage one another to learn and engage in desired social behaviors should be the focus of researchers and educators.

REFERENCES

Barrish, H. H., Saunders, M., & Wolf, M. M. (1969). Good behavior game: Effects of individual contingencies for group consequences on disruptive behavior in a classroom. *Journal of Applied Behavior Analysis, 2,* 119–124. doi10.1901/jaba.1969.2-119

Bowman-Perrott, L., Burke, M. D., Zaini, S., Zhang, N., & Vannest, K. (2016). Promoting positive behavior using the good behavior game: A meta-analysis of single-case research. *Journal of Positive Behavior Interventions, 18,* 180–190. doi:10.1177/1098300715592355

Bradshaw, C. P., Koth, K. W., Thorton, L. A., & Leaf, P. J. (2009). Altering school climate through school-wide positive behavioral interventions and supports: Findings from a group-randomized effectiveness trial. *Prevention Science, 10,* 100–115. doi:10.1007/s11121-008-0114-9

Bradshaw, C. P., Mitchell, M. M., & Leaf, P. J. (2010). Examining the effects of schoolwide positive behavioral interventions and supports on student outcomes: Results from a randomized controlled effectiveness trial in elementary schools. *Journal of Positive Behavior Interventions, 12,* 133–148. doi:10.1177/1098300709334798

Cashwell, C. S., Skinner, C. H., Dunn, M., & Lewis, J. (1998). Group reward programs: A humanistic approach. *Humanistic Education and Development, 37,* 47–53.

Chow, J., & Gilmour, A. (2016). Designing and implementing group contingencies in the classroom: A teacher's guide. *Teaching Exceptional Children, 48*(3), 137–143. doi:10.1177/0040059915618197

Epstein, M., Atkins, M., Cullinan, D., Kutash, K., & Weaver, R. (2008). Reducing behavior problems in the elementary school classroom: A practice guide (NCEE #2008-012). *National Center for Education Evaluation and Regional Assistance, Institute of Education Sciences, U.S. Department of Education.* Retrieved from http://ies.ed.gov/ncee/wwc/publications/practiceguides

Farkas, M. S., Simonsent, B., Migdole, S., Donovan, M. E., Clemens, K., & Cicchese, V. (2012). Schoolwide positive behaviors support in an alternative school setting: An evaluation of fidelity, outcomes, and social validity of tier I implementation. *Journal of Emotional and Behavioral Disorders, 20,* 275–288. doi:10.1177/1063426610389615

Fudge, D. L., Reece, L., Skinner, C. H., & Cowden, D. (2007). Using multiple classroom rules, public cues, and consistent transition strategies to reduce inappropriate vocalization: An investigation of the color wheel. *Journal of Evidence-Based Practices for Schools, 8,* 102–119.

Greenwood C. R., & Hops H. (1981) Group-oriented contingencies and peer behavior change. In P. S. Strain, Ed., *The utilization of classroom peers as behavior change agents. Applied clinical psychology* (pp. 189–259). Boston, MA: Springer. doi:10.1007/978-1-4899-2180-2_7

Greenwood, C. R., Hops, H., Delquadri, J., & Guild, J. (1974). Group contingencies for group consequences in classroom management: A further analysis. *Journal of Applied Behavior Analysis, 7*(3), 413–425. doi:10.1901/jaba.1974.7-413

Heering, P. W., & Wilder, D. A. (2006). The use of dependent group contingencies to increase on-task behavior in two general education classrooms. *Education and Treatment of Children, 29,* 459–467.

Horner, R. H., Sugai, G., Smolkowski, K., Eber, L., Nakasato, J. Todd, A. W., & Experanza, J. (2009). A randomized, wait-list controlled effectiveness trial assessing schoolwide positive behavior support in elementary schools. *Journal of Positive Behavior Intervention, 11,* 133–144. doi:10.1177/1098300709332067

Kagan, S. (1985). Dimensions of cooperative classroom structures. In R. Slavin, S. Sharan, S. Kagan, R. H. Lazarowitz, C. Webb, & R. Schmuck (Eds.), *Learning to cooperate, cooperating to learn* (pp. 67–96). New York, NY: Plenum.

Kirk, E. R, Becker, J. A., Skinner, C. H., Fearrington, J. Y., McCane-Bowling, S. J., Amburn, C., . . . Greear, C. (2010). Deceasing inappropriate vocalizations using group contingencies and color wheel procedures: A component analysis. *Psychology in the Schools, 47,* 931–943.

Lewis, T. J., Hudson, S., Richter, M., & Johnson, N. (2004). Scientifically supported practices in emotional and behavioral disorders: A proposed approach and brief review of current practices. *Behavioral Disorders, 29,* 247–259.

Lewis, T. J., McIntosh, K., Simonsen, B., Mitchell, B. S., & Hatton, H. L. (2017). Schoolwide systems of positive behavior support: Implications for students at risk and with emotional/behavioral disorders. *AERA Open, 3*(2), 1–11. doi:10.1177/2332858417711428

Litow, L., & Pumroy, D. K. (1975). A brief review of classroom group-oriented contingencies. *Journal of Applied Behavior Analysis, 8*, 341–347.

McCurdy, M, Skinner, C. H., McClurg, V., Whitsitt, L. & Moore, T. (2020). Bonus rewards for everyone: Enhancing mathematics performance with supplemental interdependent group contingencies. *Preventing School Failure, 64*(1), 77–88.

Moore, T. C., Alpers, A. J., Rhyne, R., Coleman, M. B., Gordon, J. R., Daniels, S., . . . Park, Y. (2019). Brief prompting to improve classroom behavior: A first-pass intervention option. *Journal of Positive Behavioral Interventions, 21*, 30–41. doi:10.1177/1098300718774881

Muscott, H. S., Mann, E. L., & LeBrun, M. R. (2008). Positive behavioral interventions and supports in New Hampshire: Effects of large-scale implementation of schoolwide positive behavior support on student discipline and academic achievement. *Journal of Positive Behavior Interventions, 10*, 190–205. doi:10.1177/1098300708316258

Popkin, J., & Skinner, C. H. (2003). Enhancing academic performance in a classroom serving students with serious emotional disturbance: Interdependent group contingencies with randomly selected components. *School Psychology Review, 32*, 271–284.

Pumroy, D., K., & McIntire, R. (1991). Behavior analysis/modification for everyone. *Journal of Behavioral Education, 1*, 283–294. doi:10.1007/BF00947183

Romeo, F. F. (1998). The negative effects of using a group contingency system of classroom management. *Journal of Instructional Psychology, 25*(2), 130–133.

Scott, K. C., Skinner, C. H., Moore, T. C., McCurdy, M., Ciancio, D., & Cihak, D. (2017). Evaluating and comparing the effects of group contingencies on mathematics accuracy in a first-grade classroom: Class average criteria versus unknown small-group average criteria. *School Psychology Review, 46*, 262–271.

Simonsen, B., Britton, L., & Young, D. (2010). School-wide positive behavior support in an alternative school setting: A case study. *Journal of Positive Behavioral Interventions, 12*, 180–191. doi:10.1177/1098300708330495

Simonsen, B., Fairbanks, S., Briesch, A., Myers, D., & Sugai, G. (2008). Evidence-based practices in classroom management: Considerations for research to practice. *Education and Treatment of Children, 31*, 351–380.

Skinner, C. H., Cashwell, T. H., & Skinner, A. L. (2000). Increasing tootling: The effects of a peer monitored interdependent group contingencies on students' reports of peers' prosocial behaviors. *Psychology in the Schools, 37*, 263–270.

Skinner, C. H., Neddenriep, C. E., Robinson, S. L., Ervin, R., & Jones, K. (2002). Altering educational environments through positive peer reporting: Prevention and remediation of social problems associated with behavior disorders. *Psychology in the Schools, 39*, 191–202.

Skinner, C. H., & Skinner, A. L. (2007). Establishing an evidence base for a classroom management procedure with a series of studies: Evaluating the color wheel. *Journal of Evidence-Based Practices for Schools, 8*, 88–101.

Skinner, C. H., Skinner, A. L., & Burton, B. (2009). Applying group-oriented contingencies in classrooms. In K. A. Akin-Little, S. G. Little, M. Bray, & T. Kehle (Eds.), *Behavioral interventions in schools: Evidence-based positive strategies* (pp. 157–170). Washington, DC: APA Press. doi:10.1037/11886-010

Skinner, C. H., Skinner, C. F., Skinner, A. L., & Cashwell, T. C. (1999). Using interdependent contingencies with groups of students: Why the principal kissed a pig at assembly. *Educational Administration Quarterly, 35*, 806–820. doi:10.1177/00131619921968833

Skinner, C. H., Williams, R. L., & Neddenriep, C. E. (2004). Using interdependent group-oriented reinforcement to enhance academic performance in general education classrooms. *School Psychology Review, 33*, 384–397.

Speltz, M. L., Shimamura, J. W., & McReynolds, W. T. (1982). Procedural variations in group contingencies: Effects on children's academic and social behaviors. *Journal of Applied Behavior Analysis, 15*(4), 533–544. doi:10.1901/jaba.1982.15-533

Sprague, J., Colvin, G., & Irvin, L. (1996). *The Oregon school safety survey.* Eugene, OR: University of Oregon.

Sugai, G. & Horner, R. (2002). The evolution of discipline practices: School-wide positive behavior supports. *Behavior Psychology in the Schools, 24*(1–2), 23–50. doi:10.1300/J019v24n01_03

Sugai, G., Horner, R. H., Dunlap, G., Heineman, M., Lewis, T. J., Nelson, C. M., . . . Reuf, M. (2000). Applying positive behavioral support and functional behavioral assessment in schools. *Journal of Positive Behavioral Interventions, 2*, 131–143. doi:10.1177/109830070000200302

Theodore, L. A., Bray, M. A., & Kehle, T. J. (2004). A comparative study of group contingencies and randomized reinforcers to reduce disruptive classroom behavior. *School Psychology Quarterly, 19*(3), 253–271. doi:10.1521/scpq.19.3.253.40280/

Tingstrom, D. H., Sterling-Turner, H. E., & Wilczynski, S. M. (2006). The Good Behavior Game: 1969–2002. *Behavior Modification, 30*, 225–253. doi:10.1177/0145445503261165

Waasdorp, T. E., Bradshaw, C. P., & Leaf, P. J. (2012). The impact of schoolwide positive behavioral interventions and supports on bullying and peer rejection: A randomized controlled effectiveness trial. *Archives of Pediatrics and Adolescent Medicine, 166*, 149–156. doi:10.1001/archpediatrics.2011.755

Wright, S., Skinner, C. H., Kirkpatrick, B. A., Daniels, S., & Moore, T. (2019, February). *Generalizing social skills with a positive peer reporting intervention.* Paper presented at the annual meeting of the National Association of School Psychologists, Atlanta, GA.

Zaheer, I., Maggin, D., McDaniel, S., McIntosh, K., Rodriquez, B. J., & Fogt, J. B. (2019). Implementation of promising practices that support students with emotional and behavioral disorders. *Behavioral Disorders, 44*, 117–128. doi:10.1177/0198742918821331

School-Wide Positive Behavioral Interventions and Supports

KENT MCINTOSH AND ANGUS KITTELMAN ∎

Schools implementing evidence-based social-emotional practices and programs learn that successful implementation hinges on the systems supporting ongoing delivery. Systems include structures and strategies that assist school personnel in delivering these practices with fidelity. School-Wide Positive Behavioral Interventions and Supports (SWPBIS; Horner & Sugai, 2015) is one example of an empirically supported framework with systems designed to enhance the delivery of evidence-based practices promoting prosocial behaviors in schools (Horner & Sugai, 2015; Swain-Bradway, Lindstrom Johnson, Bradshaw, & McIntosh, 2017).

SWPBIS FRAMEWORK

As opposed to being a practice in itself, SWPBIS is a framework designed to support the implementation of many evidence-based practices. The framework helps ensure that practices are connected (e.g., similar features and goals) and delivered across all relevant school settings (e.g., classrooms, hallways, playgrounds, buses). Additionally, the framework ensures all school personnel have a common understanding of how practices are linked and share common goals (e.g., improving student prosocial behaviors, attendance, school climate).

Multitiered. Within the framework, SWPBIS is comprised of three tiers of support. At each tier, school personnel deliver evidence-based practices to students, based on their level of need. As with a public health model, all students receive a universal layer of social-emotional support (Tier

1). However, some students will need some more support (low effort, sometimes delivered in groups; Tier 2), and a few will need intensive and individualized support (Tier 3; Gage, Whitford, & Katsiyannis, 2018).

Preventive and instructional. As intensive and individualized supports are costly and time-intensive to deliver, investing in preventing minor unwanted student behaviors before they intensify is a proactive strategy. Research indicates that investing in strong Tier 1 prevention systems improves student outcomes and can reduce the high financial burden associated long-term negative student behaviors (e.g., student dropout; Swain-Bradway et al., 2017). A strategy for preventing unwanted behaviors is to provide explicit instruction and reinforce students' engagement in positive behavior expectations (Horner & Sugai, 2015).

Systems focus. SWPBIS is comprised of organizational systems that support implementation and continuous improvement. SWPBIS teams develop, implement, and improve on school systems. These systems are critical for ensuring that (a) school personnel have ongoing professional development to implement SWPBIS with fidelity, (b) school leadership support implementation, and (c) teams use data to guide implementation efforts (i.e., allocation of resources, identifying areas for improvement; Swain-Bradway et al., 2017).

SWPBIS Evidence of Effectiveness

The evidence base of SWPBIS in documenting improvements in student and school outcomes has increasingly grown over the last 20 years. Validation studies include randomized control trials, single-case experimental studies, longitudinal and correlational studies, and descriptive case evaluations (Gage et al., 2018; Horner & Sugai, 2015; Solomon, Klein, Hintze, Cressey, & Peller, 2012). For example, Solomon and colleagues (2012) conducted a meta-analysis of single-case studies spanning 16 years examining the effects of SWPBIS on student behaviors across school contexts (e.g., classrooms, hallways, recesses). Effect sizes across studies were positive and ranged from small to moderate, with larger effects occurring for students in unstructured contexts (i.e., recess and hallways). More recently, Gage et al. (2018) conducted a systemic review and meta-analysis of experimental and quasi-experimental group designs examining the effects of Tier 1 SWPBIS on reducing exclusionary disciplinary practices. Using schools as the unit of analysis, the authors found that implementing Tier 1 had a significant, large effect on reducing suspensions.

Core Features of Tier 1 SWPBIS

Tier 1 is comprised of several core features (Horner & Sugai, 2015). First, Tier 1 teams *define* the important and valued student and/or school outcomes to improve upon after consulting with families and community stakeholders. These may include decreasing the disproportionality with which students of color receive office discipline referrals, increasing student attendance, or improving school safety. Valued school outcomes may also overlap well with district improvement goals (e.g., increasing graduation rates). Once outcomes are defined, Tier 1 teams are responsible for providing professional development to school personnel on how to teach, monitor, and respond to students engaging in prosocial behaviors that match these valued outcomes. For example, school personnel will *teach* students a small number of schoolwide behavior expectations and consistently reinforce them across all school contexts (Solomon et al., 2012).

Once students have learned these schoolwide expectations, school personnel will continue to *monitor* and positively *respond* to students engaging in these expectations throughout the school year. By monitoring and positively responding to students (e.g., verbal praise, small tangible incentives), expectations are continually reinforced (Horner & Sugai, 2015). In addition, when students engage in unwanted behaviors that conflict with these expectations, it presents valuable learning opportunities for school personnel to reteach them to students. Finally, teams *use data for decision making* when monitoring implementation of the core Tier 1 features (Gage et al., 2018; Horner & Sugai, 2015). Ongoing monitoring of school-level data helps Tier 1 teams identify areas for improvement. For example, data could indicate the need for reteaching students the schoolwide behavior expectations in specific settings where unwanted behaviors are more often occurring (Gage et al., 2018).

Peer-Mediated Intervention Within SWPBIS

Although ensuring that schools and classrooms are safe, predictable, and positive is primarily the responsibility of school personnel and administrators, there can be a strong and active leadership role for students in SWPBIS. These opportunities can be categorized into the avenues of representation, peer modeling, peer management, and peer-mediated instruction.

Representation. As described earlier, SWPBIS implementation is guided through a team-based approach. Especially at the secondary level, teams can improve outcomes through including a student representative or even a student subcommittee on the Tier 1 team (Good, McIntosh, & Gietz, 2011). Students can contribute to the school SWPBIS team's efforts by sharing student perspectives and having student voice shape the creation and refinement of systems. In fact, high schools cannot achieve the highest fidelity score for team representation on the SWPBIS Tiered Fidelity Inventory (TFI, a fidelity of implementation measure; Algozzine et al., 2014) without having a student member. Moreover, when students participate in designing the imagery of SWPBIS in a school (e.g., develop expectations posters), students can see themselves in the systems and may be more invested in them.

Peer modeling. Because SWPBIS is a schoolwide effort and all students receive instruction in the schoolwide expectations and norms, students can serve as potential models of positive behavior for each other throughout the day (see Chapter 14, this volume). When students see their peers acting in line with the school values, they have access to continuous prompting for positive behavior. Hence, in a school with strong SWPBIS systems, students who are unsure of the correct behavior can use the "look around you" approach to find cues for prosocial interactions (McIntosh & Goodman, 2016).

Peer management. Beyond allowing for abundant peer modeling by teaching the expectations to all students, strong SWPBIS systems allow an opportunity for students to intervene with each other, either to acknowledge the use of prosocial behavior or provide an instructional correction (see Chapter 10, this volume). When teachers and other school personnel regularly use the language of the schoolwide expectations to describe student behavior, they provide a tool that anyone in the school—especially students—can use to interact regarding the need for prosocial behavior. For example, if a student is being treated disrespectfully by a peer, that student could use the language of the expectations to intervene (e.g., "At Lincoln, we use respectful words"), with the knowledge that the peer has received the expectations lessons and is familiar with them.

Peer-mediated instruction. Finally, a SWPBIS system implemented fully provides students with the opportunities to teach and demonstrate the schoolwide lessons themselves. During lesson plan design, students can provide valuable contextual information to help the lessons have better match with the students. Within the lesson and with proper guidance, students can teach the lessons in ways that provide clear instruction but are also potentially more engaging to peers. One particularly important area for peer-mediated instruction is bullying prevention. Without student input into desired responses to bullying behavior or delivery by trusted peers or respected student leaders, students may disregard lessons and choose to continue potentially maladaptive responses instead of intervening as a bystander or notifying school personnel. As an example, a middle school in western Canada used the freely available SWPBIS bullying prevention curriculum (Ross, Horner, & Stiller, 2008) and asked students to provide input into lesson design and deliver the lessons themselves. The school team deliberately selected a range of students (including popular students and those who had previously engaged in bullying behavior) to teach lessons, which resulted in a dramatic reduction in referrals for bullying and harassment (Good et al., 2011).

RECOMMENDATIONS FOR IMPLEMENTATION

Implementing Tier 1 involves unified efforts from administration and school personnel. Districts can also be a powerful implementation driver by providing leadership support, resources (e.g., funding, access to evidence-based practices, research-validated fidelity tools), and technical expertise (e.g., training and ongoing coaching; Mercer, McIntosh, & Hoselton, 2017). At the school level, we offer several recommendations for achieving successful Tier 1 implementation: (a) using a team-based approach to service delivery; (b) gathering input from school personnel, students, families, and community members; (c) measuring fidelity with validated tools; and (d) collecting and using data to guide decision making.

Team-Based Approach

As Tier 1 is designed to be universally implemented, we recommend including members with varying levels of knowledge about Tier 1 core features, students, and the school context on the Tier 1 team (Algozzine et al., 2014). Members typically include personnel with different roles and functions in a school (e.g., general and special education teachers, counselors, classified personnel, family members, student representative). Although members may cycle on and off the team over time, it is critical that an administrator (e.g., someone who can allocate funding for implementation, dedicate personnel time for professional development) and a person with applied behavioral expertise (e.g., knowledge of behavior interventions and systems; Algozzine et al., 2014) be present on the team throughout implementation. Tier 1 teams are responsible for overseeing implementation by collecting and summarizing data (fidelity and student and/or school outcomes), and making decisions about where to improve ongoing implementation, based on where the data indicate the biggest needs. Research indicates that when teams use data for decision-making during Tier 1 implementation, they are more likely to continue implementing with fidelity two years later (McIntosh, Mercer, et al., 2018).

Input from School Personnel, Students, Families, and Community

We also recommend that Tier 1 teams obtain at least yearly feedback from all relevant stakeholders (e.g., students, families, community members). Obtaining input from multiple sources ensures that different populations and perspectives are represented. During initial implementation, this step is a powerful way to gather consensus on whether Tier 1 core features are culturally appropriate and teams have buy-in for implementation from stakeholders. Input from stakeholders can be gathered at school events or workshops or through surveys (e.g., McIntosh, Pinkelman, Girvan, & Sugai, 2017). As described earlier with peer-mediated instruction, students can provide valuable contributions on how to contextualize and teach Tier 1 lessons so they are relevant for peers (Good et al., 2011; Ross et al., 2008).

Measuring Fidelity With Validated Tools

Assessing fidelity is a powerful way to measure adherence (i.e., that school personnel are consistently and appropriately delivering core features of Tier 1) and quality of implementation delivery (Fritz, Harn, Biancarosa, Lucero, & Flannery, 2019). We recommend assessing fidelity with the assistance of an internal or external coach with applied behavioral and systems expertise, as including a coach has been shown to lead to more accurate self-reports of fidelity (McIntosh, Massar, et al., 2017). We also recommend that Tier 1 teams identify fidelity tools that are both reliable and valid, while also sensitive to detecting implementation change over time (Fritz et al., 2019). Recently, Mercer, McIntosh, and Hoselton (2017) published an article comparing the psychometric properties of five different fidelity measures assessing Tier 1 fidelity and found the measures to be largely comparable in assessing overall Tier 1 fidelity (Mercer et al., 2017).

Collecting and Using Data to Guide Decision-Making

Once fidelity data are collected using research-validated measures, Tier 1 teams can use fidelity and outcome data (e.g., number of suspensions or referrals, perceptions of school climate, outcomes across different student groups) to serve two purposes: guiding ongoing implementation efforts and summarizing and reporting on data annually to stakeholders (Algozzine et al., 2014). In terms of the first, more frequent assessments of fidelity and student or school outcomes (e.g., every two to three months; Algozzine et al., 2014) assist teams with identifying areas for improvement and where progress has been made with implementation, improving outcomes, or both. We have found the ability for teams to collect, summarize, and share data to be a powerful implementation strategy. For example, research indicates that the frequency Tier 1 teams collect and share data with all school personnel is significantly related to four factors (school priority, team use of data, district priority, and district capacity) that predict sustained implementation of Tier 1 SWPBIS with fidelity (McIntosh, Kim, Mercer, Strickland-Cohen, & Horner, 2015). Finally, we recommend summarizing and reporting on fidelity and outcome data annually to stakeholders (e.g., families, community members) to increase implementation transparency (Algozzine et al., 2014). Having year-by-year comparisons of fidelity and outcome data show school personnel and other stakeholders the extent that schools are making progress toward implementation and improving student and school outcomes.

CONSIDERATIONS OF DIVERSITY AND EQUITY IN SWPBIS

Although the effects of SWPBIS on general student outcomes are well-documented, there is also evidence showing that SWPBIS can be effective in reducing the discipline gap between students of color and their White peers, as well as between students with disabilities and those without disabilities. For example, a recent nationwide evaluation showed that schools implementing SWPBIS with adequate fidelity of implementation suspended a lower percentage of African American,

Table 18.1. Interventions with Promising Evidence for Increasing Equity in School Discipline

Element	Studies
Tier 1 SWPBIS	McIntosh, Gion, and Bastable (2019)
	Swain-Bradway et al. (2019)
	Vincent, Swain-Bradway, Tobin, and May (2011)
Formal Acknowledgement/ Reward Systems	Barclay (2017)
	Tobin and Vincent (2011)
Use of Disaggregated Data for Decision Making	Tobin and Vincent (2011)
	McIntosh, Ellwood, McCall, and Girvan (2018)
Brief Classroom Strategies	Cook, Doung, Pullman, McIntosh, McGinnis, Fiat, and Larson (2018)
	Gion, McIntosh, and Falcon (2019)
	Okonofua, Paunesku, and Walton (2016)
Classroom Coaching	Bradshaw et al. (2018)
	Gion et al. (2019)
	Gregory, Hafen, Ruzek, Mikami, Allen, and Pianta (2016)

Pacific Islander, and multiracial students than the national average (McIntosh, Gion, & Bastable, 2018). These results are consistent with previous studies showing lower suspension or office discipline referral risk for students of color in schools implementing SWPBIS (Nkomo & Baker, 2017; Vincent, Cartledge, May, & Tobin, 2009, October; Vincent, Swain-Bradway, Tobin, & May, 2011). There is also evidence of SWPBIS reducing disciplinary risk for students with disabilities as well (Tobin, Horner, Vincent, & Swain-Bradway, 2012). However, these results also show that typical SWPBIS implementation should not be expected to eliminate the discipline gap entirely.

An explicit focus on disciplinary equity within SWPBIS can even further narrow the discipline gap. For example, schools in Wisconsin that completed professional development in PBIS, early literacy, and cultural responsiveness decreased the discipline gap for African American students and students with disabilities (Swain-Bradway, Gulbrandson, Galston, & McIntosh, 2019). In addition, embedding equity-specific interventions within SWPBIS systems has increased equity in school discipline (Gion, McIntosh, & Falcon, 2019; McIntosh, Ellwood, McCall, & Girvan, 2018). Table 18.1 provides a list of interventions with initial evidence for improving equity in school discipline.

Potential Mechanisms for SWPBIS Increasing Disciplinary Equity

Given that SWPBIS appears to be effective in increasing disciplinary equity and there is little evidence that cultural responsiveness training is effective (Bottiani,

Larson, Debnam, Bischoff, & Bradshaw, 2018), it seems plausible that there are specific features of the SWPBIS framework that enable equity interventions to be effective. This section describes core features of SWPBIS and potential effects on equity.

Defining and teaching expectations. The actions of defining and explicitly teaching expectations serves to make the hidden curriculum visible, removing assumptions about student knowledge and instead teaching each student what is expected. Involving students in activities selecting salient schoolwide expectations that fit the values of families and the community and identifying how expectations for their behavior vary across settings (e.g., school, home, neighborhood) has been shown to be effective in making student–teacher interactions more positive (Gion et al., 2019).

Acknowledging prosocial behavior. Two separate studies using separate fidelity of implementation measures have shown that schools with higher fidelity of formal systems for acknowledging positive behavior have more equitable discipline practices (Barclay, 2017; Tobin & Vincent, 2011). Such findings could indicate that reducing disparities in school discipline may start with reducing disparities in student acknowledgment. Although rates of reinforcement may be the primary driver of these findings, it is also possible that perceived fairness (e.g., students noticing which student groups are disproportionately acknowledged) could also be a factor (Gion et al., 2019).

Responding instructionally to unwanted behavior. Because patterns of teacher responses to student behavior indicate the influence of implicit racial bias (Girvan, Gion, McIntosh, & Smolkowski, 2017), it is important to give teachers strategies to neutralize their implicit biases and respond instructionally to unwanted behaviors instead of a knee-jerk reaction of excluding some students from instruction (McIntosh, Girvan, Horner, & Smolkowski, 2014). Training teachers in a neutralizing routine can allow them to respond instructionally instead of harshly, decreasing disproportionality (Cook et al., 2018).

Using data for decision-making. Finally, there is evidence that schools that have greater use of discipline data for decision-making have increased disciplinary equity (Tobin & Vincent, 2011). To ensure that PBIS systems are effective for all student groups (e.g., by race/ethnicity, special education status), teams can disaggregate their discipline data and examine effects for each group of interest (McIntosh, Barnes, Morris, & Eliason, 2014). A particularly promising approach is to examine data for vulnerable decision points, that is, specific discipline situations that are more prone to implicit bias (Smolkowski, Girvan, McIntosh, Nese, & Horner, 2016). Selecting interventions based on vulnerable decision points has been shown to be effective in increasing equity (McIntosh, Ellwood, et al., 2018).

CONCLUSION

As a framework for implementing evidence-based practices, PBIS represents an important avenue for engaging students in the goal of improving valued outcomes. Using a systems approach provides an opportunity for ensuring meaningful participation and peer intervention in a way that centers students in the school culture. As such, it also represents an important avenue for increasing equity in school discipline.

ACKNOWLEDGMENTS

The research reported here was supported by the Institute of Education Sciences, U.S. Department of Education, through Grant R324A1800027 to the University of Oregon. The opinions expressed are those of the authors and do not represent views of the Institute or the U.S. Department of Education.

REFERENCES

Algozzine, R. F., Barrett, S., Eber, L., George, H., Horner, R. H., Lewis, T. J., . . . Sugai, G. (2014). *SWPBIS tiered fidelity inventory.* Eugene, OR: OSEP Technical Assistance Center on Positive Behavioral Interventions and Supports. http://www.pbis.org

Barclay, C. M. (2017). *Benchmarks of equality? School-wide positive behavior interventions and supports and school discipline risk and disparities for Black and Hispanic students* (Unpublished doctoral dissertation). University of South Florida, Tampa, FL.

Bottiani, J. H., Larson, K. E., Debnam, K. J., Bischoff, C. M., & Bradshaw, C. P. (2018). Promoting educators' use of culturally responsive practices: A systematic review of inservice interventions. *Journal of Teacher Education, 69,* 367–385. doi:10.1177/0022487117722553

Cook, C. R., Doung, M. T., Pullmann, M., McIntosh, K., McGinnis, J., Fiat, A. E., & Larson, M. F. (2018). Addressing discipline disparities for Black male students: Linking malleable root causes to feasible and effective practices. *School Psychology Review, 47*(2), 135–152. doi:10.1177/1098300717753831

Fritz, R., Harn, B., Biancarosa, G., Lucero, A., & Flannery, K. B. (2019). How much is enough? Evaluating intervention implementation efficiently. *Assessment for Effective Intervention, 44,* 135–144. doi:10.1177/1534508418772909

Gage, N. A., Whitford, D. K., & Katsiyannis, A. (2018). A review of schoolwide positive behavior interventions and supports as a framework for reducing disciplinary exclusions. *Journal of Special Education, 52,* 142–151.

Gion, C., McIntosh, K., & Falcon, S. F. (2019). *Effects of a multicomponent classroom intervention on racial disproportionality in school discipline.* Manuscript under review.

Girvan, E. J., Gion, C., McIntosh, K., & Smolkowski, K. (2017). The relative contribution of subjective office referrals to racial disproportionality in school discipline. *School Psychology Quarterly, 32,* 392–404. doi:10.1037/spq0000178

Good, C., McIntosh, K., & Gietz, C. (2011). Integrating bullying prevention into schoolwide positive behavior support. *Teaching Exceptional Children, 44*(1), 48–56.

Horner, R. H., & Sugai, G. (2015). School-wide PBIS: An example of applied behavior analysis implemented at a scale of social importance. *Behavior Analysis in Practice, 8,* 80–85. doi:10.1007/s40617-015-0045-4

McIntosh, K., Barnes, A., Morris, K., & Eliason, B. M. (2014). *Using discipline data within SWPBIS to identify and address disproportionality: A guide for school teams.* Eugene, OR: OSEP Technical Assistance Center on Positive Behavioral Interventions and Supports. University of Oregon.

McIntosh, K., Ellwood, K., McCall, L., & Girvan, E. J. (2018). Using discipline data within a PBIS framework to enhance equity in school discipline. *Intervention in School and Clinic, 53,* 146–152.

McIntosh, K., Gion, C., & Bastable, E. (2018). *Do schools implementing SWPBIS have decreased racial disproportionality in school discipline?* (PBIS evaluation brief). Eugene, OR: OSEP TA Center on Positive Behavioral Interventions and Supports.

McIntosh, K., Girvan, E. J., Horner, R. H., & Smolkowski, K. (2014). Education not incarceration: A conceptual model for reducing racial and ethnic disproportionality in school discipline. *Journal of Applied Research on Children, 5*(2), 1–22.

McIntosh, K., & Goodman, S. (2016). *Integrated multi-tiered systems of support: Blending RTI and PBIS.* New York, NY: Guilford Press.

McIntosh, K., Kim, J., Mercer, S. H., Strickland-Cohen, M. K., & Horner, R. H. (2015). Variables associated with enhanced sustainability of school-wide positive behavioral interventions and supports. *Assessment for Effective Intervention, 40,* 184–191.

McIntosh, K., Massar, M., Algozzine, R. F., George, H. P., Horner, R. H., Lewis, T. J., & Swain-Bradway, J. (2017). Technical adequacy of the SWPBIS Tiered Fidelity Inventory. *Journal of Positive Behavior Interventions, 19,* 3–13.

McIntosh, K., Mercer, S. H., Nese, R. N. T., Strickland-Cohen, M. K., Kittelman, A., Hoselton, R., & Horner, R. H. (2018). Factors predicting sustained implementation of a universal behavior support framework. *Educational Researcher, 47,* 307–316.

McIntosh, K., Pinkelman, S., Girvan, E. J., & Sugai, G. (2017). *Stakeholder Input and Satisfaction Survey–Student (SISS-Student).* Unpublished instrument, University of Oregon, Eugene, OR. http://www.pbisapps.org

Mercer, S. H., McIntosh, K., & Hoselton, R. (2017). Comparability of fidelity measures for assessing tier 1 school-wide positive behavioral interventions and supports. *Journal of Positive Behavior Interventions, 19,* 195–204.

Nkomo, L., & Baker, M. (2017). *Rhode Island PBIS annual report 2016–17.* Providence, RI: Paul V. Sherlock Center on Disabilities, Rhode Island College.

Ross, S. W., Horner, R. H., & Stiller, B. (2008). Bully prevention in positive behavior support. *Educational and Community Supports.* Retrieved from http://www.pbis.org/common/pbisresources/publications/bullyprevention_ES.pdf

Smolkowski, K., Girvan, E. J., McIntosh, K., Nese, R. N. T., & Horner, R. H. (2016). Vulnerable decision points in school discipline: Comparison of discipline for African American compared to White students in elementary schools. *Behavioral Disorders, 41,* 178–195.

Solomon, B. G., Klein, S. A., Hintze, J. M., Cressey, J. M., & Peller, S. L. (2012). A meta-analysis of school-wide positive behavior support: An exploratory study using single-case synthesis. *Psychology in the Schools, 49,* 105–121.

Swain-Bradway, J., Gulbrandson, K., Galston, A., & McIntosh, K. (2019). Do Wisconsin schools implementing an integrated academic and behavior support framework improve equity in academic and school discipline outcomes? (PBIS evaluation brief). *OSEP TA Center on Positive Behavioral Interventions and Supports.* Retrieved from https://www.pbis.org/resource/

do-wisconsin-schools-implementing-an-integrated-academic-and-behavior-support-framework-improve-equity-in-academic-and-school-discipline-outcomes

Swain-Bradway, J., Lindstrom Johnson, S., Bradshaw, C. P., & McIntosh, K. (2017). What are the economic costs of implementing SWPBIS in comparison to the benefits from reducing suspensions? *OSEP Technical Assistance Center of Positive Behavioral Interventions and Supports.* Retrieved from https://www.pbis.org/resource/what-are-the-economic-costs-of-implementing-swpbis-in-comparison-to-the-benefits-from-reducing-suspensions

Tobin, T. J., Horner, R. H., Vincent, C. G., & Swain-Bradway, J. (2012). *If discipline referral rates for the school as a whole are reduced, will rates for students with disabilities also be reduced?* (PBIS evaluation brief). Eugene, OR: OSEP TA Center on Positive Behavioral Interventions and Supports.

Tobin, T. J., & Vincent, C. G. (2011). Strategies for preventing disproportionate exclusions of African American students. *Preventing School Failure, 55*, 192–201. doi:10.1080/1045988X.2010.532520

Vincent, C. G., Cartledge, G., May, S. L., & Tobin, T. J. (2009, October). *Do elementary schools that document reductions in overall office discipline referrals document reductions across all student races and ethnicities?* (PBIS evaluation brief). Eugene, OR: OSEP TA Center on Positive Behavioral Interventions and Supports.

Vincent, C. G., Swain-Bradway, J., Tobin, T. J., & May, S. (2011). Disciplinary referrals for culturally and linguistically diverse students with and without disabilities: Patterns resulting from school-wide positive behavior support. *Exceptionality, 19*, 175–190.

## 19

Classroom Management

TODD F. HAYDON, CARA L. DILLON, ALANA M. KENNEDY,
AND MEAGAN N. SCOTT ■

Difficulty managing classroom behavior is often an acknowledged problem for teachers, especially teachers early in their careers (Alter & Haydon, 2017). One of the primary tasks of teachers is to help students learn; however, it is problematic for learning to take place in chaotic environments (Barbetta, Norona, & Bicard, 2005). Stress and frustration in response to managing chronic challenging behaviors is burdensome and disempowering and may well manifest in teachers as low self-efficacy and low job satisfaction (Haydon, Stevens, & Leko, 2018; Landers, Servilio, Tuttle, Alter, & Haydon, 2011). As a result, teachers have a daily challenge to establish and maintain a positive, productive classroom environment conducive to learning (Jones, & Jones, 2016). As a result, teachers may have to repeat directions, reprimand those who did not follow directions, often apply consequences for rule-breaking behaviors, or wait until all students comply (Fudge, Reece, Skinner, & Cowden, 2007).

Researchers have identified the implementation of classroom rules as an integral part of establishing an effective classroom environment. Rules provide the structure and organization for how students may respond appropriately in the classroom (Boostrom, 1991; Maag, 2004). Rules represent a social agreement recognized between the students and their teacher. The implementation of rules is cost-effective in that they are very easily implemented and focus on the prevention of challenging behaviors before they occur (Alter & Haydon, 2017). As a result, teachers spend more time and effort in teaching academic content and less time reprimanding students (Scott, Anderson, & Alter, 2011). Furthermore, when students play an active role in rule development, they have a better chance of learning, remembering the rules, and have ownership of rules (Barbetta, et al., 2005).

The purpose of this chapter is to present guidelines for establishing effective classroom rules based on the literature, recommendations for implementation of classroom rules, and describing the Color Wheel System, as well as implementation guidelines. We selected the Color Wheel System because this system incorporates different sets of rules for different classroom activities. In addition, procedures are used to transition the classroom from one activity to another, while simultaneously transitioning from one set of rules to another (Blondin, Skinner, Parkhurst, Wood, & Snyder, 2012; Kirk et al., 2010).

GUIDELINES FOR RULES AND ROUTINES

Alter and Haydon (2017) conducted a literature review on the characteristics of effective classroom rules both as a stand-alone intervention and part of a package intervention. In the reviewed studies, teachers taught rules to the students either through recitation, classroom discussion, or modeling of examples and nonexamples. Alter and Haydon (2017) identified seven features of effective classroom rules based on empirical evidence that, when followed, help create orderly, productive classrooms that teach appropriate social skills along with the academic curriculum. These features are provided in Table 19.1 and are detailed as follows.

Classroom rules should be stated positively. Classroom rules should be posted and positively written (Gable, Hester, Rock, & Hughes, 2009). Positively stated rules provide students with the necessary information to behave appropriately. Positively stated rules have a higher probability to be followed by teacher praise (Barbetta, et al., 2005). Stating rules in the negative does not help students understand what they should be doing, only what they should not be doing. Therefore, "No calling out" should be changed to "Raise your hand to speak."

Table 19.1. SEVEN EFFECTIVE FEATURES OF CLASSROOM RULES

Key Feature	Description of Key Feature
Stated positively	Use wording that describes desired behaviors rather than undesired behaviors when creating rules.
Number of rules	Teachers should aim to include fewer rather than more classroom rules. A suggested number of rules is around four.
Specific in nature	Rules should be specific, as short as possible, explicit, and observable.
Taught to students	Directly teach rules to students. It is recommended to review rules on an ongoing basis.
Publicly posted	Display rules in the classroom in writing so they are visible to all students. Rules can be given out as handouts or placed on students' desks.
Tied to positive and negative consequences	Tie rules to consequences that reinforce rule compliance and punish rule breaking.
Created collaboratively with students	Request and integrate student input when creating classroom rules to increase student buy in.

Fewer number of rules. It is recommended that teachers aim to include fewer rather than more classroom rules (Alter & Haydon, 2017). Although there is no clear consensus on the ideal number, one general recommendation is that there be a smaller rather than larger number of rules. Barbetta and colleagues (2005) recommend that there should be no greater than four to six positively stated classroom rules. This ensures that students are able to remember the rules and teachers are able to consistently enforce them.

Rules should be specific in nature. Rules should be specific, as short as possible, explicit, and observable (Barbetta, et al., 2005), which enables students to understand clearly what is expected of them and allows the teacher to provide specific praise for appropriate behavior that is connected to the classroom rules. Whereas global statements such as "Be respectful" may be used when developing a school's core Positive Behavior Interventions and Supports (PBIS) framework, classroom rules should be defined more concisely in terms of observable behaviors (Olsen, 2015). For example, "Follow adult directions" may fall under the domain of "Be respectful," but it is much clearer for students to understand and abide by in the classroom setting. In addition, rules and expectations must be directly taught to students (Gable, Hester, Rock, & Hughes, 2009).

Rules should be taught to students. Students should be given ample time to practice the classroom rules and should be shown examples and nonexamples of what "following the rules" looks like. This includes practicing what appropriate behavior looks like during different classroom activities and routines. For example, it may be expected that students remain silent during assessments but are expected to speak quietly to one another during collaborative group work. These differences in expectations should be made explicit and should be practiced systematically until students can consistently demonstrate their understanding. In this sense, classroom routines and procedures should be predictable to foster consistent appropriate behavior (Bear & Manning, 2014).

Rules should be publicly posted. Classroom rules should be posted in a location that can be easily seen by students and referenced by adults (Barbetta, et al., 2005). The inclusion of pictures is indicated for younger students and prereaders. Publicly posting rules serves as a visual prompt for teaching and reminding students to engage in prosocial behavior (Alter & Haydon, 2017; Scott et al., 2011). Slight variations on visual posting of rules are giving the rules as a handout to students, (Johnson, Stoner, & Green, 1996) and posting the rules on the participant students' desks. (Musser, Bray, Kehle, & Jenson, 2001).

Rules should be tied to positive and negative consequences. Instances of rule-following behavior should be noted and reinforced by the teacher via specific verbal praise (Olsen, 2015), and misbehavior should be addressed consistently and predictably (Bear & Manning, 2014). Often, a teacher reinforces all noticed instances of appropriate behavior at a high rate when students are first learning the expectations of the learning environment. These rates of reinforcement may be decreased as students begin to master basic rules such as arriving to class with required materials, but it is essential that praise and positive acknowledgment continue throughout the school year (Alter & Haydon, 2017). In general, it is recommended that teachers make an effort to ensure they use more positive statements (i.e., praise, encouragement) than corrective or negative statements (Sabey, Charlton, & Charlton, 2019).

Rules should be created collaboratively with students. Classroom rules can often be developed jointly with students. Soliciting student input when developing rules can improve student buy-in and contribute to a sense of autonomy and connection to the classroom (Alter & Haydon, 2017). It is important that students be guided in the development of rules by sharing the general recommendations with them (four to six total, clear, positively-stated) prior to rule generation (Barbetta, et al., 2005). When students are included in the creation of rules, they can be mobilized to hold each other accountable to the shared expectations.

RECOMMENDATIONS FOR IMPLEMENTATION

A variety of methods can be implemented with classroom management in real-world settings, and varying techniques can be chosen to best fit each classroom. As previously mentioned, visual aids can support classroom rules and expectations and provide quick references to these rules and expectations. Daily schedules can also be posted in the classroom on posters, boards, and other visual systems so that students know what we be expected of them throughout the day and establish a routine. Naturally, different situations call for different rules and expectations. Behavior matrices can provide a visual for students and staff to reference in various areas and situations (Gable, Hester, Rock, & Hughes, 2009). Behavior matrices consist of a table with the columns being the various situations a student may be in throughout the day (class time, lunch, indoor recess, bathrooms, etc.) and the rows would be the rules (Have nice hands, appropriate voice level, staying in your area, etc.). Where the rows and columns intersect describes the appropriate behavior for the situation (Having an appropriate voice at lunch would be different than having an appropriate voice at class time.). An example is shown in Table 19.2. These items should be printed large enough that staff and students can reference them from most areas of the classroom. These visual aids can set the stage for the day and prevent problems before they occur.

These visual aids must be paired with direct instruction of the rules and expectations to be effective (Gable, Hester, Rock, & Hughes, 2009). This would include setting aside a short period of time to state each rule and give examples and nonexamples of the rule when students first arrive for the school year. Further

Table 19.2. EXAMPLE BEHAVIOR MATRIX

Rules and Expectations

	Recess	Lunch	Class Time	Group Work
Be in your area	Stay on blacktop on rainy days, and stay inside the fence.	Pick a table to sit at and remain at table until clean-up.	Stand or sit at desk space.	Stand or sit at assigned table.
Have nice hands	Keep hands in your own body space, and use gentle hands to touch friends for games like tag.	Keep hands in your own body space and only touch your own food.	Keeps hands in your own body space and only touch items on your desk.	Keeps hands in your own body space and only touch items shared by the group or on your own desk.
Have a good voice level	Voice Level 3	Voice Level 2	Voice Level 0	Voice Level 1

teaching may need to occur if there is a system like voice level as in the behavior matrix example so that students can recognize what each level means. For example, a staff member can state the rule of "staying in our area" means to keep your body in your assigned area of the classroom and give the example of sitting or standing at an assigned seat or sitting on a carpet square at story time. They could give a nonexample of standing at a friend's desk without permission or being in the play area during work time. Throughout the school year, follow-up session should occur to ensure that the students remember the rules and expectations. These can even occur weekly. After teaching these strategies, consequences for following the rules and expectations or not following the rules and expectations should be established and implemented.

Direct praise. Once the expectations and rules have been set, consequences for following and not following the expectations should be implemented to further manage classroom behaviors. Setting rules alone has been found to not be enough to change undesired behaviors (Gable, Hester, Rock, & Hughes, 2009). Direct praise and tangibles are techniques to reinforce following rules and expectations. Direct praise provides feedback to the student that the behavior they exhibited is appropriate. Increasing praise can increase the likelihood of appropriate behaviors occurring, and a ratio of at least four praises to every one reprimand is recommended. Clickers or counters are useful tools to determine how much praise is being given during class times, and these tools can help a staff member increase their number of praises throughout the day (Gable, Hester, Rock, & Hughes, 2009).

Direct praise must be specific to be most effective (Gable, Hester, Rock, & Hughes, 2009). For example, "Good job" and "Nice work" are vague statements; however, "I like how you got to work right away when I asked," or "Great job using nice hands while playing at recess," are both specific as to what behavior was appropriate. Direct praise should also be given in a timely manner and as quickly after the behavior occurs as possible, and praise should be given in a way that is socially appropriate for the student (Bear, 2010). For example, a student may be embarrassed to be praised in front of the class and would then avoid doing that appropriate behavior again to avoid the public praise.

Tangibles. In some instances, praise is not reinforcing enough for a student to continue performing appropriate behaviors more so than an inappropriate one. A tangible reward may then be paired with praise so the student is more likely to perform the appropriate behavior. A small tangible could be given when an appropriate behavior occurs, or the student could earn stickers or tokens that can later be exchanged for a tangible when a goal is met. For example, a student can earn a sticker and praise when they raise their hand, and earning five stickers earns them a piece of candy. However, direct praise is often the first choice for teachers, and increasing praise can be an effective strategy to attempt before adding a tangible (Gable, Hester, Rock, & Hughes, 2009).

Other antecedent strategies. Antecedent strategies for classroom management are proactive strategies that occur before problem behaviors begin. Establishing routines and preteaching rules and expectations are antecedent strategies discussed previously. Other antecedent strategies are used for classroom management include precorrection, arranging seats, and interspersing easy and difficult tasks (Kern & Clemens, 2007). Precorrection is an antecedent strategy where a teacher reminds students of rules and expectations before a situation where inappropriate behaviors typically occur (Ennis, Royer, Lane, & Griffith, 2017). For example, a teacher may remind students before starting story time to sit on their mat and raise their hands to answer questions if out-of-seat and talk-out behaviors are common. Students can benefit from a classroom arranged to match the task, which would ensure that students can easily face the teacher and materials and minimize distractions from other students. Desks in rows may prove more effective for direct instruction, and grouping desks may assist with group projects or discussions (Kern & Clemens, 2007). Multiple difficult tasks may overwhelm students. An easy task placed between these difficult tasks can alleviate this problem and allow students a mental break (Kern & Clemens, 2007). For example, after a lengthy task that requires students to practice new spelling words, a short review of the previous week's spelling words can provide a useful break before starting the next task.

Planned ignoring. Concurrently with praising appropriate behaviors, there should also be consequences for inappropriate behaviors. A consequence for inappropriate behaviors could be planned ignoring, time-outs, or reprimands. Planned ignoring involves not acknowledging an inappropriate behavior so that the behavior will no longer be performed as the desired result no longer occurs (Gable, Hester, Rock, & Hughes, 2009). Often, a cue is given to prompt an appropriate behavior. For example, a teacher may ignore a student that answers a question without raising their hand and raises their own hand to remind the student of the appropriate behavior. When the student does perform the appropriate behavior, praise should be given. While this method can be useful, there can be some unforeseen effects because of the method. A student, when ignored, may exhibit a more extreme version of the inappropriate behavior. This can be difficult for teachers to further ignore this more extreme behavior; however, pairing ignoring with prompts for the appropriate behavior and following up with praise when the appropriate behavior is performed can mitigate this problem (Gable, Hester, Rock, & Hughes, 2009).

Reprimands. While praise recognizes when students perform appropriate behaviors, reprimands bring attention to inappropriate behaviors. Reprimands should be short, private, and paired with a reminder of the appropriate behaviors (Gable, Hester, Rock, & Hughes, 2009). However, this method may not be effective for students who enjoy teacher attention. The attention the student gains from the teacher may be more reinforcing than the reprimand is punishing. This can lead to more inappropriate behaviors to gain that teacher attention.

Greeting at the Door Routine

An effective classroom routine that has empirical evidence is positive greetings at the classroom door. Positively greeting individual students at the door when they arrive to school helps to set a foundation for a positive student–teacher relationship (Anyon et al., 2018) and positive classroom climate (Cook et al., 2018b) and helps to prevent challenging behavior before it occurs (Cook et al., 2018a). Previous research has demonstrated that positive greetings at the door are associated with decreases in student off-task behavior (Allday & Pakurar, 2007) as well as increases in students' time spent academically engaged and decreases in disruptive behavior when combined with precorrection, specific behavioral praise, and private connections with students who appear to struggle (Cook et al., 2018b). Greeting students at the door also provides an opportunity for the teacher to gauge student emotion/attitude and address any issues or concerns that may have occurred before the start of the instructional day. The type of greeting can vary according to teacher preference and student age, but it should be positive, include some form of individual student attention (i.e., using the student's name), and convey sincere warmth. Often, teachers greet students in this way at the start of the school year, but do not continue to do so as the year progresses. To maintain the positive effects of morning greetings, teachers should continue to do so throughout the school year.

Positive greetings at the door in conjunction with specific verbal praise of instances of appropriate behavior and best-practice in classroom rules development are conceptualized as proactive behavior management strategies that help to prevent problem behavior before it occurs (Allday & Pakurar, 2007). This contributes to a positive classroom climate that is characterized by predictability and in which students are provided with high rates of positive acknowledgment and thus feel connected to the school environment and that includes less use of reactive and punitive behavior management strategies.

The Color Wheel System

Utilized as a solution to mitigate problems associated with unclear classroom expectations, the Color Wheel System is a classwide technique used to create behavioral expectations for various classroom activities (Skinner, Scala, Dendas, & Lentz, 2007). Instead of having one set of behavioral expectations for all activities across the school day, the Color Wheel System has specific rules that corresponds to three different colors: red, yellow, and green. Red rules typically are intended to grasp the students' attention for teachers to provide instructions or directions for a task (Watson et. al, 2016). "Eye on the teacher" and "Mouths closed" are examples of red rules (Skinner & Skinner, 2007). As an attempt to limit distractions during academic work, yellow rules include statements such as "Remain in your seat," "Eyes on your own work," or "Raise your hand to speak." As for green rules, they are implemented during activities where getting up from one's seat and interacting with other classmates is encouraged. Such statements for green rules include "Use your indoor voice" or "Keep hands and feet to yourself" (Aspiranti, Bebech, Ruffo, & Skinner, 2018; Watson et al., 2016). Once the rules are selected, visual cues in the form of a color wheel and a rule poster board are publicly displayed throughout the classroom, so that the students, as well as the teacher, can discriminate behavioral expectations at any given time. Students can also be prompted to state the current expectations individually or as a group.

Implementation of the Color Wheel System has been proven to improve multiple areas of concern in the classroom. Transition time is reduced significantly (Fudge et al., 2007), by having teachers repeat procedures for moving to one activity to another as well as providing warning signals. For example, a teacher may give their students a two-minute warning about how the color wheel is going to change colors as well as what the expectations for the new color are. Another area of improvement is having more time for quality instructions without disruptions. Choate et al. (2007), implemented the Color Wheel System in a first-grade classroom and saw an immediate decrease in out-of-seat behavior. Prior to implementing the management technique, the percentage of out-of-seat behavior was approximately 19% to 41% and reduced to 6.7% to 11%. Additionally, Kirk et al. (2010) supported previous investigations of the Color Wheel System's ability to reduce inappropriate classroom behaviors (Choate et al., 2007; Fudge et al., 2007; Saecker et al., 2008) by providing evidence of a reduction of inappropriate vocalizations when implemented. A procedural script for the Color Wheel System is presented in Figure 19.1.

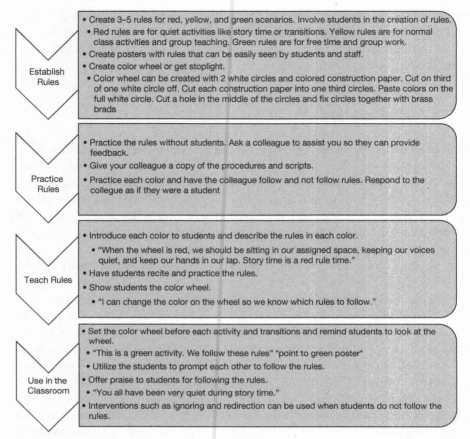

Establish Rules
- Create 3–5 rules for red, yellow, and green scenarios. Involve students in the creation of rules.
  - Red rules are for quiet activities like story time or transitions. Yellow rules are for normal class activities and group teaching. Green rules are for free time and group work.
- Create posters with rules that can be easily seen by students and staff.
- Create color wheel or get stoplight.
  - Color wheel can be created with 2 white circles and colored construction paper. Cut on third of one white circle off. Cut each construction paper into one third circles. Paste colors on the full white circle. Cut a hole in the middle of the circles and fix circles together with brass brads

Practice Rules
- Practice the rules without students. Ask a colleague to assist you so they can provide feedback.
- Give your colleague a copy of the procedures and scripts.
- Practice each color and have the colleague follow and not follow rules. Respond to the collegue as if they were a student

Teach Rules
- Introduce each color to students and describe the rules in each color.
  - "When the wheel is red, we should be sitting in our assigned space, keeping our voices quiet, and keep our hands in our lap. Story time is a red rule time."
- Have students recite and practice the rules.
- Show students the color wheel.
  - "I can change the color on the wheel so we know which rules to follow."

Use in the Classroom
- Set the color wheel before each activity and transitions and remind students to look at the wheel.
  - "This is a green activity. We follow these rules" *point to green poster*
  - Utilize the students to prompt each other to follow the rules.
- Offer praise to students for following the rules.
  - "You all have been very quiet during story time."
- Interventions such as ignoring and redirection can be used when students do not follow the rules.

Figure 19.1. Procedural script for the Color Wheel.

CONSIDERATIONS OF DIVERSITY AND EQUITY IN CLASSROOM MANAGEMENT

Although there is supporting evidence that has shown that the Color Wheel System is effective across different settings, populations, teachers, and general education classrooms, there is limited research on the intervention's effect on self-contained classrooms, specifically with students with autism spectrum disorder (ASD). However, there are some components of the Color Wheel System that may be beneficial to students with ASD. Some students with ASD have shown to have high disruptive behaviors during instructional periods (Aspiranti, Bebech, Ruffo, & Skinner, 2018); thus, implementing the Color Wheel System could be utilized to support these students as it has been shown evidence of reducing inappropriate and disruptive classroom behaviors. Being distracted easily, having trouble attending, and/or having trouble ending an activity are all areas of concern for some children with ASD (Aspiranti et al., 2018). Having consistent procedures while transitioning from activity to activity as well as having verbal warnings would provide structure and predictability, which would aid to mitigate those areas of concern for those students. The visual rule poster and color wheel components of the intervention add to the level of predictability as well as children with ASD respond well to visual stimuli and will be able to easily discriminate among behavioral expectations.

When using the Color Wheel System in an integrated, inclusive classroom, specific guidelines should be implemented appropriately to see a reduction in unwanted behaviors from the students. Teachers should be encouraged to use red rules frequently, but be mindful of how long they are making the students follow the red rules as this should be a brief time period since the rules can be difficult to follow (Aspiranti, Bebech, & Osiniak, 2018). Students should not associate the red with punishment as with many other techniques the color red can correspond with negative consequences; thus, teachers should make sure that the distinction between red and punishment is known. Additionally, although the Color Wheel System aids in classroom management, the teacher still has full control of the reinforcement and consequences that their class receives. For instance, a teacher may use being on green as a group reward for their students as that color encourages more free communication with peers. The time on each color is not necessarily fixed. Hence, to avoid time for potential disruptive behaviors to occur, the class can transition to a new color if the whole class is ready before the warnings are up. Lastly, individual behavior plans override the Color Wheel System guidelines previously mentioned as supplemental help may be needed in conjunction with the intervention (Aspiranti, Bebech, & Osiniak, 2018).

When teaching the rules and procedures for the Color Wheel System, additional supports may be needed when implementing in a classroom with students with ASD. In previous studies, techniques such as role playing have been used, however, Aspiranti, Bebech, Ruffo, and Skinner's (2018) study provided evidence that adding a social story component while explaining procedures for the intervention for individuals with ASD will aid in a reduction in disruptive and inappropriate behaviors. Social stories have been shown to be effective in helping students with ASD navigate how to obtain and maintain social skills. Students are provided with short stories with pictorial cues that aid in understanding a complex social situation as well as learning the appropriate behavioral response to that social situation. The study not only showed a reduction of disruptive behaviors, but it also suggested that the conjunction of the social story and Color Wheel System can be effective for children with ASD who are nonverbal (Aspiranti, Bebech, Ruffo, & Skinner, 2018).

REFERENCES

Allday, R. A., Pakurar, K. (2007). Effects of teacher greetings on student on-task behavior. *Journal of Applied Behavior Analysis, 40,* 317–320.

Alter, P., & Haydon, T. (2017). Characteristics of effective classroom rules: A review of the literature. *Teacher Education and Special Education, 40*(2), 114–127.

Anyon, Y., Atteberry-Ash, B., Yang, J., Pauline, M., Wiley, K., Cash, D., . . . Pisciotta, L. (2018). It's all about the relationships": Educators' rationales and strategies for building connections with students to prevent exclusionary school discipline outcomes. *Children and Schools, 40*(4), 221–230. doi:10.1093/cs/cdy017

Aspiranti, K. B., Bebech, A., & Osiniak, K. (2018). Incorporating a class-wide behavioral system to decrease disruptive behaviors in the inclusive classroom. *Journal of Catholic Education, 21*(2), 10. doi:10.15365/joce.2102102018

Aspiranti, K. B., Bebech, A., Ruffo, B., & Skinner, C. H. (2018). Classroom management in self-contained classrooms for children with autism: Extending research on the Color Wheel System. *Behavior Analysis in Practice, 12*(1), 143–153. doi:10.1007/s40617-018-0264-6

Barbetta, P. M., Norona, K. L., & Bicard, D. F. (2005). Classroom behavior management: A dozen common mistakes and what to do instead. *Preventing School Failure: Alternative Education for Children and Youth, 49*(3), 11–19. doi:10.3200/PSFL.49.3.11-19

Bear, G.G. (2010). *School discipline and self-discipline: A practical guide to promoting prosocial student behavior.* New York, NY: Guilford Press.

Bear, G. G., & Manning, M. A. (2014). Best practices in classroom discipline. In P. L. Harrison & A. Thomas (Eds.), *Best practices in school psychology: student-level services* (pp. 251–268). Bethesda, MD: National Association of School Psychologists.

Blondin, C, Skinner, C., Parkhurst, J., Wood, A., & Snyder, J. (2012). Enhancing on-task behavior in fourth-grade students using a modified Color Wheel System. *Journal of Applied School Psychology, 28*, 37–58.

Boostrom, R. (1991). The nature and functions of classroom rules. *Curriculum Inquiry, 21*, 193–216. doi:10.2307/1179942

Choate, S. M., Skinner, C. H., Fearrington, J., Kohler, B., & Skolits, J. (2007). Extending the external validity of the color wheel procedures: Decreasing out-of-seat behavior in an intact, rural, 1st grade classroom. *Journal of Evidence-Based Practices for Schools, 8*, 120–133.

Cook, C. R., Coco, S., Zhang, Y., Fiat, A. E., Duong, M. T., Renshaw, T. L., . . . Frank, S. (2018a). Cultivating positive teacher–student relationships: Preliminary evaluation of the establish–maintain–restore (EMR) method. *School Psychology Review, 47*(3), 226–243. doi:10.17105/SPR-2017-0025.V47-3

Cook, C. R., Fiat, A., Larson, M., Daikos, C., Slemrod, T., Holland, E. A., . . . Renshaw, T. (2018b). Positive greetings at the door: Evaluation of a low-cost, high-yield proactive classroom management strategy. *Journal of Positive Behavior Interventions, 20*(3), 149–159. doi:10.1177/1098300717753831

Ennis, R. P., Royer, D. J., Lane, K. L., & Griffith, C. E. (2017). A systematic review of precorrection in PK–12 settings. *Education and treatment of children, 40*(4), 465–495.

Fudge, D. L, Reece, L., Skinner, C. H., & Cowden, D. (2007). Using multiple class-room rules, public cues, and consistent transition strategies to reduce inappropriate transitions: An investigation of the color wheel. *Journal of Evidence-Based Practices for Schools, 8*, 102–119.

Gable, R. A., Hester, P. H., Rock, M. L., & Hughes, K. G. (2009). Back to basics: Rules, praise, ignoring, and reprimands revisited. *Intervention in School and Clinic, 44*(4), 195–205. doi:10.1177/1053451208328831

Haydon, T., Stevens, D., & Leko, M. (2018). Source and protective factor: The role of the principal in special education teacher stress. *Journal of Special Education Leadership, 31*(2), 99–107.

Johnson, T. C., Stoner, G., & Green, S. K. (1996). Demonstrating the experimenting society model with classwide behavior management interventions. *School Psychology Review, 25*, 199–214.

Jones, V., & Jones, L. (2016). *Comprehensive classroom management: Creating communities of support and solving problems* (11th ed.). Boston, MA: Pearson.

Kern, L., & Clemens, N. H. (2007). Antecedent strategies to promote appropriate classroom behavior. *Psychology in the Schools, 44*(1), 65–75.

Kirk, E. R., Becker, J. A., Skinner, C. H., Yarbrough Fearrington, J., McCane-Bowling, S. J., Amburn, C., . . . Greear, C. (2010). Decreasing inappropriate vocalizations using class-wide group contingencies and color wheel procedures: A component analysis. *Psychology in the Schools, 47*, 931-943. doi:10.1002/pits.20515

Landers, E., Servilio, K., Tuttle, T., Alter, P. A., & Haydon, T. (2011). Defining disrespect: A teacher's perspective. *Rural Special Education Quarterly, 30*(2), 13–18.

Maag, J. W. (2004). *Behavior management: From theoretical implications to practical applications* (2nd ed.). Belmont, CA: Wadsworth/Thomson Learning.

Musser, E. H., Bray, M. A., Kehle, T. J., & Jenson, W. R. (2001). Reducing disruptive behaviors in students with serious emotional disturbance. *School Psychology Review, 30*, 294–304.

Olsen, J. (2015, December). PBIS Forum 15 practice brief: PBIS in the classroom. *Positive Behavioral Interventions and Supports*. Retrieved from https://assets-global.website-files.com/5d3725188825e071f1670246/5d6ffd3b72843e1a87d4c36a_rdq%204%20brief%20-%20classroom.pdf

Sabey, C. V., Charlton, C., & Charlton, S. R. (2019). The "magic" positive-to-negative interaction ratio: Benefits, applications, cautions, and recommendations. *Journal of Emotional and Behavioral Disorders, 27*(3), 154–164. doi:10.1177/1063426618763106

Saecker, L., Sager, K., Skinner, C. H., Williams, J. L., Luna, E., & Spurgeon, S. (2008). Decreasing a fifth-grade teacher's repeated directions and students' inappropriate talking using color wheel procedures. *Journal of Evidence-Based Practices for Schools, 9*, 18–32.

Scott, T. M., Anderson, C. M., & Alter, P. J. (2011). *Managing classroom behavior using positive behavior supports.* Upper Saddle River, NJ: Pearson.

Skinner, C.H., Scala, G., Denda, D., & Lentz, F.E. (2007). The color wheel: Implementation guidelines. *Journal of Evidence-Based Practices for Schools, 8*, 134.

Skinner, C. H., & Skinner, A. L. (2007). Establishing an evidence base for a classroom management procedure with a series of studies: Evaluating the color wheel. *Journal of Evidence-Based Practices for Schools, 8*, 88–101.

Watson, T. L., Skinner, C. H., Skinner, A. L., Cazzell, S., Aspiranti, K. B., Moore, T., & Coleman, M. (2016). Preventing disruptive behavior via classroom management: Validating the Color Wheel System in kindergarten classrooms. *Behavior Modification, 40*(4), 518–540. doi:10.1177/0145445515626890

## 20

Technology-Based Classroom Management

SHELLEY KATHLEEN KRACH AND LORI R. KERN ■

Classroom management (Certo & Fox, 2002) and time management (Grayson & Alvarez, 2008) are among the most common work-related problems described by teachers. Classroom management problems range from mild issues such as student inattention (Harrison, Vannest, Davis, & Reynolds, 2012) to extreme concerns such as fighting (Barth, Dunlap, Dane, Lochman & Wells, 2004). Time management issues arise because teachers are required to juggle interventions and lesson planning across multiple classes (Certo & Fox, 2002), complete mountains of paperwork (Certo & Fox, 2002), differentiate instruction (Marshall, 2016), and manage classroom behavior (Certo & Fox, 2002).

As will be discussed in this chapter, technology-based tools may fix some of these problems for some teachers. Often, teachers who are open to technology use (early adopters) are eager to try new technologies when they become available (Li & Huang, 2016). This is because early adopters may have previously benefited from home-based technologies (e.g., vacuuming with Roomba™, InstantPot™ for dinner, etc.). Early adopters may generalize these personal benefits to classroom benefits. However, when a home-based technology fails to make life easier, the cost is a financial one. The cost of using an unproven, school-based technology may be long-term student academic and behavioral problems for students.

Therefore, it is important that the use of any school-based technology be supported by data. Unfortunately, data-supported, efficacy studies of technology-based tools often take several years to become published in a journal. Early adopters don't want to wait years to get started when they believe that a program can help their students; they want to get started right away! And, if the early adopter tried the program and liked it, they want to tell their friends about how great the program was as well (anecdotal support for efficacy). Unfortunately, this anecdotal support is not sufficient to say that the program actually works, because the plural

Table 20.1. Guidelines for Choosing a Technology-Based Intervention

Guideline	Descriptor	Yes	No
Effective	Are the desired outcomes obtainable?		
	Does research evidence support use?		
	Does personal evidence support use?		
	Does this match my goals for my students?		
Efficient	Do the benefits outweigh the costs?		
	Does the cost include new technology?		
	How long does it take to learn?		
	How long does it take to use?		
Relevant	Does the intervention fit the context?		
	Was it designed for my children (age, SES, etc.)?		
	Am I a person who enjoys using technology?		
	Do I believe that this program will work?		
Durable	Is this sustainable?		
	Is there a yearly fee?		
	Will the children have access to it next year?		
	Does my administration support the use of the program?		

Note: Derived from Sugai and Horner (2006).

of *anecdote* is not *data* (Kernaghan & Kuruvilla, 1982). Therefore, this gap between research and practice often leads to widespread adoption of technology-based tools that are not supported by data-based research (Ahuja, 2016).

Fortunately, there is a clear method that teachers can use to evaluate new technology-based tools before using them. Sugai and Horner (2006) provide a set of guidelines for choosing general interventions; these have been adapted in this chapter to address specific concerns related to technology-based tools (see Table 20.1). These guidelines require that interventions be effective, efficient, relevant, and durable (Sugai & Horner, 2006). While some of the guidelines require published research to make decisions about program adoption, other factors can be evaluated at a personal or system level.

RECOMMENDATIONS FOR IMPLEMENTATION

Empirical Support for Effectiveness

To meet the guideline of *effectiveness*, the main considerations are if the intervention (a) is designed to do what the user wants it to do and (b) has data to support its use. Ideally, support for the tool will be presented in a research, peer-reviewed journal article. Data provided by the manufacturer of the intervention should not be used to determine effectiveness of the program. Only independent, unbiased research on effectiveness should be used to be certain that the program works.

Self-Assessment for Effectiveness

Even if research demonstrates the effectiveness of a technology-based tool, how well it actually works may depend on the user. Higgins and Moseley (2001) found that if teachers did not view technology-based interventions positively, then the intervention was less effective overall.

Similarly, some untested technology-based tools may work regardless of previous research (or lack thereof). Findings by McIntosh, Rizza, and Bliss (2000) indicate that increased child–teacher interactions can result in improved student behavior. Therefore, children's behavior may be improving simply due to increased teacher attention and not the actual intervention itself. Given that teachers may decrease their direct-child contact by using a computer-based intervention, an unproven technology may result in a worsening of behavior unrelated to the intervention used.

Additionally, teachers may report that an intervention worked due to a placebo effect (Boot, Simons, Stothart, & Stutts, 2013). Sandler and Bodfish (2008) found that teachers rated children's behavioral changes similarly for those who received 100% of a dose of their ADHD medication, 50% of their dose of ADHD medication, or 0% of their dose when examined in a blind study. This indicates that teachers may think (and rate) children's behaviors as improved just because they are aware that an intervention is happening. Therefore, individual teacher's opinions of effectiveness should always be weighed against systematic, research-based findings.

Efficiency

To meet the guideline of *efficiency*, the main consideration is if the intervention is worth (a) the time, (b) the money, and (c) the effort. Some technologies take a while to get started, but they save time over the long term. Some are too difficult to use without considerable training or staff so they aren't worth the costs. Any consideration of worth needs to include the entire costs of the project from implementation to program evaluation.

Costs and benefits of technology change from district to district and person to person. Davis (1989) developed the Technology Acceptance Model (TAM) to describe factors that influence technological decision-making and acceptance; Persico, Manca, and Pozzi (2014) expanded this model. Part of this expansion was a development of an assessment metric for technology-based interventions. Each part of this model must be evaluated to determine if the amount of effort needed to implement the intervention is worth what the children will get out of it.

First, an analysis of pre-existing system support must be completed prior to any consideration. Do students have access to the hardware and/or software required? If not, how much will this cost financially? Do the users (i.e., teachers, parents, administrators, and students) have the necessary skills to use the technology? If not, how long will it take to prepare training materials and provide the training needed? What staff will be needed to provide this training? Finally, once the new intervention starts, what is the cost of keeping it running and the cost to evaluate the effectiveness of the program? These costs may include instructional technology support staff for hardware maintenance and software troubleshooting, annual licensing costs for each user for the programs, training costs for the users, and hiring costs for data management specialists.

A benefits' analysis involves many of the same considerations. Who will benefit from this program? Teachers may benefit because of less stress due to decreased behavioral problems in the classroom (Certo & Fox, 2002). Other children in the classroom may benefit due to decreases in bullying (Espelage, Low, Van Ryzin, & Polanin, 2015) or increases in classroom instructional time (Luiselli, Putnam, Handler, & Feinberg, 2005). Parents may benefit due to more positive school interactions (Dotterer & Wehrspann, 2016) and the availability of specific information about their child's behaviors (Krach, McCreery, & Rimel, 2017). Finally, administrators may benefit because students' academics often improve when behavioral problems decrease (Luiselli et al., 2005). The level of benefits for each of these stakeholders will change from intervention to intervention.

As with effectiveness, the efficiency of a specific, technology-based assessment depends on the nature of the school. Just knowing the cost of a single piece of software is not sufficient in making efficiency decisions. All aspects of the extended TAM(Davis, 1989; Persico et al., 2014) must be considered.

Relevance

To meet the guideline of *relevancy*, the main consideration is if the intervention is going to work for specific teachers and/or their students. For example, if an intervention was validated with third graders, but the teacher works with ninth graders, this might not be the right intervention. But, if the same teacher's ninth graders are functioning on the level of third graders, then the intervention may be relevant. Additional relevancy considerations include child and teacher characteristics such as race, socioeconomic status, disability status, and language.

Studies show that teacher variables may influence how different teachers feel about, select, and use different instructional technology. For example, in a study by Weber and Custer (2005), male teachers prefer tasks where the students interact with building or using a technology whereas female teachers prefer tasks where the students use the technology for social interactions. In another example, Higgins and Moseley (2001) found that teachers of younger children were less likely to use technology-based interventions than those who work with older children. Therefore, the relevancy of an intervention may change based on the teacher or student using it.

Finally, certain technology-based programs may not be legally relevant for school use. The Family Educational Rights and Privacy Act (FERPA,1974) requires that all educational data are protected; protected data include anything providing both the child's name and evaluative information. If a specific program allows for

Table 20.2. Web-Accessibility Standards (Partial List)

Guideline	Description	Groups Effected
1	Provide <alt> text for images or tables	Blind Visually impaired
2	Captions for multimedia	Deaf/hard of hearing
4	Easily seen and heard	Color blind Deaf/hard of hearing Visually impaired
6	Enough time provided to access materials	Processing speed deficits Reading disabilities Motor skills deficits
7	No blinking lights	Seizure disorders Visually impaired
8	Clear navigation tools	Spatial processing deficits
9	Readable and understandable text	Reading disabilities

Note: World Wide Web Consortium (2008), based on U.S. Department of Justice (2010).

any grades, scores, or points to be easily viewed along with a student's name, then that program is not appropriate for school use.

An additional, legal question related to relevancy addresses users with disabilities. As with buildings and bathrooms, there is an access requirement for computers and websites (U.S. Department of Justice, 2010). Therefore, all internet-based materials must be "web-accessible" (World Wide Web Consortium, 2008). A partial list of the criteria for determining web accessibility can be found in Table 20.2. These criteria should be used when deciding on the use of any website, video, podcast, or interactive media. Many websites do not indicate if they provide compliant materials (World Wide Web Consortium, 2008). To determine if a website is accessible, there are many free accessibility checkers available at this website: https://www.w3.org/WAI/ER/tools/

Durability

To meet the guideline of *durable*, the main concern is if the intervention is going to last. There are several examples here as to why a specific intervention may not be durable. In one example, a grant provided funds for two years for a software program, and then the grant ends. In another, elementary school children have access to the program, but middle school children do not. In a third, the previous principal was supportive of the intervention, but the new one does not wish to continue it. Each of these examples are system-specific. Intervention-specific examples include sturdiness of the equipment, room to store the equipment, and availability of staff to help maintain the equipment. Durability must be considered for both of these continuation variables: intervention-specific (Will it function?) and system-specific (Will it be available?).

If a program is not durable within a specific school, then children who were doing well using the program may show limited or no improvement when it is removed. For example, short-term improvement is common for situations where a contingency-based reward or punishment is involved; however, the improvement goes away when the consequences do (Frey & Rogers, 2014). This only makes sense: if your job stopped paying you, then you are less likely to continue working.

Long-term improvement may be seen for interventions that focus on skill building or learning tasks (Frey & Rogers, 2014). Therefore, certain types of interventions (e.g., those teaching skills) may be preferred over others (i.e., those providing rewards/punishments) if there is a concern about durability. If long-term improvements are desired for interventions based on reward-based or punishment-based interventions, this may be accomplished through the use of fading.

Fading is a common method for maintaining change after the removal of a contingency (reward and/or punishment). This is usually done by monitoring a child's progress throughout the intervention to determine when the child's behavior meets the teacher's expectations. When the child meets expectation, then the intervention is slowly removed until the child no longer needs the support to continue (Rock & Thead, 2007). Therefore, when choosing any contingency-based intervention program, the software must provide methods for monitoring the child's progress, slowly removing the intervention, and finally stopping the intervention entirely. Otherwise, fading is not a viable option and the improvements in behavior will be temporary.

CASE STUDY—AN EVALUATION OF CLASS DOJO

Users must evaluate all of the guidelines (i.e., effectiveness, efficiency, relevance, and durability; Sugai & Horner, 2006) before implementing an intervention in a classroom. In the following section, a popular program, Class Dojo, will be evaluated against these standards. Class Dojo (https://www.classdojo.com) is a technology-based, behavioral-tracking tool. It allows teachers to add or remove "Dojo Points" for individual children or for the whole class.

Case Study Effectiveness

In 2019, the Class Dojo website stated that 95% of U.S. schools are using the program. Yet, there are still very few studies to support its use. There were only three methodologically sound studies identified at the time of this writing. These studies find that Class Dojo is a good method of tracking behavior and works well when paired with another empirically supported intervention such as Check-In/

Check-Out (Dadakhodjaeva, 2017; Dillon, 2019; Chiarelli, Szabo, & Williams, 2015; Krach et al., 2017). What else supports the use of this program? The website provides teachers' anecdotal comments citing ease of use, engaging images, clear data, student interest, and parent involvement. The website does not provide empirical support for the use of the program.

Therefore, it seems that Class Dojo is only as effective as the teacher using it and/or the intervention paired with it. For example, if the teacher is using Dojo Points to trade in for rewards, then any problems associated with token economies become problems with Class Dojo (Krach, McCreery, Wilcox, & Focaracci, 2017). These types of problems might include teachers failing to provide or remove points when appropriate. Teachers may also set rewards as too difficult (or too easy) to obtain (Kazdin, 1982; Sran & Borrero, 2010). In addition, if Dojo Points are removed, then problems associated with response cost may be expected (e.g., anger, temper tantrums, etc.; Doll McLaughlin, & Barretto, 2013). None of these are native to Class Dojo. These issues are commonly associated with any behavioral tracking method.

Case Study Efficiency

Class Dojo is free and does not take much effort to use or to learn for anyone who knows how to use the internet. Therefore, on the surface, it meets the requirement for efficiency. Class Dojo needs to be used in conjunction with another empirically supported intervention (e.g., Check-In/Check-Out, token economy, etc.). These coordinating interventions may take time to learn and mentorship to have them incorporated into the classroom for the first time.

Case Study Relevance

Determining the relevancy of a technology-based program is a personal decision. Is the user the type of person who enjoys working with technology-based tools? Do the users think that this intervention method will work for their children? Is there enough technology in the classroom to be able to put this system in place? Based on the answers to these questions, Class Dojo may be relevant for some teachers but not for others.

It may also be relevant for some children but not for others. For example, the images are culturally neutral (e.g., the representative avatar is green). However, some parents find these monster-like images offensive and concerning (Singer, 2014). A positive cultural issue is that the program is available in several different languages (https://www.classdojo.com/). One final cultural relevancy issue is race-/ethnicity-/gender-based cyberbullying; the chatrooms and discussion boards in Class Dojo need to be monitored closely (Patchin & Hinduja, 2010).

There are legal issues related to the relevancy of the use of Class Dojo in public schools. For example, at least 30 different web-accessibility compliance issues were noted for the homepage using a compliance checker (U.S. Department of Justice, 2010; https://achecker.ca/). In addition, there are FERPA concerns related to teachers projecting Dojo Points alongside student's names onto a projection screen or SMART board (Singer, 2014). To not violate tFERPA, teachers need to keep identifiable information in a private location (e.g., personal computer screen, tablet, smart phone, etc.) and not project it in a manner visible to the whole class.

Durability

Durability is also a personal decision. Although there is no cost to use Class Dojo, there may be concerns about long-term maintenance of effects because it is a contingency-based program (Frey & Rogers, 2014). In addition, the user has to be committed to stick with the program and not move on to the next trend or idea. Therefore, as with relevancy, Class Dojo may be durable for some teachers but not for others.

CONSIDERATIONS OF DIVERSITY AND EQUITY IN TECHNOLOGY-BASED CLASSROOM MANAGEMENT

Each of these four evaluation standards must be considered in more detail when working with culturally and linguistically diverse populations.

Effectiveness. It is important to pay close attention to the sample description when reviewing efficacy studies for any intervention. If the student and teacher school population is divergent from the sample used in the study, the findings may not be applicable for their use (Hunsley, 2007).

Efficiency. There are still many schools and families that do not have computer access for students to use in their homes and classrooms (Auxier & Anderson, 2020). Therefore, socioeconomics and hardware availability must be considered as part of the cost-benefit analysis. If the school and or families do not have access to technology, then the monetary cost portion of cost-benefit analysis increases. The time and effort portions may also increase for teachers, children, and parents who have not had easy access to these tools and are therefore less familiar with their use.

Relevancy. In addition to teacher variables, it is equally important to make sure that any materials are culturally relevant to the students using them. For example, verbal information should be provided in the child's/parent's appropriate language. Any images, videos, and animations should include representative, multicultural examples. If the program uses social interactions (e.g., discussion boards, posts, comments sections, etc.), then there must be consideration for how these will be monitored for hate speech, bullying, and inappropriate language.

Durability. There are high rates of teacher turn-over in urban and low-income schools (Guin, 2004). Oftentimes, teachers new to these types of schools are also new to teaching or may be less qualified to teach than those who work in higher-income schools (Sass et al., 2012). This means that school-wide technology intervention will have to be taught every year to the teachers that are new to the school. If the task is too onerous for these teachers, they will not maintain it in their day-to-day practice.

DISCUSSION

In conclusion, technology can be fun for children, and it may make teacher's lives simpler. However, before using any technology-based tool, a systematic evaluation should be conducted to ensure that it is appropriate for everyone involved. This evaluation should include a review of effectiveness, efficiency, relevance, and durability of the program (Sugai & Horner, 2006). These evaluation guidelines should allow teachers to make decisions on all future technology-based interventions.

REFERENCES

Ahuja, S. (2016). Research results for quality schooling: Bridging the gap between research and practice. *MIER Journal of Educational Studies, Trends and Practices*, 2(2), 206–214.

Auxier, B., & Anderson, M. (2020, March). As schools close due to the coronavirus, some U.S. students face a digital 'homework gap'. *Pew Research – FactTank*. https://www.pewresearch.org/fact-tank/2020/03/16/as-schools-close-due-to-the-coronavirus-some-u-s-students-face-a-digital-homework-gap/

Barth, J. M., Dunlap, S. T., Dane, H., Lochman, J. E., & Wells, K. C. (2004). Classroom environment influences on aggression, peer relations, and academic focus. *Journal of School Psychology*, 42, 115–133. doi:10.1016/j.jsp.2003.11.004

Boot, W. R., Simons, D. J., Stothart, C., & Stutts, C. (2013). The pervasive problem with placebos in psychology: Why active control groups are not sufficient to rule out placebo effects. *Perspectives on Psychological Science*, 8(4), 445–454. doi:10.1177/1745691613491271

Certo, J. L., & Fox, J. E. (2002). Retaining quality teachers. *High School Journal*, 86, 57–75. doi:10.1353/hsj.2002.0015

Chiarelli, M., Szabo, S., & Williams, S. (2015). Using ClassDojo to help with classroom management during guided reading. *Texas Journal of Literacy Education*, 3(2), 81–88. ERIC: EJ1110950

Dadakhodjaeva, K. (2017). *The good behavior game: Effects on and maintenance of behavior in middle-school classrooms using Class Dojo* (Unpublished doctoral dissertation). University of Southern Mississippi, Hattiesburg, MS.

Davis, F. D. (1989). Perceived usefulness, perceived ease of use, and user acceptance of information technology. *MIS Quarterly*, 13, 319–340. doi:10.2307/249008

Dillon, M. B. M., Radley, K. C., Tingstrom, D. H., Dart, E. H., Barry, C. T., & Codding, R. (2019). The effects of tootling via ClassDojo on student behavior in elementary classrooms. *School Psychology Review*, 48(1). doi:10.17105/SPR-2017-0090.V48-1

Doll, C., McLaughlin, T. F., & Barretto, A. (2013). The token economy: A recent review and evaluation. *International Journal of Basic and Applied Science, 2*(1), 131–149.

Dotterer, A. M., & Wehrspann, E. (2016). Parent involvement and academic outcomes among urban adolescents: Examining the role of school engagement. *Educational Psychology, 36*(4), 812–830. doi:10.1080/01443410.2015.1099617

Espelage, D. L., Low, S., Van Ryzin, M. J., & Polanin, J. R. (2015). Clinical trial of second step middle school program: Impact on bullying, cyberbullying, homophobic teasing, and sexual harassment perpetration. *School Psychology Review, 44*(4), 464–479. doi:10.17105/spr-15-0052.1

Family Educational Rights and Privacy Act of 1974, 20 U.S.C. § 1232g (1974).

Frey, E., & Rogers, T. (2014). Persistence: How treatment effects persist after interventions stop. Policy Insights from the *Behavioral and Brain Sciences, 1*(1), 172–179. doi:10.1177/2372732214550405

Grayson, J. L., & Alvarez, H. K. (2008). School climate factors relating to teacher burnout: A mediator model. *Teaching and Teacher Education, 24*, 1349–1363. doi:10.1016/j.tate.2007.06.005

Guin, K. (2004, August 16). Chronic teacher turnover in urban elementary schools. *Education Policy Analysis Archives, 12*(42). Retrieved [date] from http://epaa.asu.edu/epaa/v12n42/

Harrison, J. R., Vannest, K., Davis, J., & Reynolds, C. (2012). Common problem behaviors of children and adolescents in general education classrooms in the United States. *Journal of Emotional & Behavioral Disorders, 20*(1), 55–64. doi:10.1177/1063426611421157

Higgins, S., & Moseley, D. (2001). Teachers' thinking about information and communications technology and learning: Beliefs and outcomes. *Teacher Development, 5*(2), 191–210. doi:10.1080/13664530100200138

Hunsley, J. (2007). Addressing key challenges in evidence-based practice in psychology. Professional Psychology: Research and Practice, 38(2), 113–121. https://doi.org/10.1037/0735-7028.38.2.113

Kazdin, A. E. (1982). The token economy: A decade later. *Journal of Applied Behavior Analysis, 15*, 431–445. doi:10.1901/jaba.1982.15-431

Krach, S. K., McCreery, M. P., & Rimel, H. (2017). Examining teachers' behavioral management charts: A comparison of Class Dojo and paper-pencil methods. *Contemporary School Psychology, 21*(3), 267–275. doi:10.1007/s40688-016-0111-0

Krach, S. K., McCreery, M. P., Wilcox, R., & Focaracci, S. (2017). Positive behavioral supports: Empirically supported use of behavioral logs. *Intervention in School and Clinic, 53*, 67–73. doi:10.1177/1053451217693366

Kernaghan, K., & Kuruvilla, P. K. (1982). Merit and motivation: Public personnel management in Canada. *Canadian Public Administration, 25*, 696–712. doi:10.1111/j.1754-7121.1982.tb02102.x

Li, S. C. S., & Huang, W. C. (2016). Lifestyles, innovation attributes, and teachers' adoption of game-based learning: Comparing non-adopters with early adopters, adopters and likely adopters in Taiwan. *Computers & Education, 96*, 29–41. doi:10.1016/j.compedu.2016.02.009

Luiselli, J. K., Putnam, R. F., Handler, M. W., & Feinberg, A. B. (2005). Whole-school positive behaviour support: Effects on student discipline problems and academic performance. *Educational Psychology, 25*, 183–198. doi:10.1080/0144341042000301265

Marshall, K. (2016). Rethinking differentiation: Using teachers' time most effectively. *Phi Delta Kappan, 98*(1), 8–13. doi:10.1177/0031721716666046

McIntosh, D. E., Rizza, M. G., & Bliss, L. (2000). Implementing empirically supported interventions: Teacher–child interaction therapy. *Psychology in the Schools, 37*(5), 453–462. doi:10.1002/1520-6807

Patchin, J. W., & Hinduja, S. (2010). Cyberbullying and self-esteem. *Journal of School Health, 80*(12), 614–621. doi:10.1111/j.1746-1561.2010.00548.x

Persico, D., Manca, S., & Pozzi, F. (2014). Adapting the technology acceptance model to evaluate the innovative potential of e-learning systems. *Computers in Human Behavior, 30*, 614–622. doi:10.1016/j.chb.2013.07.045

Rock, M. L., & Thead, B. K. (2007). The effects of fading a strategic self-monitoring intervention on students' academic engagement, accuracy, and productivity. *Journal of Behavioral Education, 16*(4), 389–412. doi:10.1007/s10864-007-9049-7

Sandler, A. D., & Bodfish, J. W. (2008). Open-label use of placebos in the treatment of ADHD: A pilot study. *Child: Care, Health and Development, 34*(1), 104–110. doi:10.1111/j.1365-2214.2007.00797.x

Sass, T. R., Hannaway, J., Xu, Z., Figlio, D. N., & Feng, L. (2012). Value added of teachers in high-poverty schools and lower poverty schools. *Journal of Urban Economics, 72*(2–3), 104–122. https://doi.org/10.1016/j.jue.2012.04.004

Singer, N. (2014, November 19). School tracking app won't keep data. *The New York Times*, p. B.6.

Sran, S. K., & Borrero, J. C. (2010). Assessing the value of choice in a token system. *Journal of Applied Behavior Analysis, 43*(3), 553–557. doi:10.1901/jaba.2010.43-553

Sugai, G., & Horner, R. R. (2006). A promising approach for expanding and sustaining school-wide positive behavior support. *School Psychology Review, 35*, 245–259.

U.S. Department of Justice. (2010, September 15). 2010 ADA standards for accessible design. Retrieved from https://www.ada.gov/regs2010/2010ADAStandards/2010ADAstandards.htm

Weber, K., & Custer, R. (2005). Gender-based preferences toward technology education content, activities, and instructional methods. *Journal of Technology Education, 16*(2), 55–71.

World Wide Web Consortium. (2008). Web content accessibility guidelines (WCAG) 2.0. Retrieved from https://www.w3.org/TR/2008/REC-WCAG20-20081211/

## 21

Interdependent Group Contingencies

DANIEL M. MAGGIN, CHRISTERALLYN A. J. BROWN, AND SKIP KUMM ∎

Interdependent group contingencies refer to a class of interventions in which students receive a consequence contingent on the behavior of the entire group (Litow & Pumroy, 1975). While most approaches to classroom management involve implementing supports to individual students and delivering consequences based on individual behavior, interdependent group contingencies require groups of students to meet a behavioral criterion to receive the reward. As such, interdependent group contingencies increase the efficiency and consistency of intervention implementation by demarcating common expectations, goals, and outcomes to all students in the class. Rather than manage each of these elements for individual students, therefore, interdependent group contingencies provide a framework for communicating each of these elements to the entire group and supporting greater intervention fidelity (Weeden, Wills, Kottwitz, & Kamps, 2016).

Interdependent group contingencies represents a set of adaptable procedures that researchers and practitioners can modify and extend to meet the needs of students. For instance, Barrish, Saunders, and Wolf (1969) introduced interdependent group contingencies for use in classrooms and termed the intervention the Good Behavior Game (GBG). Using a peer-teaming approach, the GBG provides rewards for groups of students who remain under a predetermined set of rule violations over an established time period. The GBG remains among the most widely used and researched interdependent group contingency frameworks, but others modified the procedures to target a variety of additional outcomes and improve the match to student developmental and behavioral needs. For instance, Murphy, Theodore, Aloiso, Alric-Edwards, and Hughes (2007) noted that students might become sated on a reward if given repeatedly over time. To address this concern, the research team introduced random rewards—termed *mystery motivators*—to increase responsiveness to the intervention over time. Radley, Dart, and O'Handley (2016) extended the GBG model to address noise levels in three elementary classrooms. Noting that previous research on interdependent group contingencies require teachers to use their judgment when recording student behavior, this research team used a more objective measure of classroom behavior—decibel levels—to document student behavior. Finally, Chaffee, Briesch, Volpe, Johnson, and Dudley (2019) extended the GBG model to include a peer-reporting component for middle school students. Specifically, these researchers moved the emphasis on student inappropriate and disruptive behaviors to positive outcomes based on peer comments. Within this form of the interdependent group contingency, the research team instructed students to provide positive comments to peers engaging in appropriate classroom behavior and dispensed rewards based on the number of positive comments reported. Results indicated increased academic engagement and decreased disruptive behaviors for the classroom.

Research examining the effectiveness of interdependent group contingencies as a means for promoting student academic engagement and reducing disruptive behaviors indicates that the intervention consistently produces positive results (Maggin, Pustejovsky, & Johnson, 2017). However, the implementation of interdependent group contingencies requires careful forethought because, despite having a common arrangement of providing rewards to students based on the behavioral performance of the group, there are several procedural options available for maximizing the intervention's potency. In the following chapter, we describe a standard model for classroom-based interdependent group contingency interventions based on the GBG (Barrish et al., 1969), expand on procedural variants available for increasing the match with student needs, provide recommendations for overcoming common obstacles and challenges, and conclude with considerations for increasing the cultural relevance for students from diverse backgrounds.

INTERDEPENDENT GROUP CONTINGENCY BASE MODEL

As previously noted, the defining feature of an interdependent group contingency is that students receive rewards for meeting behavioral expectations based on the performance of the whole group (Litow & Pumroy, 1975). Conceptually, interdependent group contingencies provide a straightforward approach to classroom management with enough flexibility to apply it across a range of target behaviors, classroom arrangements, and developmental stages. While the malleability of the procedure is appealing, there is a need to develop a well-defined implementation plan to ensure consistent enforcement of behavioral expectations and positive and negative consequences to students. Given the versatility of interdependent group contingency procedures, there is not a singular, standard model of implementation. For the current purposes, therefore, we draw on the most common model of the interdependent group contingency, the GBG, to describe the base model.

Pre-Intervention Planning

Table 21.1 provides an overview of the steps involved in planning to implement a standard model of interdependent group contingencies. As can be seen, the planning phase requires the implementer to consider several issues ranging from the most appropriate time period for the intervention, establishing positively stated behavioral expectations, selecting positive and negative consequences, developing methods for responding and recording violations of classroom expectations, and creating procedures for acknowledging appropriate student behavior. The purpose of the pre-intervention planning phase is to establish the intervention procedures to support consistent implementation of the intervention across students and contexts. Given research indicating that teachers often provide a disproportionate number of negative consequences to students exhibiting behavior problems and students from minority backgrounds (Bal, Betters-Bourbon, & Fish, 2019), consistent and equitable implementation is paramount.

Selecting a time period. For interdependent group contingencies, intervention planning begins with selecting a time period to apply the intervention. Research

Table 21.1. INTERDEPENDENT GROUP CONTINGENCY PLANNING CONSIDERATIONS

Planning Consideration	Description
1. Select target class period	Teacher selects a specific time-period in which students exhibit challenging behaviors to implement the group contingency intervention
2. Develop classroom expectations	Establish the behavioral expectations of the classroom and state them in positive, easy-to-remember phrases
3. Select behavioral criterion	Establish a criterion that students must collectively meet to earn the established reward
4. Determine positive consequences	Select rewards for students when their group meets the established behavioral criterion
5. Develop method for responding to student violations	Outline a process for communicating to students when behavioral expectations are not met
6. Develop method for recording student violations and recognizing positive behavior	Outline a process for publicly recording student breaches of the classroom expectations
7. Develop contingency groupings	Divide the class into groups who will work together to earn the established reward for meeting the behavioral expectations
8. Review expectations, recording system, and criteria with class	Develop process for reviewing the results of the intervention and distributing rewards to student groups meeting the established criteria

examining the literature on interdependent group contingencies indicates that implementation typically occurs between 30 and 60 minutes (Maggin, Pustejovsky, & Johnson, 2017). Practitioners considering the use of interdependent group contingencies for their classroom, therefore, should consider this intervention for discrete time periods that correspond to particularly challenging class periods due to the potency of the intervention. Moreover, implementing the intervention for select time periods will increase the likelihood that the strength of the intervention is maintained over time (Naylor et al., 2018).

Develop classroom expectations. Following the selection of a discrete time period, practitioners should consider the classroom expectations and associated rules for students to follow. Behavioral expectations refer to the conventions that guide social interactions and classroom comportment (Zaheer, Maggin, McDaniel, McIntosh, Rodriguez, & Fogt, 2019). Within an interdependent group contingency, the behavioral expectations become the basis for the criterion on which students receive the reward or not. That is, students receive rewards based on the group meeting a predefined criterion for behavioral performance. Developing clear and positively stated behavioral expectations establish the behavioral standards for the students and communicates the rules when the intervention is in place. Perhaps the most common approach for using behavioral expectations as a means for tracking student behavior is to award points based on student performance. In some versions of the interdependent group contingencies, students receive points for meeting behavioral expectations while in others, students receive points for violating expectations or established rules (Maggin et al., 2017). For some students, particularly those who are younger, assigning points might seem immaterial and, therefore, might benefit from concrete methods such as dropping tokens or coins into a jar or moving the hands of a reward clock. Regardless of the basis and process for rewarding points, it is important for implementers to establish these procedures to support consistent implementation across time points and students.

Select behavioral criterion. Following the development of behavioral expectations and the methods for enforcing them, implementers must select the criterion for rewarding student behavior. While the expectations establish the standards for classroom comportment and behavior, the criterion represents the contingency for students to earn rewards and, in turn, reinforce their behavior. Selecting an appropriate criterion requires balancing the methods for enforcing the expectations with students' ability to meet them. That is, the criterion should be stringent enough to support positive behavior and sufficiently relaxed for students to earn rewards. For instance, Sy, Gratz, and Donaldson (2016) compared different approaches for selecting an appropriate criterion. The methods used included (a) basing the selection on the number of student violations recorded during the previous intervention session and (b) determining a desirable percentage drop from the previous session. For this latter option, if groups earning rewards committed 10 violations, and the goal was a 10% drop, the next day's criterion would be set at 9 violations or fewer for group to earn the reward. Ultimately, implementer knowledge of student behavior, the length of the target time period, and the stringency of the expectations are essential for selecting an appropriate criterion. Particularly at the outset of implementation, research supports the use of more lenient criteria to ensure students experience success with gradual tightening of the criteria as students demonstrate the capacity to meet the criterion consistently (Theodore, Bray, Kehle, & Dioguardi, 2004).

Determine positive consequences. Inherent within interdependent group contingencies is the delivery of a reward contingent on groups of students meeting the established criterion. As such, it is important for implementers to select rewards that motivate students to meet the behavioral criterion and sufficiently feasible to accrue and deliver on a daily basis. Rewards can range from material items such as stickers, stamps, and small toys to activities including computer or phone time, homework passes, or free time to edibles such as chips, crackers, or fruit. Implementers planning to use an interdependent group contingency should check with school policies and consider the developmental stage and interests of the classroom. Many school personnel find it useful to employ a preference assessment with students to determine the most desired rewards. For students not meeting the behavioral criterion, the consequence is not receiving the reward. It is through the process of rewarding students for meeting the established behavioral goal and withholding rewards for not meeting the goal that shapes student behavior over time.

Develop method for responding to student behavior. The effectiveness of interdependent group contingencies is grounded in the delivery of reward to students depending on whether the behavioral criterion is met. In addition to delivering or withholding rewards following the intervention time period, it is also necessary to let students know when there is a violation of the behavioral expectations and to record these violations in a public manner to make students aware of their proximity to the criterion. Developing a procedure for responding to student violations allows the implementer to communicate in a consistent, clear, and neutral manner that emphasizes the expectations rather than the encroachment. For instance, when a violation occurs, the implementer could acknowledge the student in a neutral tone, state clearly the behavior and the expectation impinged, encourage the student to do better moving forward, and record the violation using the method developed in the earlier stages of the planning process. If the emphasis is on acknowledging appropriate behavior, then a similar approach remains viable with the implementer not recording the violation but rather praising the appropriate behavior and documenting its occurrence. Regardless, it remains important to recognize violations to assist students' differentiation between appropriate and inappropriate classroom behaviors.

Develop contingency groupings. Interdependent group contingencies requires dividing the class into collections or teams of students on which the delivery—or withholding—of rewards is based. That is, the collective behavior of the student group dictates whether students receive the reward, rather than the comportment of a single student. For instance, if the group of students meets the established threshold, each student receives the reward. Interdependent group contingencies increase the potency of the intervention by leveraging group dynamics to encourage students to remain on task and meet the behavioral expectations. For most classes, implementers must consider the arrangement of students carefully to ensure a particular group is not comprised of a disproportionate number of students with behavioral problems or to avoid grouping students with adversarial histories or conflicting dispositions. Collecting individual data on the number of violations, particularly during the early stages of implementation, might provide objective data on which to inform revisions to the student groupings. In addition, randomly assigning students to teams each day provides an opportunity to ensure equitable distribution of students with varying intensities of behavior over time. Random assignment to groups provides implementers with a strategy to reduce frustration across students and increase interest in demonstrating positive behavior (McKenna & Flower, 2014). Ultimately, it is likely that implementers will need to make modifications to the teams but initial thoughtfulness can reduce the extent of those changes.

Review expectations, recording system, and criteria with class. The final step before implementing an interdependent group contingency is to teach students the behavioral expectations, criteria for earning the reward, and related intervention procedures. Ensuring students understand the classroom standards and the methods for earning rewards based on group behavior is critical for the success of the intervention. As such, implementers should review the behavioral expectations, recording system, methods for acknowledging rule violations, and the rewards available for meeting expectations. While there are many methods for teaching students about the intervention, students tend to learn best from those using modeling, student role play, and feedback (Naylor, Kamps, & Wills, 2018). Implementers may, therefore, introduce the game in a time period that is shorter than the target timeframe and allow students to play different roles and demonstrate behaviors that meet and violate the established expectations. Regardless of the particular teaching methods, it is important to orient students to the intervention procedures and classroom expectations for them to respond positively to the framework.

Intervention implementation. Table 21.2 provides an overview of the steps involved in implementing a standard model of interdependent group contingencies. Following implementation planning, school personnel should be prepared to put the interdependent group contingency into action. Procedurally, implementers should be sure to announce the beginning of the intervention period to make students aware that the behavioral expectations and contingencies are operational. Making clear that the intervention is in effect increases the likelihood of positive responding over time because students come to associate the intervention with earning rewards for meeting the behavioral expectations. Critical to the implementation of an interdependent group contingency is to respond to violations and responsiveness to the behavioral expectations in a consistent, neutral manner, recording these instances systematically, and only delivering positive consequences to those student groups meeting the established threshold. It is through the process of rewarding positive behavior and ignoring or providing explicit feedback to unwanted behaviors that students learn to discriminate between constructive and detrimental classroom comportment.

Table 21.2. INTERDEPENDENT GROUP CONTINGENCY IMPLEMENTATION PROCEDURES

Implementation Consideration	Description
1. Announce start of intervention period	Teacher states that the intervention period begins making clear that initiation of the contingencies
2. Respond and record student violations as planned	Teachers monitor student adherence to the established behavioral expectations, responds, and records violations
3. Announce end of intervention period	Teacher states that the intervention period is complete and the contingencies for receiving the reward is over
4. Repeat criterion for reward	Teacher reminds students of the criteria for earning the reward for that intervention period
5. Review each group's performance	Teacher publicly reviews the performance for each group and provides praise to groups meeting the criteria and encouragement to groups not meeting the criteria to do better next time
6. Announce groups that will receive the reward	Teacher publicly announces the groups earning the reward
7. Deliver reward	Teacher delivers the reward for the intervention period to students in groups remaining below the established number of violations
8. Record each team's score to monitor progress	Teacher writes the number of student violations to the expectations to monitor progress and determine if revision to group compositions is needed

Following completion of the intervention time period, the implementer should announce the end of the intervention period and deliver rewards expeditiously. Distributing rewards to students quickly strengthens their association between meeting expectations and a positive outcome, thereby increasing the likelihood of continued positive responding during the intervention in the future. Providing those groups of students that did not earn the reward with encouragement and a reminder of the next intervention time period can assist with offsetting any negative responses. Finally, implementers should record the score for each student grouping to monitor progress and inform any decisions to revise them in the future.

Procedural Variants

In the initial part of this chapter, we described the process of planning to implement an interdependent group contingency and outlined a standard model based on the GBG (Barrish et al., 1969). Among the most appealing aspects of interdependent group contingencies, however, is the malleability of the procedures with a variety of options available for implementers to modify the base model to promote improved student responding. In the following sections, we highlight three procedural variants of interdependent group contingency interventions to demonstrate ways implementers might extend the base model to increase potency.

Mystery motivator. As noted previously, interdependent group contingencies require the delivery of a reward to encourage students to meet the established behavioral expectations. While positive outcomes represent an important part of encouraging appropriate behavior, students sometimes become sated on receiving the same reward each time, and their incentive to meet the behavioral expectations diminishes over time. When students no longer feel motivated to meet the expectations, responsiveness is difficult to maintain. To encourage ongoing interest and motivation to meet the behavioral expectations, many practitioners use a procedure called the *mystery motivator*. Mystery motivators require the implementer to develop a menu of reward options to choose rather than the selection of a single reward (Pokorski & Barton, 2019). Following the development of the reward menu, the implementer randomly selects rewards for delivery during a given intervention time period. Rewards remain masked from the students until after the intervention period is complete, although it is important to deliver them expeditiously. Procedures for selecting mystery motivators include selecting them prior to the intervention period or immediately following its completion. For instance, implementers might randomly select rewards for each day, record them on a calendar, and reveal them directly after the intervention ends. In contrast, an implementer could place envelopes with rewards in a hat or raffle drum and have students select the reward. Regardless of the particular procedures used, the purpose is to increase student interest and motivation to adhere to the classroom expectations over time.

Peer reporting. Most interdependent group contingency interventions involve the teacher monitoring student behavior and tallying violations of the behavioral expectations. Understandably, many school personnel find the focus on student violations unpalatable and prefer to emphasize positive classroom behaviors. As such, implementers interested in focusing on positive sets of behaviors such as preparedness, engagement, and hand-raising, might use peer reporting to assist with recognizing occurrences of constructive student behavior. Positive peer reporting is useful because students learn a structured approach for acknowledging appropriate classroom behavior effectively extending the number of opportunities for students to receive praise and interact positively with their peers (Lum, et al., 2019). Providing students with a process for recognizing prosocial classroom behaviors is particularly effective for supporting those who are socially withdrawn or isolated by increasing the likelihood of having positive interactions with peers. Tootling—the opposite of tattling—is an example of a codified peer reporting intervention used within the context of an interdependent group contingency (Dillon et al., 2019). Within this intervention framework, students learn to identify established positive classroom behaviors and the procedure for reporting peer occurrences of the behavior. For instance, if a student sees a peer assist a classmate academically, the student who observes the act might record it on a sheet and submit it via a box designated for tootles. If the class reaches the established number of tootles over the course of a period, day, or week, students receive the specified reward. Positive peer reporting is most effective for low-frequency pro-social behaviors, such as a peer providing assistance on a class assignment, extra effort on cleaning the classroom, or instances where students demonstrate leadership, caring, or thoughtfulness. When coupled within an interdependent group contingency framework, positive peer reporting is useful for emphasizing appropriate classroom behavior and increasing the opportunities for acknowledging positive student behavior.

RECOMMENDATIONS FOR IMPLEMENTATION

Interdependent group contingency interventions afford many advantages such as having a strong evidence base, capacity to focus on a range of behaviors and outcomes, and a clear structure that supports consistent implementation. As with any intervention, however, challenges with implementing interdependent group contingencies arise for a variety of reasons. For interdependent group contingencies in particular, implementers must prepare to address potential interpersonal conflict within individual teams. Moreover, because the intervention requires the delivery of rewards to students, school personnel must manage the inventory and delivery. In the following section, we address both of these issues.

Limit Interpersonal Conflict and Group Sabotage

Interdependent group contingencies leverage group dynamics to encourage students to meet behavioral expectations. Because of the procedures for acknowledging student violations of classroom expectations and tallying them and delivering rewards to students based on the collective behavioral performance of the group, there is an opportunity for interpersonal conflict across team members to arise. For instance, some students react negatively toward group members for earning their team a tally while others may actively seek to sabotage their team's chances by repeatedly acting out. Fortunately, there are strategies implementers employ to prevent or account for such challenges. For students who get upset with their groupmates over earning a tally, perhaps the most effective approach is to incorporate specific training during the student orientation to the intervention around positive responding to others if a tally is assigned. Following earlier recommendations, explicit instruction and role-playing around appropriate responses might mitigate these issues. Within the context of implementation, school personnel anticipating a problem with peers belittling each other should emphasize the criteria for earning rewards to make clear that a single violation does not preclude the group from access to the incentive. Moreover, implementers should select criteria that is appropriate for the classroom and not overly stringent to ensure students experience success, particularly in the initial stages of implementing the intervention. For students actively sabotaging the intervention for others in their group, implementers should track the number of violations each student commits to ensure an objective assessment that the student is exhibiting extreme rates of behavior. Assuming the student is committing violations at an elevated rate, implementers can use the data to demonstrate to the student that their behavior is an outlier and preventing others from earning rewards. In addition, it is possible to move students onto their own team until they consistently meet the behavioral expectations. Moving students to their own team might be particularly effective for students motivated by peer attention because it is likely that saboteurs seek opportunities for attention regardless of whether it is positive or negative attention from peers or adults. However, due to potential stigmatization, it is important that implementers use data to inform decisions to isolate a student on their own team and to undertake these decisions cautiously.

Manage Contingencies and Rewards

Interdependent group contingencies rely on the prompt delivery of rewards to students following the intervention period. Immediacy of the reward is critical because the longer students must wait to receive the reward, the greater the dissociation from the reason for earning the reward. As such, the quicker students receive the reward, the greater their association with meeting the behavioral expectations and the greater the likelihood in the future that they will respond positively during the intervention condition. Because the speed with which students receive rewards relates to the overall effectiveness of the intervention, it is important for implementers to manage the contingencies and rewards in a manner that ensures their availability when the intervention is used. Too often, implementers find themselves without an inventory of established rewards to deliver to students and must wait for order placements and deliveries. In the interim, days and even weeks might go by before students receive their rewards, and the value of those rewards is lost and disconnected from the original intent. Perhaps the easiest approach to avoid these issues is to use rewards that are readily available and do not require purchasing such as homework passes and access to preferred activities. For instance, implementers might use indirect items such as stickers, tokens, or points to ensure students receive acknowledgement of meeting the behavioral expectations. Indirect reinforcers can then be exchanged for backup reinforcers, which are preferred items provided based on the number of indirect reinforcers earned. For those reward systems that require purchasing including tangible items or edibles, implementers should take regular inventory and place orders as needed.

CONSIDERATIONS OF DIVERSITY AND EQUITY IN INTERDEPENDENT GROUP CONTINGENCIES

The purpose of using a structured approach for classroom management is to assist teachers in applying rules and consequences in a fair and equitable manner across all students. Research, however, indicates that teachers use negative consequences and exclusionary practices with students from culturally and linguistically diverse backgrounds at a substantially higher rate than those from majority backgrounds (Gion, McIntosh, & Smolkowski, 2018). The adaptable nature of interdependent group contingencies provide an opportunity to enhance their fit for students from a range of backgrounds by matching the procedures to the cultural contexts for students. That is, many scholars argue for the need to consider the contextual fit of evidence-based interventions to the practical realities of the settings in which they are applied. Among the approaches advanced to enhance the contextual fit of interventions for students is to adapt the procedures to enhance the cultural relevance for students (Barrera, Castro, Stryker, & Toobert, 2013). Recently, Brown, Maggin, and Buren (2018) proposed a framework for making cultural adaptations to school behavioral interventions that include modifying the procedures, content, and methods for delivering classroom management supports for students with intensive behavioral needs. In the following sections, we define each type of cultural adaptation and provide examples for modifying the base interdependent group contingency model.

Procedural Adaptations

Procedural adaptations refers to the use of process-oriented methods to inform the development of cultural adaptations. For instance, when considering modifications to existing interventions, it is useful to use a process that actively accounts for the purpose of the intervention, the rationale for why the intervention is expected to work, and the resources available to school personnel. In particular, those considering adjustments to the interdependent group contingency base model might consider engaging members of the school and local communities to ensure consistency between the proposed cultural adaptations and the norms of the student population. Collecting information on the cultural characteristics, rather than assuming one knows, provides insight into making the intervention more meaningful and targeted to students' interests. Following the collection of this information, implementers can adjust the expectations, rewards, and procedures to ensure greater match between the student population and the cultural backgrounds of students. Regardless of the specific adaptations made, school personnel are encouraged to document the modifications selected to determine if these led to better student outcomes.

Content Adaptations

Content adaptations refers to adjustments made to the substantive elements of the interventions to make the material more relatable, comprehensible, and representative of student experiences. Perhaps the most straightforward example of content adaptations is modifying the language of instruction to match the primary language of students (Brown et al., 2018). School personnel employing interdependent group contingencies might consider representing the classroom expectations and intervention rules in the primary language of students if it differs from the language used in the school or classroom. Moreover, interventionists can further adapt the content of interdependent group contingencies by using metaphors, concepts, and examples that relate directly to the cultural experiences of students or perhaps making the rewards aligned to the interests and experiences of students. For instance, some communities use gardens as a representation for calmness and serenity. Implementers might consider infusing these cultural metaphors when teaching the intervention to students to emphasize that the goal is to establish a classroom context that is safe and free of distractions. Using these terms when instructing students on the rules and procedures of the intervention can increase the students' understanding of the intervention's methods and increase the rate of responsiveness.

Implementation Adaptations

Implementation adaptations refer to modifications to the methods for putting the intervention into practice. Examples of implementation adaptations include taking into consideration the cultural characteristics of the individual charged with implementation, making the outcomes goals and outcomes of the intervention more culturally appropriate, and aligning the intervention context to the values, customs, and traditions of the student population. For example, Indigenous students might respond to interdependent group contingencies implemented by a trusted member of the community members or aligning the goals of the intervention to behaviors that align with selected community values. Another example of implementation adaptations is to change the implementer from a classroom teacher to a trusted paraprofessional if their cultural characteristics align better with the student's cultural background.

CONCLUSION

Interdependent group contingencies are an evidence-based and adaptable class of interventions in which students receive consequences contingent on the behavior of the entire group. Research consistently demonstrates the effectiveness of interdependent group contingencies on student classroom behavior and academic engagement (Maggin et al., 2017). Interdependent group contingencies consist of multiple components with several options for maximizing their potency including modifying the intervention procedures, manipulating the positive contingencies for students meeting behavioral expectations, and adapting the intervention framework to more closely align with student cultural and linguistic characteristics. Because interdependent group contingencies are adaptable, school-based implementers must carefully plan to ensure accurate and consistent implementation to maximize effectiveness and ensure contextual fit with the particular needs of students. In this chapter, we provided implementers with an overview of the considerations needed to operationalize interdependent group contingencies, provided an overview of research-based approaches for customizing the intervention to an array of classroom settings, and recommended practices for addressing common challenges associated with implementation.

REFERENCES

Bal, A., Betters-Bubon, J., & Fish, R. E. (2019). A multilevel analysis of statewide disproportionality in exclusionary discipline and the identification of emotional disturbance. *Education and Urban Society, 51*, 247–268.

Barrera, M., Jr., Castro, F. G., Strycker, L. A., & Toobert, D. J. (2013). Cultural adaptations of behavioral health interventions: A progress report. *Journal of Consulting and Clinical Psychology, 81*(2), 196–205.

Barrish, H. H., Saunders, M., & Wolf, M. M. (1969). Good behavior game: Effects of individual contingencies for group consequences on disruptive behavior in a classroom. *Journal of Applied Behavior Analysis, 2*, 119–124.

Brown, C., Maggin, D. M., & Buren, M. (2018). Systematic review of cultural adaptations of school-based social, emotional, and behavioral interventions for students of color. *Education and Treatment of Children, 41*(4), 431–456.

Dillon, M. B. M., Radley, K. C., Tingstrom, D. H., Dart, E. H., Barry, C. T., & Codding, R. (2019). The effects of tootling via ClassDojo on student behavior in elementary classrooms. *School Psychology Review, 48*(1), 18–30.

Gion, C., McIntosh, K., & Smolkowski, K. (2018). Examination of American Indian/Alaska Native school discipline disproportionality using the vulnerable decision points approach. *Behavioral Disorders, V44*(1), 40–52.

Litow, L., & Pumroy, D. K. (1975). A brief review of classroom group-oriented contingencies. *Journal of Applied Behavior Analysis, 8*(3), 341–347.

Lum, J. D., Radley, K. C., Tingstrom, D. H., Dufrene, B. A., Olmi, D. J., & Wright, S. J. (2019). Tootling with a randomized independent group contingency to improve high school classwide behavior. *Journal of Positive Behavior Interventions, 21*(2), 93–105.

Maggin, D. M., Pustejovsky, J. E., & Johnson, A. H. (2017). A meta-analysis of school-based group contingency interventions for students with challenging behavior: An update. *Remedial and Special Education, 38*(6), 353–370.

Mckenna, J. W., & Flower, A. (2014). Get them back on track: Use of the good behavior game to improve student behavior. *Beyond Behavior, 23*(2), 20–26.

Naylor, A. S., Kamps, D., & Wills, H. (2018). The effects of the CW-FIT group contingency on class-wide and individual behavior in an urban first grade classroom. *Education and Treatment of Children, 41,* 1–30.

Pokorski, E. A., Barton, E. E., & Ledford, J. R. (2019). Assessing the differential effects of known and mystery rewards in a preschool-based group contingency. *Journal of Early Intervention, 41*(3), 256–275.

Radley, K. C., Dart, E. H., & O'Handley, R. D. (2016). The quiet classroom game: A class-wide intervention to increase academic engagement and reduce disruptive behavior. *School Psychology Review, 45,* 93–108.

Theodore, L. A., Bray, M. A., Kehle, T. J., & Dioguardi, R. J. (2004). Contemporary review of group-oriented contingencies for disruptive behavior. *Journal of Applied School Psychology, 20*(1), 79–101.

Weeden, M., Wills, H. P., Kottwitz, E., & Kamps, D. (2016). The effects of a class-wide behavior intervention for students with emotional and behavioral disorders. *Behavioral Disorders, 42*(1), 285–293.

Zaheer, I., Maggin, D., McDaniel, S., McIntosh, K., Rodriguez, B. J., & Fogt, J. B. (2019). Implementation of promising practices that support students with emotional and behavioral disorders. *Behavioral Disorders, 44*(2), 117–128.

## 22

Independent and Dependent Group Contingencies

TOM CARIVEAU ■

Group contingencies are often touted for their effectiveness and economic and practical feasibility compared to individualized contingencies (Gresham & Gresham, 1982; Hayes, 1976; Litow & Pumroy, 1975), but they also provide a method for teachers to structure their classroom to promote greater cooperation and engagement between students. By arranging a common consequence for various members, classmates may assist one another in reaching a behavioral criterion and reduce the likelihood that peers will reinforce problem behaviors (Solomon & Wahler, 1973; Sulzbacher & Houser, 1968). In a hypothetical extension, you may engage in similar supportive behaviors if your neighbor's speeding produced a ticket for everyone in your neighborhood. Under this arrangement, you would likely praise your neighbor for appropriate driving, monitor their driving, and prompt them to take their time on errands. In all group contingency arrangements, a predetermined behavioral criterion is set and reaching this criterion produces some consequence for members of the group. The three types of group contingencies (i.e., interdependent, independent, and dependent) differ based on the arrangement of students who inform the criterion and who receives the reward. The focus of this chapter is on the application of independent and dependent group contingencies in applied settings. Advantages of each arrangement and variables that may be adapted to meet the needs of a specific classroom are described.

INDEPENDENT GROUP CONTINGENCIES

In independent group contingencies, a criterion is set and each students' access to the reward is based on their own behavior meeting the criterion. In this way, each student's access is independent of the behavior of her peers. This system is so common in classroom settings that these procedures often are used without any reference to the intervention being an independent group contingency. Take, for example, a study by Osborne (1969) in which an independent group contingency was arranged for six girls at a school for the deaf. Students were required to remain in their seat for 15 minutes. If a student met this criterion, they were given five minutes of free time. If a student left their seat, that student did not receive free time. Low rates of out-of-seat behavior were observed when this contingency was arranged. The most common independent group contingency is schoolwide rules. Adherence to these rules produce some consequence (e.g., rewards), while nonadherence produces some other consequence (e.g., an office discipline referral). These systems are arranged throughout an entire school with individual students' behavior producing consequences for that student alone.

Although effective, independent group contingencies do not necessitate any level of peer interaction for a reward to be received by a member. That is, because each student must meet the criterion separately to access the reward, no interaction among students is required. Nevertheless, independent group contingencies have been shown to be more effective than no intervention (Deshais, Fisher, & Kahng, 2019; Gresham & Gresham, 1982) and may be more feasible to implement compared to individualized contingencies.

DEPENDENT GROUP CONTINGENCIES

In dependent group contingencies, a criterion is set and the reward is delivered to the entire class based on the responding by one member or a small group. That is, all members' access to the reward is dependent on the behavior of the individual(s) whose behavior will inform the contingency. As a result, dependent group contingencies are more commonly associated with interaction among groupmates, which may not occur in independent group contingencies. One concern is that this type of arrangement may put undue pressure on the target student or group of students and that these members may commonly experience aversive interactions if a criterion is not met (Davis & Blankenship, 1996; Romeo, 1998). Nevertheless, dependent group contingencies have often been described as producing positive interactions among peers (Alden, Pettigrew, & Skiba, 1970; Williamson, Williamson, Watkins, & Hughes, 1992).

Research suggests that dependent group contingencies may be effective in promoting more positive interactions among students who may exhibit problem behaviors and their peers (Alden et al., 1970). The teacher may increase the likelihood that the target students' peers are more likely to deliver praise and attention to the target student by setting a criterion that is attainable (discussed later). One method for ensuring that the criterion is attainable is to expose the participant to the contingency outside of the group, before applying the group contingency. Pretraining procedures may occur with the target student in a one-on-one setting to ensure that the participant can emit the target responses at the criterion level (e.g., Coleman, 1970). One example is First Steps to Success, an intervention for young children who engage in problem behavior in classroom settings (Walker et al., 1998). Prior to the group contingency, the eventual target student receives individualized pretraining with a staff member that includes role-playing positive and negative examples of appropriate classroom behavior for 30 min. Once preintervention is completed, the student rejoins the class and receives points for demonstrating appropriate behavior in the classroom. If the student meets the criterion by the end of the class, all students receive access to some reward (e.g., story time or extra recess). This pre-intervention arrangement may serve two important functions. First, the target response is defined, and she is allowed to practice the response. Second, the criterion for the reward is clearly defined. Both of these aspects may be critical for the student to be successful in meeting the criterion when the intervention is introduced in the classroom.

Although dependent group contingencies may be used to target problem behavior emitted by one student or a small group of students, it has additional advantages. First, dependent group contingencies may facilitate cooperation among students to produce a shared reward. Second, using randomized components, such as randomized selection of a student, may be associated with high levels of appropriate behavior by all students, as any member's behavior may inform the contingency (Deshais et al., 2019; Williamson, Campbell-Whatley, & Lo, 2009). Finally, dependent group contingencies may be the most feasible to implement as the teacher only needs to monitor the behavior of one or a small group of students. In interdependent and independent group contingencies, behavior must be recorded for all students.

Once a group contingency is selected, the teacher must consider additional components of the intervention: (a) selecting a target behavior, (b) selecting a behavioral criterion, (c) selecting a reward, (d) reducing delays to the reward, and (e) describing the intervention.

RECOMMENDATIONS FOR IMPLEMENTATION

Selecting a Target Behavior

Group contingency interventions have been applied to a range of target behaviors in educational settings. These include problem behaviors (Gresham & Gresham, 1982), academic engagement or on-task behavior (Heering & Wilder, 2006; Williamson et al., 2009), and academic responding (Deshais et al., 2019). Because the contingency will be arranged for the entire class, the target behavior must be relevant to each student, although not necessarily a problem for all members. For example, although certain problem behaviors (e.g., talking out) may be emitted by only a few students, it may still be appropriate to arrange a group contingency for the entire class as low rates of these behaviors is ideal for all students. Although group contingencies may commonly be applied to address problem behaviors, teachers may also arrange these interventions to target skill fluency, prosocial responses (e.g., tootling; Cihak, Kirk, & Boon, 2009), or self-management behaviors.

One potential consideration when selecting a target behavior is whether the behavior is likely to increase the student's success in other environments. Although targeting problem behavior may be valuable in the classroom, targeting other appropriate alternatives may be more generalizable to other settings. Moreover, selecting specific target behaviors, such as academic tasks, may increase the likelihood that students emit other collateral responses, such as helping peers (e.g., Williamson et al., 1992). In contrast, when the group contingency is defined based on problem behavior, other students may be more likely to issue reprimands when problem behaviors occur, rather than delivering praise in the absence of problem behavior.

Questions to ask when selecting a target behavior include the following:

- Is the target behavior relevant to all students?
- Is the target behavior important for these students in other settings or situations?
- Are all students capable of emitting the target behavior?
- Can the students assist one another in emitting the target behavior?

Selecting a Behavioral Criterion

After selecting a target behavior, the teacher must determine how much of the target behavior must be emitted to produce the reward. This criterion may often be set arbitrarily, leading to ineffective contingencies. Instead, the criterion should be set based on prior performance of the target members. Selecting a behavioral criterion has received little attention in research on group contingencies, but it is likely best to arrange the criterion so that students will receive the reward more often than not. This means that the criterion should be set within the students' current abilities and be raised over time until the terminal goal is met.

Percentile schedules are one method for identifying a behavioral criterion based on past performance (Galbicka, 1994). Although the equation for determining a percentile schedule is somewhat complex, the logic is not. The teacher must first identify the number of past days/observations that the current performance should be compared and the proportion of these past performances that should be exceeded to produce the reward. This arrangement is ideal as the criterion is based on past performance, which may increase the likelihood that students are contacting the reward frequently at the beginning of the intervention. In addition, meeting the criterion will subsequently result in the criterion increasing as it is based on this performance. The teacher must also identify the terminal criterion as performance may not constantly improve above some level and arranging a criterion above this level would be unattainable, leading to a failed group contingency. For example, the percentile schedule may be used to set a criterion for the number of words read per minute; however, a cap based on normative data would be appropriate.

Under some circumstances, arranging for the behavioral criterion to be unknown may be advantageous. That is, additional problems may arise if the criterion can no longer be met in a given period. If the criterion is unknown, this reactivity would be unlikely as the criterion has yet to be selected or identified to the group.

Questions to ask when selecting a criterion include the following:

- What is the terminal goal?
- What can the student(s) do now?
- How many prior days of student performance should the current performance be compared?
- What proportion of past performances should the students need to exceed?

Selecting a Reward

Group contingencies involve the delivery of the same consequence to members of the group. The teacher should select a consequence that is feasible to present to individual students or the entire class, depending on the type of group contingency. Consequences that can be delivered immediately are ideal, which will also depend on other features of the group contingency and students' preferences. Common immediate consequences include classwide games (e.g., Heads Up, Seven Up), access to small tangible items (e.g., stickers, erasers, or pencils), a free period for the entire class, or showing a clip of a movie. More delayed rewards can also be included such as additional time at recess, free periods at the end of the day, or special games during physical education courses. Unique arrangements may also be made available based on the features of the class and management systems in the school more broadly. Capitalizing on larger behavior management programs across multiple classes may allow for consequences to be arranged that are costlier, although still more feasible when compared to individualized systems. Yet, sometimes the best things in life and group contingencies are free, such as having the principal kiss a pig (see Skinner, Skinner, Skinner, & Cashwell, 1999).

Additional considerations must be made when preferred consequences differ between students. For example, extra recess may not be preferred by some students. In these instances, arranging for students to select a consequence from a prescribed menu may be more effective than arranging for a single consequence across the group. As an alternative, arranging for unknown or randomized rewards may increase the effectiveness of the intervention and the probability, or at least the opportunity, a student's preferred reward would be delivered. This may include having the teacher or a student select a reward from a bag if the criterion is met (Cariveau & Kodak, 2017; Heering & Wilder, 2006). A critical feature of this arrangement is that there is an opportunity for a students' preferred activity to be selected. Selecting unknown rewards may be particularly useful for entire classrooms as it is not dependent on the student whose responding met the criterion. In this way, student 1 could have informed the contingency, but student 2's most-preferred activity may be selected. Adaptations to how a reward is selected also may come to function as a reward itself. For example, if there are five activities that may be selected of varying value from a bag. Requiring that a specific activity be pulled from the bag a total of three times may increase the value of a reward, even if the preferred activity is not eventually selected. This arrangement may be similar to almost hitting a BINGO or the jackpot on a slot machine, termed the *near-miss effect* (Foxall & Sigurdsson, 2012). Anecdotally, Cariveau and Kodak (2017) included an unknown reinforcer and noted that one group repeatedly received access to toy cars on consecutive selections. The students' loud and incredulous statements when cars were selected yet again might suggest that the selection procedure increased the value of the reward, even when these students were satiated on the item.

Selecting an unknown reward may serve a variety of advantages; however, there are a variety of components of this system that may be altered to best serve the needs of the classroom or target other relevant skills. For example, instead of selecting an unknown reward in a dependent group contingency, the teacher may have the student who informed the contingency select the reward and share it with the class (e.g., Coleman, 1970). As an alternative, the class may vote anonymously (or publicly) on which reward they would prefer, which may allow for students to practice other social skills (e.g., considering other members' preferred rewards or allowing others to vote without coercion).

Questions to ask when selecting a reward include the following:

- Is the reward valuable to all students?
  - If no, how might we increase the value to the group?
  - If no, how might we make it unclear what reward will be delivered?
- Can the reward be delivered so that other problem behavior does not occur?
  - Example: Ending recess early is likely associated with more problem behavior as compared to having them go to recess later.
- Can the reward be delivered immediately, or will there be some delay between the criterion being met and the reward?

Reducing Delays to the Reward

The behavioral criterion may be initially set so that a reward is delivered numerous times throughout the day or at least once per day. Under ideal circumstances, many rewards would be earned throughout the day and delivered immediately following the target response. In a typical classroom, this arrangement is likely not feasible. Instead, it may be most effective to arrange for other intermediate rewards, such as points or stickers to be accumulated by the student (independent group contingency) or entire group (dependent group contingency) before exchanging these for the final reward. These arrangements are consistent with token economies. Tokens are commonly used to break up delays that may exist between the target behavior and the delivery of a reward (Hackenberg, 2009). These delays commonly exist in group contingencies as certain group rewards cannot be presented immediately (e.g., extra recess or a pizza party). Although rules may be included (described later), it is recommended that some form of token be used when a delayed reward is arranged.

Including tokens or other feedback systems in group contingencies are common. Although explicit feedback may be commonly recommended, one issue that may arise is when the criterion can no longer be met during the group contingency. For example, some group contingency interventions have included tallying instances of problem behavior publicly with a reward available if fewer than five tallies occur during a single class period (e.g., Barrish et al., 1969). Once five tallies have been earned, problem behaviors may be more likely as the criterion may no longer be met. If teachers choose to include a token or feedback system, including an unknown criterion may reduce the likelihood that reactive behavior occurs as it is unknown whether the criterion has been met.

A final consideration when attempting to break up delays to a reward is whether there should be the potential for the reward to be lost once it is earned. For example, if the criterion is met, but high rates of problem behavior occur before the reward is delivered, the teacher may want to remove the reward. Instead, it is recommended that any reward that is earned is delivered. Nevertheless, if the teacher determines that losing the reward is an option, this possibility should be described to the class at the outset of the intervention.

Earning Versus Losing Rewards

Another consideration when selecting a consequence is whether the reward should be earned or lost. Earning may be commonly recommend; however, research has shown that both procedures may be effective (Donaldson, DeLeon, Fisher, & Kahng, 2014; Iwata & Bailey, 1974), and some students may prefer reward-loss over reward-gain arrangements (Donaldson et al., 2014). In either system, the contingencies for reward gain or reward loss should be explicitly defined and adhered to by the teacher. For example, if emitting five or more disruptive behaviors during the day results in a student losing access to a free period at the end of the day, this should be the only way for the student to lose access to the free period. A major consideration when using reward loss is to ensure that rewards earned through other systems are not lost.

Reward-loss and reward-gain procedures may be arranged in a complementary fashion such that the same behavior and reward are arranged. In fact, the teacher may only need to change the description of the group contingency. Specifically, in a reward-gain procedure, the students would be informed that they would need to meet some criterion for the reward to be delivered. In reward loss, the students would be informed that if they did not meet some criterion, they would lose access to the reward. Either condition may be effective and differentially preferred by students. Moreover, some teachers may not endorse having students earn rewards for specific behaviors. Instead, the reward-loss procedures may fit more closely with their theoretical perspectives.

Describing the Intervention

Describing the group contingency plays an important role in the effectiveness of the intervention. As previously noted, the target behavior, criterion, and reward should be clearly defined so that every student knows (a) what they are supposed to do, (b) how long/how many times they are supposed to do it, and (c) what reward will be available. If these components are unknown, then the options should be explicitly identified and the method for selecting the option should be stated.

Target behavior. When describing the target behavior, a brief version of behavioral skills training should be used. First, operational definitions should be provided for each target behavior. The students might be included in generating these definitions, although the teacher must ensure that the definitions include behaviors that are directly observable and students should be able to identify examples and nonexamples of each target response. The teacher should then model examples and nonexamples, give the students the opportunity to practice examples and nonexamples (if appropriate), and then provide feedback to the students based on their performance. Operational definitions may be refined based on the responses emitted during this modeling or practice period.

Example procedure:

1. The teacher and class generate definitions of the target behavior.
   Script: *Let's make sure that everyone knows what behaviors I will be looking for in our new game. I care most when you are on task. What does being on task mean* (allow students to generate their own definition)? *So being on task is when you have all of your materials ready, you are looking at your materials or me, and you are keeping your hands to yourself and only talking when you are called on. Does anything else need to be included?*
2. The teacher models examples and nonexamples.
   Script: *I am going to show you what being on task looks like and what it doesn't look like. Make sure you pay attention to our definition and tell me if I am on task or not on task.*
3. The students are given the opportunity to emit examples and nonexamples. It is recommended that examples be emphasized with only brief nonexamples.
   Script: *Now it's your turn to show me some examples of on-task behavior.*

4. The teacher provides feedback to students. The teacher should deliver descriptive praise for examples and note what components of the definition are not met if nonexamples are presented.

Criterion. Following an adequate description of the target behavior, the teacher should describe the criterion that must be met for the students to earn the reward. The students should be able to identify whether a response is supposed to occur some set number of times or for some duration and if this criterion is fixed or unknown. If the criterion will be unknown to the class, the teacher should describe the procedure for selecting the criterion. The teacher might also allow them the opportunity to practice meeting the criterion in some abbreviated fashion. For example, if each student must be on task for 80% of the class period, the teacher might ask the students to calculate how long 80% of one minute is and then have the students complete some activity for that duration. If there is some system in place to provide feedback during the intervention (e.g., tokens), then this should also be described. Finally, the teacher should identify how students will be selected to inform the contingency. That is, will each student need to meet the criterion for them to receive the reward (independent group contingency), will a selected student or small group of students need to meet the criterion for the entire group to receive the reward (dependent group contingency), or will an unknown student need to meet the criterion to produce the reward for the group (unknown dependent group contingency)? If the latter, the teacher should describe how and when this student will be selected. Depending on the age of the students, the teacher should consider generating a name for the target student that relates to the school mascot or some other preferred character (e.g., "hero eagle").

Example Procedure:

1. The teacher should describe the criterion.
   Script: *I will draw one student's name before reading begins. That student will be our "hero eagle" today. You won't know if you or one of your friends is the hero eagle, so each of you should try your best. To receive the reward, the hero eagle will need to be on task for at least 80% of our reading class. Reading lasts 50 minutes, so how many minutes does that mean you will need to be on task (40 minutes)?*
2. The teacher should ask comprehension questions to ensure that the criterion is understood by the class.

Reward. The reward is critical for arranging an effective group contingency. The teacher should describe (a) how the reward will be selected and (b) when the reward will be delivered. If the reward will be selected after the criterion is met, the teacher should make sure that it is clear when the reward will be selected and how (see previous discussion). It may be valuable to have multiple reminders throughout the room of what rewards are available. For example, McCullagh and Vaal (1975) provided students with a rewards menu that included definitions of behaviors that resulted in tokens being earned or lost. Each student received a copy of the menu and it was also posted on the classroom wall.

Example Procedure:

1. The teacher should describe how the reward will be selected and when it will be delivered.
   Script: *If the hero eagle is on task for 80% of reading, then I will share who the hero eagle was today and that person will get to pick an eagle friend who was also on task to pick a reward for everyone out of the jar. We will get to play whatever activity is selected for 10 minutes and then go to lunch. If we didn't earn the reward, then I won't share who the hero eagle was, and we won't take a break before lunch.*

CONSIDERATIONS OF DIVERSITY AND EQUITY

A defining feature of independent and dependent group contingencies is the arrangement of an identical criterion and reward across all members of a group, consistent with cooperative rather than competitive contingencies (see Cariveau, Muething, & Trapp, 2020). As a result, these group contingencies may provide opportunities for interaction and coordination among classmates that may not otherwise occur. Although this is a strength, it is imperative that the teacher recognize the implications of selecting a behavioral criterion that will likely be met as this will affect the interactions among groupmates. Ensuring that all students can earn the reward, despite varying levels of ability, is invaluable to the success of group contingencies and their positive effects on student interactions.

Inclusiveness and cooperation among group members should be emphasized in any group contingency. Nevertheless, in dependent group contingencies, concerns may arise when the criterion is inconsistently met or when one member actively sabotages the intervention. Under these conditions, a teacher might consider allowing students to choose whether they would like to work under an independent or dependent group contingency. Prior research on cooperative contingencies have included opportunities to work individually (e.g., independent group contingencies) when a partner exhibits problem behavior (e.g., taking; Schmitt & Marwell, 1971). Notably, when a choice between these two options is provided, a better reward is arranged for cooperating rather than individual work. Similar arrangements may be made in classroom settings with a better reward being made available for choosing the dependent group contingency, while still allowing for students to pick an independent group contingency if a peer is exhibiting problem behavior.

Finally, independent and dependent group contingencies have been used across a variety of classrooms and with students of different ages, ethnicities, and disability statuses. Teachers should consider how factors related to diversity may affect students' success in a group contingency and what components of these interventions may be adapted to best support all students. Best of all, students may be included in the various decisions made regarding components of the group contingency, hopefully leading to a more ecologically valid intervention for all students in the class.

CONCLUSION

Independent and dependent group contingencies are effective and feasible classroom interventions used to promote academic and behavioral success. Numerous components of a group contingency can be altered to ensure that the intervention is effective in a given situation. Selecting and describing the target behavior, the criterion for the reward, and the reward itself are all critical components of group contingencies; yet, other variables such as methods to reduce delays to the reward, including earn or loss contingencies, and including unknown components must also be considered. Finally, dependent group contingency arrangements may have pronounced effects on behaviors other than the targeted response, including their ability to promote cooperation among students. Educators should consider each of the described variables for their potential utility in programming group contingencies in their settings.

REFERENCES

Alden, S. E., Pettigrew, L. E., & Skiba, E. A. (1970). The effect of individual-contingent group reinforcement on popularity. *Child Development, 41*, 1191–1196.

Barrish, H. H., Saunders, M., & Wolf, M. M. (1969). Good behavior game: Effects of individual contingencies for group consequences on disruptive behavior in a classroom. *Journal of Applied Behavior Analysis, 2*, 119–124. doi:10.1901/jaba.1969.2-119

Cariveau, T., & Kodak, T. (2017). Programming a randomized dependent group contingency and common stimuli to promote durable behavior change. *Journal of Applied Behavior Analysis, 50*, 121–133. doi:10.1002/jaba.352

Cariveau, T., Muething, C. S., & Trapp, W. (2020). *Interpersonal and group contingencies. Perspectives on Behavior Science, 43*, 115–135.

Cihak, D. F., Kirk, E. R., & Boon, R. T. (2009). Effects of classwide positive peer "tootling" to reduce the disruptive classroom behaviors of elementary students with and without disabilities. *Journal of Behavioral Education, 18*, 267–278. doi:10.1007/s10864-0099091-8

Coleman, R. (1970). A conditioning technique applicable to elementary school classrooms. *Journal of Applied Behavior Analysis, 3*, 293–297.

Davis, P. K., & Blankenship, C. J. (1996). Group-oriented contingencies: Applications for community rehabilitation programs. *Vocational Education and Work Adjustment Bulletin, 29*, 114–118.

Deshais, M. A., Fisher, A. B., & Kahng, S. (2019). A comparison of group contingencies on academic compliance. *Journal of Applied Behavior Analysis, 52*, 116–131. doi:10.1002/jaba.505

Donaldson, J. M., DeLeon, I. G., Fisher, A. B., & Kahng, S. (2014). Effects of and preference for conditions of token earn versus token loss. *Journal of Applied Behavior Analysis, 47,* 537–548. doi:10.1002/jaba.135

Foxall, G. R., & Sigurdsson, V. (2012). When loss rewards: The near-miss effect in slot machine gambling. *The Analysis of Gambling Behavior, 6,* 5–22.

Galbicka, G. (1994). Shaping in the 21st century: Moving percentile schedules into applied settings. *Journal of Applied Behavior Analysis, 27,* 739–760.

Gresham, F. M., & Gresham, G. N. (1982). Interdependent, dependent, and independent group contingencies for controlling disruptive behavior. *The Journal of Special Education, 16,* 101–110.

Hackenberg, T. D. (2009). Token reinforcement: A review and analysis. *Journal of the Experimental Analysis of Behavior, 91,* 257–286. doi:10.1901.jeab.2009.91-257

Hayes, L. A., (1976). The use of group contingencies for behavioral control: A review. *Psychological Bulletin, 83,* 628–648.

Heering, P. W., & Wilder, D. A. (2006). The use of dependent group contingencies to increase on-task behavior in two general education classrooms. *Education and Treatment of Children, 29,* 459–468.

Iwata, B. A., & Bailey, J. S. (1974). Reward versus cost token systems: An analysis of the effects on students and teacher. *Journal of Applied Behavior Analysis, 7,* 567–576.

Litow, L., & Pumroy, D. K. (1975). A brief review of classroom group-oriented contingencies. *Journal of Applied Behavior Analysis, 8,* 341–347.

McCullagh, J., & Vaal, J. (1975). A token economy in a junior high school special education classroom. *School Applications of Learning Theory, 7,* 1–8.

Osborne, J. G. (1969). Free-time as a reinforcer in the management of classroom behavior. *Journal of Applied Behavior Analysis, 2,* 113–118.

Romeo, F. F. (1998). The negative effects of using a group contingency system of classroom management. *Journal of Instructional Psychology, 25,* 130–133.

Skinner, C. H., Skinner, C. F., Skinner, A. L., & Cashwell, T. H. (1999). Using interdependent contingencies with groups of students: Why the principle kissed a pig. *Education Administration Quarterly, 35,* 806–820.

Solomon, R. W., & Wahler, R. G. (1973). Peer reinforcement control of classroom problem behavior. *Journal of Applied Behavior Analysis, 6,* 49–56.

Sulzbacher, S. I., & Houser, J. E. (1968). A tactic to eliminate disruptive behaviors in the classroom: Group contingent consequences. *American Journal of Mental Deficiency, 73,* 88–90.

Walker, H. M., Kavanagh, K., Stiller, B., Golly, A., Severson, H. H., & Feil, E. G. (1998). First step to success: An early intervention approach for preventing school antisocial behavior. *Journal of Emotional and Behavioral Disorders, 6,* 66–80.

Williamson, B. D., Campbell-Whatley, G. D., & Lo, Y. (2009). Using a random dependent group contingency to increase on-task behaviors of high school students with high incidence disabilities. *Psychology in the Schools, 46,* 1074–1083. doi:10.1002/pits.20445

Williamson, D. A., Williamson, S. H., Watkins, P. C., & Hughes, H. H. (1992). Increasing cooperation among children using dependent group-oriented reinforcement contingencies. *Behavior Modification, 16,* 414–425.

For the benefit of digital users, indexed terms that span two pages (e.g., 52–53) may, on occasion, appear on only one of those pages.

Tables and figures are indicated by *t* and *f* following the page number

Index

Flood, W. A., 107
fluency, writing, interventions for,
38–39, 87–91
"follow target student choice of tasks"
strategy, PM-PRT, 151, 152t, 161
Fowler, S. A., 107
Fox, J. J., 131
free resource, peers as, 6
friend preference, respect for in
PM-PRT, 158
friendships, supporting development of, 10
fun, role in restorative interventions, 190
Furlow, C. M., 107–8

Gage, N. A., 216
"gain attention" strategy, PM-PRT, 152t,
155, 160, 161
game-based cooperative learning
considerations of diversity and
equity, 80–83
effectiveness and efficacy, 35–37
example, 78–80, 79t, 80t, 81f, 81t
general discussion, 83
overview, 76–77
recommendations for
implementation, 77–80
game board, Math PALS, 68f, 68
games component, TGT, 77
Ganz, J. B., 111–12
Garcia, J., 120–21
Gardner, R., 108–9
Gardner, S., 166–67
Gay, G., 18
gender matching, 8–9, 123
generalization
promoting, 7–8
of social skills following instruction,
128, 132
Gentile, C., 37
Gibbs, G., 92
Ginsburg-Block, M. D., 32
goal sheet, for writing interventions, 87–
88, 89–91, 99
Goldstein, H., 10
Good Behavior Game (GBG), 207, 249–50
Grades 2–6 Math PALS, 68–70, 69f
Grades 2–6 Reading PALS, 63–64, 63t,
66–67, 67f

Graham, S., 37–38
graph sheet, for writing interventions, 87–
88, 89–90, 91
Gratz, O., 252–53
Grauvogel-MacAleese, A. N., 119, 179
Green, K., 177
Greenwood, C., 9, 34, 49
greeting at the door routine, 232–33
Gregory, A., 113
Gresham, F. M., 107, 130–31
Griner, D., 19–20, 21–22
group contingencies. See also
interdependent group contingencies
considerations for
implementation, 209–11
considerations of diversity and
equity, 272–73
dependent, 264–65
general discussion, 273
independent, 263–64
overview, 206–8, 263
recommendations for
implementation, 265–72
reward systems, 201
strengths and challenges, 208–9
grouping methods used in PMAIs, 31
group supports. See peer-mediated group
supports; specific intervention types
Gulsrud, A., 112
Gustafson, J. R., 141

Haisley, F. B., 52
Haring, T. G., 129–30
Harper, G. F., 31, 36–37
Harris, K. R., 37
Hatton, H. L., 202–3
Haydon, T., 36–37, 227
Heitzman-Powell, L., 179
Hensley, M., 133
Hermansen, E., 165
Higgins, S., 240, 241
High School Reading PALS, 63–64, 63t,
66–67, 67f
Hocking, C., 179
home input, on restorative practices and
conflict resolution, 192
home setting, pivotal response training
in, 157–58